Mark Antliff is Associate Professor of Art History at Duke University and author of *Inventing Bergson: Cultural Politics and the Parisian Avant-Garde* (Princeton University Press, 1993). With Matthew Affron he co-edited *Fascist Visions: Art and Ideology in France and Italy* (Princeton University Press, 1997). He is currently completing two books: *The Advent of Fascism: Art, Myth and Ideology in France 1909–1940* and *Modernism and Aesthetic Closure: Fauvism, Cubism, Futurism.*

Patricia Leighten is Professor and Chair of Art History at Duke University and author of *Re-Ordering the Universe: Picasso and Anarchism, 1897–1914* (Princeton University Press, 1989) and *A Politics of Form: Art, Anarchism and Audience in Avant-Guerre France* (University of Chicago Press, forthcoming). She and Mark Antliff are currently co-editing *A Cubism Reader, 1906–1914* (University of Chicago Press, forthcoming). She serves on the Editorial Boards of *Modernism/modernity* and Duke University Press.

Thames & Hudson world of art

This famous series provides the widest available range of illustrated books on art in all its aspects. If you would like to receive a complete list of titles in print please write to:

THAMES & HUDSON
181A High Holborn
London WC1V 7QX

In the United States please write to:

THAMES & HUDSON INC.
500 Fifth Avenue
New York, New York 10110

Printed in Singapore

D0089941

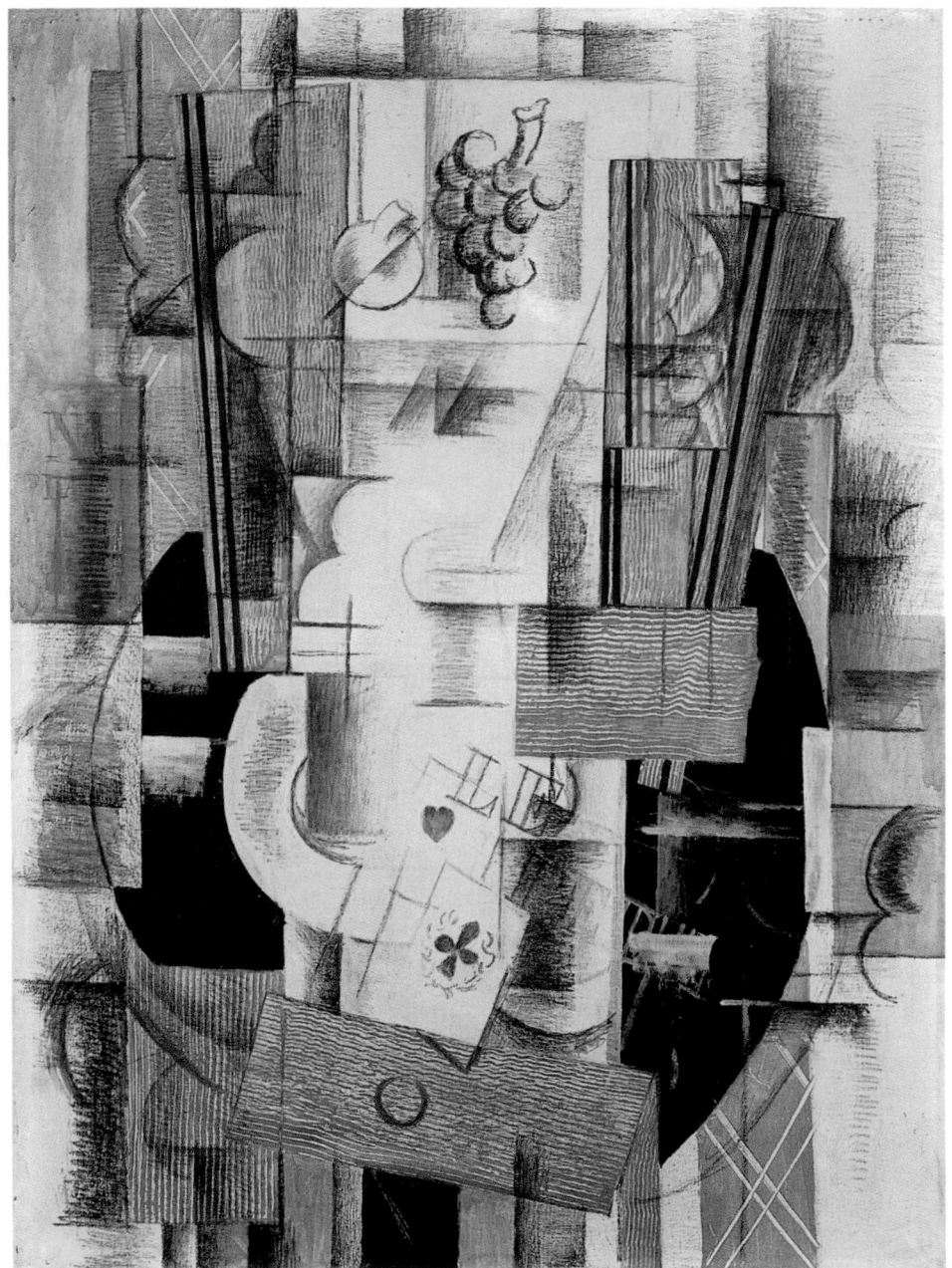

Mark Antliff and Patricia Leighten

Cubism and Culture

183 illustrations, 58 in color

Thames & Hudson world of art

Frontispiece:
1. **Georges Braque**,
Fruit Dish, Ace of Clubs, early 1913.
Braque here explores in paint numerous elements that
echo aspects of collage, probably Cubism's most
important innovation: woodgrain paper imitated in paint
with a decorator's comb, diamond-patterned wallpaper,
playing cards, and commercial lettering. These references
to manufactured objects summon forth the world of
popular culture and contrast with the geometric
abstraction that structures the overall image.

First published in paperback in the United States of America in 2001 by
Thames & Hudson Inc., 500 Fifth Avenue, New York, New York 10110

thamesandhudsonusa.com

Library of Congress Catalog Card Number 2001086844
ISBN 0-500-20342-3

Designed by Derek Birdsall
Typeset by Omnific

Printed and bound in Singapore by C. S. Graphics

Contents

To Kenneth Allen, Robert L. Herbert and Jack J. Spector

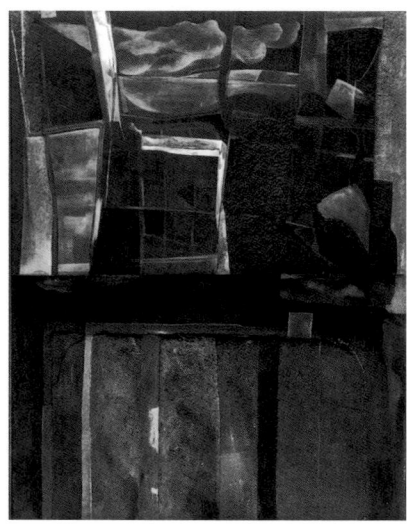

Kenneth Allen, *Night-Window No. 3*, 1985–90

Acknowledgments

A number of friends and fellow scholars played important roles during the writing of this book, and we would especially like to thank Allan Antliff, Francis Frascina, Kelly Goode, Linda Henderson, Mark Menlove, Gill Perry, and Anna Greutzner Robins. This book reached its final form during our stay at the Institute for Advanced Study, Princeton, NJ and benefited from lively discussions with Ruth Abbey, Anat Biletzki, the incomparable Pétronille Danchin, Irving Lavin, Marilyn Aronberg Lavin, Jeremy Moon, Lou Roberts and Bette Talvacchia. Special thanks go to Marilyn Lavin for her generous loan of H. W. Janson, *Modern Art in the Washington University Collection* (Saint Louis 1947), with its early colour reproduction of Picasso's *Bottle of Suze*, and to Amanda Beresford, who as Curator of the Steinberg Gallery of Art, Washington University, allowed us to examine the *Bottle of Suze* closely in spring 1999. We would also like to express our appreciation to Nikos Stangos for his encouragement and editorial wisdom and to the ms. readers for their excellent criticism. Finally, we would be remiss not to express our debt of gratitude to Phoebe and her friends Patti, Tinker, Miles, Cleo, Maisie and Tätlim for their ability to get us away from our desks and out into the woods, where our contemplative conversations shaped the book throughout.

Introduction

Cubism, arguably the seminal art movement of the twentieth century, initiated a pictorial revolution through its radical approach to imagemaking, employing some of the most important features of modernism in Europe and America: visual abstraction and obfuscation, spatial and temporal disorientation, avant-gardist rejection of past values, and breakdown of class hierarchies in the embrace of popular culture, all evident in Georges Braque's *Fruit Dish, Ace of Clubs* of early 1913. Cubist style transformed not just subsequent painting, sculpture and photography, but also architecture and design of everything from furniture to clothing to objects of everyday use. Chances are you find yourself at this moment in a room fully compatible with post-Cubist aesthetics, either because you are in a modern or postmodern building, or because the nineteenth-century building you are in was gutted and refitted in accordance with post-Cubist design principles and furnishings. How could a modernist movement developed by about a dozen people in the short period from 1907 to 1920 have such a sweeping influence on contemporary and subsequent culture?

Our premise in writing this book is that the answer to that question lies largely in the ways Cubism responded to profound aesthetic, philosophical and societal changes in the early twentieth century. A few examples: X-rays were discovered by Wilhelm Roentgen in 1895, revealing realities invisible to the naked eye and reinforcing a growing mistrust of external appearances; electric street lights replaced gas lamps in Paris in 1906; Henri Bergson, the antirationalist philosopher, gave lectures at the Collège de France so wildly popular that people climbed ladders to listen at the windows; a burgeoning women's movement agitated for female emancipation, including legal birth control, and made the then shocking demand for the right to vote; and a large-scale labour movement was growing, campaigning for fairer pay and such new demands as an 8-hour workday and 5-day workweek. Last but not least, the pictorial innovations initiated by earlier modernists, most significantly Cézanne, transformed modes of representation for subsequent avant-garde artists. Exciting and extraordinary changes were taking place, and the atmosphere heralded a future that these young artists hoped to help shape. At the same time, diplomacy

Le Meeting du Pré-Saint-Gervais contre la Guerre

Au retour, une Bagarre s'est produite, place du Combat, entre Anarchistes et Agents

Un coin du meeting du Pré-Saint-Gervais

between European powers was so frequently punctuated by crises that it seemed, to the many thousands that demonstrated at anti-war rallies, to be a system of alliances guaranteed to end in a war that would engulf the whole of Europe and its colonies, a suspicion that was proved right by the outbreak of World War I in August 1914. Cubism developed in France in this atmosphere of rapid change and impending war, shaped partly by a number of artists committed to an idealistic conception of society opposed to war. The Cubists purposely grappled in their art with contemporary ideas about modernity, society, and the 'nature of reality', and also reflected their historical period in ways less conscious and controllable, as in their responses to colonialism or the rapid development of commercialism.

In re-examining this art and its innovative modes of representation, we will be drawing on the abundant literature that has reshaped our understanding of the history of Cubism over the past two decades (see Select Bibliography). Recent study of the Cubists' responses to everything from the critical reception of Cézanne, popular culture, philosophy, science and changing gender relations to nationalist rhetoric, French colonialism, leftist politics and war has served to underscore the integral relation of such issues to the aesthetic innovations unfolding on the Cubists' canvases. In the chapters that follow we consider the movement's initial development in France with such richly cultural and social concerns in mind. How Cubism responded to these cultural currents can best be approached by structuring this book around key issues and pre-occupations. *Cubism and Culture* has therefore been organized to trace a chronological and stylistic history of the movement as it developed in France before and during World War I while simultaneously considering a variety of questions related to these profound cultural changes. How did such concerns and cultural transformations help shape the varieties of this art? What visual elements and combinations worked in response to their differing ideas? And how does awareness of the complexity of the Cubists' wider culture help us interpret individual works of art or the movement as a whole, not limited to their intentions? Thematic chapters follow various periods of the movement in roughly chronological sequence, while considering salient issues related to that period.

Chapter One, 'European Primitives', looks at the early development of the Cubist movement, between roughly 1907 and 1909, in the context of primitivist modernism. At the turn of the century, many of the late nineteenth-century avant-gardists and future Cubists embraced a shared notion of the 'primitive'. They attributed an authenticity of vision and spontaneity of expression to the art of children and to supposedly primitive cultures, ranging for them from the ancient civilizations of Egypt and Java to cultures thought to be 'without history': sub-Saharan Africa and Oceania. By incorporating stylistic features of the art of such cultures into their modernism, primitivists opposed what they viewed as the sterility of their own society and its art: overcivilized, moribund and decadent. The idea that they could revitalize themselves and their art through reference to 'innocent' art and cultures may well be the underlying motive in the development of Cubism, and it is a position from which many of them began. The important influence of Paul Cézanne (1839–1906) overlaps with these ideas and was appropriated by primitivist discourse. In this chapter, we explore the beginnings of Cubism in the enthusiasm for 'primitive' art, especially from Africa, on the part of André Derain (1880–1954), Pablo Picasso (1881–1973) and Georges Braque (1882–1963) as well as the ways the work of Cézanne was viewed in primitivist terms.

The second chapter, 'Philosophies of Time and Space', considers the period 1909 to 1912, looking at how each artist responded to different aspects of the complex ideas and theories influential in artistic and literary milieux and at the resultingly differing aims in their Cubist works. Here we consider the Cubist revolt against nineteenth-century academic techniques of perspectival illusionism and the related assumption that a painting must represent a single moment in time and be seen from a fixed position in space. The

3. **Pablo Picasso**, *Head with Scarification*, summer 1907. This work is the most direct expression of Picasso's admiration of African art, evoking several kinds of masks from French West and Central Africa with bold expressionist strokes of pure colour. The transformation of Western conventions – such as a portrait head – with 'African' forms was done with the intention of revitalizing painting, expressing the painter's direct and spontaneous feelings with an 'authenticity' often attributed to 'primitive' artists.

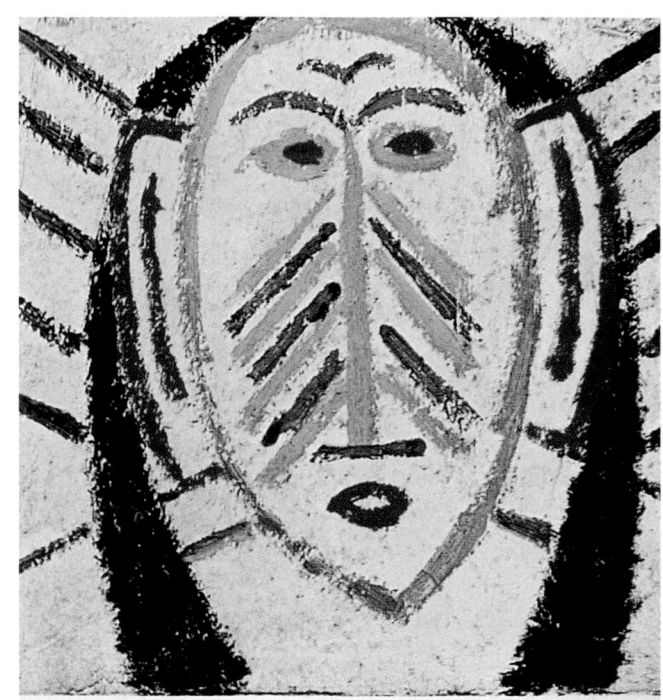

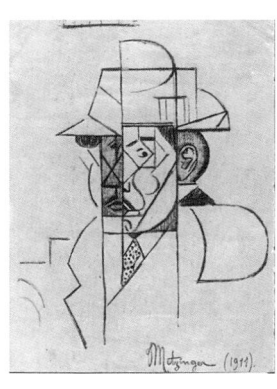

4. **Jean Metzinger**, *Study for Portrait of Albert Gleizes*, 1911. Metzinger painted this portrait of his friend Gleizes around the time that they began to collaborate on *Du Cubisme*, an aesthetic manifesto published in 1912. The surface of the work is broken into several disjunctive spaces that correspond to different moments in time. We see Gleizes's hat both in profile and from above, while the face is even more complicated, combining partial profile, frontal and three-quarter views. Gleizes and Metzinger justified such temporal and spatial disjunctions in terms of the theory of time developed by Bergson.

Cubists overturned these methods by introducing multiple viewpoints, distortions of form, and ambiguous spatial relations into their paintings, confounding viewer expectations. Several Cubists wrote texts explaining their pictorial innovations in terms of new theories of time and space propounded by such prominent figures as the mathematician Henri Poincaré and the philosopher Henri Bergson. Our study of Cubist art will underscore the stylistic diversity resulting from these shared philosophical premises, which motivated artists and critics affiliated with the movement.

Chapter Three, 'Political Uses of the Past', takes up the subject of the complex relation of Cubism to tradition, covering the movement between 1907 and 1914. In their uses of the past, especially styles of past art, the cultural politics of several Cubists become especially visible. For some, subversion of academic style operated as a critique of past traditions, which were seen as implicated in an aesthetic and social status quo. For others, Cubism was a way precisely to revitalize or regenerate the past, recuperating valuable essences of the French 'race' and even founding a new 'classicism'. This chapter undertakes to explore these cultural and political debates in which key Cubists participated. How such debates in turn shape their art and the critical reception of their work reveals

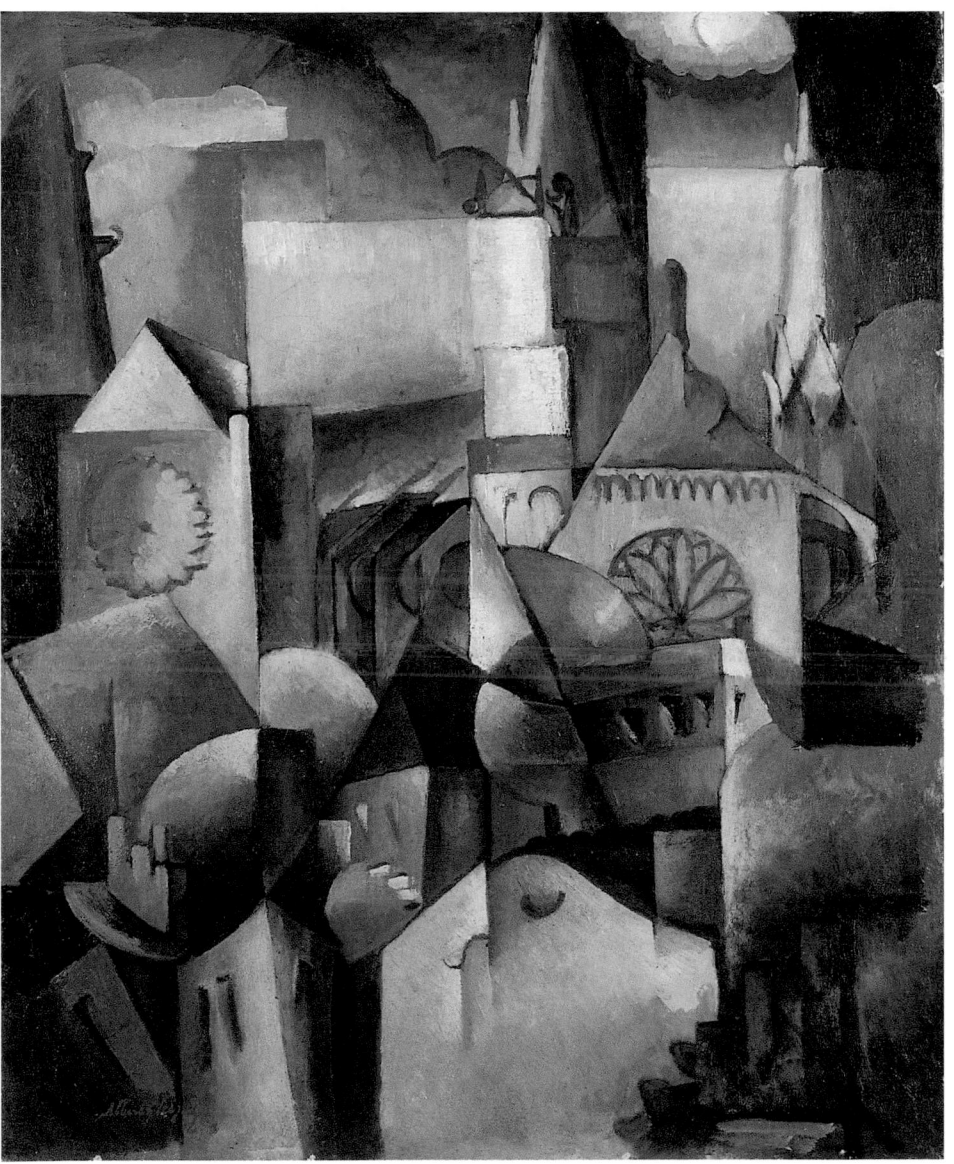

5. **Albert Gleizes**, *Chartres Cathedral*, 1912.
Gleizes's Cubist transformation of one of France's greatest Gothic monuments links
the creativity of the country's past with its present, as well as linking the image of the
cathedral to the town. By merging the geometric planes of the walls and towers with
the surrounding environment, he depicts the building as rooted in the labour of the
common people. Gleizes's theory favoured the 'Gothic north' over any identification
of French culture with the 'Latin south', which was associated with the classical and
academic tradition and with French right-wing politics.

fissures between some of the artists that problematize any notion of a unitary movement or of Cubist art occupying a single political position.

Chapter Four, 'Gender Codes', considers issues of gender as they relate to interpretations of Cubism, between 1909 and 1916. Notions of the masculine and the feminine were rife in popular culture of this period and in the critical literature on Cubism. Based on fundamental assumptions about the nature of creativity, inherited as with so much else from the Symbolist movement, artists and writers expressed concepts of gender in their art in terms of subject, style and genre. The decorative arts, mass culture and consumerism were all gendered as 'feminine' in critical writings of the day, and so the involvement of male Cubists in these cultural arenas served to problematize the status of Cubism as a style allied to the 'fine arts'. Cubist theories of creativity likewise embraced the gendered female-as-nature/male-as-culture dichotomy, leading to images of women as tied to their reproductive functions and to images of men engaged in such cultural activities as sports, expressive of male dynamism. Such assumptions led to both conflict and contradiction when male and female Cubists negotiated artistic partnerships, which we consider in the cases of Robert Delaunay (1885–1941) and Sonia Terk Delaunay (1885–1979), and Alice Halicka (1895–1975) and Louis Marcoussis (1883–1941).

Chapter Five, 'Pasted Papers and Revolution', looks at the most influential invention of the Cubist movement on subsequent twentieth-century art. Collage, *papier collé* and assemblage entail procedures of gluing coloured and commercial papers and objects onto a two-dimensional surface or of bringing them together with three-dimensional objects. Simple as it may sound to viewers a century later, with that act, modernism turned a corner. The potential of this new medium was initially explored between 1912 and 1914 by Picasso, Braque and Juan Gris (1887–1927), who pushed Cubism beyond transformations of the depictions of objects to an entirely new artistic language that problematized representation. The very materials of which collage was made constituted not only a rejection of the medium of oil-on-canvas, but a critique of the craft tradition and the sanctity of the 'hand of the artist'. The parallel medium of assemblage likewise problematized traditional sculptural materials, as well as profoundly altering the treatment of three-dimensional form, space and scale. Much of this new art operates in the name of the 'popular' (mass-produced newspapers, advertisements, song-sheets, cheap wallpaper, glass, scraps of tin), raising important questions about the relation of 'high' art to vernacular culture and about the 'cultural politics' of the works themselves. Looking at such questions, we consider the relation of collage and assemblage both to the call within modernism for the breaking down of barriers between art and life and to the more generally problematic relations of modernism to popular, commercial and political culture.

Chapter Six, 'Cubism at War', considers the impact of war on the Cubist movement. The most inventive period of Cubism ended with the outbreak of World War I in 1914, and, by the time of the Armistice in November 1918, the cosmopolitan community that had nurtured Cubism's beginnings was shattered by wartime xenophobia and the dispersal of the international European avant-garde. Most of the French Cubists joined the military, while many foreigners like the poet and art critic Guillaume Apollinaire (1880–1918) and Marcoussis, both Poles, changed their citizenship or joined the Foreign Legion. We also consider those who either resisted the war, such as the critic Alexandre Mercereau (born 1884), or refused to fight, such as Picasso, Gris and Marcel Duchamp (1887–1968). The overwhelming effect of the war, however, was a shift to nationalism even within the avant-garde artistic community. This chapter considers the art produced under the pressure of these momentous historical changes and the emergence of the 'Purist' movement as a critique of earlier Cubism. [10]

In sum, Cubism's stylistic development is integrally connected with historical events that both profoundly altered French society and inaugurated the twentieth century. In the pages that follow we examine the reciprocal relation of Cubism's formal innovations to those historical transformations, to better understand the movement's relation to French culture in its broadest and most inclusive sense.

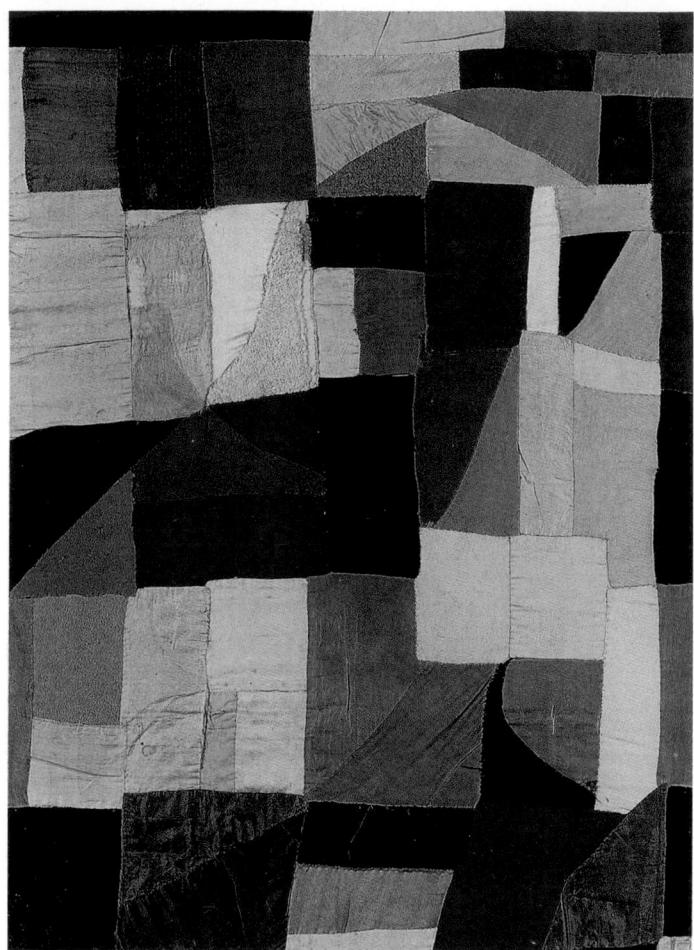

6. Sonia Terk Delaunay,
Couverture (Quilt), 1911.
Terk's hand-sewn quilt combines domesticity with abstraction in an innovative way. Terk has adapted the formal language of Cubism, with its geometricity and emphasis on surface, to the traditionally female craft of quiltmaking. In later years she would apply her Cubist abstraction to decorative design, including high-fashion clothing and china. Although successful financially, her forays into the decorative arts have only recently won the critical recognition previously reserved for her painting.

7. Juan Gris, *Breakfast*, 1914.
Here Gris presents a Cubist version of his own breakfast table, gluing in commercial papers that both present and represent objects and surfaces. The table's top and legs appear in artificial woodgrain paper, while the newspaper *Le Journal* and a packet of coffee lie on its surface in front of decorative wallpaper. Such 'real' elements contrast with the difficulty of reading the great variety of perspectives.

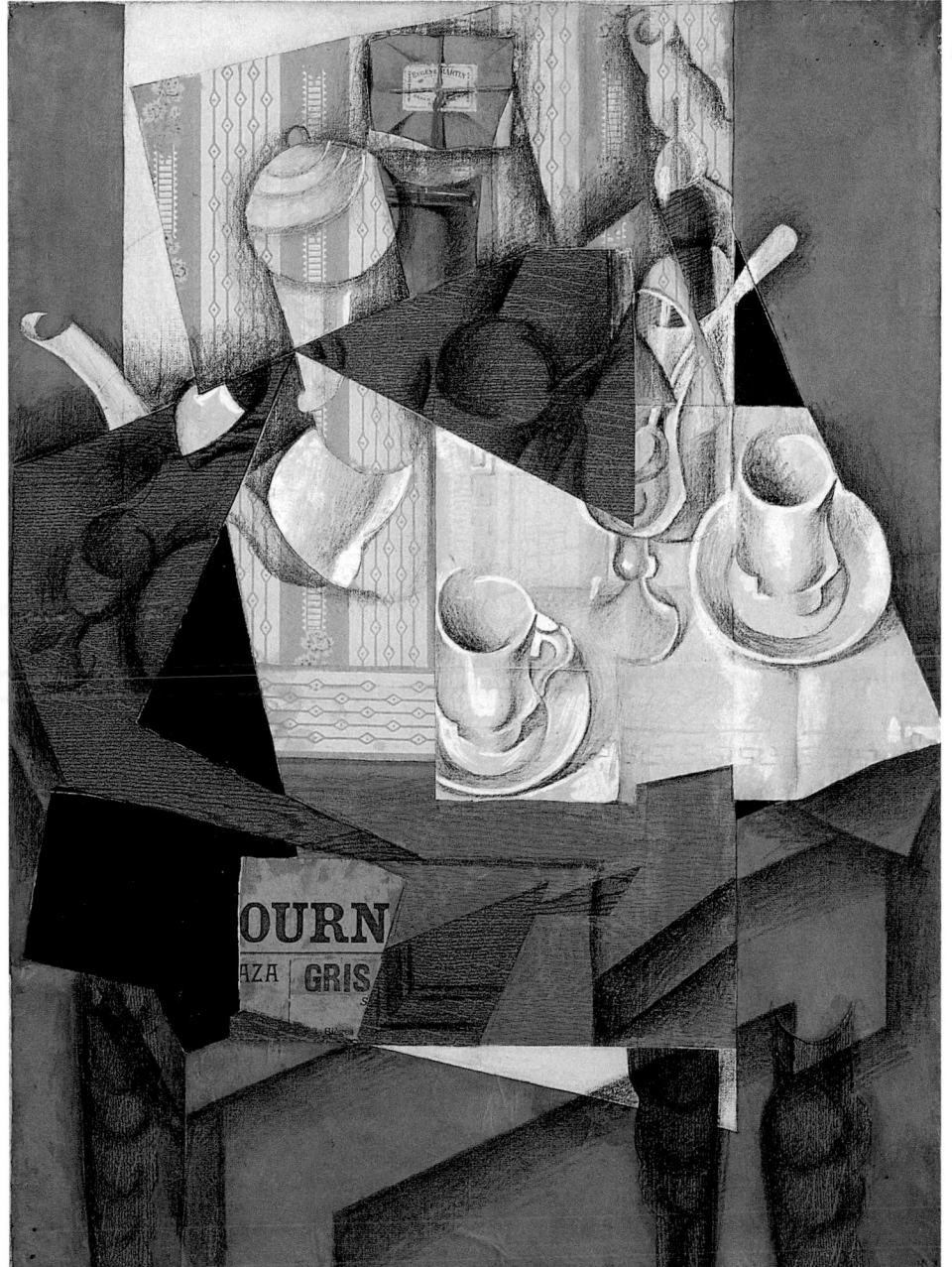

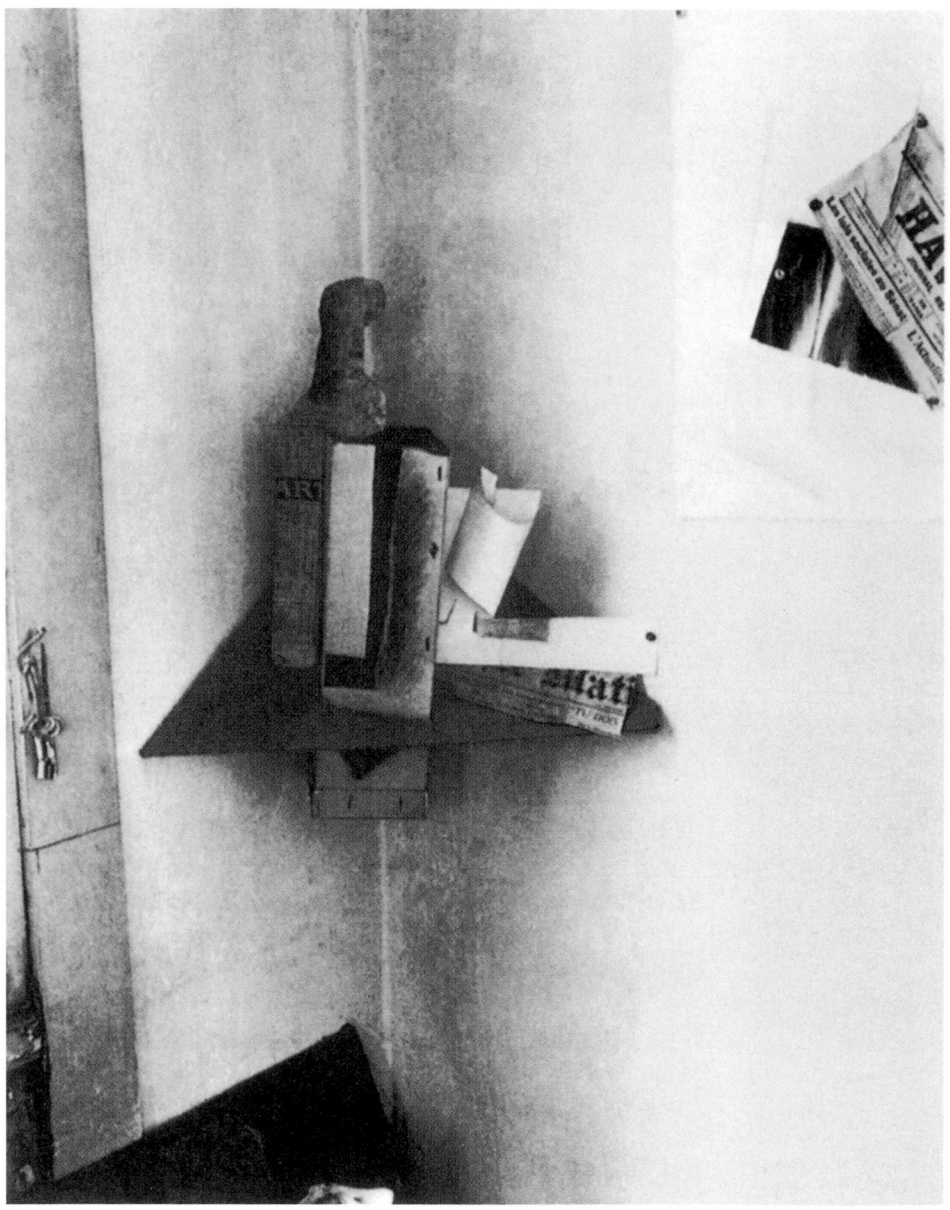

8. Georges Braque,
Construction, February 1914, no longer extant.
The concept of collage was extended into three
dimensions, first with paper sculpture, then with
other materials such as cardboard, wood, tin and
found objects. Here Braque combines cardboard
and newsprint to represent a still life of bottle and
newspaper on a table. Fitted into the corner of
the room, the walls themselves and their shadows
become part of the sculpture, fulfilling one of the
most pressing calls of modernism: the breaking
down of barriers between art and life.

9. Juan Gris,
Hommage à Picasso, 1912.
Juan Gris came to Paris in 1906, but didn't become a Cubist until around 1910. By 1912 he was a familiar face in both Cubist circles, exhibiting this homage to Picasso at the Salon des Indépendants that spring. Yet, apart from the general combination of multiple viewpoints, his own Cubist style does not imitate Picasso's closely. Instead Gris constructs the work with a regularity and precision based on his interest in mathematics and the Golden Section.

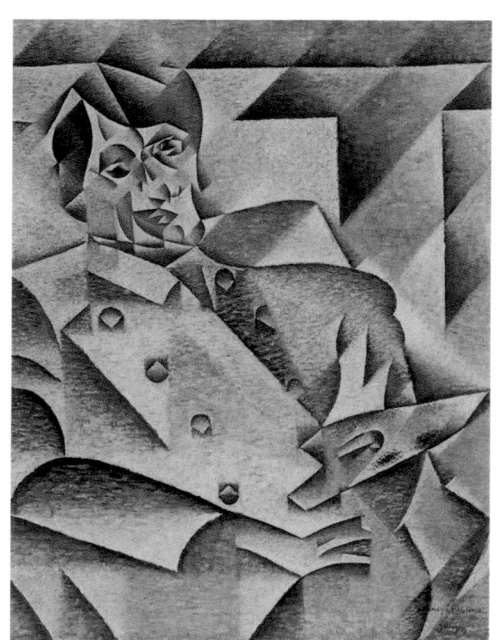

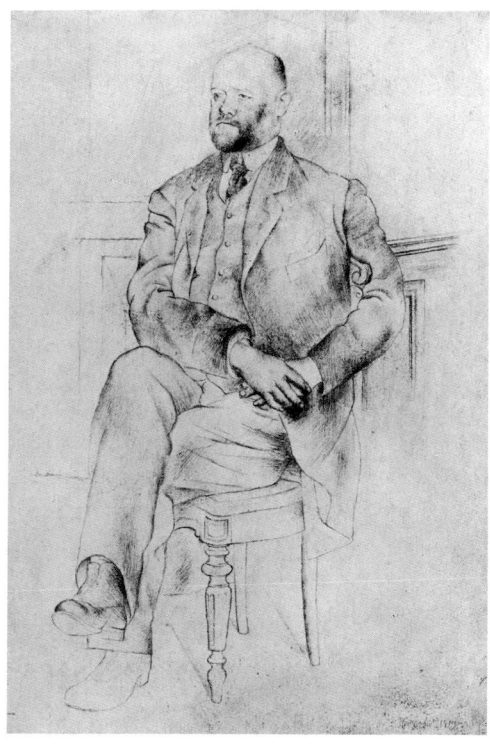

10. Pablo Picasso,
Portrait of Ambroise Vollard, 1915.
This fine line drawing was viewed as 'Ingresque' in 1915, a year after World War I broke out, when its return to realism and sheer virtuosity were considered shocking. Such works were celebrated by Apollinaire, who praised Picasso for continuing with his 'invaluable work as an artist', and for having 'outdone Ingres in his admirable drawings'. Though Picasso pushed the abstraction of Cubism further than ever during the war years, he also came under pressure as a non-combatant in the nationalistic climate of war fever.

There were two groups of Cubists, who interacted, overlapped and exchanged ideas in various ways. Picasso, Braque and their circle – including the poets and art critics Apollinaire and André Salmon (1881–1969) as well as the artist Marie Laurencin (1885–1945) – centred initially in the 'Bateau Lavoir' ('Washboat'), a rambling building on the slopes of Montmartre where Picasso, Salmon and Gris had their studios. The second Cubist group frequently met in Puteaux, a town on the outskirts of Paris where other key figures lived, including Albert Gleizes (1881–1953) and the Duchamp-Villon brothers: Jacques Villon (1875–1963), Raymond Duchamp-Villon (1876–1918) and Marcel Duchamp. These two groups are mainly separated by their exhibition practices, though their Cubist styles can also vary widely.

The Puteaux group regularly exhibited in Paris's large public venues, such as the spring Salon des Indépendants and the fall Salon d'Automne. Resultingly, they became the public face of the Cubist movement and are frequently referred to as the 'Salon Cubists'. The critic Roger Allard (1885–1961) identified Henri Le Fauconnier (1881–1945), Gleizes, and Jean Metzinger (1883–1956) as the progenitors of a new movement in his review of the 1910 Salon d'Automne. At the 1911 Salon des Indépendants, these artists proclaimed their allegiance to Cubism by exhibiting together, with

11. Installation photograph of the Salon d'Automne, October 1912. This rare photograph of a Salon installation shows large-scale works by the following artists (from left to right): František Kupka (1871–1954), *Amorpha, Fugue in Two Colours*; Francis Picabia, *The Spring*; and Jean Metzinger, *Dancer in a Café*. Sculptures by Amedeo Modigliani (1884–1920) can be seen in the foreground, alongside small paintings by other Cubists.

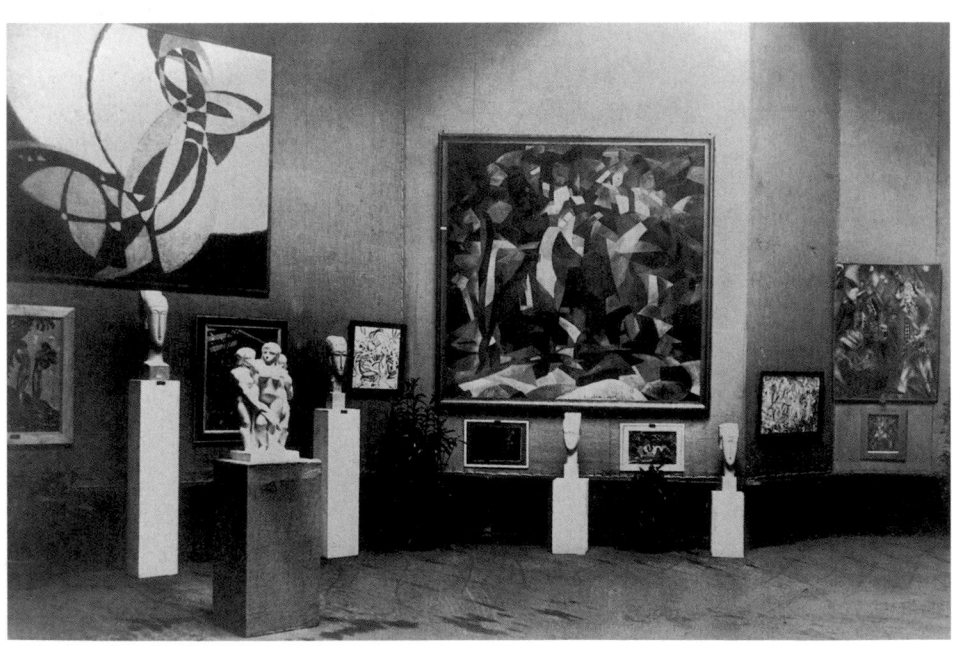

the addition of Marie Laurencin, Fernand Léger (1881–1955), and Robert Delaunay, creating a *succès de scandale* that assured the notoriety of the movement.

In the heyday of Cubism, Picasso, Braque, Derain and Gris used a private dealer, Daniel-Henry Kahnweiler (1884–1979). By 1912 he had signed contracts with these artists to buy their entire production, restricting them from showing their work anywhere in Paris other than their studios or his gallery. Kahnweiler also worked hard to exhibit his artists' work outside of Paris and abroad, where it was shown together with many of the Puteaux Cubists', for instance in Lyons, Amsterdam, Munich, Budapest, Moscow, London, New York, Chicago and Boston. Before 1912, the work of Picasso and Braque was also visible at Wilhelm Uhde's small Notre-Dame-des-Champs gallery, where Picasso held a show in May 1910; another Picasso exhibition appeared at Ambroise Vollard's gallery from December 1910 to February 1911. Additionally Braque until spring 1909, Derain until 1910 and Gris until 1912 exhibited their emerging Cubism at the public salons. As a consequence, the work of this group was visible in Paris in these years, but viewers had to work harder to find it. Several of the Salon Cubists published their ideas about Cubism — including Gleizes, Metzinger and Le Fauconnier — explaining their complex interests and aims, while no one in Kahnweiler's group did so in the early period. Debate continues as to whether these early writings are applicable to the Cubist movement as a whole.

A second wave of artists joined the movement after it was well underway, including Gris, Marcoussis, Halicka, Roger de La Fresnaye (1885–1925), Alexander Archipenko (1887–1964), Henri Laurens (1885–1954), Jacques Lipchitz (1891–1973), Francis Picabia (1879–1953) and Maria Blanchard (1881–1932). La Fresnaye showed paintings in a room adjacent to the Cubist room at the 1911 Salon des Indépendants; subsequently both he and the sculptor Archipenko joined other Cubists in attending regular meetings at Gleizes's studio in Courbevoie, a Paris suburb adjacent to Puteaux. Archipenko, like Duchamp-Villon, was one of the originators of Cubist sculpture; following his arrival in Paris in 1908 he befriended Léger and joined the Duchamp-Villon circle in 1911. Marcoussis arrived in France in 1903 and began working in a Cubist style in 1911. Halicka came to Paris in May 1912 and studied briefly at the Académie Ranson, founded by Paul Ranson and Maurice Denis in 1908. The Académie followed the Symbolist aesthetic principles of the Nabi group, who modelled their art after the early work of Paul Gauguin (1848–1903), as in his *Vision After the Sermon* of 1888, with 12

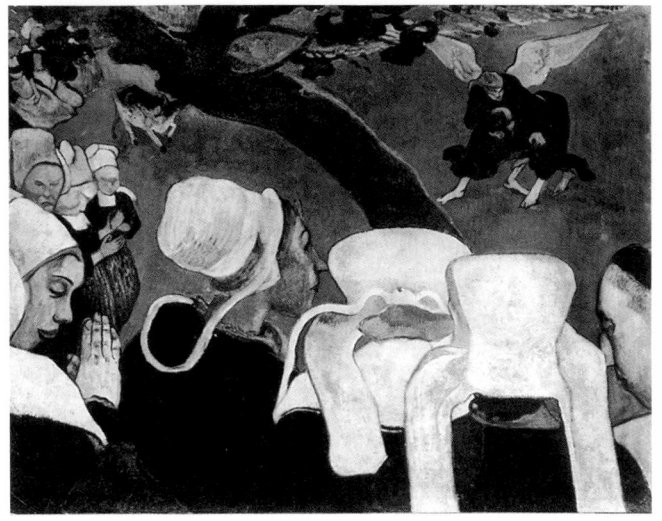

12. Paul Gauguin,
Vision After the Sermon, 1888. This signature painting from Gauguin's period of retreat to Pont Aven, Brittany exhibits all the hallmarks of his Symbolist style. In a primitivist attempt to evoke the Breton women's 'great and rustic superstitious simplicity', Gauguin employs flat simplified shapes outlined in black, an abrupt psychological division between the space of the worshippers and that of the wrestlers (whom they experience as Jacob wrestling with the Angel), spatial distortion, and colour reversal, such as red grass.

its matte colours, flattened space, and simplified forms outlined in black. Halicka was thus first influenced by the Nabis and only developed a Cubist aesthetic after 1914. Picabia met Apollinaire in 1911, working thereafter on his own blend of Cubism and abstraction. Blanchard in turn explored Fauvism following her arrival in Paris in 1909 and only turned to Cubism in 1916, when she formed a close friendship with Gris. Each of these artists played a significant role in the movement but they cannot be considered as its principal progenitors during the prewar era.

Between 1907 and 1912, the various artists associated with Cubism came to know one another's work. In 1909 Metzinger began publishing what the poet Max Jacob (1876–1944), a close friend of Picasso, called 'Mallarméen' poetry in neo-Symbolist journals like *Ile sonnante* and *Pan*. Metzinger later recalled that Jacob introduced him to Apollinaire and the Picasso circle in late 1907. Metzinger lived in Montmartre from 1906 to 1912, and from 1907 on he frequented Picasso's nearby studio and often joined the *bande à Picasso* with Braque, Derain, Jacob, Salmon and Apollinaire, whose Cézannesque portrait he painted in 1910. In December 1908, [13] Metzinger exhibited paintings alongside those of Braque and Picasso at Uhde's Notre-Dame-des-Champs Gallery.

The Italian Futurist Gino Severini, who lived in Montmartre [15] from 1906 to 1913, later recalled that the café La Closerie des Lilas, on the corner of boulevard Montparnasse and avenue de l'Observatoire, was at the epicentre of the movement. In the winter of 1908 a group associated with the neo-Symbolist journal *Vers et*

13. **Jean Metzinger**,
Portrait of Apollinaire, 1910.
Metzinger's role as an intermediary between the *bande à Picasso* in Montmartre and the Puteaux Cubists was paralleled by Apollinaire, whom he depicted in this early portrait. Painted the same year that Metzinger developed a fully Cubist style, the work is still representative of his Cézannesque phase, using a muted palette and broadly visible brushstrokes to generalize the forms of the face and body. Many of the Cubists painted portraits of Apollinaire, who performed the role of defender for the entire group.

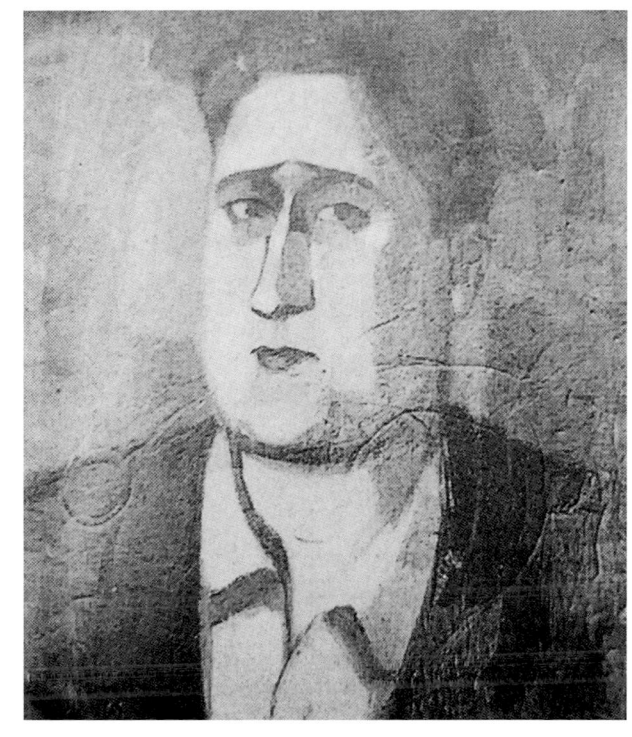

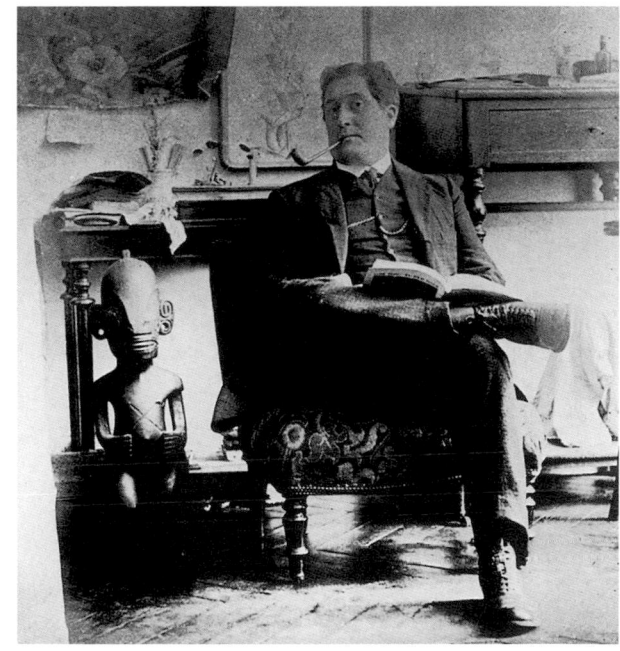

14. Photograph of Guillaume Apollinaire, taken by Pablo Picasso in his studio, boulevard de Clichy, c. 1910.

Prose gathered around the Symbolist poet Paul Fort and, with Salmon as its secretary, began to hold their weekly Tuesday *soirées* at the café. Severini notes that the attendees included older Symbolist writers and their younger neo-Symbolist admirers Gustave Kahn, Maurice Maeterlinck, Apollinaire and Allard, as well the 'Unanimist' poet Jules Romains (1885–1972) and art critic Alexandre Mercereau. Severini mentions Metzinger, Gleizes, Le Fauconnier, Villon, Duchamp-Villon, Duchamp and Léger, and according to literary historian Roger Shattuck, Apollinaire, Jacob and Picasso walked down from Montmartre on a weekly basis to join these meetings of poets and painters at the Closerie.

Similar interactions took place in Montmartre, the bohemian counterpart to Montparnasse. Braque, Derain, Duchamp, Gris, Marcoussis, Metzinger and Picasso all lived in Montmartre before 1913, with the latter two residing at the infamous Bateau Lavoir, on rue Ravignan, along with Salmon. Severini, who moved to Montmartre in 1906 and lived alongside Braque on the impasse Guelma, recalled that the artists met frequently at a restaurant on rue Cavalotti near Gris's studio, where the proprietor, Monsieur Vernin, let them eat on credit. 'Besides the group of painters

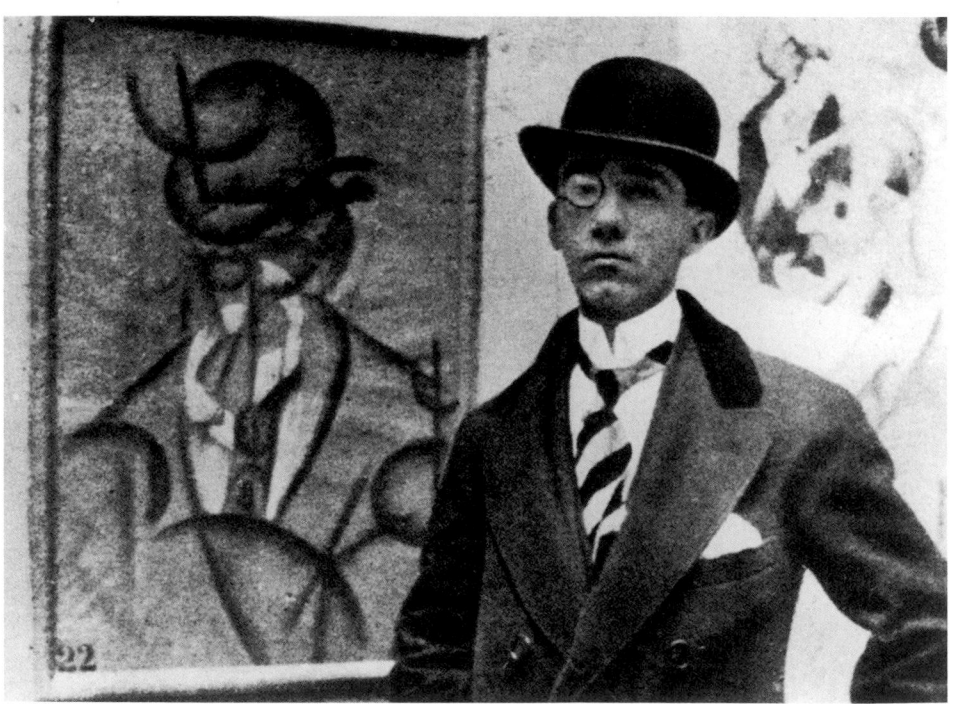

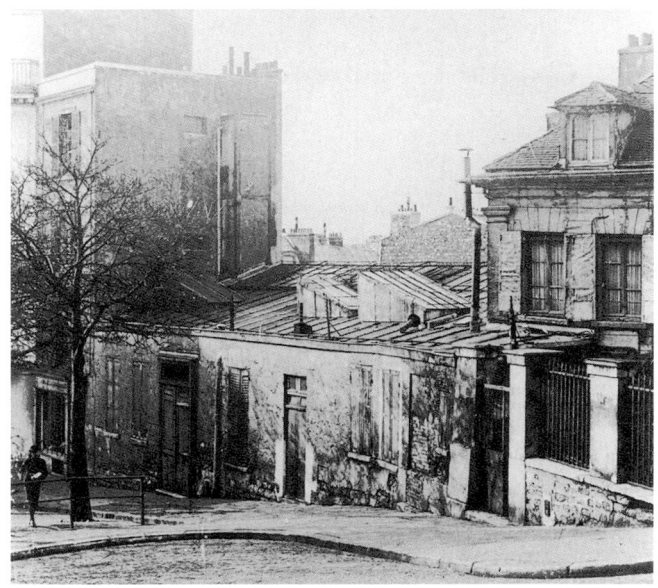

[Braque, Kees Van Dongen, Gris, and Picasso] there was a comparable flock of writers made up of Apollinaire, Salmon, Jacob, and [Maurice] Raynal [1884–1954]'. By 1912 Vernin's bistro had attained a reputation similar to the Closerie des Lilas, since an article published in the journal *Fantasio* in October 1912 described the rue Cavalotti restaurant as a 'Cubist bar'. The author noted that, on any given evening, Gris, Marcoussis, Jacob, Apollinaire and Picasso could be seen in the company of Léger, Derain, and Le Fauconnier discussing the thought of '[Henri] Bergson and Leonardo da Vinci'. This suggests a lively exchange between the Montmartre *bande à Picasso* and those Cubists residing in Montparnasse or Puteaux. As the reference to the French philosopher Bergson suggests, the shared aesthetic interests uniting these Cubists also facilitated an important exchange of ideas, contributing to the many competing Cubist styles and meanings. The ways that these ideas underlie Cubist works of art is one of the central subjects of this book.

Chapter I   European Primitives

In the winter of 1908 to 1909, the American writer Gelett Burgess visited Paris and toured the art scene, seeking out the most 'shocking' new developments and in so doing interviewing a number of key modernists, including Henri Matisse (1869–1956), Derain, Braque, Picasso and Metzinger. Thus in 1910 the author of 'I've Never Seen a Purple Cow' and 'Why Be A Goop?' published a lively and entertaining record of his quest in New York's *Architectural Record*, called 'The Wild Men of Paris', giving us one of the earliest documentations of the beginnings of Cubism, albeit rather tongue-in-cheek. It was not the mere geometricity of such works as Braque's *Grand Nu (Large Nude)* (1908), the drawing for it that Burgess published, Derain's *Bathers* (1907), Picasso's *Demoiselles d'Avignon* (1907) or *Three Women* (1908) that struck him. What interested Burgess most was the 'ugliness' and 'primitive' character of what he saw, and – although he did not like this development any more than the laughing crowds he observed at the Salon – he saw pretty clearly what was at stake:

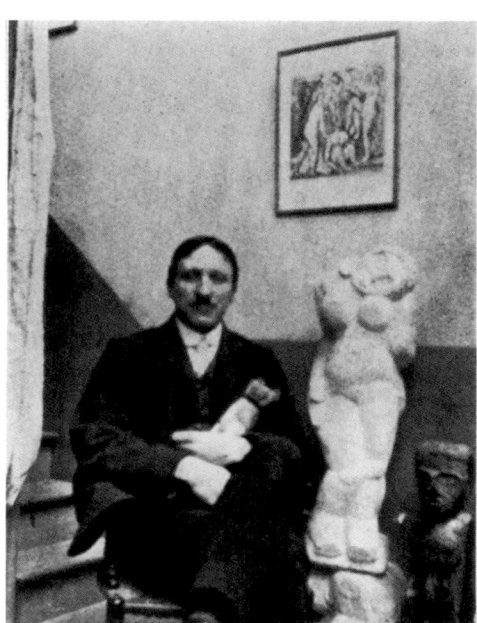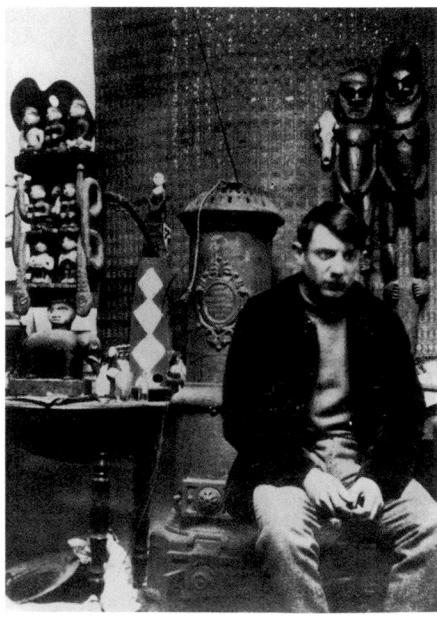

Had they attempted to invent a new form of humor? Were they merely practical jokers? Or must we seriously attempt anew to solve the old question:'What is art?'

It was an affording quest, analyzing such madness as this. I had studied the gargoyles of Oxford and Notre Dame, I had mused over the art of the Niger and of Dahomey, I had gazed at Hindu monstrosities, Aztec mysteries and many other primitive grotesques; and it had come over me that there was a rationale of ugliness as there was a rationale of beauty; that, perhaps, one was but the negative of the other, an image reversed, which might have its own value and esoteric meaning. Men had painted and carved grim and obscene things when the world was young. Was this revival a sign of some second childhood of the race, or a true rebirth of art?

Burgess has pointed out here the key to this moment in early Cubism: a purposeful simplification and distortion of forms in the spirit of seeking a direct expressiveness associated with what modernists took to be the 'primitive' art of non-European cultures, from Egypt to sub-Saharan Africa to Oceania. This complex phenomenon needs discussion before we can look at the art created in its name.

The concept of 'primitive'

The term 'primitive' does not constitute an essentialist category but exemplifies a relationship of binary opposition to the 'civilized'. Within the context of modernism, 'primitivism' is an act on the part of artists and writers seeking to celebrate features of the art and culture of peoples deemed 'primitive' and to appropriate their supposed simplicity and authenticity to the project of transforming Western art. In Western culture the term 'primitive' has been applied with positive as well as negative valences, but historically, when ascribed to cultures external to Europe, its connotations have been predominantly negative. Above all, the concept of the primitive in this period is the product of the historical experience of the West and more specifically is an ideological construct of colonial conquest and exploitation best understood in terms of time/space, gender, race, and class.

In Western discourse a distinction between collective and individual forms of expression in art production is viewed as part of a temporal progression from a 'less developed' ('primitive') condition, wherein cultural production is related to material needs or instinctual drives, to the state of 'advanced' societies, in which the individual creative intellect gains ascendancy over the realm of

17. André Derain in his studio holding a sculpture of a cat, 1908.

18. Pablo Picasso in his rue Ravignan studio, 1908.

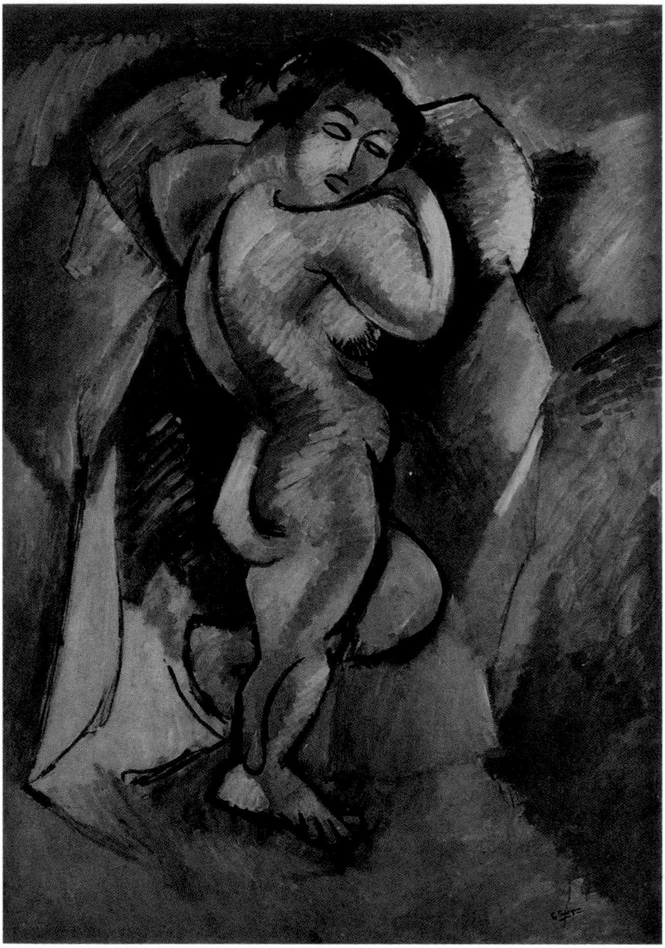

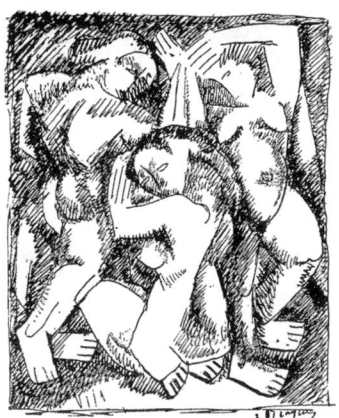

19. **Georges Braque**,
Grand Nu (Large Nude), 1907–8.

20. **Georges Braque**,
Drawing for *Large Nude*, 1907–8.

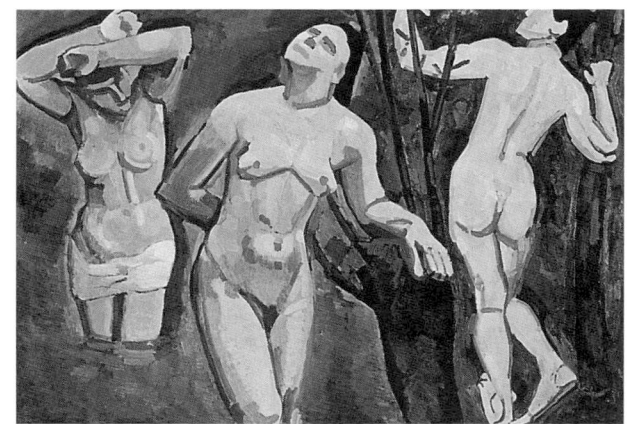

21. **André Derain**,
Bathers, 1907.

22. **Pablo Picasso**,
Les Demoiselles d'Avignon, 1907.

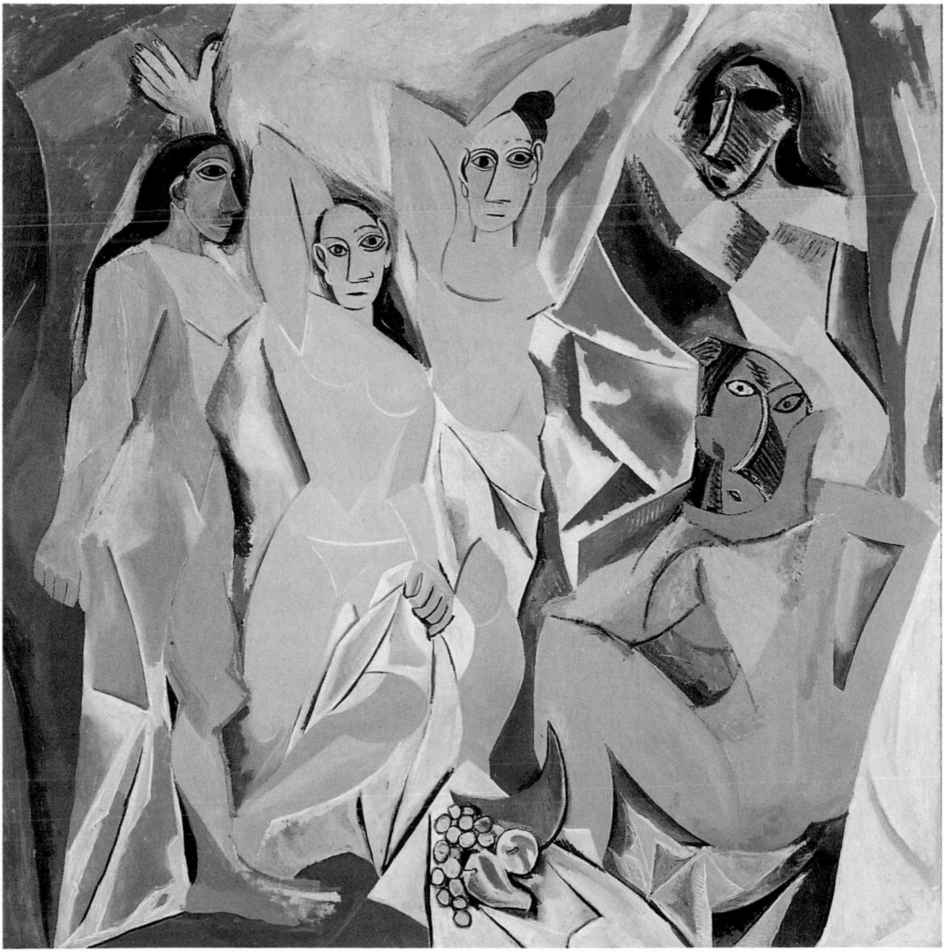

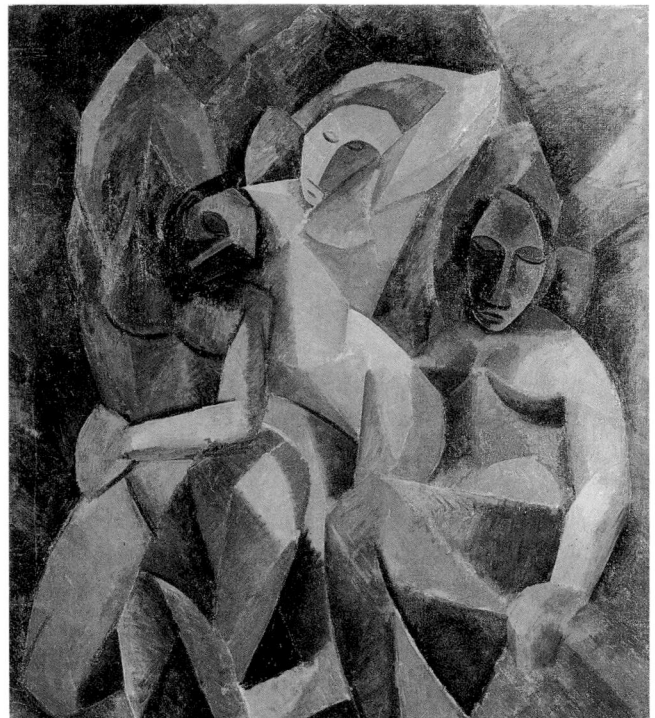

23. **Pablo Picasso,**
Three Women, 1907–8.
Picasso creates ambiguities in *Three Women,* a work that embodies his transition from africanism to Cézannism. Using only two basic colours throughout, he juxtaposes figural forms – legs, arms, ribs – with background forms rendered in identical colours, purposely confusing the viewer as to relative locations of form and space. The calf and thigh of the figure on the right perform the same function as the buildings in Braque's *Houses at L'Estaque* (1908), intentionally creating a breakdown between foreground and background, form and space, flesh and cloth, and 'opening' his Cubist forms to *passage* on a large scale. 1909 has sometimes been considered the turning point in this 'opening' of Cubist form – no longer bounded by an outline – though it is already visible here.

the irrational. If one were to conceive of such art as changeless and primeval, it would deny what anthropologist Johannes Fabian terms 'coevalness', the temporal coexistence of the producer of 'primitive' art with his or her Western counterpart. In this discourse the actuality of physical synchronicity is replaced by a typological timeframe defined in terms of Western progress and primitive regression. The spatial and temporal are frequently combined in such discourse, for to leave the West and enter into a foreign culture is to leave one's own 'mature' culture and enter into an 'infantile' past, as if traveling through time rather than space: African, Oceanic and even Middle Eastern and North African cultures have been said to mirror the 'childhood' of Western civilization, or as Burgess put it, a time 'when the world was young'. As such the term 'primitive' is part of a larger discourse concerning the role of temporal constructs in power relations between cultures, propped up by racial theories of inferiority.

At the same time, Western conceptions of the primitive could have positive valences, particularly when Western culture itself was thought to be 'overly civilized' and thus in need of rejuvenation through contact with societies in an 'earlier stage of development'.

(Burgess captures this ambivalence when he rhetorically asks whether avant-garde primitivism is 'a sign of some second childhood of the race, or a true rebirth of art?') Nineteenth-century social critics frequently bemoaned the shift of the rural peasantry to industrial towns for similar reasons. Writers like John Ruskin saw the transferral of populations from country to city as a sign of the loss within Western culture of a pre-industrial, and thus 'primitive', agrarian society whose communitarian values and religiosity contrasted sharply with the decadent effects of urbanism. Here we can observe social class as an element in the 'primitive', operative when applied to peasants, or the 'folk', within Europe's borders.

Gender distinctions are also fundamental to notions of the primitive, as the second-class status of women in all societies relates to an association of women with the natural and men with the cultural sphere. Although women obviously play a role in the cultural life of any society they are nevertheless seen as less transcendental of nature than men. The restriction of female activities to those that supposedly possess this 'natural' relation does not impinge on men, whose physiology is not viewed as delimiting their capacities in the field of cultural production.

All of the Cubists express notions of the 'primitive' in various ways. Turn-of-the-century avant-garde artists and their primitivist aesthetic manoeuvres operated in and against their social world. Modernists could simultaneously share in and be sharply critical of colonial attitudes in an atmosphere we can no longer experience. In regard to Africa, for example, far from extending their social criticism to a radical critique of the reductive view of Africans promoted by the French government for colonial justification, the modernists embraced a deeply romanticized view of 'Africa' (conflating many cultures into one) as the embodiment of humankind in a precivilized state, whose cultural practices they mythified. The modernists subverted colonial stereotypes, both of the right and the left, but their subversive revisions remained implicated in the prejudices from which they derived, so that they now appear no less stereotypical and reductive than the racist caricatures they opposed. Their aim was to critique civilization by embracing an imagined primitiveness whose authenticity they opposed to a 'decadent' West. In wanting to subvert Western artistic traditions and the social order in which they were implicated, modernists celebrated a return to those imagined 'primitive' spiritual states whose suppression they viewed as having cut off a necessary vitality. Burgess quotes Derain, who equates his embrace of African art – including that of Egypt – with a return to 'nature':

These Africans being primitive, uncomplex, uncultured, can express their thought by a direct appeal to the instinct. Their carvings are informed with emotion. So Nature gives me the material with which to construct a world of my own, governed not by literal limitations, but by instinct and sentiment.

Primitivism focuses colonial issues tellingly, revealing complex and ambivalent relations to issues of race, gender, and power on the part of modernists grappling with new ideas and difficult material, sometimes from a socially critical perspective. In this light, it is important to recognize how little primitivism, in the hands of all the modernists, addresses the alien cultures they want to appropriate and how much it speaks of the European culture to whom their works were addressed, even if only purposely to scandalize it. By evoking an alien, exotic, or paradisal world, they speak of the inadequacies and oppressions of 'home'. At the deepest level, primitivists sought a contemporary parallel to an edenic moment in the artists' own white European 'races', looking to what they took to be 'primitive' cultures – visible in Paris via the French colonies – for a naiveté, spontaneity, and directness that European culture had putatively lost. Certainty that Europeans once enjoyed political and amoral freedom on the model of an imagined and utopian 'savagery' in Tahiti, Guinea, and the Congo animated the critique of France's 'civilizing mission' to those lands as tainting those colonies' hitherto uncorrupted primitiveness.

Africanism

The discovery of African sculpture by modernists took place within the circle of Fauves or 'wild beasts', so named for the outrageous style of their painting at the salons of 1905 and 1906. Matisse, Derain and Maurice Vlaminck (1876–1958), among others, exhibited works whose hallmarks included a purposeful lack of definition of form and arbitrary colour. Matisse's pastoral *Bonheur de vivre* or *Joy of Life* (1905–6) had an enormous impact when it was shown at the Salon des Indépendants in 1906 for its absolute updating of an ancient – indeed academic – theme: the *paysage champêtre* (rural landscape), whose most admired model was Giorgione's *Fête champêtre* (now thought possibly to be Titian). The unsettling lack of spatial consistency in the Matisse, combined with its arbitrary colour, free brushwork and lack of 'finished' form seemed even more shocking when applied to its pastoral subject, and on the scale of the more important *paysage historique* (historical landscape). Derain's *Three Trees*, on the other hand, is primitivist in a purely stylistic sense, rather than in

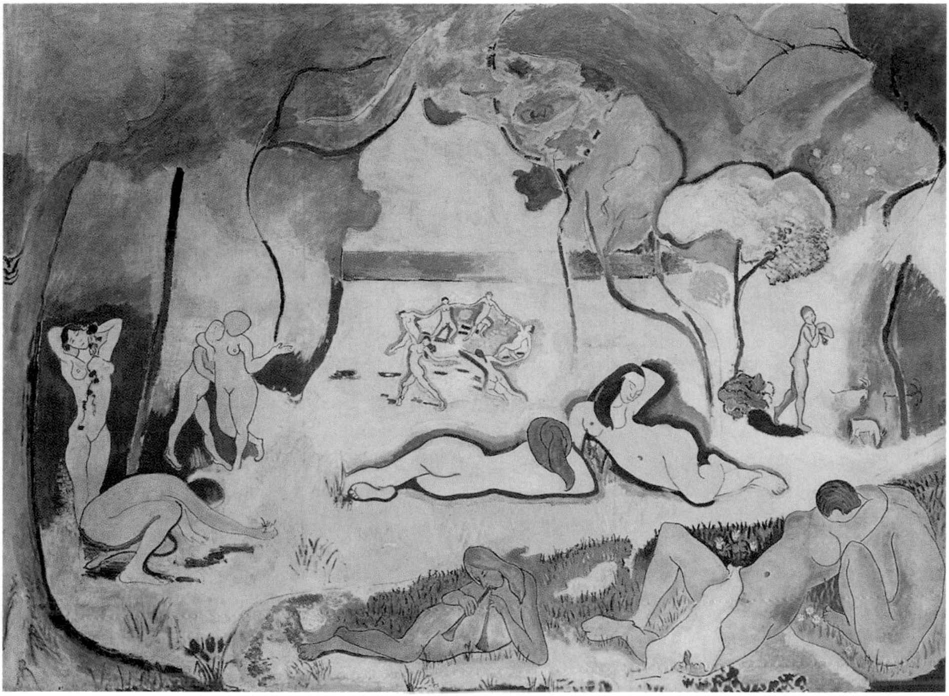

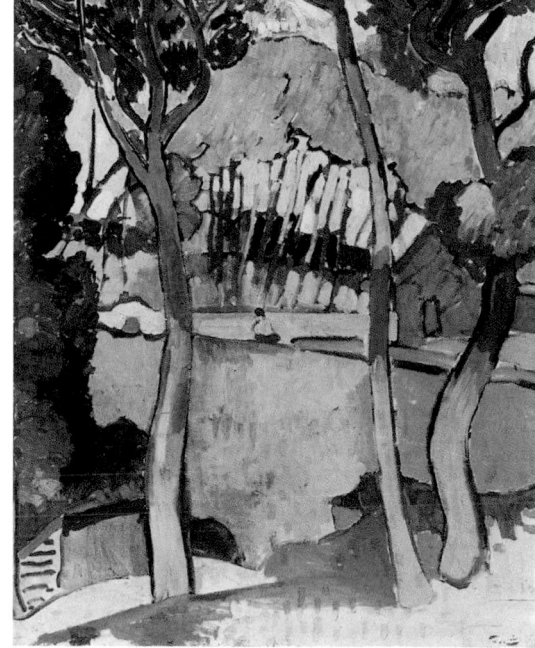

24. **Henri Matisse**,
Le Bonheur de vivre (Joy of Life),
1905–6.

25. **André Derain**,
Three Trees, L'Estaque, 1906.

subject. Numerous formal elements work to flatten space and resist a naturalistic reading of the landscape. The main figures of the trees are outlined in black and cut off by the top of the canvas; their trunks shift in colour not in relation to their own forms but rather as they pass in front of shapes and colour changes in the background, violating as they do so academic principles of appropriate placement of 'warm' (red, orange, yellow) and 'cold' (purple, blue, green) colours; the background itself is simplified to the point of unreadability of form, as for example in the amorphous mass of yellow foliage above the flat geometric house on the right. Such structuring of the linear rhythms and colours of the work were viewed by critics at the time, whether positively or negatively, as both 'abstract' and 'decorative'. The radical spatial inventions that Derain used during his Fauve period were a major influence on Braque; more than this, however, by 1907 Braque, Picasso and Derain began to spend a great deal of time together and worked towards a radically abstract version of Cézannism – in the name of the 'primitive' – that soon came to represent the earliest form of Cubism.

In autumn 1906 Vlaminck procured an African mask, which he sold to Derain; Derain in turn showed it to Picasso and Matisse. A Fang mask from France's colony in the Congo, its abstract forms 26, 2 were adopted by all three artists in subsequent works: Derain in his *Bathers* of 1907, with their sculptural forms and masklike faces; 2 Vlaminck in his *Bathers* of 1908 (private collection), whose rounded, schematic faces virtually quote the Fang mask; and Picasso in a whole series of works culminating in his major work of 1907, *Les Demoiselles d'Avignon*, and continuing in *Three Women* of 1908. In all 22, 2 four cases, African masks obscure and transform the physiognomy of nude females, who serve as tropes for the primitivist regression into 'nature'.

Derain was at this time moving away from Fauvism and paying concentrated attention to the work of Gauguin, who had a large retrospective at the Salon d'Automne in 1906. Among the works on display there were Gauguin's primitivist mock-Tahitian cylindrical carvings such as *Hina and Te Fatou* (1892–93); their influence on Derain mingled with the African carvings he began to collect and resulted in the two carvings visible in the Burgess photograph: in 1 Derain's arms a cylindrical carved wooden cat, painted green with touches of red, and on the lower right a compact wooden standing figure with a masklike face.

26. Fang mask, Gabon
(former French Congo).
Fang masks were among the
earliest Central African sculptures
to be seen in Paris. The oval shape,
tiny facial features concentrated
along central horizontal and
vertical axes, and whitish painted
face helped inspire the Fauves' and
Cubists' subsequent geometric
simplifications. Many Fang masks
had concave faces, upon which
scarification marks were
sometimes incised, an influence
visible in Picasso's *Demoiselles
d'Avignon* and *Three Women*.

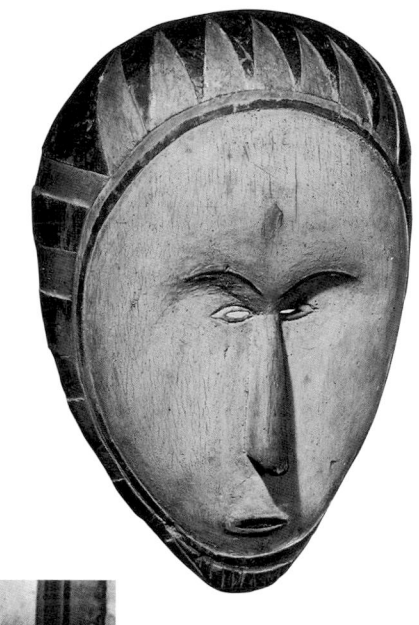

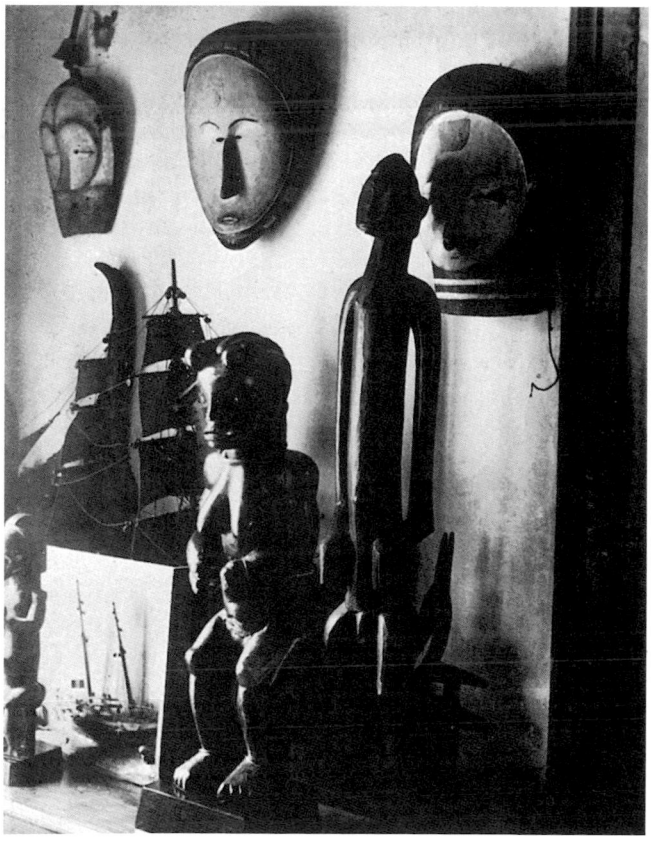

27. Derain's studio with Fang
mask on the wall, *c.* 1912–13.

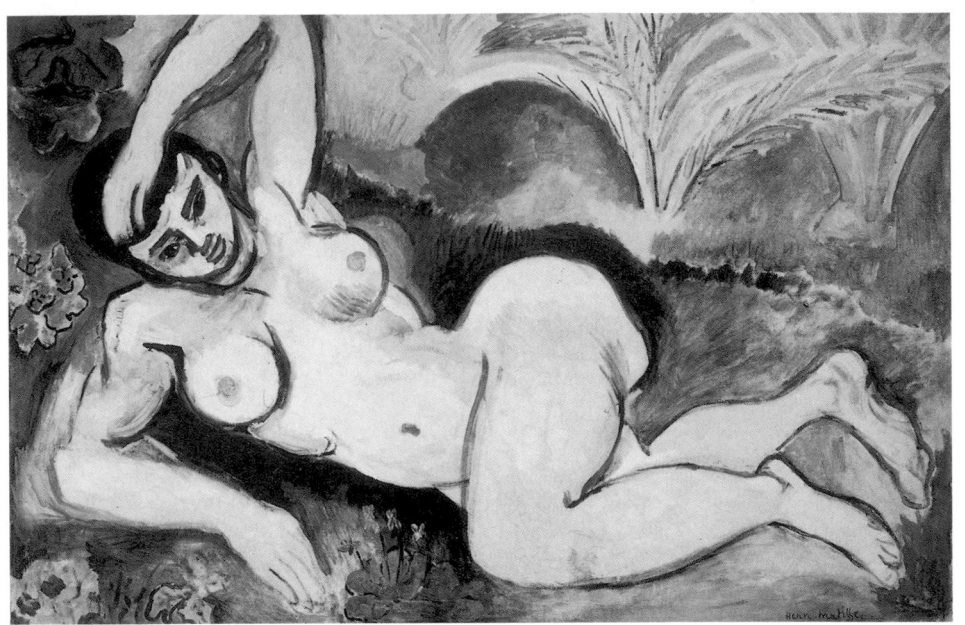

Matisse too moved the Arcadian primitivism of his Fauve work towards a more sculptural primitivism responding to African sculpture. An important example is *The Blue Nude (Souvenir of Biskra)* (1907), which the critic Louis Vauxcelles bluntly described as 'a nude woman, ugly, spread out on opaque blue grass under some palm trees'. This North African *odalisque* revitalizes or parodies, depending on your point of view, a traditional pose of Venus. Its African allusions combine North and sub-Saharan Africa and include the Algerian oasis of the title; the figure's short hair, exaggerated breasts and buttocks, and elongated torso reminiscent of Baule and Fang figurines; the blue-tinted skin, a practice of the Tuareg people; and the tropical oasis vegetation of North Africa.

Following his move to Paris, Picasso's manoeuvres as an artist increasingly expressed contempt for mainstream, bourgeois culture. He made an important shift from a politics of subject matter – as in the Blue Period – to a politics of form, through his studied and ideologically informed rejection of academic styles. He had initially embraced simplification and a purposeful appearance of 'crudity' under the influence of the Barcelona *modernistes*, who in the 1880s and 1890s admired ancient Iberian art of the Spanish peninsula (5th–3rd century B.C.), such as the *Head of a Man* from Cerro de los Santos, and Catalan Romanesque art, viewed as reflecting the elemental power of the 'folk'. Picasso first introduced Iberian forms in works like his *Portrait of Gertrude Stein* and *Self-Portrait with a Palette* of 1906, with their exaggeratedly Iberian features: large staring eyes with hard linear rims, geometric arcs of eyebrow, a simplified helmet of hair, and an oversized ear on an elongated oval head. By identifying himself with Iberian art as the 'primitive' expression of his own allegiance to the supposed elemental 'roots' of Catalan culture, Picasso strikes an adversary pose. And by making his own art, and his own image, in terms of this Spanish primitivism, he embraced its more 'genuine' forms and feelings as a challenge to the outworn decadence of the still-powerful Parisian academic tradition. The secrets of the Iberian sculptures, Picasso assured Apollinaire, were 'at once ancient and barbarian'.

88, 30

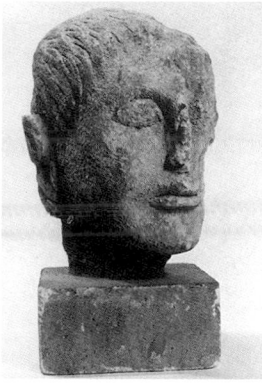

29. *Head of a Man*, Iberian, Cerro de los Santos, 5th–3rd century B.C.
A form of provincial Archaic Greek art found along ancient Mediterranean trade routes, Iberian sculpture was viewed as both 'primitive' and quintessentially Catalan by the Barcelona *modernistes* of the 1890s, in whose company Picasso had spent time as a young artist. Picasso's awareness of Iberian art was renewed by the Louvre's exhibition in spring 1906 of newly excavated bas-reliefs from Osuna, and his own acquisition in March 1907 of the Iberian head illustrated here, which had been stolen from the Salle des Antiquités Ibériques in the Louvre by a friend of Apollinaire.

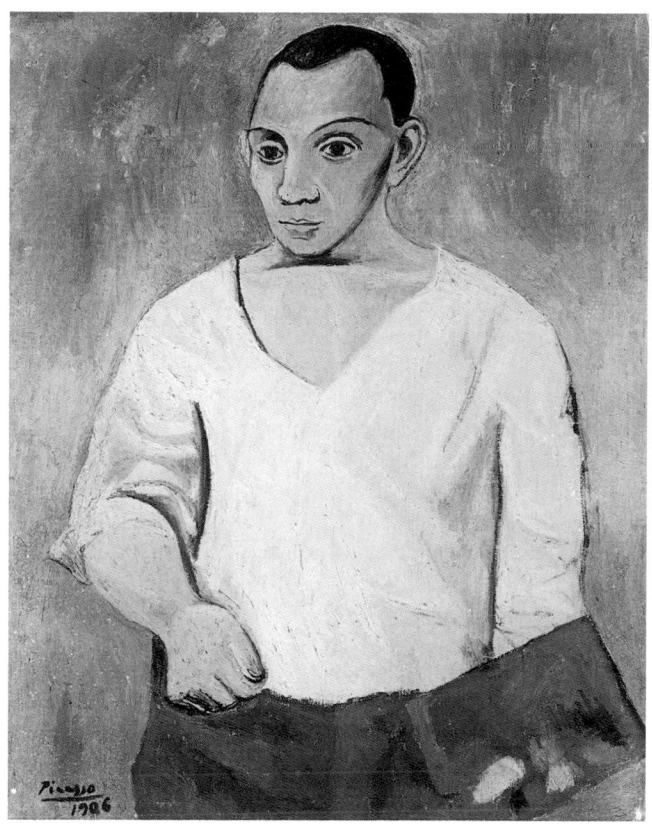

30. **Pablo Picasso**, *Self-Portrait with a Palette*, 1906.

When Picasso came to 'discover' or admire African art as a complement to his Iberian 'barbarism', he like Derain made several direct wood carvings, partly in response to Gauguin (though like Matisse he had long been interested in sculpture). *Doll* of 1907 reveals Picasso's attempt to absorb various features of Derain's Fang mask and such standing figures as the Kota reliquary and Teke figure from the former French Congo; these works were acquired in 1883 and 1904 respectively by the Musée d'Ethnographie in Paris, which Picasso, Derain and others visited when it was little more than a warehouse open to the public.

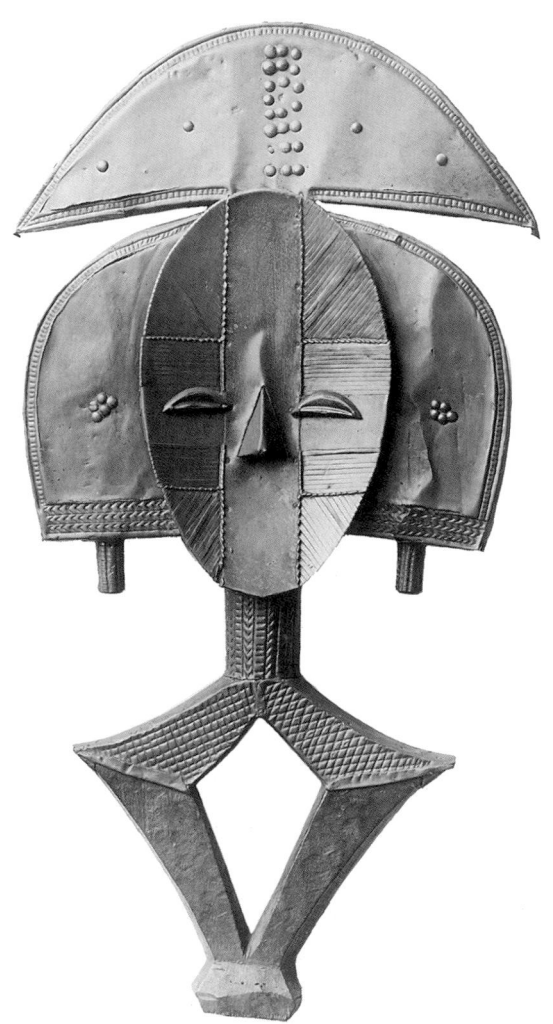

31. Kota reliquary, People's Republic of the Congo (former French Congo). This guardian figure from a Kota reliquary was brought to France by Pierre de Brazza's second expedition to Central Africa. The highly abstract forms of the head and face are layered with copper strips. Though the diamond shape of the lower part was viewed by modernists as a stunningly abstract representation of the legs, this part of the figure was normally obscured by raffia which covered and hid the dancer when it was used for ceremonial purposes.

We can glimpse in the 'africanizing' work of these artists not only a more crudely primitivist style, but resonances of the popular view of Africa and its part in the French Empire. The 'dark continent' captured the imaginations of artists and writers at this time, when news of French colonial abuses in Africa resulted in protests by an anticolonial opposition largely made up of anarchists and socialists. These revelations broke upon the world in 1905 and 1906, the same period that Picasso, Vlaminck, Derain and others were inspired to 'discover' an African art that had been visible in Paris since at least the 1890s. In *Les Demoiselles d'Avignon* and related

22

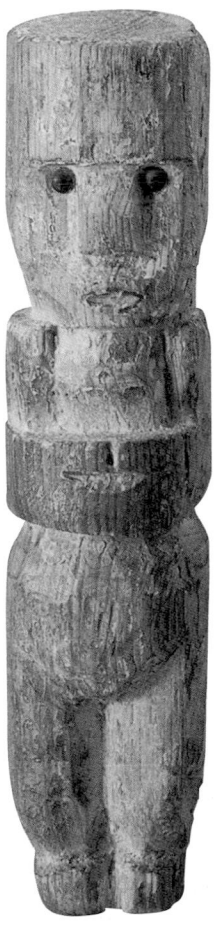

33. **Pablo Picasso**, *Doll*, 1907

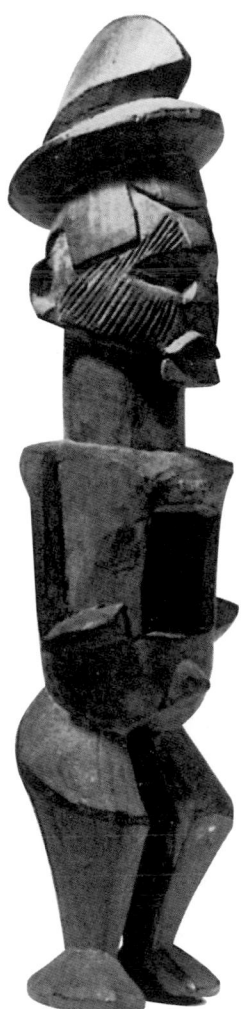

32. Teke figure, People's Republic of the Congo (former French Congo). Like Fang reliquary figures from Gabon and Baga figures from Guinea, this sculpture employs figural proportions entirely at odds with the Western canon, including a large head, simplified face, short legs, prominent navel, and elongated trunk and neck.

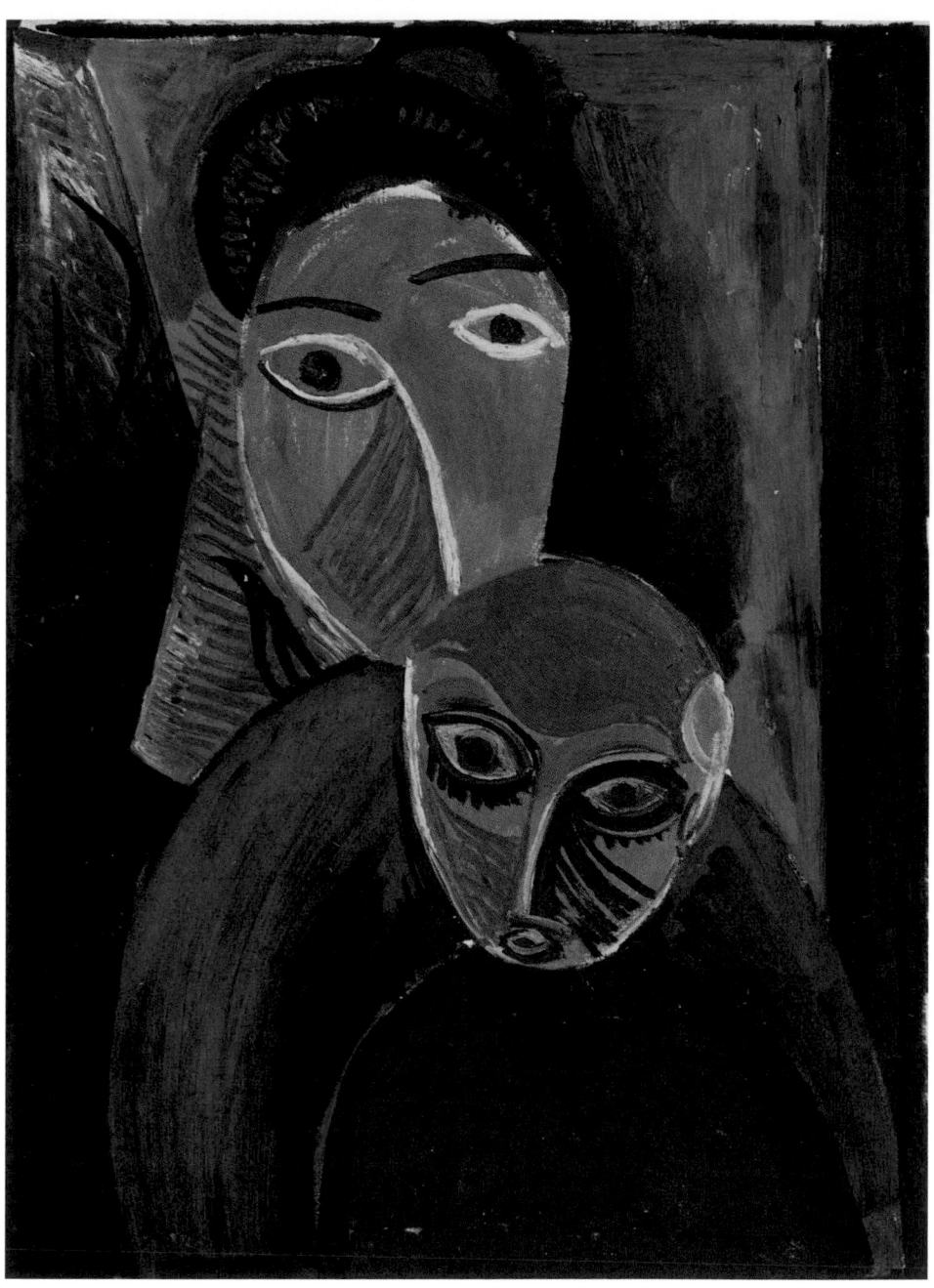

34. **Pablo Picasso**,
Mother and Child, 1907.

works of 1907 and 1908, such as *Mother and Child* and *Three Women*, 34, 23 reference to African art not only allowed Picasso to primitivize his figures, it allowed him to confront his audience with their own assumptions about 'Africa' and the relation of Picasso's work to that widely publicized discourse. By conflating his figures with recognizably African forms – such as the Kota sculpture – he violently subverted academic conventions for the human figure as evidenced in Jean-Auguste-Dominique Ingres's *Venus Anadyomene* (1808–48). 35 Synthesizing aspects of a variety of masks and statues from various parts of the French Empire, it was also the *idea* of Africa that Picasso sought. His painting necessarily constituted both an act of valuing the products of African culture and an affront to academic tradition, itself an embodiment of French civilization comparable to the 'civilizing mission' that justified French incursions in Africa. Like academic art, French colonial policy could appear morally bankrupt and its 'civilizing' ideals corrupt.

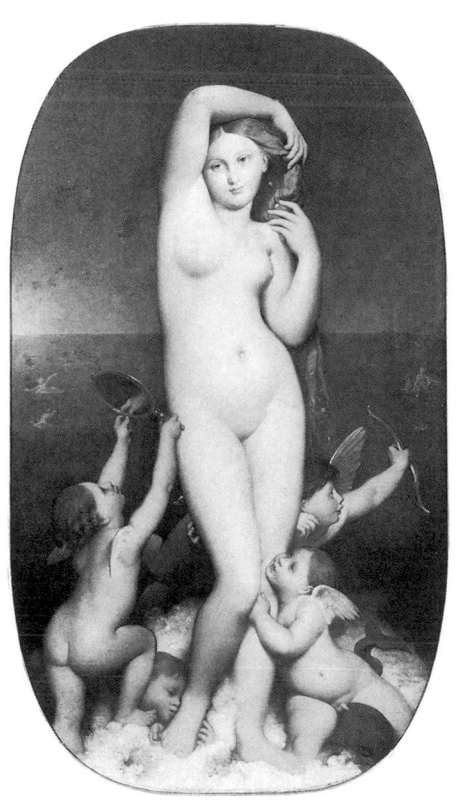

35. **Jean-Auguste-Dominique Ingres**,
Venus Anadyomene, 1808–48.

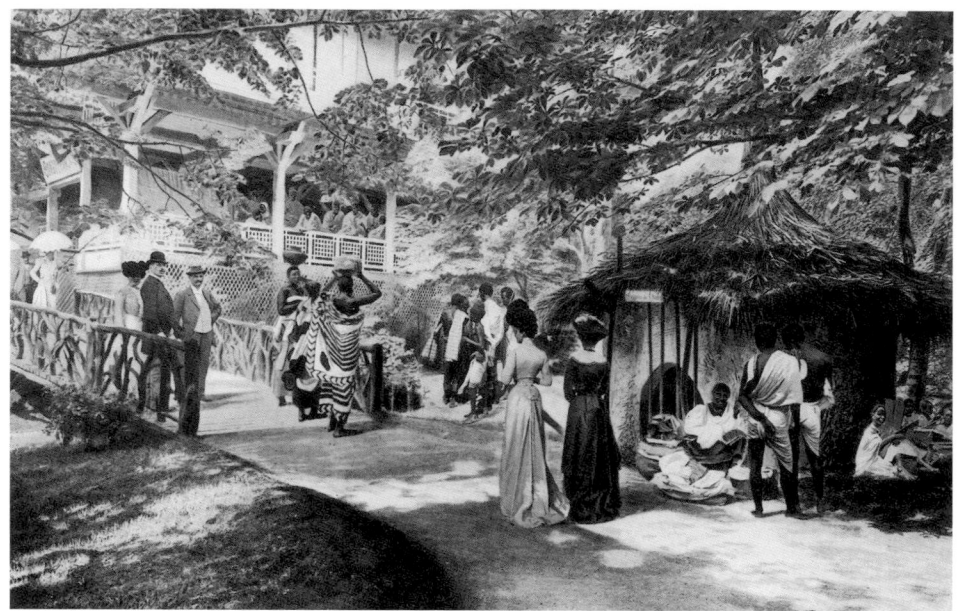

Like the rest of France, the modernists were influenced by popular sources of information about Africa. Beginning in the late nineteenth century, international expositions concocted displays of colonial peoples in live exhibits. Prior to 1906, African peoples, supplied by wild animal importers, were regularly exhibited in the zoo. Another major source of images and information about Africa was the popular press – itself influenced by prejudice, fantasy, and political interests – reinforced by novels as well as soldiers', missionaries' and explorers' accounts, often accompanied by lurid and exotic illustrations.

In the Dahomean Wars of 1890 and 1892, during the 'scramble' for colonies, the French conquered Dahomey, a kingdom on the coast of West Africa. Travellers who ventured into the interior earlier in the century had returned with fantastic tales of fetish worship, human sacrifice and cannibalism – forming a frightening image of Africans as savage, primeval spirits – that were made much of in the French press. Mass-circulation magazines such as *Le Journal Illustré* and *L'Illustration* emphasized the purported savagery of customs they misconstrued in accordance with their preconceptions. For example, in an engraving entitled 'Human Sacrifices in Dahomey' published in *Tour du Monde* in 1863, the Dahomean King watches from beneath a canopy while the priests sacrifice his chosen victims, holding their heads aloft. During the Dahomean

36. 'Congolese village',
International Exposition,
Paris, 1900.

37. 'Human Sacrifices in
Dahomey', etching from
Dr Répin, 'Voyage au Dahomey',
Tour du Monde, VII, 1863.

Wars the French popular press played up such tales in an attempt to justify French conquest. The press followed the wars only superficially, concentrating instead on the legendarily grotesque practices of the natives and illustrating their accounts with uncredited and rather free reworkings of earlier engravings. This engraving, for instance, accompanies a text whose author confesses that he himself had only witnessed the sacrifice of a hyena. The implication of cannibalism in these rites was likewise asserted and popularly believed. The sensationalism of such accounts was given lurid play in the popular press, and in a remarkably short time Dahomey came to represent in France all that was most thrillingly barbaric, savage and elemental on the 'dark continent'.

Whereas Dahomey came to symbolize the savagery of a barbaric culture in need of the civilizing effects of European rule, the French and Belgian Congos in Central Africa came to exemplify the barbarity of the Europeans themselves and the hypocrisy of governments claiming cultural superiority to those they governed. In the Belgian Congo, colonial administrators suppressed slavery only to replace it with a system of forced labour wherein Africans were compelled to harvest rubber under threat of mutilation and execution. Colonial administrators in the nearby French Congo employed similar methods, which led to a public inquiry in 1905

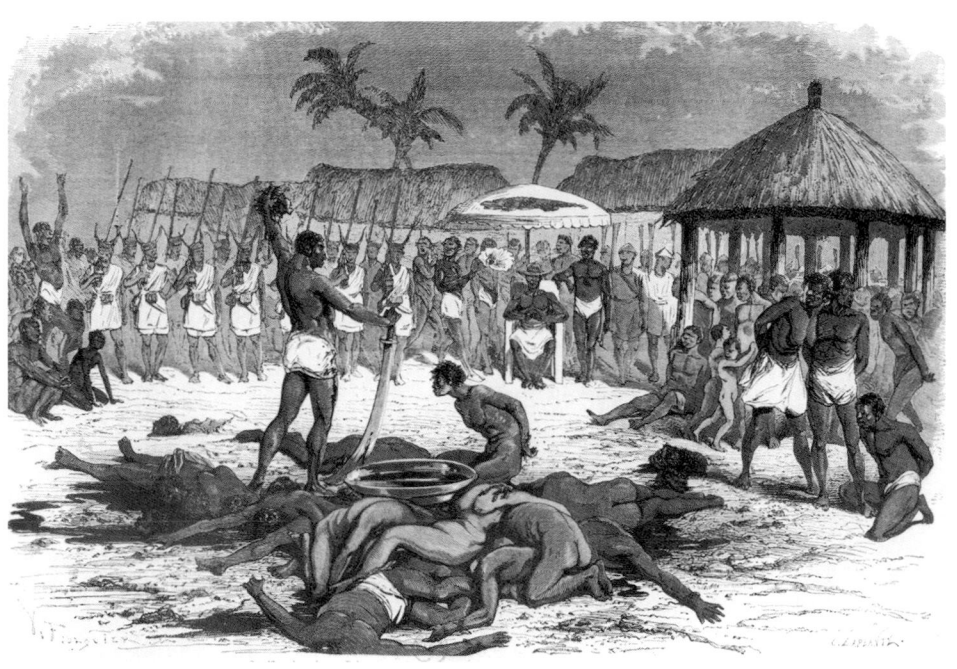

into colonial abuses, including acts of horrific cruelty, known as the Gaud-Toqué Affair. The scandals following government inquiries into atrocities committed by colonial administrators in both the French and Belgian Congos aroused controversy and opposition, inspiring a heated debate of which modernist writers and artists could not possibly have been unaware, even had they been uninterested.

Indeed, members of Picasso's circle articulated forcefully critical attitudes towards events in the Congo in a series of political cartoons in the anarchist journal *L'Assiette au beurre*. For example, anarchist leader Charles Malato and Juan Gris suggest that the infamously cruel Turks can learn cruelty from the French, whose deeds – as outlined in the inquiries – Gris illustrates in 1908 in a special issue on Turkey. The Turks are shown bayoneting the African babies they would pretend to rule; but the Turks never invaded sub-Saharan Africa, the French did. By casting a people the French

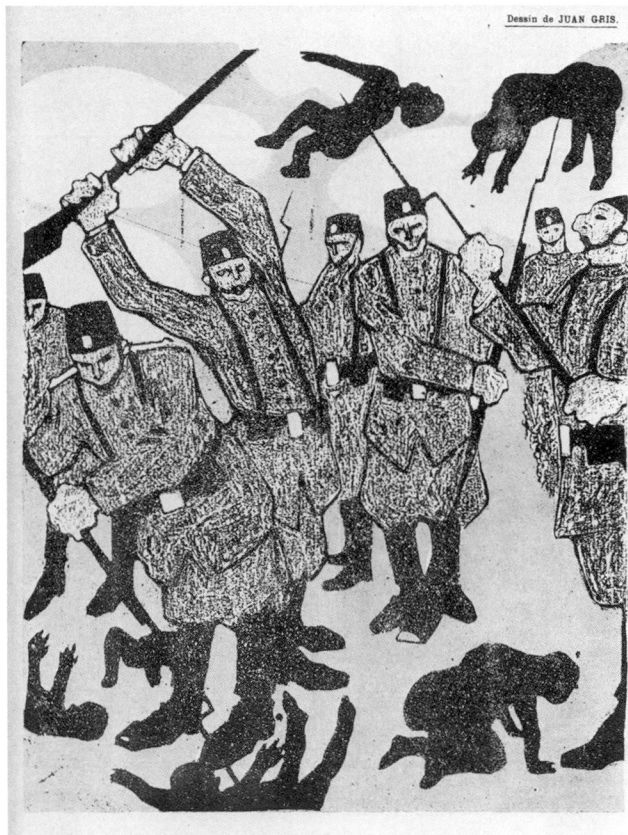

Dessin de JUAN GRIS.

Guidés par un besoin d'expansion propre à toute nation civilisée, les Turcs iront dans les pays sauvages, porter les procédés de civilisation.

38. **Juan Gris**,
'Guided by a need',
L'Assiette au beurre, 29 August 1908.

popularly considered to be cruel and backward in the mould not of French ideals but of grisly actualities, Gris parodies the foundation of French colonial philosophy with its 'civilizing mission', turns the trope of the 'barbaric' back on the complacent French, and criticizes the government in the severest terms. One hardly needs the caption to send the message home: 'Guided by a need for expansion proper to every civilized nation, the Turks will go into the savage lands to bring civilized ways'.

The arguments of the 'anticolonialists' ranged from critics who wanted a colonial empire, but one that was both more humanitarian and more efficient, to those who refused to recognize the right of France to impose its will, even in the name of civilization, upon other people. The Comité de Protection et de Défense des Indigènes (Committee for Protection and Defence of Indigenous Peoples) held protest meetings and published numerous pamphlets from 1905 until at least 1910. The debates and scandals brought a new and heightened awareness of France's African colonies and, for a politicized avant-garde, concentrated a range of politically charged meanings on everything to do with 'Africa'.

Picasso's allegiance to concepts of primitivism that date back to his fin-de-siècle period and his parallel anarchism would have encouraged an interest in the Congo revelations and subsequent debates, and this could very well have led him and others to look freshly at African art. Vlaminck, by his own account, had looked at African art with Derain at the Musée d'Ethnographie – at the time of the scandals – before his purchase of the Fang mask in 1904. 26 African sculpture offered a model of formal simplification based on folk traditions that were believed to pre-date recorded history, representing to modernists 'authentic' primitive expressions of thought and feeling. As early as the sixteenth century, French aestheticians connected concepts of the 'grotesque' in two dimensions with caricature, ornament, and the fantastical, while the 'grotesque' in three dimensions suggested the monstrous and the horrific and was specifically associated with Africa. African sculptures, resultingly, were viewed as 'idols' and 'fetishes' and represented to Europeans manifestations of the 'irrational, mute, and fearful world' in which they imagined the 'primitive' to live.

Thus an imagined primal savagery was thoroughly merged with images of and references to African sculpture for any artist or audience of prewar France, and their appearance in Picasso's already 'grotesque' *Demoiselles d'Avignon* echoed inherited images and 22 associations of superstition, irrationality, darkness, and horror, adding to his already considerable anti-academic arsenal. Salmon asserted in *La jeune peinture française* (1912) that 'in choosing savage artists as guides', Picasso 'was not unaware of their barbarity'. He was 'the apprentice sorcerer always consulting the Oceanic and African enchanters'. Elsewhere, Salmon called Picasso's collection of African and Oceanian sculptures 'grimacing idols' and 'primitive marvels'. What Picasso produced in response to this influence were 'forbidding nudes, grimacing and perfectly worthy of execration', a human effigy that 'appears to us so inhuman and inspires in us a sort of horror'. Apollinaire used similar language in 'The Beginnings of Cubism', published in *Le Temps*, 14 October 1912, to characterize the Congolese objects owned by Vlaminck and Derain, admiringly naming them 'masks and fetishes', 'grotesque and crudely mystical works', and 'barbaric sculptures'.

In *Les Demoiselles d'Avignon* (named by Salmon *The Philosophical Brothel*), Picasso sets five female nudes in a house of prostitution, placing them in a variety of postures of availability strongly reminiscent of academic precedents. His style dramatically contrasts with such earlier models as Ingres's *Venus Anadyomene*. With its clear anatomical forms, smooth transition from light to shadow, and sensual beauty, Ingres's work can stand as a superlative example of the idealization of the female nude that Picasso overthrows in his picture. Picasso's nudes in each case are stylistically transformed through allusions to Iberian, African and Oceanic art. The Iberian faces of the two central figures and their crudely simplified forms ally them with Spain's prehistoric past and announce Picasso's origins and preoccupations as outside (and against) the French classical tradition signalled by his focus on the female nude. The context of the brothel points up the prostitutes' lack of freedom. At the same time, exaggerating their sexual display, they turn their attention from the room to the world beyond the frame. Their 'primitive' power and hypnotic gaze are anything but alluring, yet they pale in comparison with the 'violence' of the two right-hand figures, whose faces are transformed by African masks and whose presences considerably increase the voltage of the work; they mock such sexual display and aggressively challenge the 'bankrupt' Western imagery of the classical 'nude'.

Picasso's primitivist attack on European art also attacks Europe's idealizations of sexuality. The radical treatment of the traditional nude female – going well beyond Matisse's *Blue Nude* – announces the end of the old world of art with a new violence. The violence comes not only from the distortion of the faces and forms of the two africanized figures, and from the transformation of passive academic nudes in tamed attitudes – such as Ingres's *Venus* –

into aggressively challenging mock-temptresses, but also from the very allusion to 'Africa' embedded in them. The tremendous powers of 'primitive' spirituality overwhelm the European tradition in a flamboyant act of rebellion. More than this, all those thrillingly nightmarish and well-publicized tales of 'Dahomey' echo in the African forms imported into this work, summoning up an imagined ruthless barbarity that the male modernist makes it his mission to confront.

As historian of medicine Sander Gilman has shown, racist assumptions about African female sexuality spilled over to the European prostitute, linked by what was seen in medical discourse as a parallel process of physical and social degeneration. The late nineteenth century saw the initiation of sociological and police classification systems for categorizing the 'biological determinants' of criminal behaviour, the very concept of which denies economic motive. The physiognomic traits attributed to the prostitute were precisely those associated with the African female, suggesting a view of prostitutes as physiognomically 'primitive'. The logical conclusion of this chain of signifiers was that the sexual activity and resulting syphilis of the European prostitute became a sign for Europeans of her physiological regression to the condition of the sexualized African female. Picasso's prostitutes – in the early sketches attendant on both customer (the sailor) and 'medical student' (or inspector) – may function within this system, as their overt and aggressive sexuality affirms cultural and racial attitudes shared by the artist and his audience even as their formal treatment underscores their aggression towards the client/viewer.

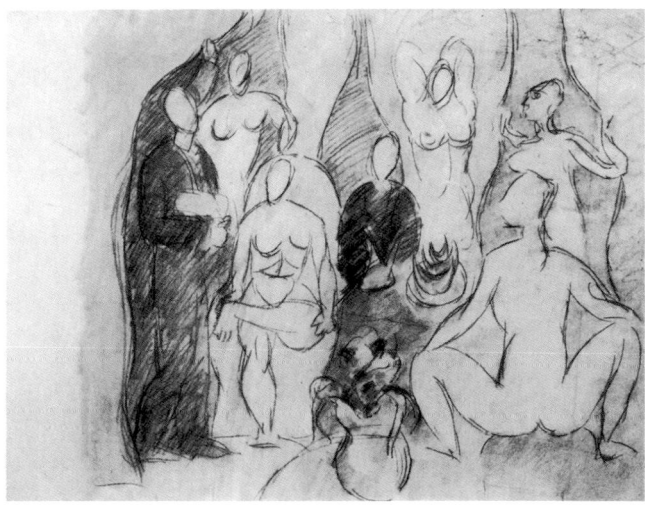

39. **Pablo Picasso**,
Study for *Les Demoiselles d'Avignon*,
spring 1907.

Picasso's primitivizing style aspires, like the African sculptures he so admired, to an act not of mere decoration, but of power, a bid to recapture kinds of representational 'magic' that the arts of civilized, Enlightened Europe had lost. The multivalent strategies of his work speak to many levels of public and private experience as well as to conventions of inherited tradition, which this public would have recognized and which Picasso would have expected it to recognize. Modernist painting for a century and more – Jacques-Louis David, Théodore Géricault, Eugène Delacroix, and Gustave Courbet – had offered finely calculated provocations of subject and theme at moments of political anxiety, crisis, and scandal. Picasso's provocation is similarly motivated, but also grapples with a central problem of modernism in general: how to radicalize structure and form, and abandon realism and narrative, without also abandoning centrally important real-life concerns. Picasso by 'masking' his figures conflates an exotic and exploited group external to Western society with an equally exploited group within Western society, analogizing the ironically more visible periphery with the corrupt centre of French culture. In their power both to attract and repel the male beholder, the africanized prostitutes capture the ambivalent character of Picasso's primitivism. While Picasso identifies the prostitute as a 'grotesque other', he identifies his own avant-garde status as a self-styled 'primitive', thus overturning European cultural values that would identify the 'primitive' with the degenerate. For colonialists France had a civilizing mission in Africa; for anarchist avant-gardists, African culture had a primitivizing mission for Europe.

The European 'primitive'

Within Europe itself modernists could also find models of the 'primitive'. In the present, glimpses of the 'natural' were viewed in children, gypsies and peasants, including in child art and in folk art; Paul Gauguin went to Tahiti not only in search of an idyllic society but in search of the child in himself. Artists also looked to the past for models of the primitive, viewing rural medieval sculpture and stained glass as authentic folk expressions of an admirably naive Catholic faith. Between 1906 and 1908, Henri Le Fauconnier focused his artistic attention on Brittany, where Gauguin and his Nabi associates had gone to escape to an 'earlier time'. Le Fauconnier painted Nabi- and Fauve-inspired images of young Breton children and of the rocky coast, with its dramatic granite 40, 4 rock formations. Le Fauconnier's coastal landscapes not only reveal his method of abstraction but more fundamentally his correlation

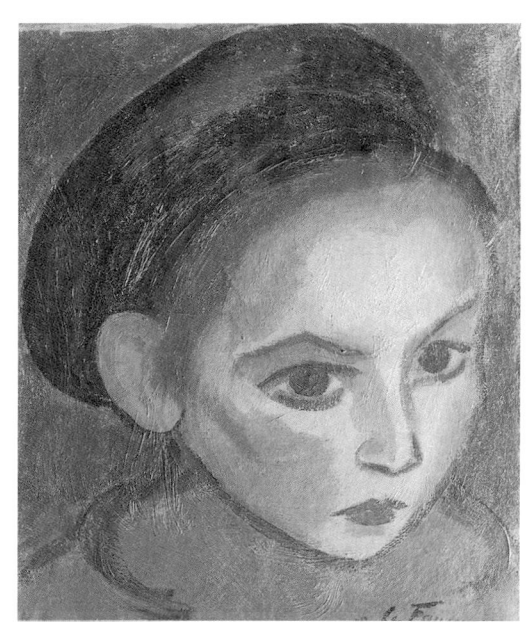

40. **Henri Le Fauconnier**,
Breton Girl, 1908.

41. **Henri Le Fauconnier**,
Village in the Rocks, 1908.

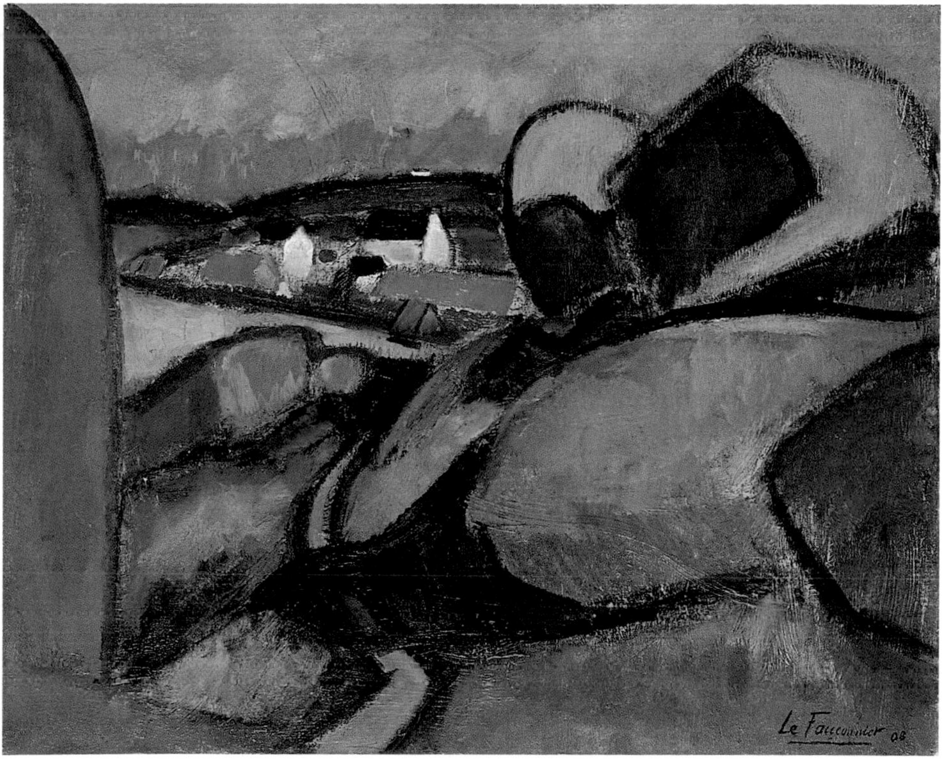

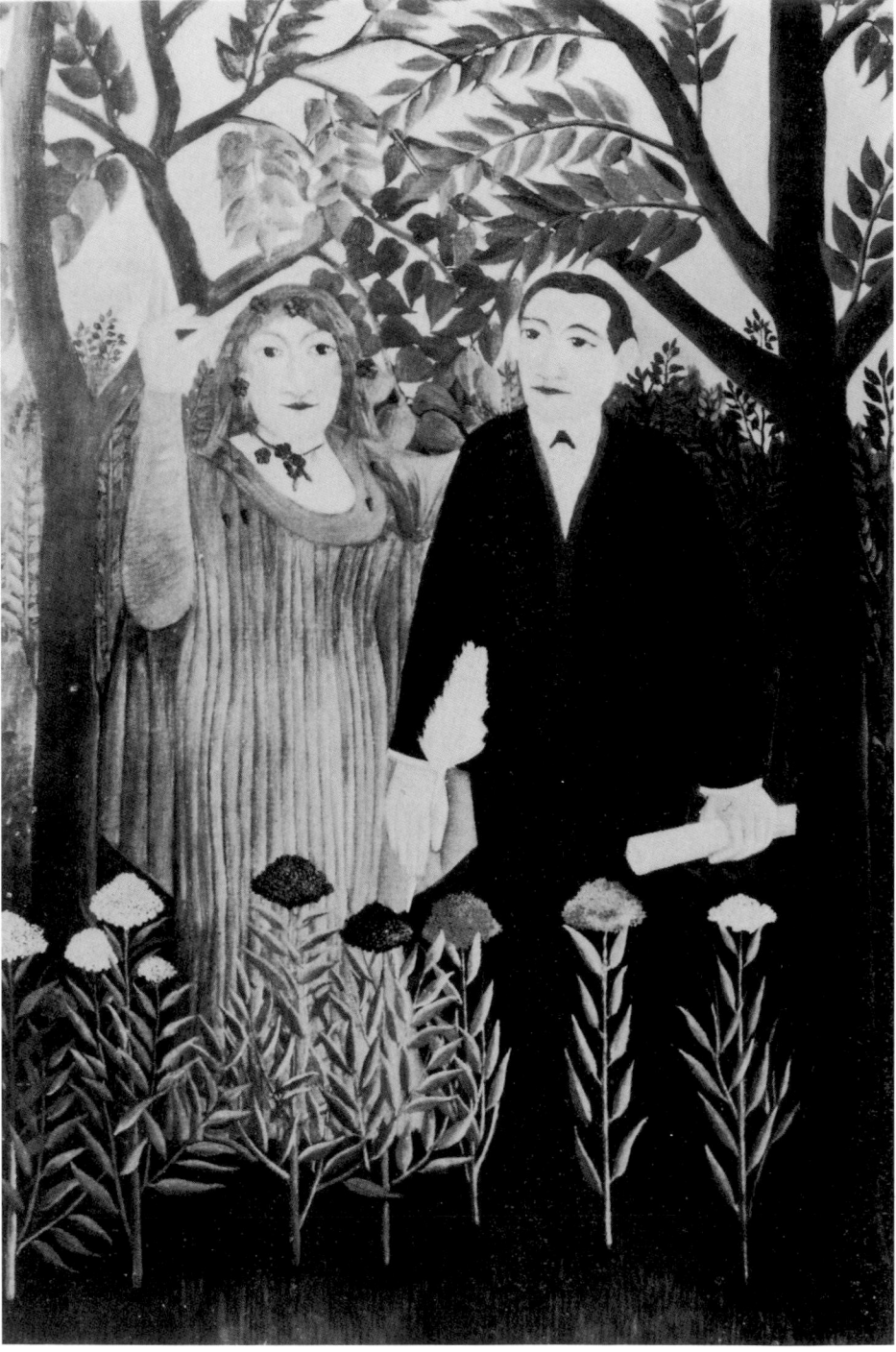

between the abstract structure of his paintings and the crystalline rock. For Le Fauconnier these granite formations were the 'primordial' counterpart to the Celtic megaliths that dotted Brittany, and like Gauguin before him he associated the form and content of his images with what he thought was the primitive character of the region. In contrast to his Nabi predecessors, however, Le Fauconnier eschewed any association of Catholicism with the primitive in favour of more primordial features, such as the extended time governing the earth's geological formation.

Modernist primitivism as an act of self-authentication – whether modelled on the art of children, the folk, or 'savages' – locates the source of creativity within the artist, in a romantic merger with the elemental that serves to liberate the self. The idea of the unique perspective of the individual in turn justifies the sorts of 'naive' distortions and extreme simplifications that emulate 'primitive' art and intimately connect with the first steps towards what would become Cubism. In this light, the appeal of the work of Henri 'Le Douanier' Rousseau (1844–1910) and Paul Cézanne in this same period is no contradiction.

Apollinaire included Rousseau, who had been a tollbooth inspector or 'douanier', among 'the most daring and most significant French artists of the last few generations', along with Degas, Cézanne, Matisse, Picasso and Braque. Rousseau was for him a 'French folk artist of unparalleled freshness and originality', who 'painted with the purity, the grace, and the consciousness of a primitive'. *The Poet and His Muse* (1909) is a double portrait of Apollinaire and Marie Laurencin depicting the two figures and surrounding trees, flowers and foliage, each element carefully delineated and lacking shadows. The only perspective techniques used are the changed scale between foreground and background, visible in the size of the leaves, and overlapping forms. A highly traditional subject, Rousseau organizes the composition with deadpan straightforwardness, and viewers then and now have debated whether to view the artist as genuinely naive or boldly modernist. His friend Apollinaire saw him as combining these two elements:

42

I tend to think that that portrait was such a good likeness – at once so striking and so new – that it dazzled even those who were not aware of the resemblance and did not want to believe in it. Painting is the most pious art. In 1909, we witnessed a phenomenon of mass suggestion similar to those that gave birth to the purest religions. It was a sublime adventure that was definitely worth living through. My face served in a unique experiment that I shall never forget.

42. **Henri 'Le Douanier' Rousseau**, *The Poet and His Muse (Portrait of Guillaume Apollinaire and Marie Laurencin)*, 1909.

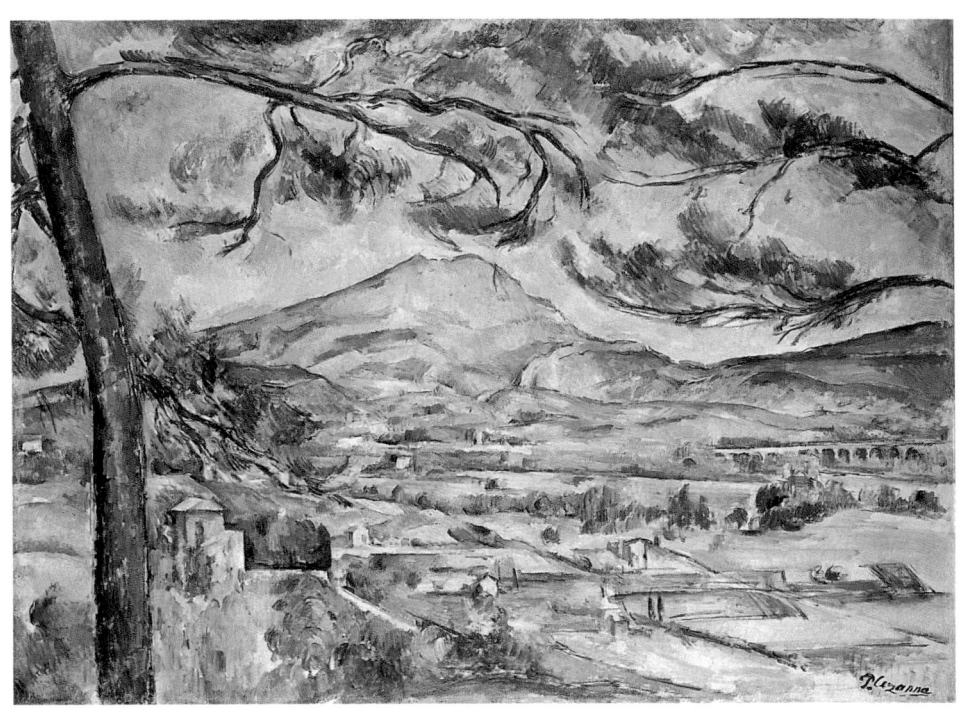

43. **Paul Cézanne**, *Mont Sainte-Victoire*, 1885–87.

Cézanne's departures from traditional structures of space and form, as in his *Mont Sainte-Victoire* (1885–87), are also made in the name of the individual sensibility and perception of the artist. Rather than representing a break from the africanized primitivism of 1907 and 1908, Derain, Picasso and Braque's embrace of Cézanne could represent their identification with a contemporary critical discourse that labelled Cézanne a modernist primitive. The concept of the 'primitive' *naïf* – the artist whose *gaucherie* guarantees his sincerity, spontaneity and originality – informs criticism of Cézanne by such contemporary writers as Maurice Denis, Gustave Geffroy and Georges Lecomte. Cézanne to some extent embraced this interpretation, identifying himself with the 'folk' of his native Provence. His Provençal landscapes – especially those depicting Mont Sainte-Victoire – signalled his allegiance to his 'race', rooted in a Latin 'Golden Age'. According to local legend the mountain's name commemorated a famous Roman military victory against barbarian invaders, and Cézanne laid claim to this popular collective heritage by repeatedly returning to the theme.

In this painting, the Provençal pine structures the foreground through the repeated arcs of its branches; the curves of these branches are echoed in the shapes of the middleground and distance, especially the outline of the mountain itself, an effect that works against the illusion of depth. Straight lines likewise parallel each other – for example in the edges of fields and buildings – reinforcing the dominance of abstract design over naturalistic observation. Parallel lines in turn are repeated on the smaller scale of the brushstrokes, which retain the mark of the brush and gesture of Cézanne's hand: a telling reminder of the artist's individual creative act. The myriad details in the view contemplated by Cézanne – he always carefully studied the 'motif' as he painted – have been generalized into rough areas of paint abstracted from the original forms; where these rough forms create conflicting readings, such as in the foreground foliage or in the distant foothills, he simply reconciles them by painting a transitional plane between them. This technique was called *passage* and was enthusiastically embraced by the Cubists, not – as with Cézanne – to muffle ambiguities but to enhance them. The effect of flatness that results in Cézanne's painting, especially compared with the academic tradition, was precisely the quality cited by Cézanne's supporters as evidence of his naivety and sincerity. The techniques such writers located as signs of awkwardness and the 'primitive' were the very ones adopted by Matisse, Derain, Braque and Picasso: anatomical distortions, faceting of forms and crude geometrizations.

Ambroise Vollard (1867–1939), owner of an important modern art gallery, held several exhibitions of Cézanne's work beginning in 1895; in 1899 Cézanne began taking part in group shows such as the Salon des Indépendants; more paintings were shown at the Salon d'Automne in 1904, 1905 and 1906, the year he died. Thus all the artists we have been discussing were familiar with his painting before the important retrospective at the Salon d'Automne in 1907, where 56 works were shown. Matisse bought Cézanne's *Three Bathers* (1875–77) from Vollard around 1899, and a reproduction of Cézanne's *Five Bathers* (1885–87) is visible hanging on the wall of Derain's studio in the Burgess photograph. In 1907 the impact of Cézanne's style was felt with renewed force in the works of Derain,

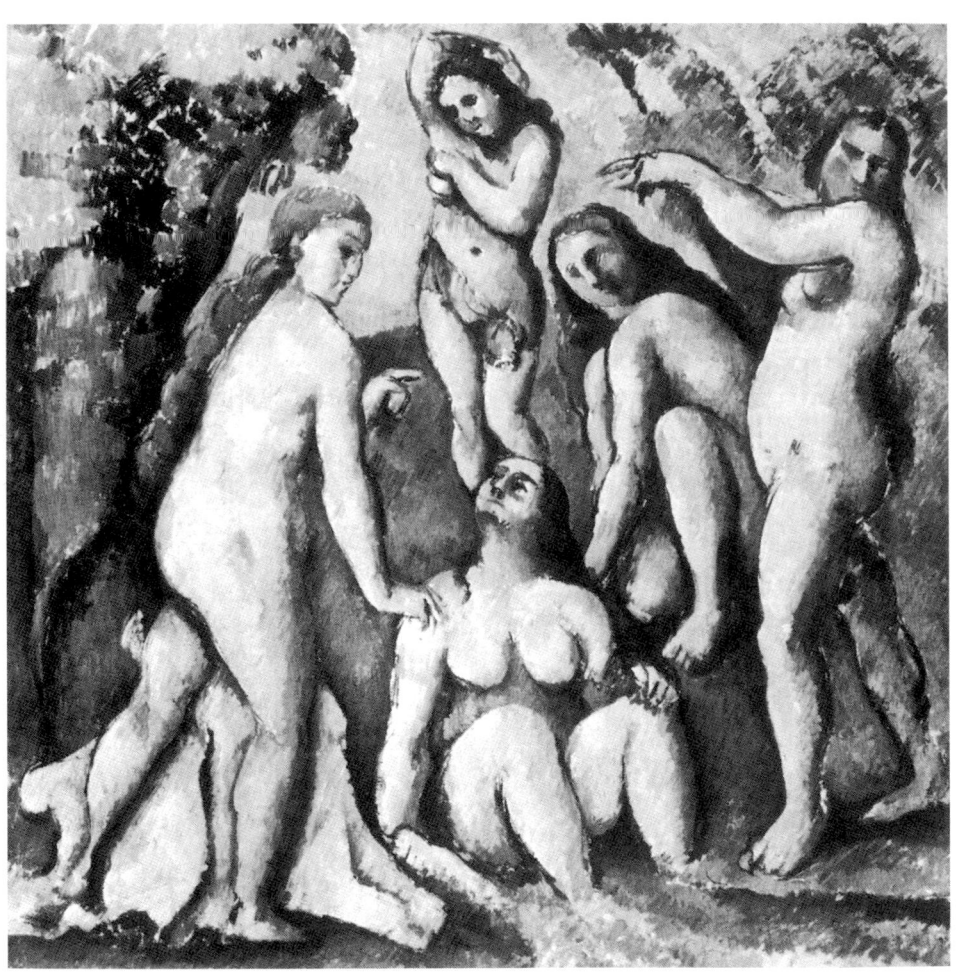

Braque and even Vlaminck, the most expressionist of the Fauves, where it mingled with their primitivism. For example, in his *Bathers* of 1907 Derain abandons the bright colours of his Fauve palette for the earthy tones used by Cézanne. He pushes his new style in a primitivist direction through what Louis Vauxcelles called his 'barbaric simplifications': crudely executed brushwork, purposely awkward figural postures and gestures, geometrification of forms and a near total lack of spatial definition. Matisse likewise combines the influences of Cézanne and African art in *The Blue Nude* of 1907, with its even more outrageously exaggerated anatomical distortions. He structures his background and figure in echoing shapes – such as the curve of hip, hill and palm leaf – that flatten the entire spatial construction, revealing that he studied Cézanne well. By 1909 such primitivism for Vauxcelles had led directly to Cubism:

> From regression to regression, Matisse goes back to the art of the caverns, to the babble of the infant who with a pointed flint traces the silhouette of a reindeer's head onto the wall.... He schematizes, he synthesizes. And the Kanaka [Polynesian] cubes of M. Braque are the direct result.

Braque's *Large Nude* of spring 1908 responded to all these works by Cézanne, Derain, Matisse and Picasso with a radically geometrized female nude. Adhering strictly to a Cézannesque palette of green, blue, ochre (dark earthy yellow) and red ochre, the angled forms of the figure are echoed throughout in the drapery in front of which she stands, most obvious in her left elbow, right forearm and left heel. As in Picasso's *Demoiselles d'Avignon*, such repeated forms flatten the space of the composition, setting up an abstract rhythm in which the figure is subsumed. The parallel brushstrokes are borrowed directly from Cézanne and are similarly used to echo the curves and angles of the abstract design, while the black outlines come from Gauguin and Van Gogh. Her squat proportions, out-of-scale feet and, above all, masklike face all suggest the important influence of African sculpture, for example Teke figures and Fang masks, in arriving at these abstractions.

44. **Paul Cézanne**, *Five Bathers*, 1885–87.

53

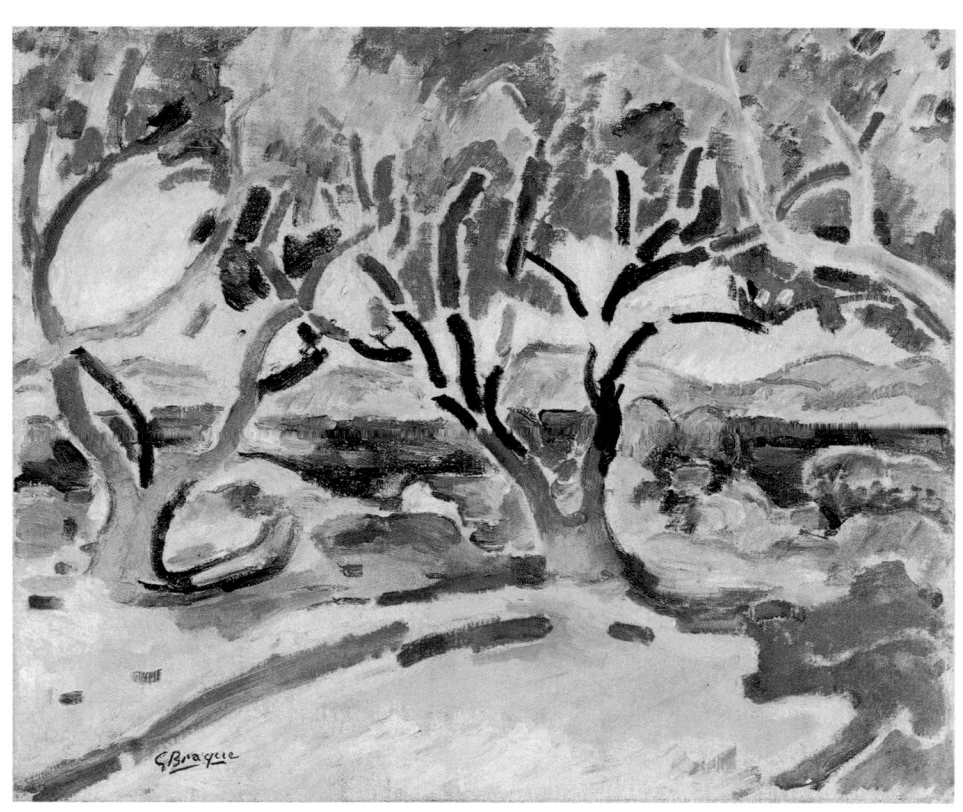

45. **Georges Braque**, *Olive Trees*, 1907.

To understand how Braque was able to respond in this way, we need briefly to consider his earlier Fauvism. In works such as *Olive Trees*, 1907, he began to simplify and distort form and space and to 45 employ the most brilliant colour, in closest imitation of similar works by Derain. Braque's Fauve paintings are distinguishable at first mainly for their stunning colour harmonies and his singular use of luminous yellows and complementary lavenders, as here. But most telling for his future work is his interest in Fauve techniques of spatial ambiguity, which he carefully studied in Matisse and Derain. In *Olive Trees*, we can readily see a landscape painted near La Ciotat on the Mediterranean coast with a foreground of trees, middle ground of water, and background of mountains.

Yet Braque works against our desire to read this as a traditional landscape by abstracting his work through a variety of techniques typical of the Fauves. No object – including the tree in the centre – is viewed whole; rather every form is cut off by the edge of the canvas, which flattens the illusion of recessive space. The repetitious forms of the branches give an impression of flat forms placed arbitrarily over the surface, while some of them join up to create an effect of visual 'holes' in the canvas, departing from the landscape illusion altogether. The colour itself inverts traditional maxims of placement: academic precepts teach that warm colours (red, orange, yellow) psychologically advance towards the viewer's eye while cool colours (green, blue, purple) recede, hence the academic artist would be careful to put warm colours on foreground objects and cool colours on distant objects, such as blue for mountains. We can see at a glance that Braque has defied these rules by placing cool green in the foreground at the bottom of the painting, blue in the middle ground, and green again at the top; similarly, warm yellows and pinks occupy bands in between these cool areas, each cancelling out the effect of the other bands, with the final ironic twist of the pink and yellow mountains in the furthest distance. All these contradictory cues work against any attempt to view this painting as a comforting 'window onto reality' and force themselves upon us as expressions of the unique sensibility of the artist: writer Emile Zola's 'nature viewed through a temperament' taken to antisocial extremes.

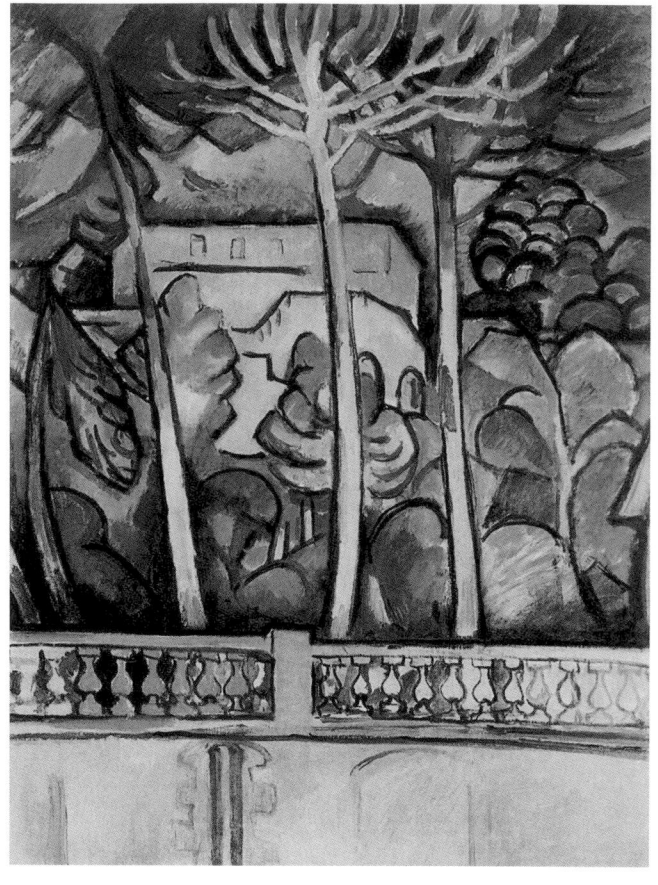

Braque brings similar techniques to his treatment of landscape in subsequent works constituting the beginnings of Cubism, painted on a trip to L'Estaque where Cézanne frequently painted. In *Terrace of Hôtel Mistral* of 1907, Braque emulates Derain's *Three Trees, L'Estaque* by cutting off the tops of the foreground trees, outlining the foliage and buildings in black and shifting colours within forms in relation to the background. But where Derain's work was saturated in sunlight, largely curvilinear and painted in a brilliant Fauve palette of reds, greens and yellows, Braque reshapes the landscape into regularly repeating geometric forms in a restricted palette of muted green, blue and ochre, with no particular light source. Further, he pivots what we are viewing — terrace, trees, bushes and distant building — to stand absolutely parallel to the canvas, so that recession into space is achieved through shapes rising in vertical lockstep. The primitivizing Cézannism of this work has taken him far from his earlier Fauvism.

Braque's *Houses at L'Estaque* was painted the following summer and, refused by the Salon d'Automne, was exhibited at Kahnweiler's gallery in November 1908. This work has been justifiably taken as the first Cubist painting, partly as a result of the critical reaction of Vauxcelles, who first used the term 'cubes' in reviewing that show. Here Braque has taken the freedoms claimed by Cézanne in the name of individual sensibility into territory that deliberately denies landscape expectations. Though there is not a real cube anywhere in the picture, a confusing plethora of straight lines and blocky shapes, virtually all the same ochre colour, vertically mount the surface of the canvas. Shadows at first suggest that there will be one light source, but they turn out to be bewilderingly inconsistent, such that in the main house in the centre two shadows actually meet at the corner. Braque purposely denies – through the use of Cézannesque *passage* – any clear spatial relation between the houses. For instance, in the foreground the first house behind the base of the tree seems at first to stand clearly in front of the one to its right, but its lower roof line is radically broken in the middle and fades out altogether at the right-hand side, with a dark ochre passage fading in a smooth transition to the wall of the other house. The result is a plane – bounded on three sides by dark lines – that diagonally faces the upper left corner of the picture, denying the recessive space necessary to view the first house as occupying three-dimensional space; this plane, however, is pierced by the upper lines of the roof, creating an impossible geometrical 'figure'. Such inconsistencies recur throughout the picture, forcing the viewer to apprehend the forms first one way, then another, while to view such an ambiguous form both ways at once would defy logic. According to some Cubists this very ambiguity induces the viewer to transcend the confines of rationality itself and to experience an 'intuitive' state of mind. We will discuss these ideas fully in the next chapter, but it is apropos here to point out that this antirational state is exactly the condition enviously attributed to 'primitive' peoples, especially when creating or viewing art, and as such is perfectly of a piece with the simplification and crudity – in a word, the 'primitivism' – of the style, as expressed by Vauxcelles above.

Picasso and Braque met in spring 1907 and were certainly aware of each other's work during this early period. By 1909, they had become close friends, visiting each other on a daily basis, discussing and viewing their work. They in fact developed the closest collaboration of any two artists within the Cubist movement, creating works between 1910 and 1912 so similar that few can distinguish them from each other. Indeed, this 'impersonality' was evidently

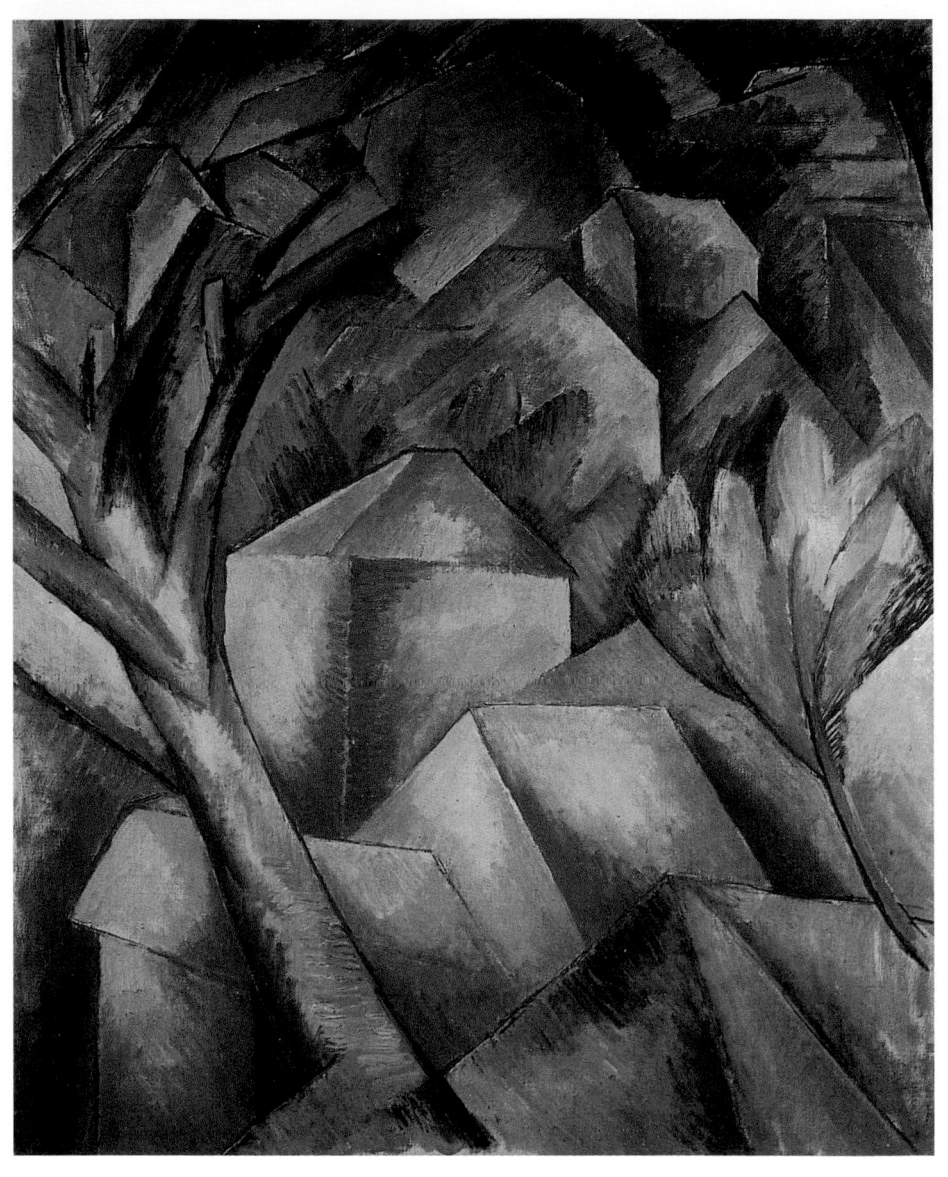

47. **Georges Braque**, *Houses at L'Estaque*, 1908.

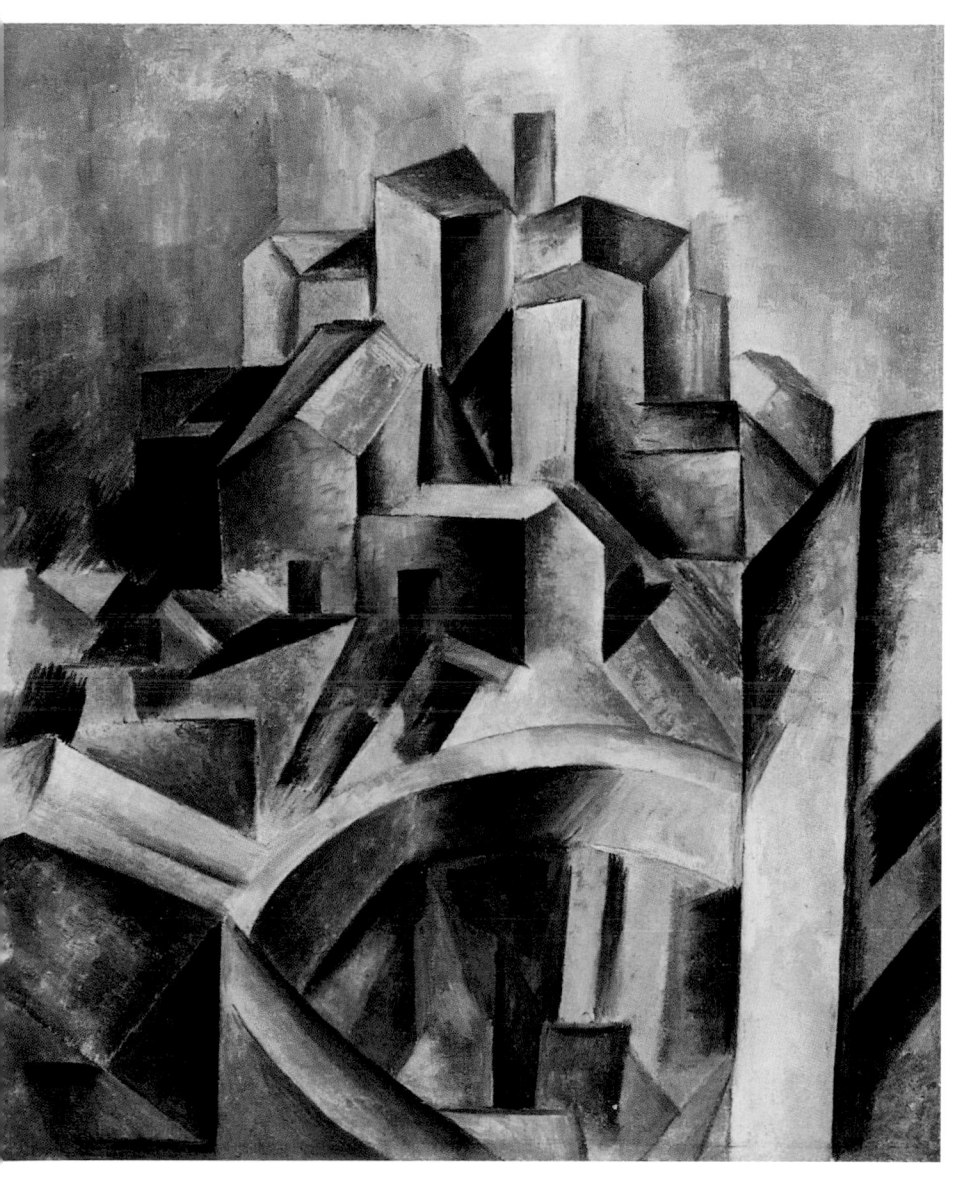

48. **Pablo Picasso**, *Reservoir at Horta*, summer 1909.

desired, as both signed their canvases only on the back until later years. Although neither artist recorded their conversations or wrote explanatory letters about this period, they shared aesthetic ideas and forms, urging each other on to ever bolder works of art. Compared with *Three Women*, Picasso goes to much greater extremes in his *Reservoir at Horta* of summer 1909, with such deformations as its twisted geometric houses in the centre left, reverse perspective on the upper right, utter lack of detail and contradictory shadows in the large form on the right edge, and purposeful obfuscation in the reflections of the reservoir water in the foreground. Additionally, the ground between the houses and reservoir and the sky to the left of the houses are broken up in such a way as to suggest echoing geometric forms, but they remain, intentionally, unresolved in the viewer's mind. Braque works in a similar vein in his *Harbour in Normandy* of 1909, where some forms are clearly contained within outlines – as with the lighthouses and pink boat hulls – while other areas break down the distinction between forms, as in the sea wall on the right and the centre foreground, which may depict a sandy beach. As with the *Houses at L'Estaque*, the viewer must have recourse to another state of mind from that of the rational Western tradition implicated in academic art.

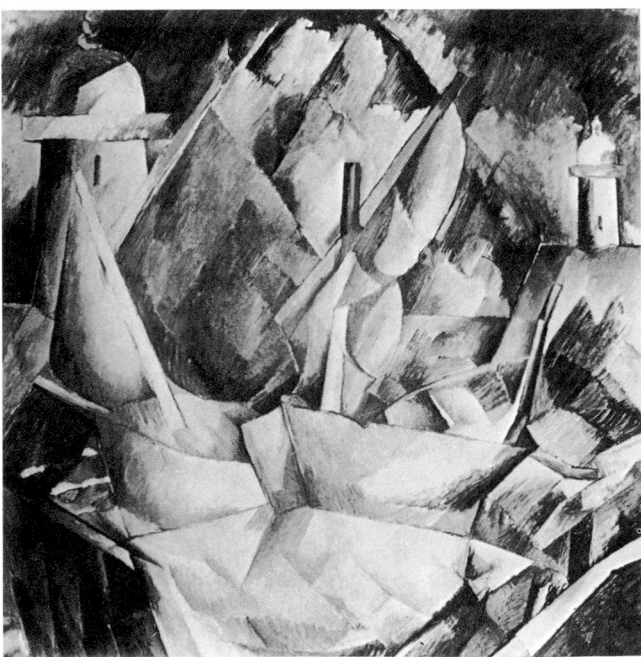

49. **Georges Braque**,
Harbour in Normandy, 1909.

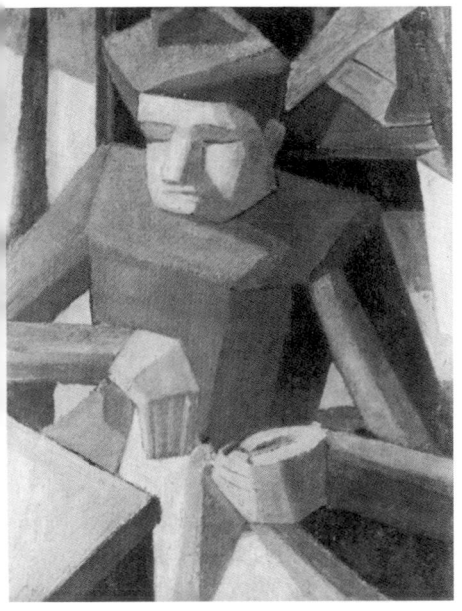
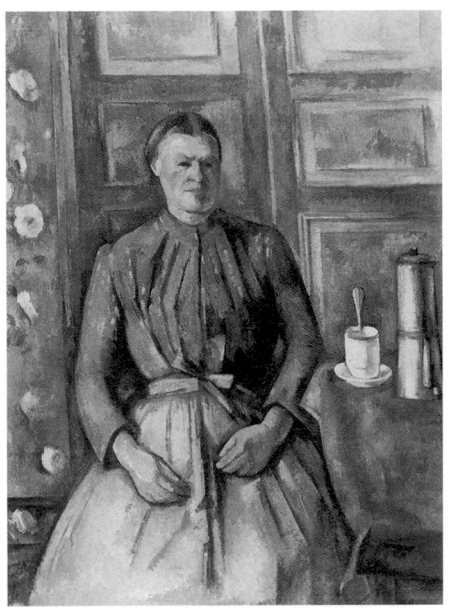

Cézanne's influence was felt by every Cubist at some stage of his or her career; in fact, early Cubism could just as easily be called 'Cézannism'. For example, another self-styled 'primitive' Fernand Léger (1881–1955) claimed both Cézanne and Rousseau as his acknowledged masters and in 1909 and 1910 developed his own style of Cubism, evident in his *Woman Sewing* from the same period. Léger credited Cézanne with showing him how to 'flatten volumes' and simplify form. Rather than emulating Braque's and Picasso's interest in *passage*, Léger emphasizes the volumetric and tonal qualities of Cézanne's work, as seen in his *Woman with a Coffeepot* (c. 1890–94). While the earthen and olive tones of Léger's *Woman Sewing* owe a great deal to the tonality of Cézanne's palette, the extreme simplification of form and greater degree of planar faceting in Léger's work is even more indebted to Rousseau's use of comparable techniques in his portraits, such as *The Poet and His Muse* (1909). To number himself among the Cubists, Léger emulated their primitivist forebears, a logical step on the road to Cubist abstraction. 50 51 42

Thus the concept of the artist as a 'primitive' – antirational, spontaneous, and above all 'authentic' – informed the entire Cubist movement throughout the pre-World War I period. And, at the same time, numerous Cubist works continued to conjure with styles of African sculpture. Later 'quotations' of African art in

50. **Fernand Léger**,
Woman Sewing, 1909–10.

51. **Paul Cézanne**,
La Femme à la cafetière (Woman with a Coffeepot), c. 1890–94.

works sometimes thought to be beyond the reach of 'content' include Picasso's *Nude* of 1910, which adopts figural proportions visible in sculptures from the French colonies on view at the Musée d'Ethnographie before 1900. Teke figures from People's Republic of the Congo, Fang reliquary figures from Gabon, and Baga figures from Guinea, all – like Picasso's nude – have simplified masklike faces, short legs, prominent buttocks, elongated trunks, and in the case of Baga figures, elongated necks. These proportions are retained in a subsequent series of increasingly abstract standing nude female figures, including the drawing visible on the wall in Picasso's photograph of Kahnweiler. Picasso likewise rendered his

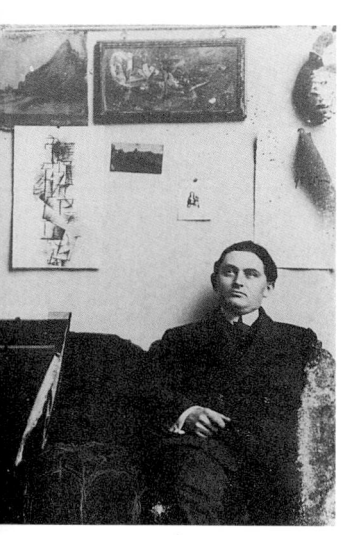

52. Photograph of Daniel-Henry Kahnweiler by Pablo Picasso, taken in Picasso's studio, boulevard de Clichy, c. 1910.

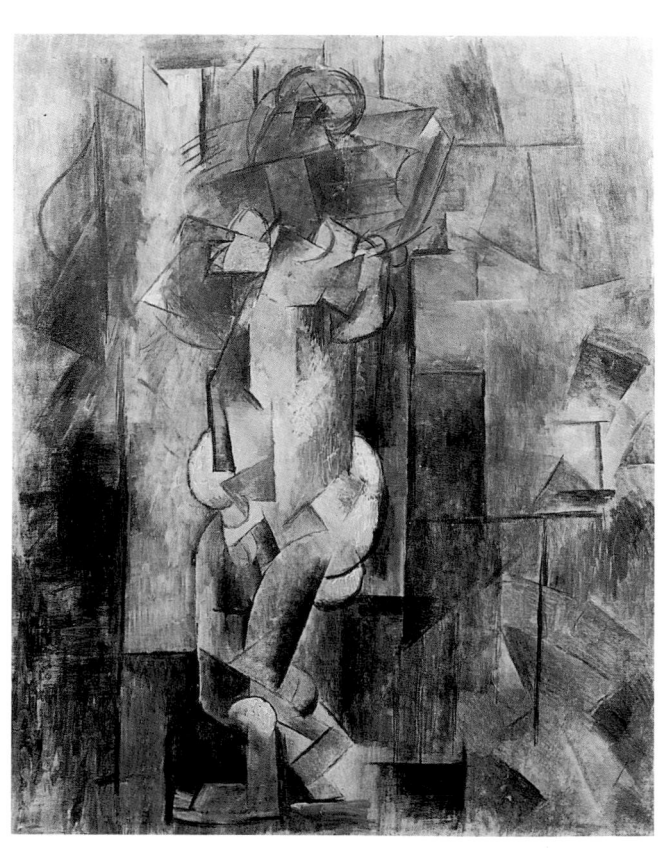

53. **Pablo Picasso**, *Nude*, 1910.

Shira-Punu mask from the former French Congo – which hangs in the upper right corner of the photograph – cryptically visible in his *Portrait of Kahnweiler* of 1910. In no way meant to be immediately discerned, aspects of the mask appear directly to the left of his sitter's head. The striated conical topknot, eye slits, straight mouth and white curve of its outer cheek coalesce to suggest the forms of the mask. However, rather than constituting an iconography or 'quotation' they inform the underlying rhythms and shapes that recur throughout the canvas, revealing that the most important aspect of African art is not by this time style per se but the acknowledgment of the primitivist roots of Cubist painting.

54

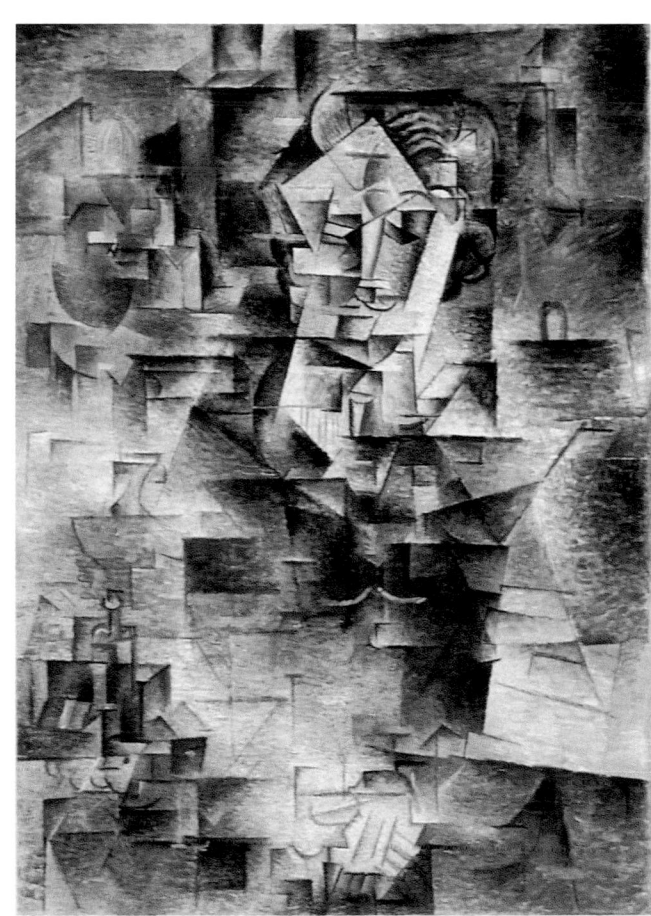

54. **Pablo Picasso**, *Portrait of Daniel-Henry Kahnweiler*, 1910. Works as difficult to 'see' as this one often employ traditional compositions to help orient the viewer. This seated half-length portrait centres the figure on the canvas and includes such readable elements as Kahnweiler's wavy hair, shadowed eyes and ochre-tinted face above a white collar, dark suit with watch fob and chain, clasped hands below and, to the left, a small table with a bottle and glass. Nonetheless, these elements should not tempt us to 'reconstruct' a realist painting; rather, they help us to discern the work's radical relation to past traditions.

Chapter 2   Philosophies of Space and Time

Before considering the philosophies that justified Cubist departures from older communal agreements about how the world 'appeared', we need to look closely at works exemplary of this radical revision of conventional pictorial illusionism. Braque's *Violin and Palette* of autumn 1909 takes his previous innovations further, breaking 'open' several of its still-life forms. In this painting, we are looking at a table with sheet music on a small music-stand and a violin resting on a green cloth; behind this, a green curtain hangs on the right and an artist's palette hangs from a nail. Yet, though these things are quite visible, so many of our expectations are denied. The table itself is not viewed in perspectival recession, but has been tilted up nearly parallel to the picture plane, receding vertically rather than into depth. The edges of the violin are not only geometrized, but discontinuous with each other; one of the shoulders of the violin is rounded, the other quite cubic (one of the rare instances in Cubism of an allusion to an actual cube!). The sound holes appear as free-floating transitions between the disjunct upper and lower halves, while, even more obviously, the strings break in the middle over the bridge. And whereas these different areas seem generally to be seen from above, the neck and scroll of the violin are viewed at a more radical angle, twisting into an expressive arabesque at the top. Most interestingly, the geometric folds of green cloth intersect with the equally arbitrarily broken planes of the brown table, so that the sense of the cloth being 'above' the table is lost in some areas. Myriad details of light and shade contradict each other, with shadows cast for example onto the left side of the violin's neck, the right side of the lower right section, and none cast at all by the strings. Light, in short, is treated as arbitrarily as form. And if this seems confusing, the lines of the sheet music trail right off the page, taking on a life of their own.

Braque's depiction of space and form clearly contradicts a 'rational' or 'orderly' treatment of space, form and light, wherein the shapes and locations of objects are clear. Following the conventions employed in traditional still-life painting, as in Jean-Baptiste-Siméon Chardin's *Musical Instruments and Parrot* (before 1732), chiaroscuro – the use of shadow and light to describe volume – aids in defining the three-dimensionality of the objects as well as their location in space. Instead Braque constructs forms seemingly viewed from a variety of perspectives rather than from only one and whose resulting spatial relations to each other are confused and disorienting. At the top of the painting the curtain, palette and nail appear far more predictable and even serve to remind us of the distance this work has come from the comforting appearance of the material world in a naturalist tradition.

Another work reveals similar techniques, although it represents a later period of development in the Cubist movement. Gleizes's *Portrait of the Publisher Figuière*, shown in the Salon d'Automne of 1913, is a nearly full-length portrait of the publisher Eugène Figuière in a dark suit, surrounded by the avant-garde books he helped produce. Seated, with his left leg crossed over his right, his pose and placement in the centre of the canvas is completely traditional. The viewer needs to be anchored in compositional conventions this way, because the abstraction of the figural forms would otherwise be overwhelming. Geometrized forms break up the left leg, left hand, right arm and head, rendering their shapes and placement in space ambiguous, though their placement relative to each other and in front of the background remains clear. Long lines cut through parts of the figure and connect up with elements of the background – such as the one running through Figuière's left shoulder and arm – working against our sense of the body as overlapping the books behind, as well as flattening and confusing the depicted space. The figure's head is broken up into geometrized sections – forehead, cheek, beard, ear – which make a reading of the head ambiguous, but one can nevertheless discern that the right-hand half of the head operates in profile as well as within an overall three-quarter view. The glimpses of this figure at different moments in time, as well as the evocation of the subjectivity of the artist's experience of Figuière over time, suggests a different sort of temporality operative within the picture, a specifically subjective temporality in contrast to the mechanical time of the clock on the upper left.

The aesthetic implications of such an approach has much in common with the books published by the sitter, which echo around – rather than 'behind' – his figure: Apollinaire's *The Cubist Painters*, Gleizes and Metzinger's own *Du Cubisme*, writings by the major Symbolist poets Paul Fort and Gustave Kahn, and works by younger neo-Symbolist writers Henri-Martin Barzun and Jacques Nayral, associated with the 'Unanimist' movement in poetry. Nayral in his capacity as Figuière's editorial assistant had selected *Du Cubisme* and *The Cubist Painters* as part of a projected series on the arts. All these writers valorize subjective experience and expression over

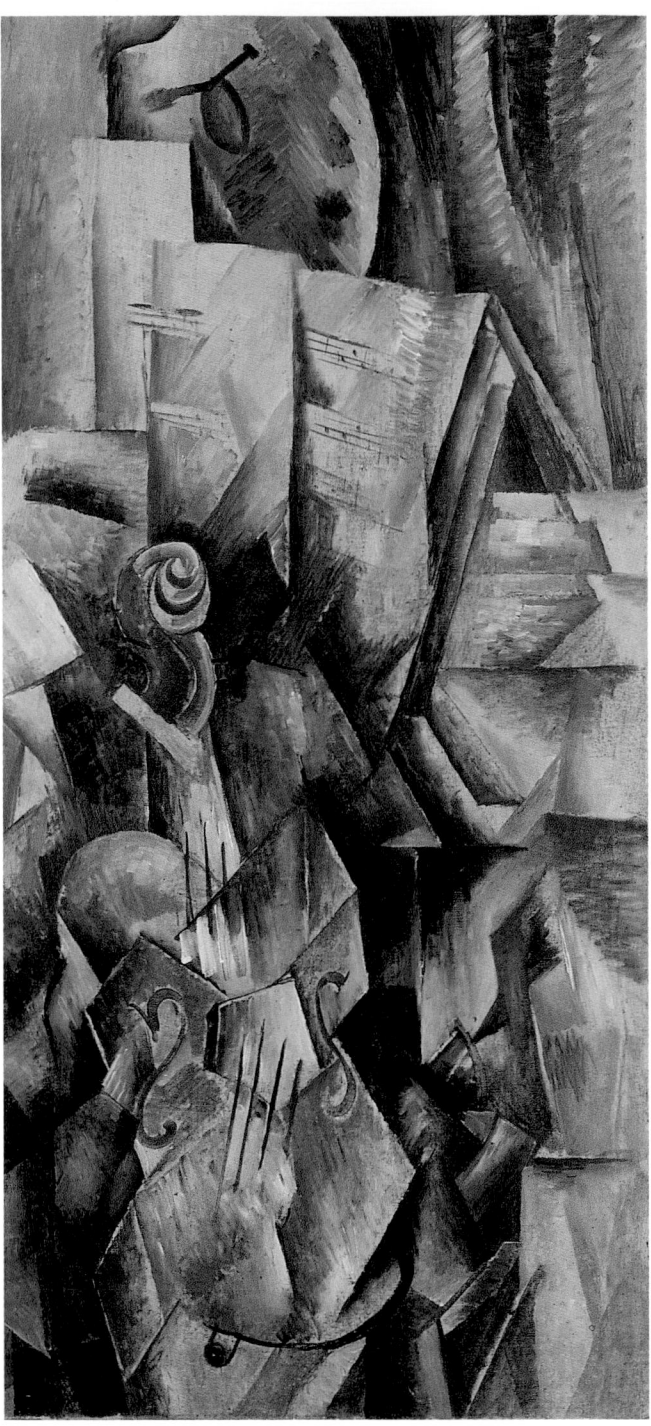

55. **Georges Braque**,
Violin and Palette, autumn 1909.

56. **Jean-Baptiste-Siméon Chardin**, *Musical Instruments and Parrot*, before 1732.

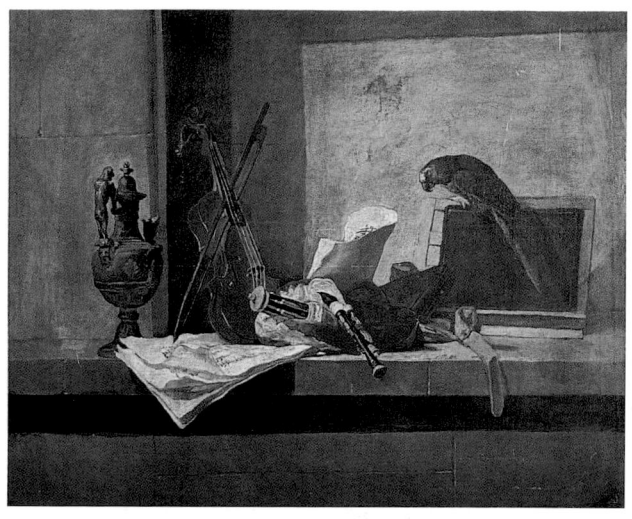

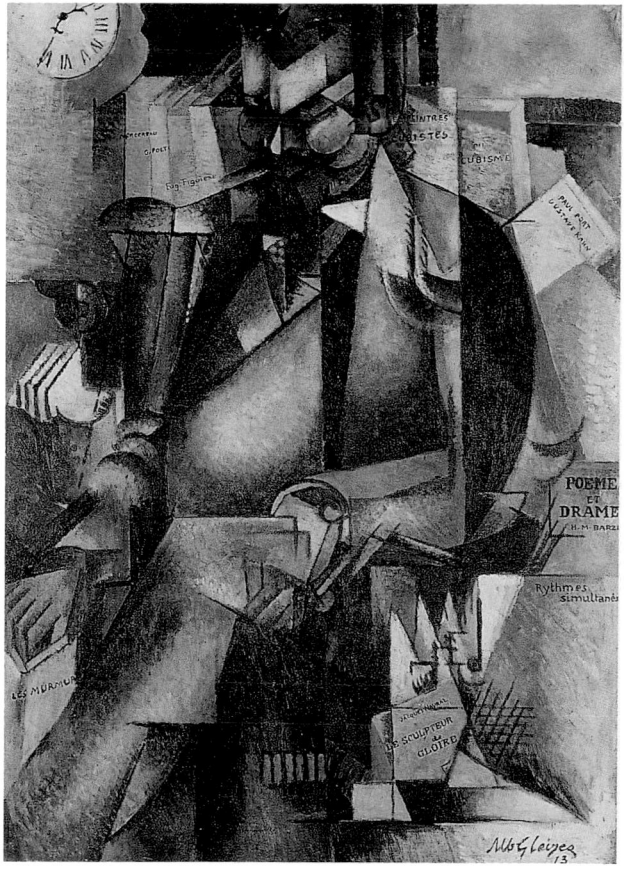

57. **Albert Gleizes**, *Portrait of the Publisher Figuière*, 1913.

an 'objective' view of the material world, that is, they embrace an antipositivist, even an antirationalist, perspective consonant with the abstraction of both Braque's *Violin and Palette* and Figuière's 'portrait'. 55, 5

What could justify such a radical turning away from the depiction of the world in recognizable terms? Cubism emerged during an era of widespread dissatisfaction with the positivism, materialism and determinism that dominated nineteenth-century thought. Underlying that positivism and materialism was a firm belief that scientific research held the key to understanding life, that the future – for living organisms and inanimate objects – could be predicted on the basis of scientific models and that such determinism could be extended to the study of human psychology. Concepts of 'free will' and 'divine providence' had no place in a world governed by determinism. Thus the narrow limitations of these nineteenth-century theories were contested by fin-de-siècle intellectuals, including the mathematician Henri Poincaré (1854–1912) and the philosophers Henri Bergson (1859–1941), Friedrich Nietzsche (1844–1900) and William James (1842–1910). Such attacks on positivism, determinism and the notion of absolute truth, as opposed to the relativity of knowledge, were not only debated in specialized journals, but popularized in widely available lay publications, read with interest by writers and artists affiliated with the Cubist movement. Equally popularized in contemporary journals were new scientific discoveries like X-rays, which affirmed doubts about the authenticity of external, material appearances by revealing realities hidden from human vision, in turn awakening for many an interest in the occult. As art historian Linda Henderson has written,

Roentgen's identification of X-rays in 1895, along with Hertz's proof of the existence of electromagnetic waves in 1888 and the development by 1900 of practicable wireless telegraphy using Hertzian waves offered laymen a new conception of space as filled with vibrating waves beyond the range of human sense perception.

In effect scientific knowledge had now outstripped the perceptual limitations of human vision, at the same time as positivist assumptions justifying nineteenth-century empiricism came under attack.

In Cubist circles this fin-de-siècle revolt inspired the rejection of Euclidean geometry and its artistic correlate, the quantitative measurement of space governing perspective, which was invented during the Renaissance and continued as an unquestioned 'given' in academic painting. A work like Jean-Léon Gérôme's *The Snake Charmer* of 1880 exhibits many of the assumptions associated with 5 traditional spatial construction. The picture plane, or fictive 'entrance' into the illusion, operates as a 'window onto the world', through which we see the material world in all its visual perfection. The room we look into, an imaginary mosque, is treated as a rectangular box, with the vanishing point to the left behind the seated figures; the gaps between the ancient stones of the flooring act as a perspectival grid revealing the spatial construction. All forms are clearly delineated, with light falling from a consistent source on the upper right, creating highlights that gradually shade, through delicate transitions, into darkness. Likewise, the figures within this space have precisely clear relationships to each other, based on overlapping and on their diminishing scale as they recede from the foreground. Such techniques are academic givens – though of course each element may be altered in the hands of different artists – and Gérôme uses his extremely polished version of this style to dramatic effect. Indeed, the academic and Western values associated with spatial clarity, measure, and naturalism are specifically contrasted within the work with the two-dimensional, decorative (and therefore 'feminine') abstraction of the tiled mosque interior, which the artist views as characteristic of the North African 'other' and which justifies the popular 'orientalism' of his subject.

58. **Jean-Léon Gérôme**,
The Snake Charmer, 1880.

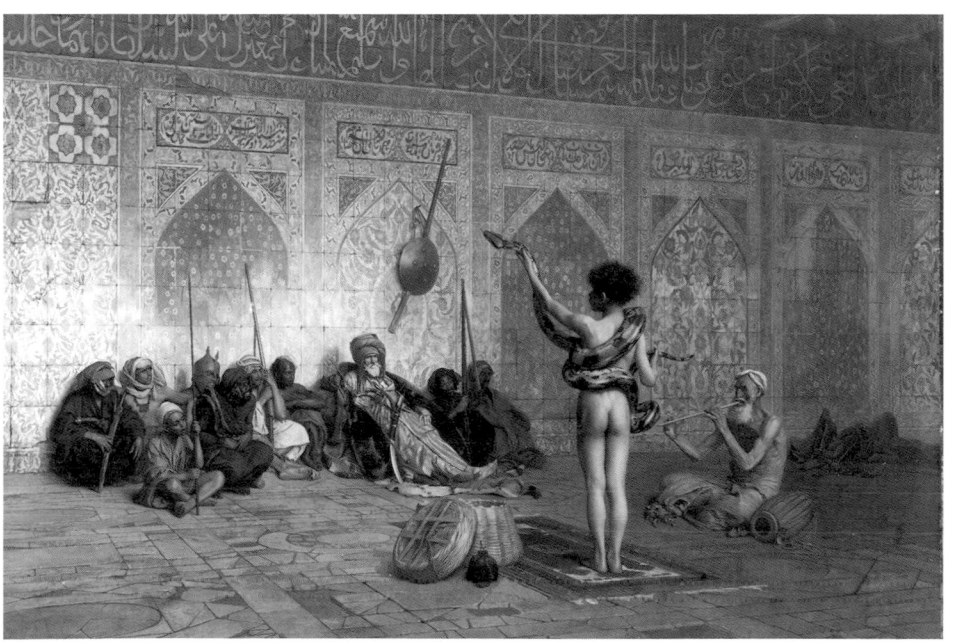

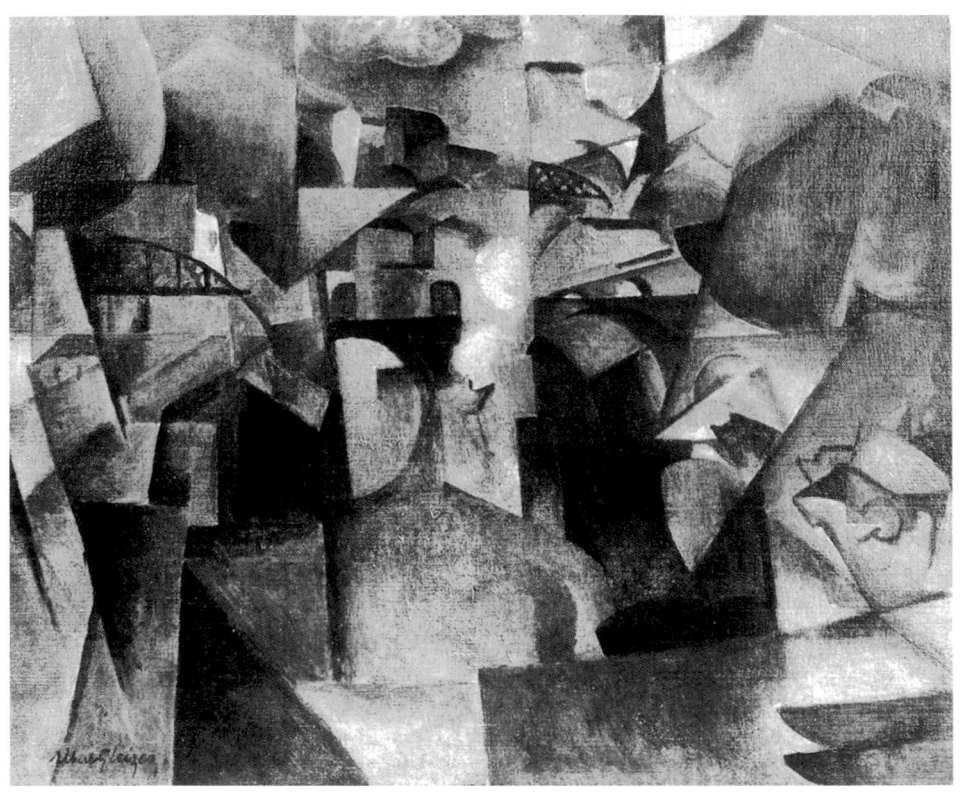

Instead of this spatial model, Cubists turned to new models of geometry and the 'fourth dimension' as inspiration for works like Gleizes's *Passy (Ponts de Paris)* of 1912, which he and Metzinger reproduced in their tract *Du Cubisme* as exemplary of art expressing their ideas. This urban landscape synthesized the river, trees, clouds, buildings, steel bridges and smoke of the modern city. Partially geometrized forms – such as the green arc of tree on the upper left or arched doors and windows on rectangular buildings in the centre – are subjectively evoked through limited colour range; shifting perspectives, signified by long vertical and diagonal bands cutting off the edges of objects contained within them; and shifting relative scales of objects, such as the two steel bridge spans. As Henderson has demonstrated, the Cubists justified this novel approach to pictorial space in part on the basis of the mathematician Henri Poincaré's theory of 'conventionalism'.

Subjectivity

Poincaré regarded all geometric models as 'contingent', as mere conventions, rather than as 'absolute'; thus Euclidean geometry was simply one geometric configuration among many equally valid alternative geometries. Cubists embraced conventionalism by declaring their freedom to transform pictorial space in response to their own subjectivity as well as to the alternative geometries championed by Poincaré. Adherence to subjectivity in turn signalled a radical break from past pictorial conventions in favour of a Nietzschean expression of individual will. In a September 1911 essay on Metzinger's Cubism, Gleizes identified his colleague as a follower of Nietzsche who 'invents his own truth' by destroying 'old values', while Apollinaire referenced Nietzsche in his May 1912 claim that the Cubist's role was to 'modify the illusions of the public in accordance with his own creation'. Gleizes's, Metzinger's and Apollinaire's enthusiasm for Nietzsche had been shared since his Barcelona days by Picasso, whose own overthrow of traditional perspective was justified by Apollinaire in similar terms.

Vanishing-point perspective also assumed a one-to-one correspondence between a fictive 'moment' in time and the placing of the beholder at a fixed position in space. Since Euclideanism thoroughly informed this spatialized concept of time, the association of a single moment in time with a single point in space was also refused in favour of the notion of 'simultaneity', wherein many different moments could be depicted in a single painting, as seen in Gleizes's *Portrait of Figuière*. Cubists justified such 'simultaneity' on the basis of the antirational concept of time or *durée* (duration) developed by the philosopher Henri Bergson and the closely related notion of 'stream of consciousness' publicized by the American pragmatist William James, with whom the avant-garde American writer Gertrude Stein (1874–1946) had studied. Stein, with her sister Sarah and brother Leo, were early collectors of the art of Matisse and Picasso; her home became an important meeting place for artists and critics associated with the Cubist movement.

Bergson claimed that the human experience of time, and the 'creative' temporality of biological evolution, were radically different from the concept of measurable, deterministic time developed by nineteenth-century positivists; likewise he rejected the concomitant division of space into separate, measurable units. Bergson (and James) described the intellect as a mere instrumental tool – a 'utilitarian' by-product of human evolution – whose rational models facilitated our daily mundane activity. The intellect, therefore, was no longer regarded as a value-neutral cognitive faculty, able to grasp

57

60. Albert Gleizes, c. 1912.

61. Jean Metzinger, c. 1912.

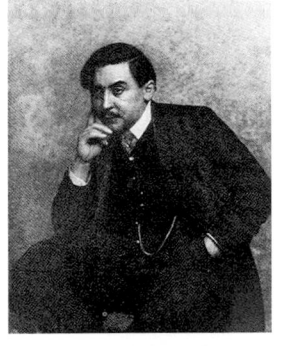

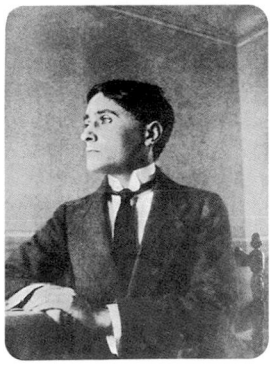

reality in an impartial manner. Instead, argued Bergson, we should rely on intuition, an empathetic form of consciousness, to discern the inner nature of reality through the flow of time, which he called 'duration'. Intuition, stated Bergson, inspired creative insights in the sciences as well as the arts: thus scientists who rejected Newtonian physics and resolved matter into energy fields and thermodynamic forces had drawn on their intuition in positing such notions. The Cubists welcomed Bergson's 'intuitive' approach to science and studied his thought to justify their adaptation of Poincaré's alternative geometries to their mode of pictorial abstraction. To properly understand the Cubists' radical transformation of pictorial form, we must explore antipositivist philosophical currents and chart their impact on Cubist theory and practice.

Space

We can begin by considering nineteenth-century rebuttals of Euclidean geometry and their influence in Cubist circles. Initially formulated in the 1820s, non-Euclidean geometry refuted one of the 'self-evident' postulates that underlay Euclid's system of three-dimensional geometry. His 'parallel postulate' held that two straight lines parallel to one another will never converge but will extend to infinity. Nineteenth-century mathematicians successfully refuted this postulate by developing concepts of 'curved' space, and visual

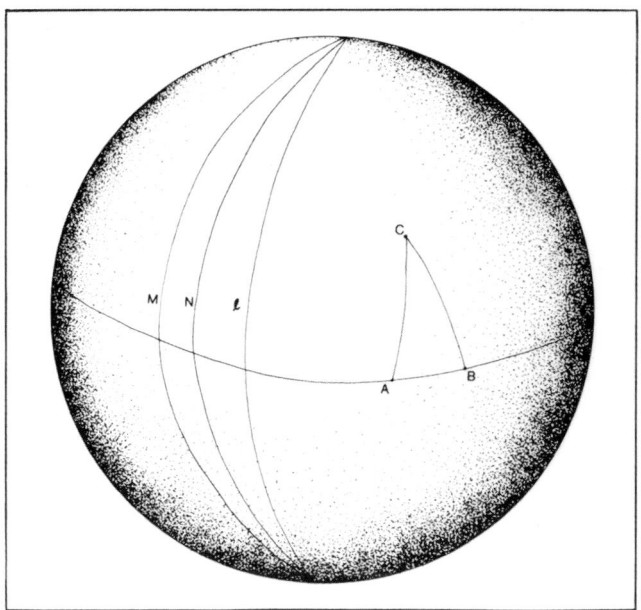

62. Riemannian geometry represented on a sphere.

models for non-Euclidean geometry published in the popular press proved particularly effective in advertising these findings. Based on the curvature of spherical space rather than the concept of flat, planar space underlying Euclid's postulates, Georg Friedrich Riemann treated space as the study of an infinite number of dimensions, subject to myriad types of curvature. Riemann's ideas inspired still others to imagine non-Euclidean geometries in which spatial curvature would be irregular rather than constant and where figures could change their shape and properties according to their position. Such deformities underscored the link between spatial geometry and the movement of shapes within that space, and this notion of 'malleable' form came to affect many of the Cubists when they developed pictorial analogues to non-Euclidean geometry.

The fourth dimension and non-Euclidean geometries were also popularly associated with the antipositivist revolt against Euclidean geometry. The mathematician Henri Poincaré played a crucial role in linking such geometries to a relativist current that would see all geometries as psycho-physical in origin, rather than as a simple reflection of external 'reality'. In his book *Science and Hypothesis* (1902), Poincaré set out to refute the neo-Kantians of his generation who endorsed the German philosopher Immanuel Kant's defence of the pre-existing or *a priori* status of three-dimensional space and of Euclidean geometry. Poincaré examined non-Euclidean geometries to demonstrate that geometrical space is a construction of the mind under the influence of practical needs before concluding that there is no geometrical space that is *a priori*. Instead, he argues, our models of space are obtained through a fusion of visual, tactile, and motor 'spaces':

Apart from the data of sight and touch, there are other sensations which contribute as much and more than they to the genesis of the notion of space. These are known to everyone; they accompany all our movements, and are usually called muscular sensations.

Poincaré concludes that our individual experience of space is nothing more than a projection of our response to bodily stimuli. The perception of three dimensions, for instance, is the result of the coordination of our two eyes, whereas the experience of two dimensions more frequently stems from our faculty of touch. To propose that Euclidean space is 'true' and uniform for everybody is thus an absurdity, for 'no geometry can be truer than another; it can only be *more convenient*', that is, a matter of mere convention.

We know that members of Picasso's circle became familiar with Poincaré's conventionalism and the related geometries described above before 1909. In 1908 the fourth dimension was already a topic of conversation at the weekly *soirées* of Gertrude Stein, according to her brother Leo. By at least 1909 Maurice Princet, an insurance actuary with training in the new geometries who may have visited the Steins, had enthusiastically conveyed his knowledge of the writings of Poincaré and other mathematicians to Picasso, Salmon and Apollinaire, the latter two key writers on Cubism. Leo Stein remembered: 'Picasso began to have ideas. Bergson's creative evolution was in the air with its seductive slogan of the *élan vital* or life force. There was a friend of the Montmartre crowd, interested in mathematics, who talked about infinities and fourth dimensions. Picasso began to have opinions on what was and what was not real.' Metzinger later recalled that Princet tutored Gris and himself in the new geometries around the same time, in the hopes that modern artists would develop a new approach to pictorial space reflective of Poincaré's philosophical premises. In his 10 May 1910 column 'Courrier des Ateliers' for *Paris-Journal*, Salmon claimed that Princet, 'a mathematician inspired to have curious reflections by the efforts of modern painters' was busy writing 'a curious work of aesthetics' (though it was never published). Metzinger in his seminal essay 'Note on Painting' (September 1910), published in the October–November issue of *Pan*, drew the following conclusion from his conversations with Princet: 'Cézanne showed us forms living in the reality of light, Picasso brings us a material account of their real life in the mind – he lays out a free, mobile perspective, from which the ingenious mathematician Maurice Princet has deduced a whole geometry'. Princet extended his circle by joining Gleizes, Metzinger, and the Duchamp brothers during their regular meetings at Jacques Villon's studio in Puteaux and Gleizes's studio at Courbevoie in 1912. Thus Princet's ideas were accessible to all of the Cubists by 1912. That same year Gleizes and Metzinger drew on Poincaré's conventionalism in their text *Du Cubisme*; Marcel Duchamp embarked on his initial study of Poincaré and other mathematicians in his notes for *The Bride Stripped Bare by her Bachelors, Even (The Large Glass)* (1915–23); and in 1913 Apollinaire summarized his own views on Cubism, conventionalism and the new geometries in *Méditations esthétiques: les peintres cubistes (Aesthetic Meditations: The Cubist Painters)* (1913).

In pictorial terms, this antipositivist approach to space resulted in three interrelated innovations: the plastic 'deformation' of objects in terms of size, shape and scale; a rejection of Renaissance perspective in favour of 'multiple views' expressive of the painter's cerebral response to 'tactile' and 'motor' space as well as 'visual' space; and the conjunction of disparate images, including 'memory' images, from widely diverse geographical locales in a single painting.

Plastic deformation: in *Du Cubisme*, Gleizes and Metzinger claimed that Cubist space should not be confused 'with pure visual space or with Euclidean space' because the Cubists did not follow Euclid in positing 'the indeformability of objects in movement'. 'If we wished to tie the painter's space to a particular geometry', Gleizes and Metzinger continued, 'we should have to refer it to the non-Euclidean scholars; we should have to study, at some length, certain of Rieman's [sic] theorems'. This association of Euclidean space with 'visual space' reflected their knowledge of Poincaré's distinction between visual, tactile, and motor spaces in *Science and Hypothesis*; moreover that same book charted the critique by Riemann and others of Euclid's assumption that figures would remain forever rigid and unchanging when moved about in his system of geometry. Instead Riemann created a geometry wherein figures change their

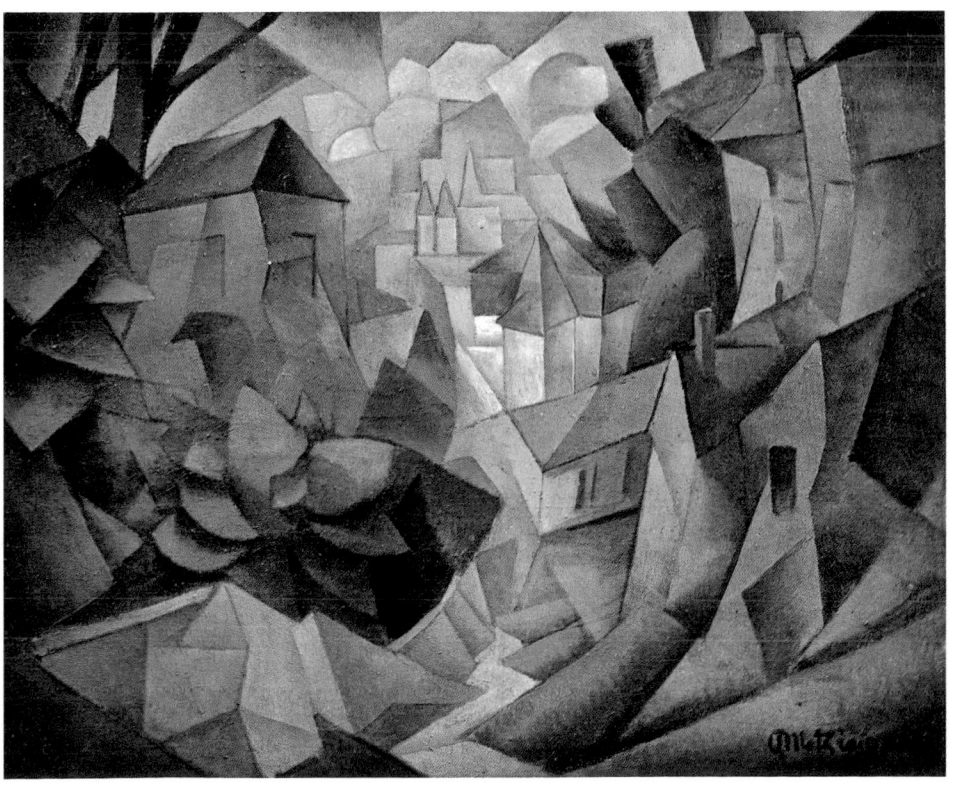

63. **Jean Metzinger,**
Cubist Landscape (The Village),
c.1911–12.

shape as they move on a surface of irregular curvature. *Du Cubisme* claimed that Cubist space expressed Riemann's precepts, and such distortions are readily apparent in Metzinger's *Cubist Landscape (The Village)* (c.1911–12). Here the foreground rocks and foliage, buildings (especially those on the right), and path leading down into a village are self-consciously deformed to correspond to a curved space.

The fourth dimension was evoked to justify figural distortions as well as distortions in scale. Apollinaire, in *The Cubist Painters*, announced that the Cubists, responding to their 'intuition [no] longer limited themselves to the three dimensions of Euclid' but instead had begun exploring the 'fourth dimension'. The fourth dimension, we are told, 'endows objects with plasticity,' thereby permitting the painter 'to proportion objects in accordance with the degree of plasticity he desires them to have'. Unlike 'the three dimensions of Euclid's geometry', that of the fourth dimension represented 'space itself, the dimension of the infinite'. According

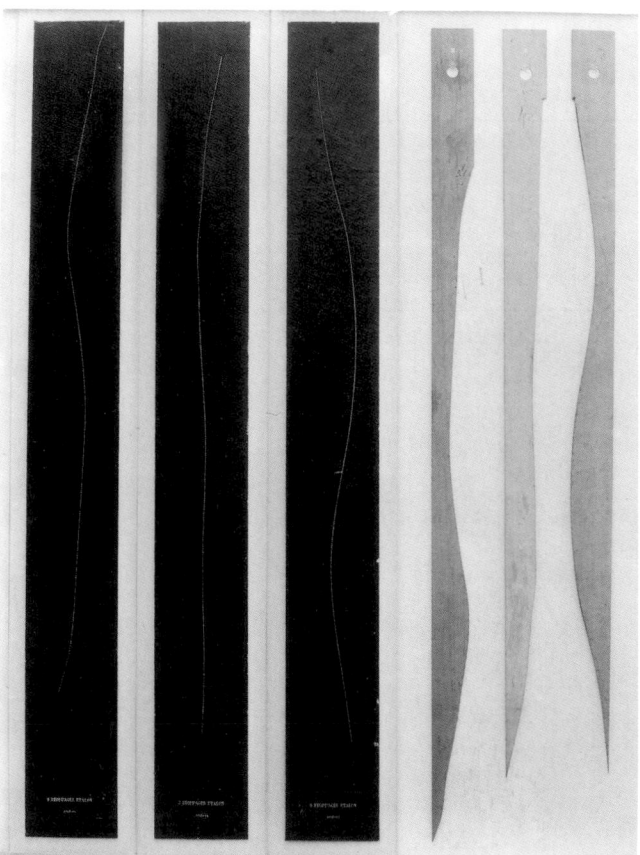

64. **Marcel Duchamp,**
Three Standard Stoppages, 1913. The deformability of objects in movement was humorously confirmed in *Three Standard Stoppages*, Duchamp's satirical (and anarchist) play on the French State's deification of the metre as an objective and 'invariable' unit of measure. In a decidedly 'non-Euclidean' gesture, Duchamp let a metre-long thread drop three times from one area of space to another, carefully recording its new 'measure' each time, to demonstrate that geometrical figures do not necessarily retain their shape when subject to movement. This subjection of the metre to the laws of 'chance' embodied Duchamp's 'freedom' from the Euclidean and Cartesian precepts informing the absolute concept of the metre itself.

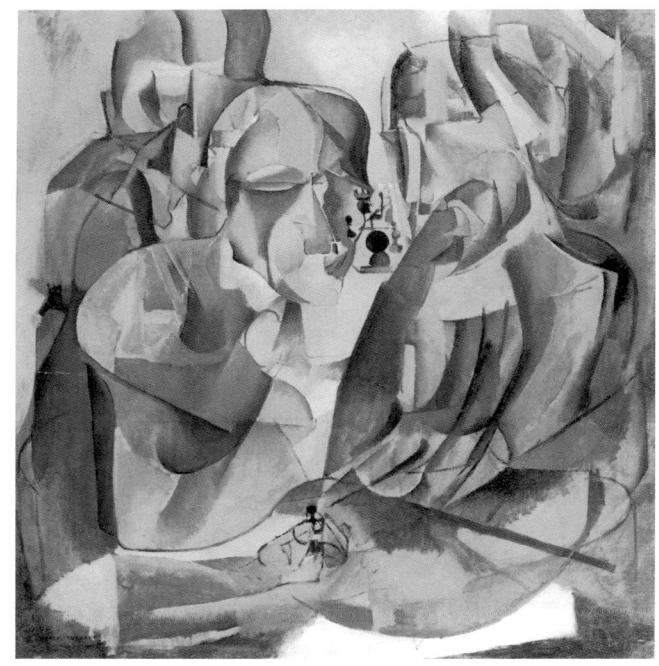

65. **Marcel Duchamp**, *Portrait of Chess Players*, 1911. Duchamp's interest in non-Euclidean geometry and enthusiasm for the fourth dimension are evident in this early portrait of his two brothers – both Cubists – engaged in a chess game. In a 1964 lecture Duchamp claimed to have placed them in an 'indefinite space', indicated by the multiple views of the head and arms of each brother. Since a chess player's skill is measured by an ability to concentrate on past and future moves, these multiple views allude to the temporal dimension of the game and the role of memory. Temporal experience is given 'spatial' form in the player's visualization of past, present, and future.

66. The Duchamp-Villon brothers in Puteaux, winter 1913. Pictured from left to right are Jacques Villon, Marcel Duchamp and Raymond Duchamp-Villon, with their dog, Pipp, and two cats.

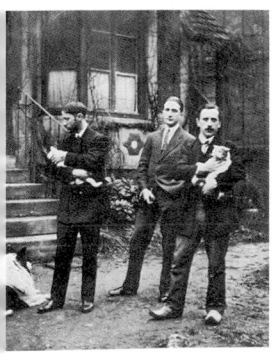

to Apollinaire, artists like Picasso and Derain anticipated such spatial plasticity through their study of African art: the bodily distortions found in Picasso's *Three Women* (1907–8), used to obscure spatial as well as formal transitions, prepared the way for the more extreme spatial disjunctions found in his later works, such as *Nude* of 1910. Here – still visibly encoding the proportions of Teke, Fang and/or Baga figures – the geometric forms of the nude's anatomy blend into the arbitrarily geometrized background, especially in the lower left leg and in the right shoulder and masklike face. The shifting views of the hips and buttocks, which appear in the white area in the centre of the canvas, imply the motion of the figure through a shifting space. In this manner the Cubists managed, to quote Apollinaire, 'to get rid of perspective', that 'infallible device for making things shrink' in favour of a new kind of pictorial space, ordered in response to 'primitive' sensations of 'intuition' and 'desire'.

Multiple views: in his 1910 'Note on Painting' Metzinger stated that Picasso conjoined 'visual perceptions' with 'tactile perceptions' to create a 'free, mobile perspective'; in *Du Cubisme* (1912) Gleizes and Metzinger returned to this paradigm, claiming that, in order to 'establish pictorial space', they had 'recourse to tactile and motor sensations, indeed to all our faculties'. By associating pure

23

53

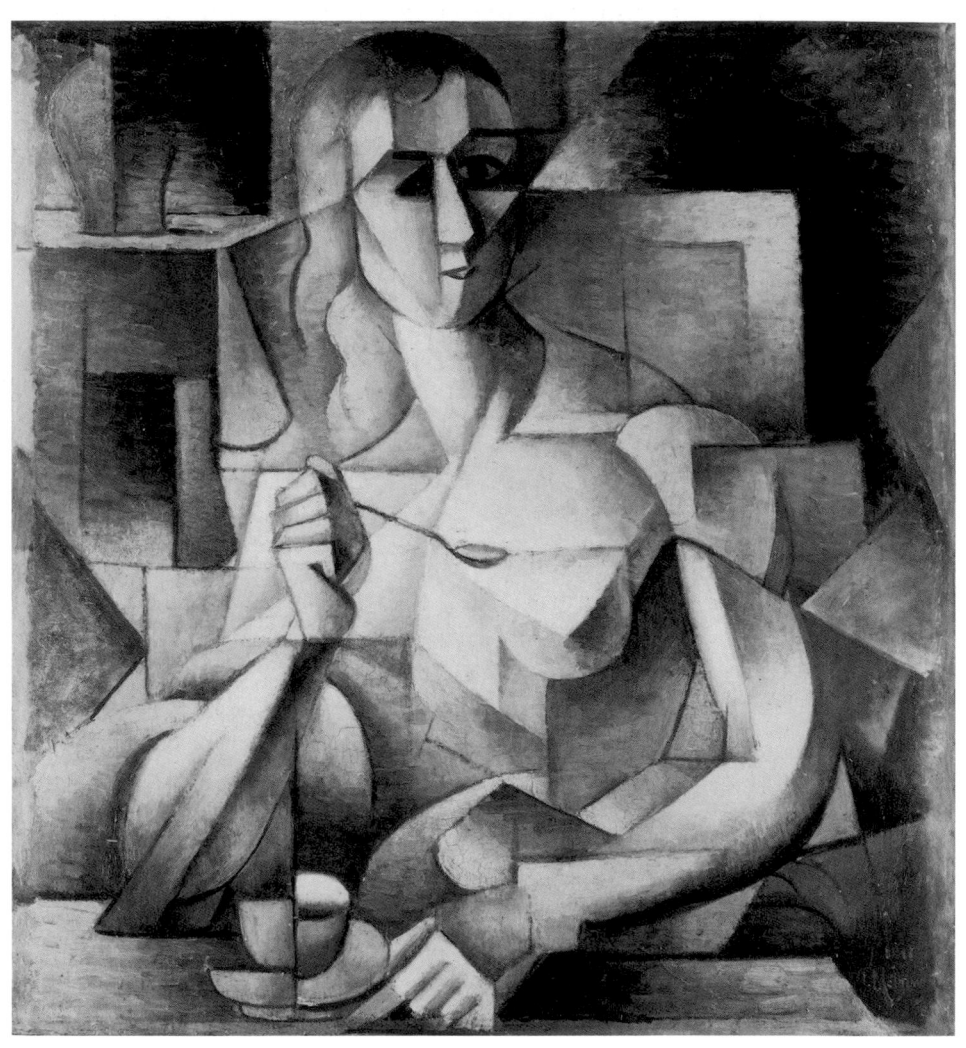

67. **Jean Metzinger**, *Le Goûter (Tea-time)*, 1911.

'visual space' with three-dimensional Euclidean space, and its stepchild, Renaissance perspective, the Cubists signalled the perceptual limitations underlying the art of the past, an art they now sought to transcend. Thus the pictorial space generated by the Cubists not only registered their visual response to a given motif, but other subjective sensations, such as touch and muscular movement (akin to proprioception). 'Motor space' has been discussed as the physical movement of the artist around a motif to capture multiple views of a subject, but Gleizes and Metzinger did not mean to reduce Cubist space to this simple formula, which was the product of memory and imagination as well as of experience. Multiple views in a Cubist painting could evoke a complex series of mental associations between past and present muscular, tactile or olfactory sensations, in addition to an artist's physical movement around a subject.

This interplay of visual, tactile, and motor spaces is fully operative in Metzinger's *Le Goûter* of 1911, an image of an artist's model, 67 semi-nude, with a cloth draped over her right arm as she takes a break between sessions. Here Metzinger alludes to a variety of sensory experiences: 'le goûter' in French means 'afternoon snack', but can also suggest 'taste' in the more abstract, artistic sense of good taste, 'le bon goût' (he includes the square frame of a canvas in the background to remind us of this). Metzinger's model is both in the act of tasting and touching. Her left hand grasps the cup and saucer, her finger touches the table, taking on its colour, and her right hand delicately suspends the spoon between cup and mouth. This suspension between two moments is given pictorial play in the 'simultaneous' conflation of moments in time throughout the painting: for instance the cup and saucer are shown both in profile and three-quarter views, as is the head of the sitter. The canvas as a whole is intersected with transparent volumetric planes, whose Cézannesque interpenetration merges the female model with the surrounding environment. Finally 'tactile space' is evoked through Metzinger's brushstrokes, whose regular marks are subsumed within the volumetric chiaroscuro of fourth-dimensional, abstract planes.

Disparate images: with the third innovation, visible in paintings such as Metzinger's *Port* of 1911 and Juan Gris's *Landscape at Céret* of 1913, space takes on a greater indeterminacy, this time in terms of locale. Both works transcend the limits of human vision as the artists include subjects at a great geographical remove from each other within a single painting, conjoined in memory and associative meaning. In the *Port* – reproduced in *Du Cubisme* as emblematic of the new art – Metzinger combines a building with shuttered windows on the right, curving in towards the centre; a sea wall in front with steps leading up from the water; and sailboats moored in a harbour, broken up and faceted into myriad shifting perspectives. Glimpsed in between these planes, he has extended the scope of our vision to include the curvature of the earth's surface and distant vessels on the high seas. Gris's *Landscape at Céret* depicts disparate landscape elements from radically different perspectives juxtaposed in a series of lozenge-shaped planes. As a result, objects both near and far, such as a distant mountain, cultivated fields, and the tiled roofs of houses, are brought together in a landscape that defies the scope of human vision.

Having liberated painting from the constraints of Renaissance perspective, the Cubists celebrated their freedom from academic conventions by inaugurating a perceptual and pictorial revolution. Artists of the Futurist, Suprematist, Constructivist, Dutch *De Stijl* and Surrealist movements all shared the Cubists' theoretical interests in their own explorations of non-Euclidean geometry and the fourth dimension.

Time and Henri Bergson

The Cubists' revolt against Renaissance perspective implicated time as well as space. In Cubist circles the theories of temporality developed by philosophers Henri Bergson and William James were both increasingly influential. Bergson strongly affected French writers associated with the development of Cubism. The Symbolist poet Tancrède de Visan had begun attending Bergson's lectures at the Collège de France before 1904, and between then and 1911 he published numerous articles in the Symbolist journal *Vers et Prose* on Bergsonian aesthetics. Visan held that the Symbolist technique of *vers libre* ('free verse') was the literary counterpart to Bergsonian 'duration' and that the rhythmic cadence of such poetry expressed each individual artist's durational state of mind. Picasso's close friend Salmon recorded the mounting enthusiasm for Bergson in Cubist circles in the popular newspaper *Paris-Journal*, noting Visan's intention to introduce the Salon Cubists to Bergson in November

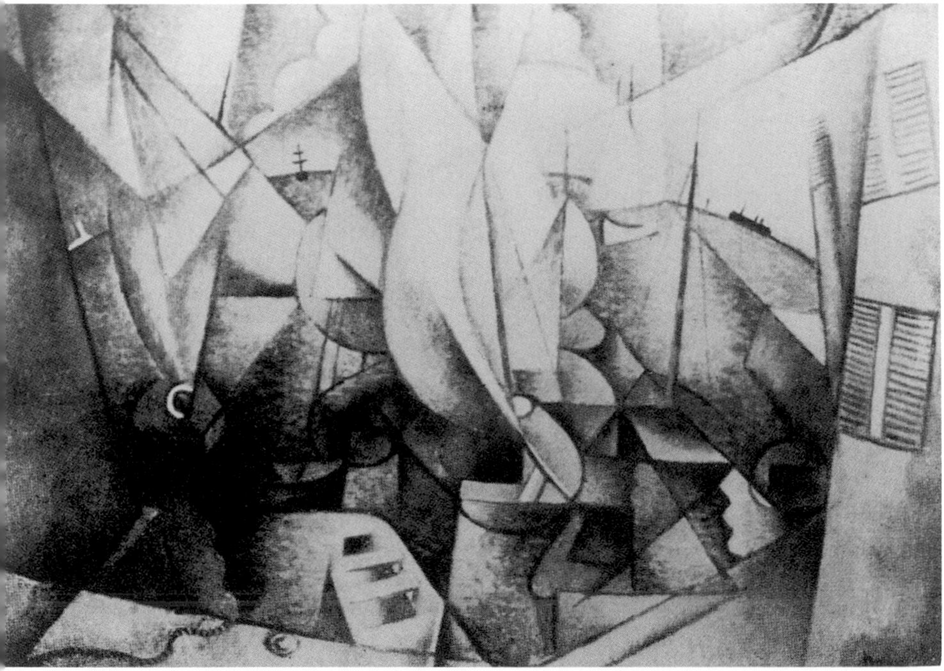

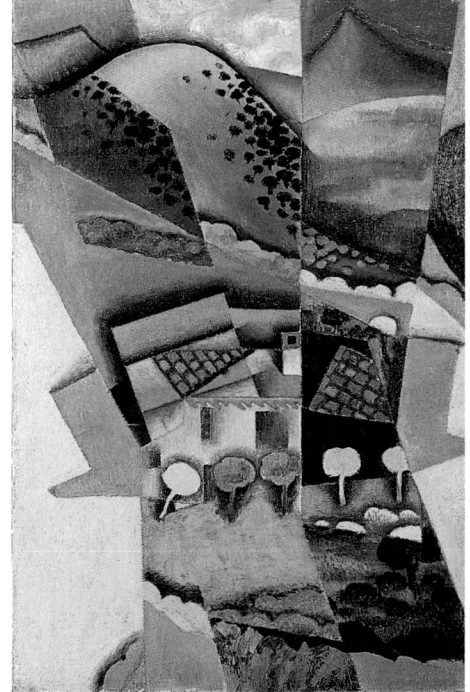

68. **Jean Metzinger**,
The Port, c. 1911–12.

69. **Juan Gris**,
Landscape at Céret, 1913.

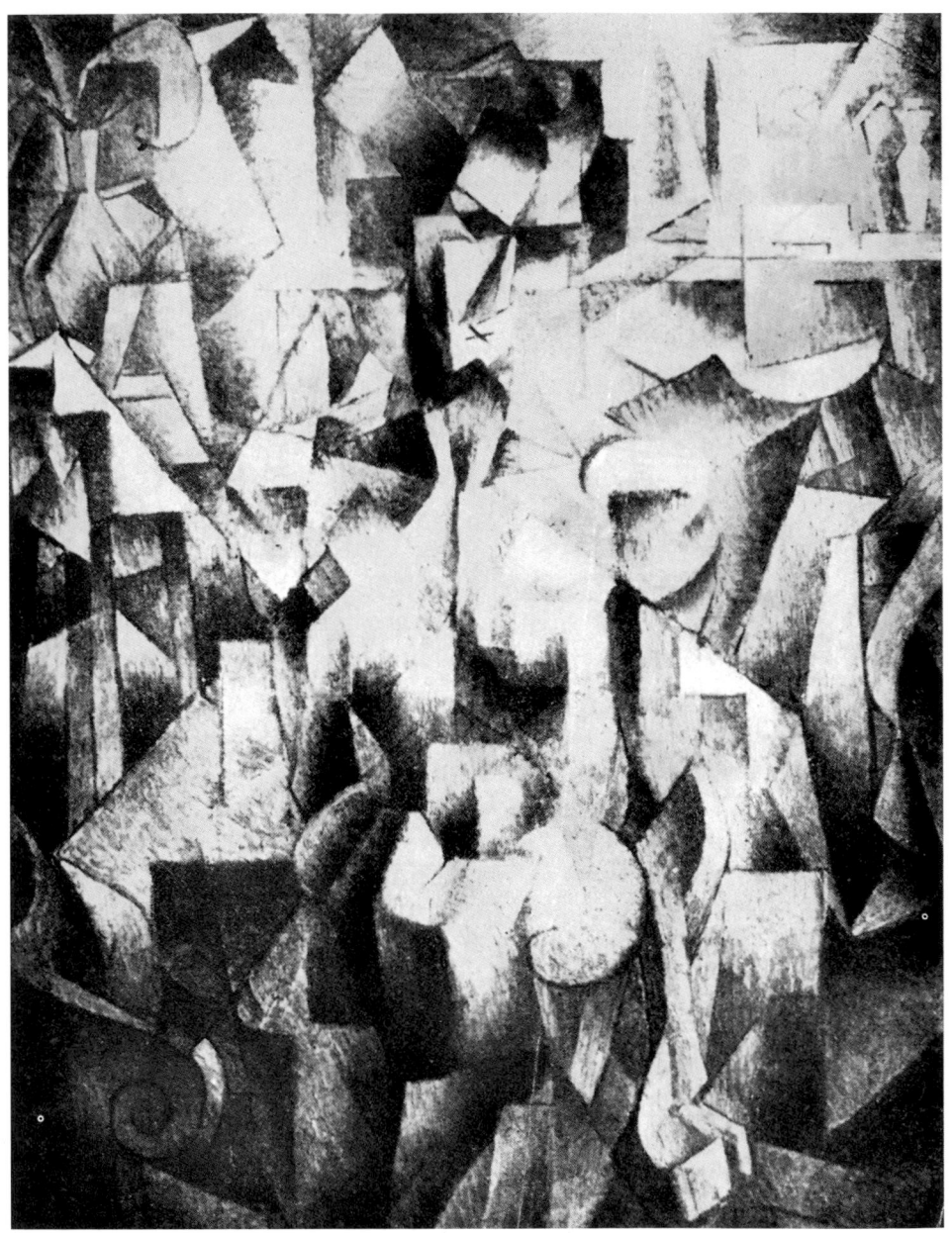

70. **Jean Metzinger**, *Nude*, 1910.

1911. He also recorded Bergson's tentative agreement to write a preface for the Section d'Or exhibition of 1912 'if he was definitely won over by their ideals'. Although Bergson never did endorse Cubism, Bergsonian paradigms appeared in art criticism of Cubism in 1910, with references to duration in Roger Allard's assessment of Metzinger's *Nude* at the 1910 Salon d'Automne. Recognizable elements of the work – later reproduced by Metzinger in *Du Cubisme* – include a three-quarter length female nude; an armchair whose scroll arm is quite visible in the lower left; a pedestal table with a vase of flowers on the upper left; and some objects on the upper right, possibly on a shelf, including a clock whose hands read 4:10. The figure of the woman dominates the centre of the composition. From top to bottom, we can see her head with its dark hair, shadowed eyes and small X-shaped mouth, the semi-circles suggesting the movement of her left shoulder, and below the partial spirals evoking both the movement and the fullness of her hips. 'Thus is born,' writes Allard, 70

at the antithesis of Impressionism, an art which, with little concern
for copying some incidental cosmic episode, offers to the viewer's
intelligence, in their full painterly quality, the elements of a synthesis
situated in the passage of time. The analytical relationships of the
objects and the details of their subordination one to another are
henceforward of little importance, since they are left out of the
picture as painted. They appear later, subjectively, in the picture
as thought by each individual who sees it.

According to this critic, we see in this abstracted and geometrized figure, nearly indistinguishable from her environment, 'the elements of a synthesis situated in the passage of time', which is later subjectively resolved by the viewer. This passage of time is in distinct contrast to the mechanical time marked off by the clock in the background.

This question of time, which is profoundly indebted to Bergson's thought, is most fully articulated in Gleizes and Metzinger's landmark text, *Du Cubisme* (1912). Here we can gain a full appreciation of Bergson's increasing impact and the manner in which the Puteaux Cubists conjoined Bergson's theories of time, space and artistic perception with Poincaré's conventionalism in their developing aesthetic. As we have seen, references to tactile and motor sensations allude to Poincaré's conventionalism, wherein notions of space are the product of the internal coordination of our sensory faculties. In *Du Cubisme* such sensory space is subsumed within a temporal concept of human consciousness: thus a Cubist painting embodies the heterogeneous nature of the artist's 'personality (unmeasurable, in which nothing is repeated)'. By subsuming pictorial space into the temporal flow of consciousness the artist has 'the power of rendering enormous that which we regard as minuscule and as infinitesimal that which we know to be considerable: he changes quantity to quality'. This 'qualitative' space is the pictorial analogue to both time *and* space: temporal heterogeneity *and* the new geometries.

Accordingly, Gleizes and Metzinger counsel artists to abandon the 'science' of 'traditional perspective' in favour of their 'creative intuition' in developing pictorial space. Creative intuition is manifest in an artist's faculty of discernment, or 'taste', which coordinates all other sensations. As we have seen Metzinger celebrated this faculty in *Le Goûter*, and Apollinaire advised artists to rely on their 'intuition' in *The Cubist Painters* (1913). The resulting dichotomy sets scientific, quantitative space – identified with traditional

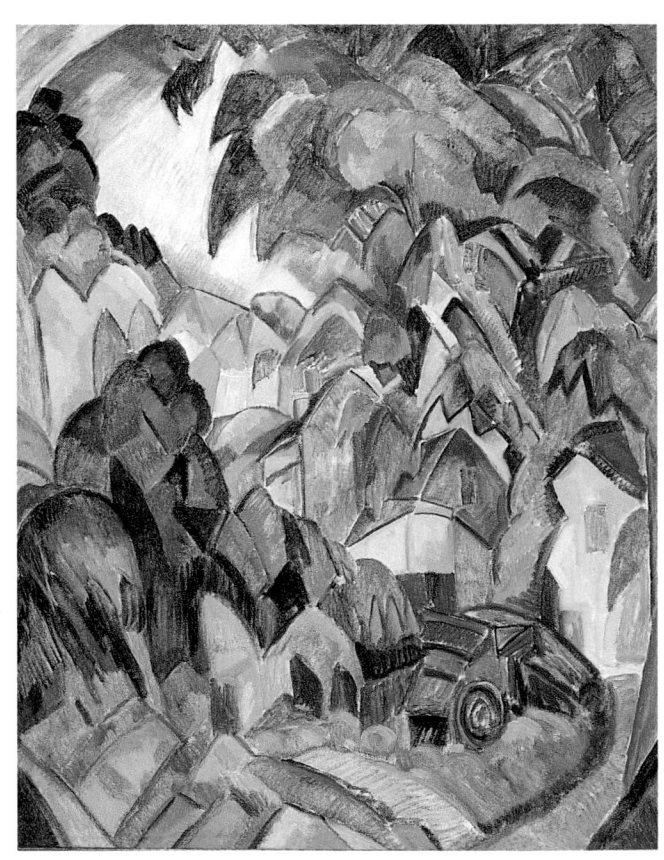

71. **Henri Le Fauconnier**, *Village in the Mountains*, 1911–12. Concurrent with the appearance of *Du Cubisme*, Le Fauconnier published his own Bergsonian tract, 'The Modern Sensibility and Painting', as a preface to a retrospective of his work at the October 1912 *Moderne Kunstkring* exhibition in Amsterdam. He claimed that repeated angular forms, vivid coloration and brushwork expressed his 'intuition' of the 'durational' dynamism of the modern world. Repeating abstract patterns of lozenges, jagged lines, and triangular and circular forms, combined with gestural brushstrokes of vivid blue, green and ochre, Le Fauconnier finds a rural equivalent to modern urban dynamism in the rugged landscape of the French Alps and the harnessing of its forces by the watermill in the right foreground.

perspective – against an artistic, 'qualitative' treatment of space, ordered in a non-quantifiable manner. The former spatial schema constitutes an impersonal, measurable medium estranged from its creator, whereas the latter qualitative projection is a synthetic expression of the whole personality, of an artist's faculty of 'taste' or 'creative intuition'.

For both Bergson and the Cubists, a work of art is a projection of our conscious reaction to deep-seated feelings. Bergson distinguishes the felt or intuitive act from a 'scientific' or non-emotive activity. Only the former is able to express the whole self, which is by definition both conscious and alogical. Gleizes and Metzinger echo Bergson when they declare their desire to give 'instinct' to their 'plastic consciousness'. The scientific temperament cedes to the artistic state of mind, and measurement is no longer the guiding principle behind the spatial organization of a canvas. Instead relations between objects are established qualitatively, that is, after the dictates of 'taste' and other senses. Linear perspective, being a mathematical system of representation, is anathema.

According to Du Cubisme's authors, qualitative space produces a 'complex rhythm' expressive of 'notions of depth, density and duration (durée)'; this concept of rhythmic space was also in line with Bergson, who envisaged an intermediary state of mind in which space is intuited, rather than conceptualized rationally. In attacking the quantitative measurement of space, Bergson arrived at a 'qualitative' notion of space/time antithetical to concepts of space developed by Euclid and Kant. Bergson argued that space was derivative of movement, that movement was fundamental to duration, and, in his later writings, that space was not unitary but multivalent, composed of differing 'degrees' of rhythmic 'extensity', Bergson's term for the mixture of time and space found in concrete experience. If 'the faculty of seeing should be made to be one with the act of willing', Bergson wrote in Creative Evolution (1907), our vision would transcend its habitual and utilitarian function and, through an effort of intuition, discern the melody of 'inner' duration. For an artist it is this rhythm that serves to bind the pattern of colours and shapes that make up a painting into an integral, organic whole.

By 1912, Gleizes and Metzinger were conversant enough in such Bergsonian theory to incorporate a conception of viewer intuition into Du Cubisme. Having determined that portions of the painting should be set in irregular relation to one another to assure that the whole remains immeasurable, qualitative and therefore 'organic', they go on to conclude: 'in order that the spectator, ready to establish unity himself, may apprehend all the elements in the order assigned to them by creative intuition, the properties of each portion must be left independent, and the plastic continuity must be broken up into a thousand surprises of light and shade'. Thus the Cubist breaks up the canvas's unity in such a way as to allow the spectator's own 'creative intuition' to 'establish unity'. The unity implicit – but in no way obvious – in the work of art now resides in the mind of the beholder. To provoke an intuitive response, the pictorial elements of the canvas must first arouse the viewer's emotions. 'Lines, surfaces, volumes, are only nuances of the notion of fullness'; they should not delineate form so much as suggest it. To achieve this, the Cubists use Cézanne's technique of *passage* to evoke an apprehension of 'the dynamism of form'. 'Between sculpturally bold reliefs, let us throw slender shafts which do not define, but which suggest. Certain forms must remain implicit, so that the mind of the spectator is the chosen place of their concrete birth'. The 'dynamism' of form therefore resides in the beholder's own unfolding response to the 'qualitative' properties of the work of art.

Metzinger's *Woman with a Horse* (1911–12) – illustrated in *Du Cubisme* and owned by the poet Jacques Nayral – is structured according to these precepts. The beholder must contemplate the work for an extended period, for the more legible forms only appear gradually, and their spatial arrangement remains ambiguous. In the foreground one can make out a vase in the bottom left, placed next to fruit and grapes, set in an imaginary locale made up of studio props and landscape elements. Dominating the central portion of the canvas is the improbable figure of a nude woman with pearl necklace and a horse: she is seated on a model's pedestal and is flanked by a tree on the left. The horse occupies the upper right-hand quadrant; shown as if from above, it appears to move forward, arching its shaggy mane and head in the direction of the nude. The monumental nude strokes the horse's right ear with her left hand while she cups her right hand to offer the docile animal a piece of fruit. The anatomy of both horse and rider is so fragmented that any sense of this image as a narrative is defeated. Taken as a whole the various elements of the canvas – blue flowers in the foreground, tree, horse, seated nude, vase, and fragment of a house in the distance – bear little proportional relation to each other. No longer governed by Renaissance perspective, these subjects are organized according to Metzinger's intuition and 'taste'. The play of lines, colours, their mutual interaction, and the 'transparency' of solid objects, further enhance the spatial ambiguity Gleizes and Metzinger associate with their 'creative intuition' of 'qualitative' space. The

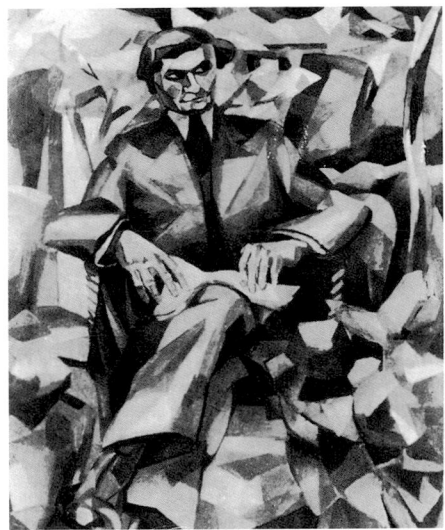

body of the female nude is composed of alternating ellipses and curvilinear forms, which merge, through *passage*, with a series of rectilinear planes that criss-cross the canvas in myriad complex combinations. Thus an interplay of volumetric forms has been 'abstracted' from the subject matter and distributed throughout the canvas. These complex forms serve not to 'define' the underlying imagery but to 'suggest' it, thus allowing the beholder's own 'creative intuition' to be brought into play to 'establish unity'.

A comparable example of this technique is Gleizes's portrait – also reproduced in *Du Cubisme* – of his close friend and future brother-in-law, Jacques Nayral. Nayral, whose interest in Bergson led him to correspond with the philosopher, asked Gleizes to paint his portrait in 1910, a task the artist completed over the course of 1911. For Gleizes this portrait, like Metzinger's *Le Goûter*, exemplified ideas that were later codified in *Du Cubisme*; in fact Gleizes's autobiographical notes suggest that the theory of intuition propounded in that text may have been broached in Cubist circles as early as 1910. In his *Souvenirs* (1957) Gleizes recalls that he completed the painting from memory, thus testing Bergson's claim in *Matter and Memory* (1896) that our duration is filled with memory images retrievable through intuition. Though he did a number of sketches of Nayral and set the writer in the tangible space of his garden, the portrait itself was 'executed without recourse to the model'. The artist and writer developed a strong friendship over the course of preparatory encounters in which Gleizes lengthily observed his way of walking, speaking and gesturing; Gleizes later described Nayral as

72

67

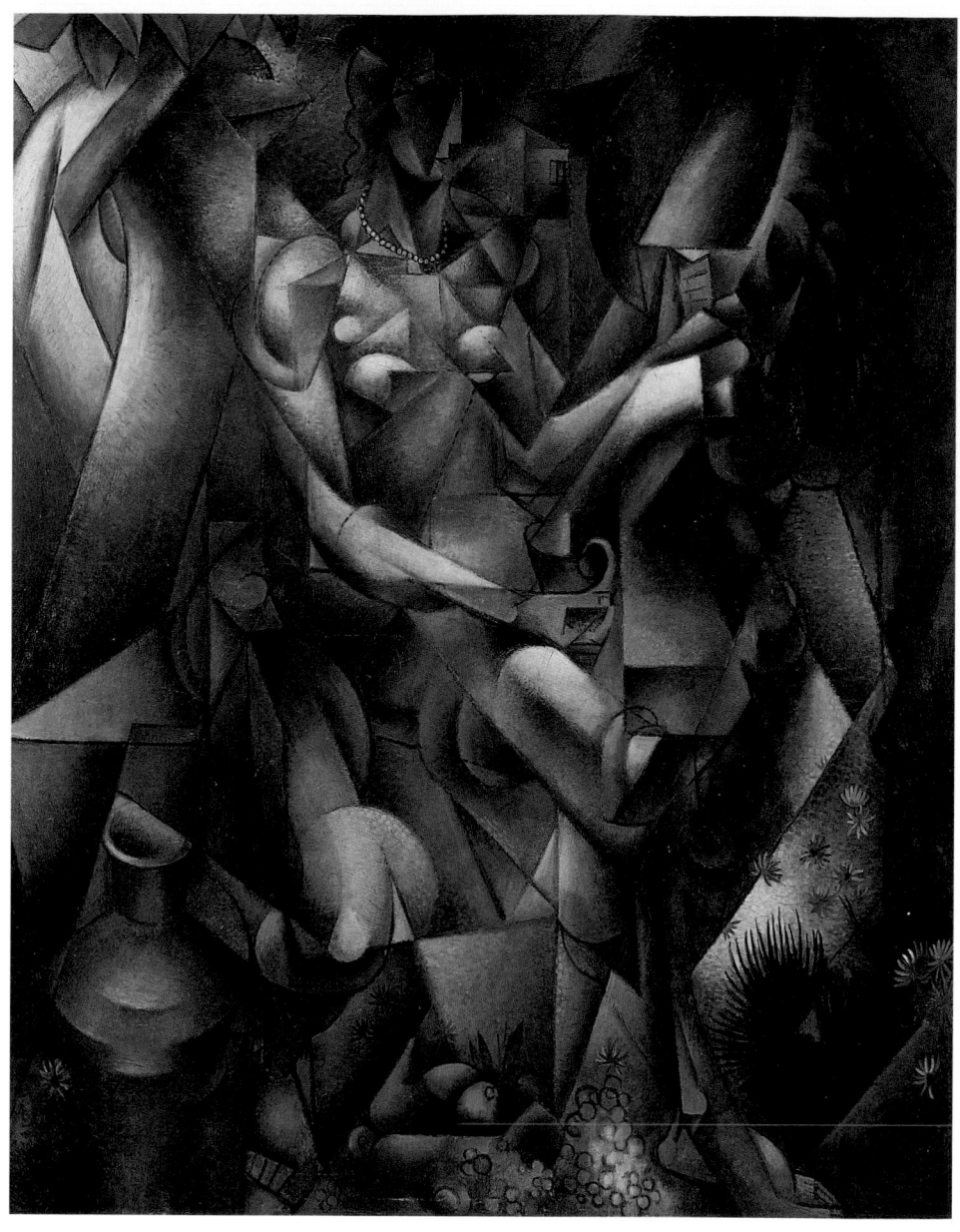

73. **Jean Metzinger**, *Woman with a Horse*, 1911–12.

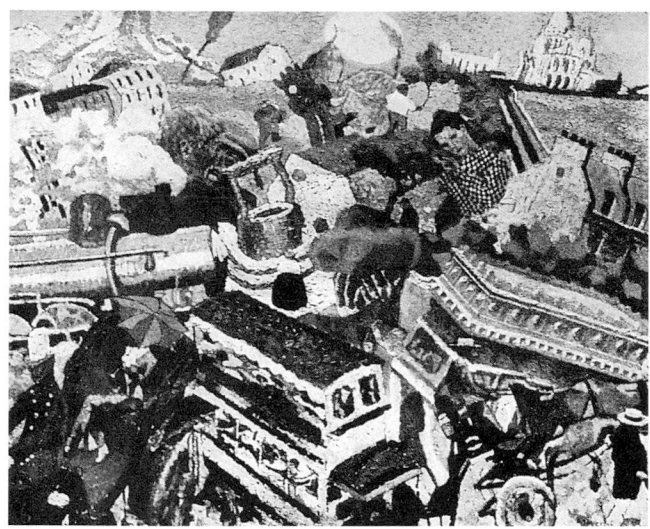

74. Gino Severini,
Travel Memories, 1910–11.
The Futurist Severini introduced memory images into his art after reading Bergson's 'Introduction to Metaphysics' (1903). In this work he combines a vast array of remembered images evoking his journey from Italy to Paris and distributes them around the well in his home town of Cortona. These images defy perspectival 'logic' by virtue of their scale, while their radial 'convergence' around the well reinforces their thematic unity.

75. Pablo Picasso, *Still Life (Memory of Le Havre),* May 1912. In his memoirs, Severini recalled showing *Travel Memories* in January 1912 to Picasso, who later invited Severini to his studio to see this Cubist response to his painting. Picasso's work differed radically from Severini's by virtue of its muted colouring, oval format, imitation of stenciled lettering and greater fragmentation of objects evoking his trip to Braque's hometown on the Normandy coast.

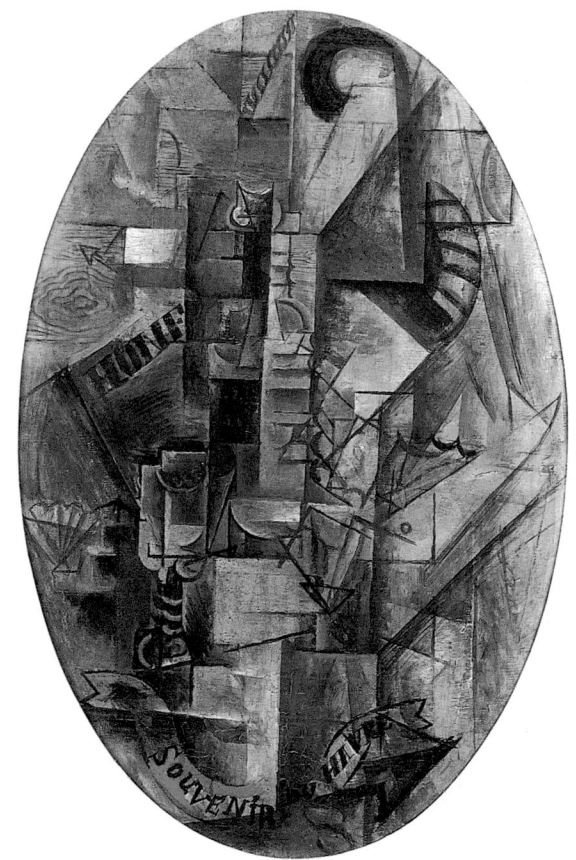

one of the most sympathetic people he had ever met. This interaction allowed him to extract 'some essential traits' from the 'jumble of details and picturesque elements' that obscured 'the permanent essence of a being'. In addition the artist focused on physiognomic elements, such as the 'well-defined planes' of Nayral's face and the 'undulations' of his hair, that served as the springboard for the volumetric treatment of form in the portrait. Nayral's expressive acts and physical appearance 'suggested to me immediately recollections, relationships, penetrations, and correspondences with the elements of environment, the land, the trees, the houses'. Nayral himself celebrated this associative process in his preface to the exhibition of Cubist art held at the Gallery Dalmau in Barcelona in April and May 1912. 'You see a portrait in a landscape' wrote Nayral; 'is it simply the reproduction of some lines that permit our eye to recognize a head, clothes, trees? Photography would be sufficient'. Instead, Nayral continues, to situate 'a thinking human in harmony with the surroundings, in accordance with them', one must 'reveal the concert of all these forms of life that are the thought of this man, the perfume of this flower, the brilliance of this plant, the vibration of this light, this is the task of the artist'. In short, this synthetic vision was the product of Gleizes's *sympathetic* response to the

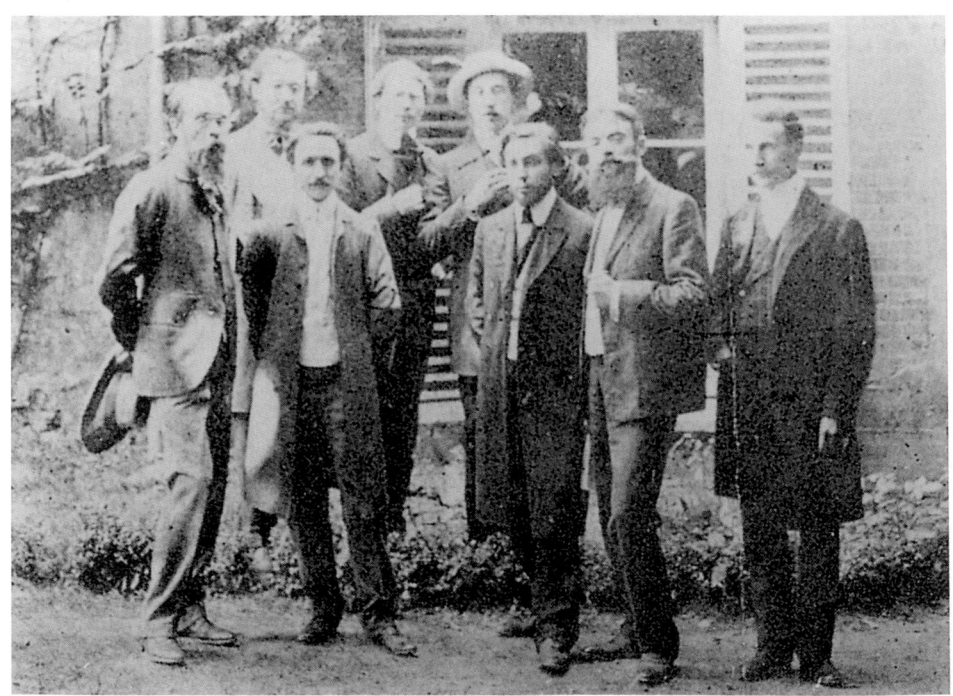

77. Albert Gleizes,
Portrait of René Arcos, 1910.
Gleizes first befriended the poet René Arcos in 1900, and it was Arcos who introduced Gleizes to his future Abbaye associates. In later years they shared an enthusiasm for the writings of Bergson and both endorsed pacifism during World War I. In his memoirs published in 1957, Gleizes recorded the profound effect Le Fauconnier's paintings of 1909 had on his developing style, stating that they reinforced his own simplification of form. Here Gleizes adapts the geometrized form and muted colouring of Le Fauconnier's *Ploumanach* landscapes to his heroic portrayal of the solitary Arcos, striding across a mountainous rural landscape in the first rays of dawn.

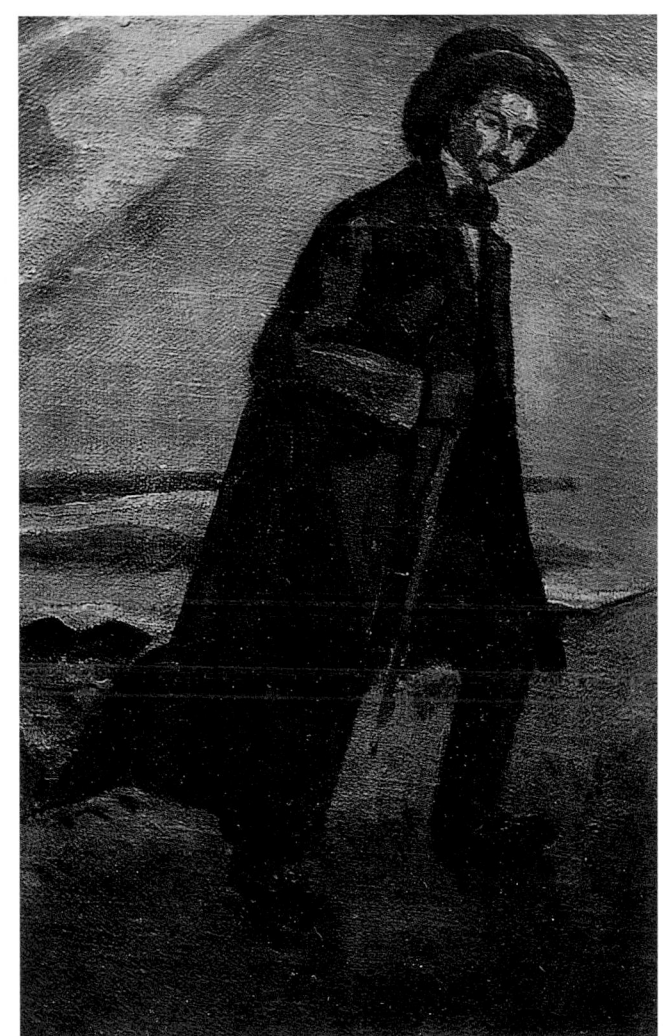

76. The members of the Abbaye de Créteil.
From left to right in the first row are the poet Charles Vildrac, painter-poet René Arcos, Albert Gleizes, and the poets Henri-Martin Barzun and Alexandre Mercereau; in the second row are Vildrac's brother-in-law, the poet Georges Duhamel, and the painters Berthold Mahn and Jacques d'Otémar. Together with the master printer Lucien Linard, the group sought to create an egalitarian artists' cooperative, modelled after the self-sufficient communities envisioned by the anarchist Peter Kropotkin. To signal their leftist ideals, Vildrac coined the name Abbaye de Créteil in emulation of Rabelais's description of the Abbaye de Thélème in his book *Gargantua* (1534). Rabelais – a writer championed in anarchist circles – had envisioned Thélème as an utopian abbey where artists could pursue their activities free of institutional and economic restraints.

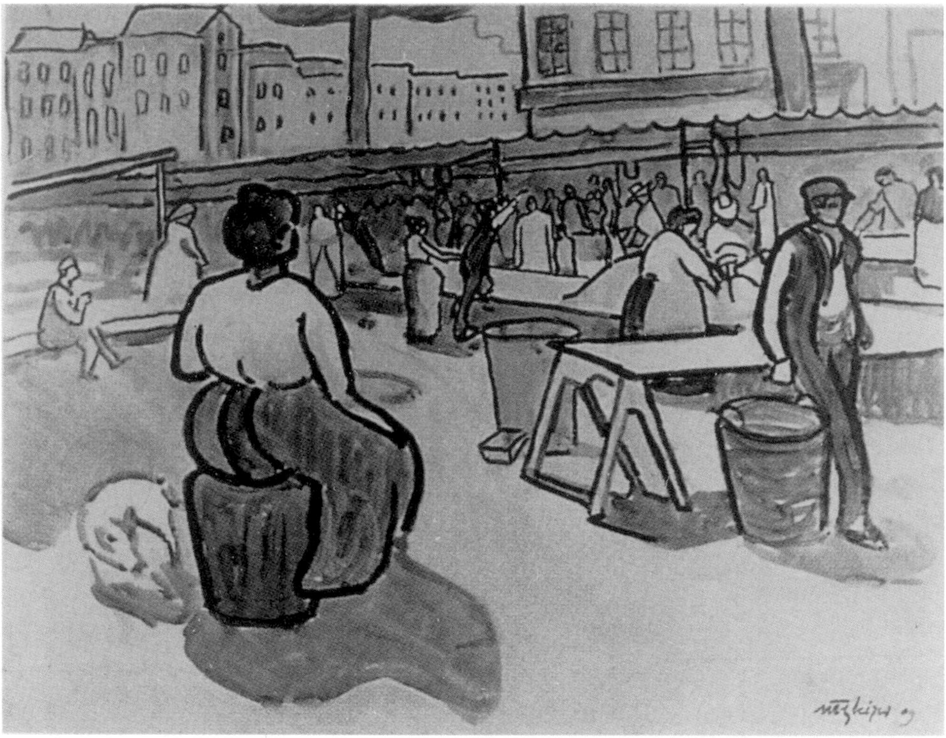

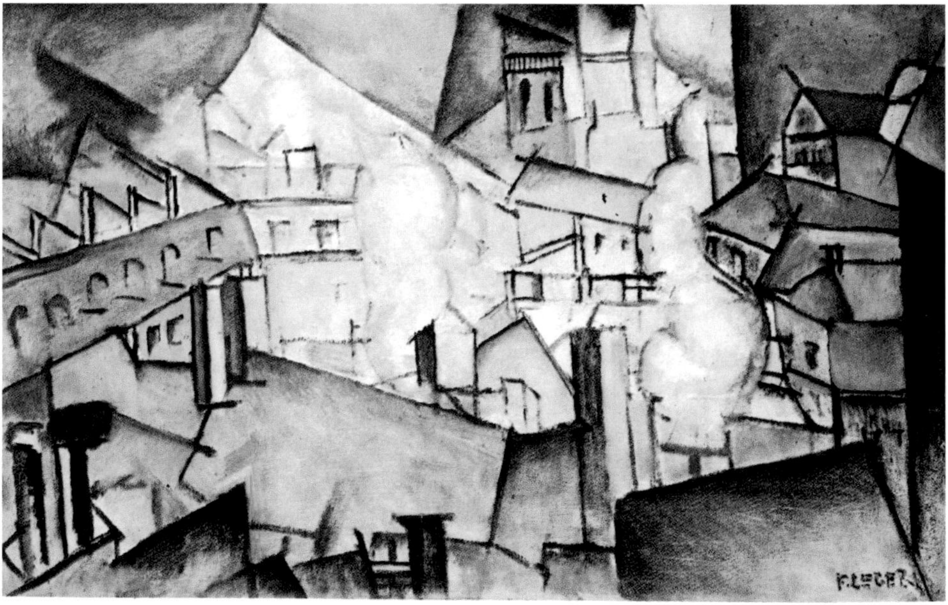

expressive acts and physiognomic traits he deemed indicative of the poet's character. Both form and content in the work were the result of Gleizes's mental associations while working from memory.

Bergson, Poetry, and Painting

Other Bergson enthusiasts included the poets René Arcos, Henri-Martin Barzun, Jules Romains, and Alexandre Mercereau, all of whom had joined Gleizes in founding the Abbaye de Créteil (1906–8), a short-lived artist's commune situated near Paris. Arcos and Mercereau followed Romains in advocating the doctrine of Unanimism, which held that an individual could directly experience the thoughts and feelings of others, thereby creating a collective consciousness. Intuition, defined by Bergson as the ability to discern one's own inner being as well as that of others, is rightly associated with Unanimism. Romains underscored the relation by titling one of his earliest Unanimist poems 'Intuitions' (1907), and in *La Grande Revue* (August 1910) he declared Bergson the most important philosopher of the era. Romain's epic *La vie unanime* (1908) attempted to capture the rhythmic pulse of collective life in the modern city. Arcos's poem *Ce qui naît* ('What is Born') of 1911 stressed the durational continuity uniting all life forms, while Mercereau's *Paroles devant la vie* (1911) focused on generative themes, evoking the Bergsonian *élan vital* coursing through a pregnant woman.

Unanimist poetry clearly set a precedent for Cubist painting with its theme of interpenetration, destroying physical barriers in favour of rhythmic continuity. For both poets and painters, the city became a powerful symbol of the rhythmic interpenetration of living things and duration. Romains's use of urban smoke as a poetic image seems to have inspired Fernand Léger to utilize this motif in his panoramic views of the city of Paris, painted from Léger's rooftop studio in the Latin quarter, which faced the Ile de la Cité and Notre Dame. In Romains's poem *La vie unanime* the rhythmic intermingling of chimney smoke figures as a symbol of a Unanimist experience of the city: 'buses grunt and chimneys smoke; people are bound together by their confused rhythms'. The ascent of smoke through the air amounts to an apotheosis of the Unanimist spirit; Romains refers to 'proud plumes of smoke that stretch beyond the fog to taste the stars'. 'My soul stretches out above me; and flutters like the plumes of smoke.... Beloved city, my consciousness will go / Wherever your smoke plumes go'. In Léger's painting the arabesque play of smoke plumes acts both to fragment the angular rooftops and to dissolve their forms, introducing the element of *passage* as the pictorial equivalent to Romains's Unanimist rhythms.

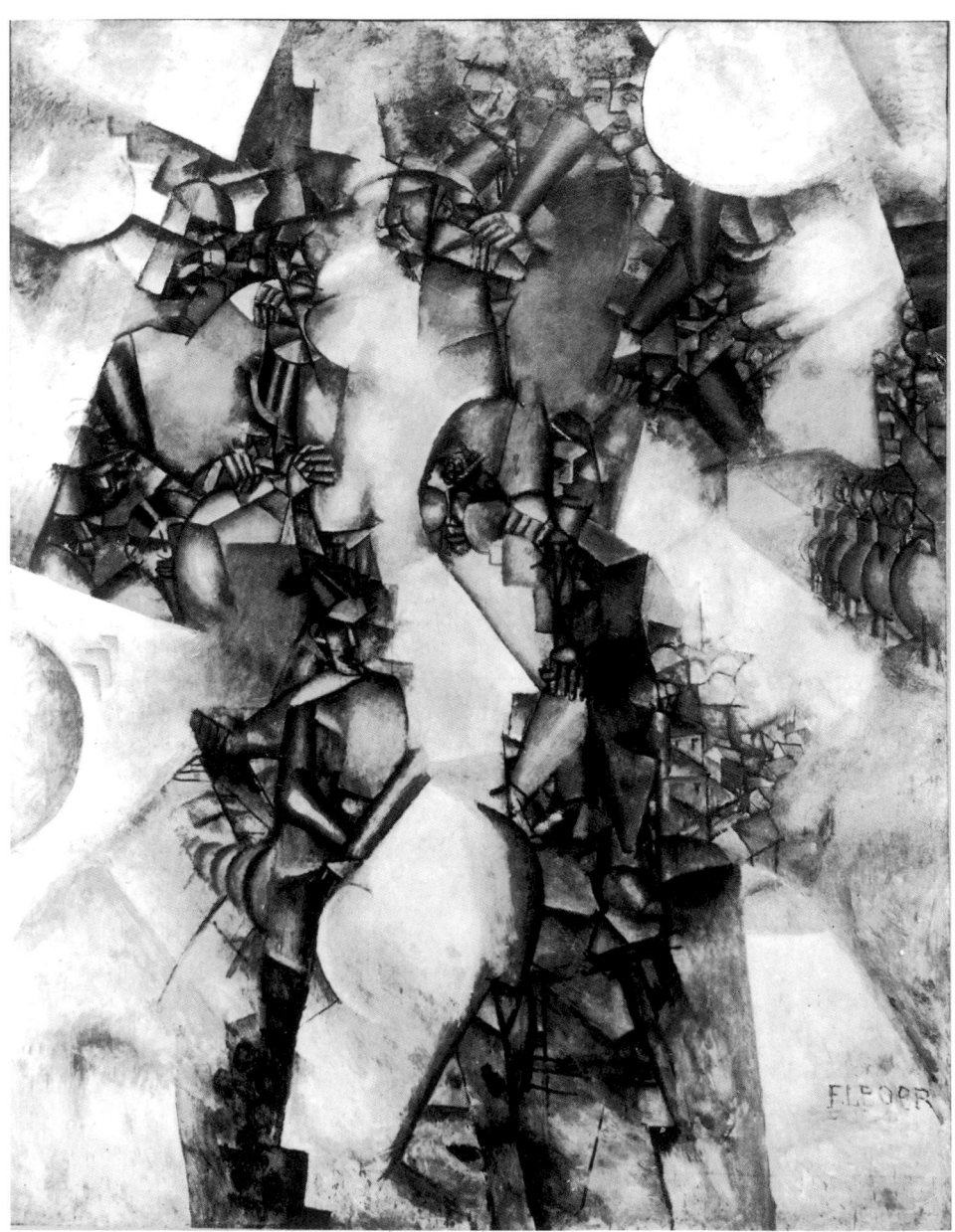

80. **Fernand Léger**,
The Wedding, 1910–11.

Since Romains's poetry conveyed the collective emotions resulting from group activities – whether they took the form of a tram ride or a funeral procession – Cubists frequently turned to equivalent communal themes as a vehicle for their abstractions. For instance in *The Wedding* (1910–11), Léger adapted his pictorial techniques to the portrayal of a wedding procession, set against the panoramic backdrop of the small market town of Argentan, as evidenced by the diminutive houses and trees on the right half of the painting. At the painting's centre are the bride and groom, both facing us with arms folded, but the bride's virginal dress forms a white quadrant that serves to obscure their bodily features and to partially hide her future partner who stands to her left. Behind these two protagonists is a tumult of top-hatted relatives and guests whose chaotic interaction lends a sense of momentous excitement to the life-changing event.

Léger's humorous treatment of familial rituals had a religious counterpart in Francis Picabia's *Procession, Seville* of 1912. Here Picabia portrays a religious procession of cowled Spanish monks whose slow advance down a street spreads from the top centre to encompass the lower third of the painting. Picabia's abstract composition reduces the monks to an unbroken series of regulated, angular volumes, painted with a restricted palette of grey, orange and white in contrast to the blue of the street and adjacent buildings. This repetition of forms and colours serves to submerge each individual figure into an overall rhythmic pattern identifiable with the group's processional function and physical activity. In effect Léger and Picabia utilized the tools of pictorial abstraction to emphasize the spirit of collectivity so crucial to *la vie unanime*.

80

81

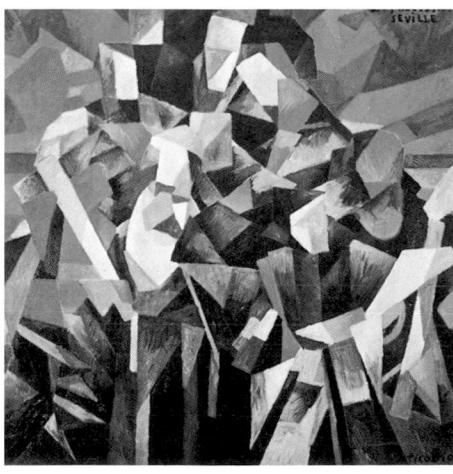

81. **Francis Picabia**,
Procession, Seville, 1912.

Memory played a fundamental role in other Cubist works influenced by Unanimism, such as Robert Delaunay's *Eiffel Tower* paintings. Bergson developed a theory of images in 'The Introduction to Metaphysics' (1903), where he argued that an accumulation of images in literature, 'taken from quite different orders of things, will be able, through the convergence of their action, to direct consciousness to the precise point where there is a certain intuition to seize on'. Bearing no logical relation to one another, such images would draw the mind into a particular alogical disposition, divorced from intellectual modes of thought. Visan, who regularly met the Cubists at the poet Paul Fort's weekly *soirées* at the Closerie des Lilas, related this notion of 'successive or accumulated images' to the poetry of Maeterlinck in 1907, and in 1910 he championed the technique in an essay for *Vers et Prose*.

In his 'Note on Painting' (autumn 1910), Metzinger discussed Delaunay's paintings of the Eiffel Tower as combining in one image many different views, each recording the public's varying experience of the tower over the course of a single day: 'Intuitive, Delaunay has defined intuition as the brusque deflagration of all the reasonings accumulated each day.' The 'accumulated images' are like those of the Unanimist poet, who intuits collective consciousness and translates that experience into poetic form. In Delaunay's case the monumental tower is the catalyst for his Unanimist experience of the metropolis, and these memory images – all focused on the tower – defy the 'logical' conventions of Renaissance perspective, confounding our rational expectations. By combining multiple views in a single image, Delaunay has set our minds in a certain 'direction' so that we too may intuit the epic significance of the tower in the minds of the Parisian populace.

82. **Robert Delaunay**, *Eiffel Tower*, 1911.
Delaunay's series of paintings of the Eiffel Tower celebrate this emblem of modernity, which, he wrote in 1909, 'calls out to the Universe'. Built as the centrepiece of the Universal Exposition of 1889, this triumph of structural engineering became an experimental station for meteorology and aerodynamics, served as a relay station for the latest in international communication – telegraphy – and flashed electric light for 120 miles in the colours of the French flag. Combining simultaneous viewpoints, Delaunay evokes the poet Blaise Cendrars's description of the two friends' trip to the Tower: 'None of the known techniques of art can claim to have solved the pictorial problem of the Eiffel Tower. Realism diminishes it; the ancient laws of Italian perspective attenuate it.... Seen from the first platform, it spiralled upward; seen from the top, it sank into itself with straddling legs and indrawn neck. Delaunay wanted to show Paris simultaneously, to incorporate the Tower into its surroundings.'

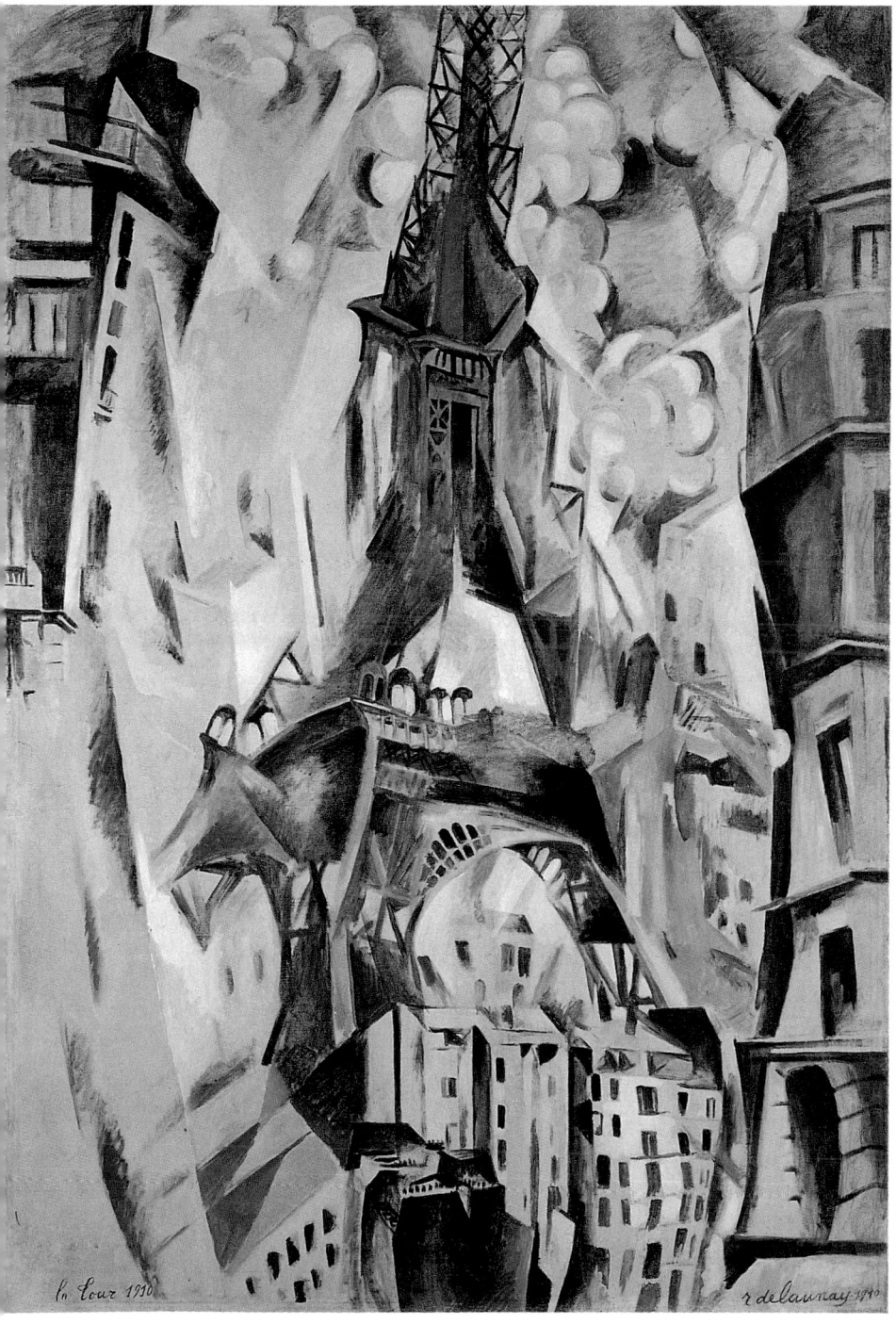

Bergson and Sculpture

Bergsonian thought played an equally important role in Cubist sculpture. Beginning in 1912, the Ukrainian-born Alexander Archipenko (1887–1964) experimented with the dynamic interchange of convex and concave forms, which culminated in his novel introduction of voids into works such as *Woman Combing Her Hair* of 1915. In his earlier *Woman with Fan* of 1914, he made a high-relief sculpture that combined with painting to create striking illusions of space and volume. The geometrized head has decorative wooden cones attached as curls of hair next to a flat painted fringe; a glass bottle forms the woman's neck; a parallel cylinder forms her right arm resting on her hip; and a piece of sheet metal bent into a convex cone forms the torso. Most strikingly, her right breast is formed by a funnel and seems to hang suspended before a deep space painted dark green. Below, Archipenko has painted her fan – also formed out of convex sheet metal – in gradations suggesting both the individual spines of the fan, the movement of the fan, and the movement of light across its surface. Because of the three-dimensionality of the material structure of this work, actual highlights and shadows cleverly play a role in rendering the shape and placement of forms ambiguous.

In 1956 Archipenko recalled that his use of sculptural voids was inspired by a section of Bergson's *Creative Evolution* (1907) on the manner in which our intellect distorts our understanding of reality. If we encounter an object or circumstance we have not anticipated, Bergson asserted, our intellect tends to define that reality negatively rather than positively. 'If the present reality is not the one we are seeking, we speak of an *absence* of this sought reality wherever we find the *presence* of another', thereby expressing 'what we have as a function of what we want'. Bergson applied this critique to ideas negatively defined in contrasting pairs, such as Hegel's dialectic, with its thesis and antithesis, and to concepts of contradiction and disorder, declaring them to be illusory constructs imposed on the plenitude of durational change. Archipenko's sculptural void allows us to fill this illusory gap with our own durational consciousness.

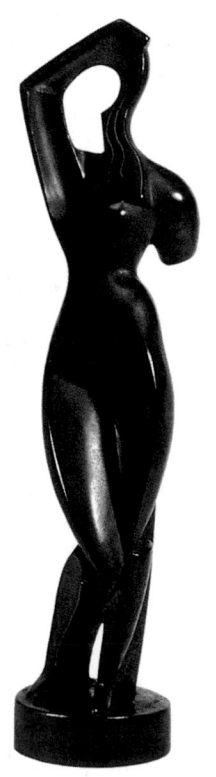

83. **Alexander Archipenko**, *Woman Combing Her Hair*, 1915. This work takes the concept of ambiguity of form a step further. Depending on the effects of lighting and our movement around the sculpture, concave and convex forms appear variously to protrude and recede. Archipenko takes this optical reversal to extremes through the play of solid and void, presence and absence. The delineated void within the figure's arm paradoxically resolves into a presence: a female head in profile. Fullness is thus expressed through emptiness, and the human imagination intuitively enacts the conversion.

84. **Alexander Archipenko**, *Woman with a Fan*, 1914

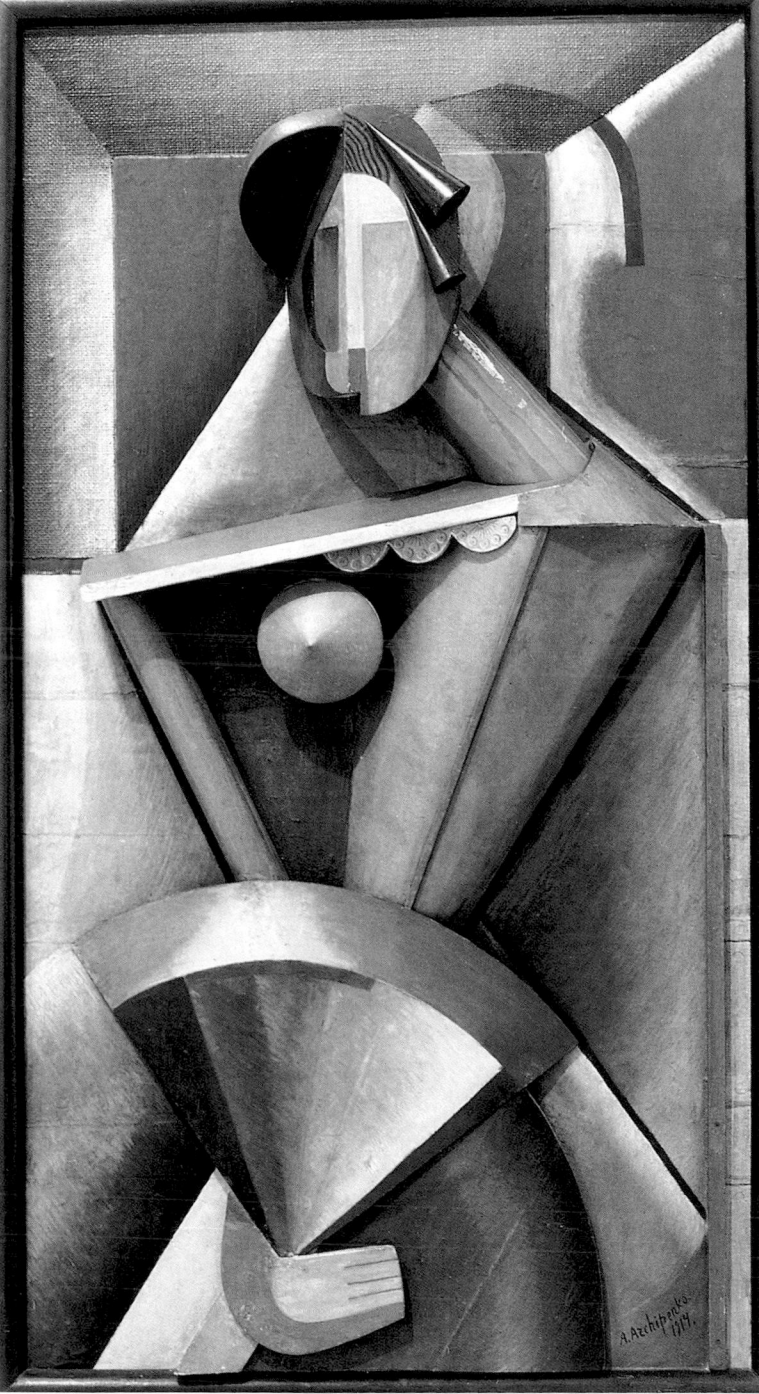

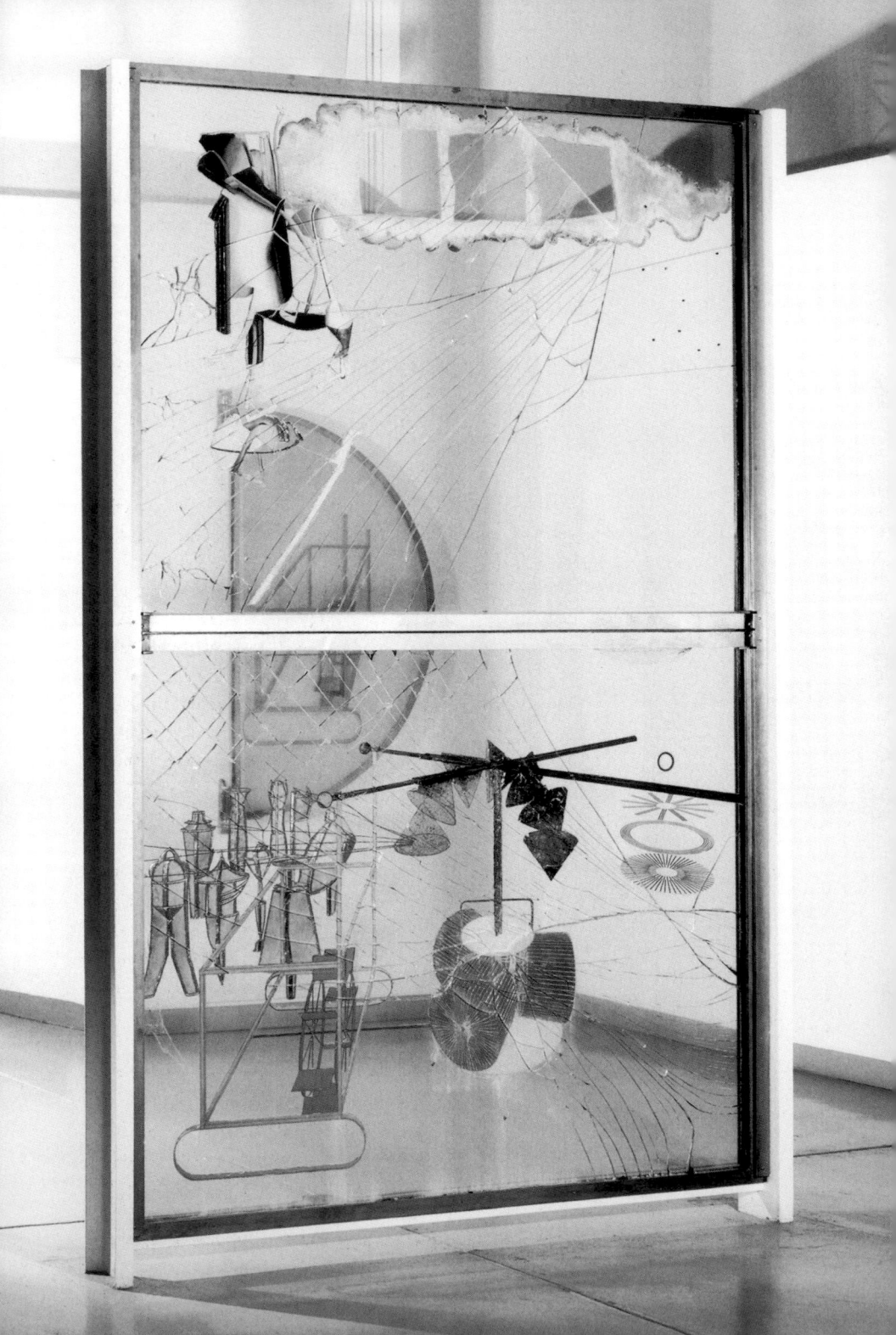

Anti-Bergsonists

The Salon Cubists' interest in Bergson and the fourth dimension inspired Marcel Duchamp to satirize his colleagues' lofty aspirations in his 9-foot composition, *The Bride Stripped Bare by Her Bachelors, Even*, known as the *Large Glass*. A multimedia work on glass begun in 1915 and left unfinished in 1923, the *Large Glass* was an allegorical parody of an industrialized multidimensional sexual encounter between the 'bachelors', found in the lower half of the glass, and the 'bride', positioned above. The bride takes the form of a machine whose sexual function is partially figured as a modern gasoline combustion engine, while the bachelors are composed of old-fashioned, uniformed tailor's dummies with ancillary mechanical apparatus for 'organs', such as a 'chocolate grinder'. In her comprehensive study of Duchamp's whimsical creation, art historian Linda Henderson has analysed the scientific and philosophical sources for this complex work, as well as the ways in which Duchamp systematically upstaged his fellow Cubists. The contrast between the realm of the bachelors and that of the bride was figured in terms of geometry as Duchamp confined the bachelors to a three-dimensional 'measured' space, subject to gravity, whereas the bride hovered in the ether-filled medium of fourth-dimensional space, permeated by electro-magnetic vibrations. The bride's means of communication with her erstwhile bachelors took the form of Hertzian waves of wireless 'spark' telegraphy; the bachelors responded mechanically to the bride's command but failed to 'consummate' the relationship by breaking through to her spatial locale. Here the potential for polygamous union between bride and bachelors is short-circuited by a spatial disjunction between the earthbound world of three dimensions and the 'heavenly' realm of the fourth dimension, a division compounded by Duchamp's anticlerical association of the bride with the Virgin Mary, whose manner of 'conception' can only be 'immaculate'. Duchamp's ridiculing of religion and the institution of marriage, combined with his unveiling of the sexuality behind these social façades, underscores his sympathies with aspects of the anarchist movement, which critiqued both marriage and the Church, proclaiming the alternative of *amour libre* or 'free love'.

Duchamp's reduction of human sexuality to a mechanical means of procreation also parodied the Bergsonian underpinnings dear to the Cubists, including his own brother Raymond Duchamp-Villon. In *Laughter* (1900), Bergson had identified as 'intellectual' the humour in a comedian's ability to evoke 'the rigid, the ready-made, the mechanical, in contrast to the supple, the ever-changing and the living ... in a word automatism in contrast to free activity'. By casting

85. **Marcel Duchamp**, *The Bride Stripped Bare by Her Bachelors, Even (The Large Glass)*, 1915–23.

86. **Marcel Duchamp**, *Bottlerack*, 1961 replica of the 1914 original. Bergson's contrast between intuitive processes of art making and what he termed the 'ready-made' designs of our intellect inspired Duchamp to appropriate mass-produced objects such as this bottle-drying rack (*égouttoir*) and to label them 'ready-mades'. Duchamp attacks the notion of intuition, championed by Gleizes and Metzinger in *Du Cubisme* (1912), both through his presentation of an unaltered 'found object' as a work of art and in the *égouttoir*'s punning rejection of *goût* or artistic 'taste'.

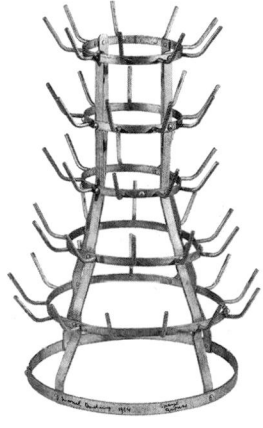

the sexual activity of both bride and bachelors as a series of mechanical movements, Duchamp subjects the rituals of courtship and consummation to a Bergsonian mode of satire. This 'intellectualized' treatment of human sexuality would even be an affront to Bergson himself, who described sexual communion between human beings as akin to empathetic intuition. Duchamp's predilection for satire rather than sincerity, cold intellect as opposed to empathetic intuition, was shared by others. For instance Juan Gris's interest in both Bergson and caricature may have inspired the rigid geometry governing the bodily fragmentation and caricatural physiognomy of his bourgeois *Man in the Café* (1912). Christopher Green argues that the caricatural 'deformations' in Gris's work were likely informed by his familiarity with Paul Gaultier's *Le Rire et la caricature*. Thus Duchamp and Gris stand somewhat apart from their fellow Cubists by virtue of the 'intellectual' irony and wit behind their aesthetic innovations.

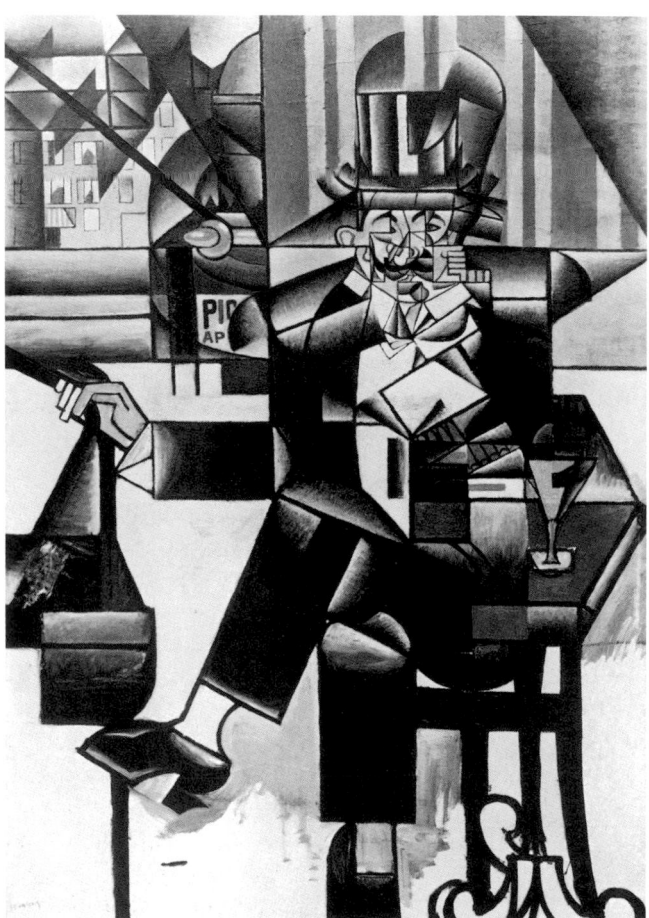

87. **Juan Gris**, *Man in a Café*, 1912.

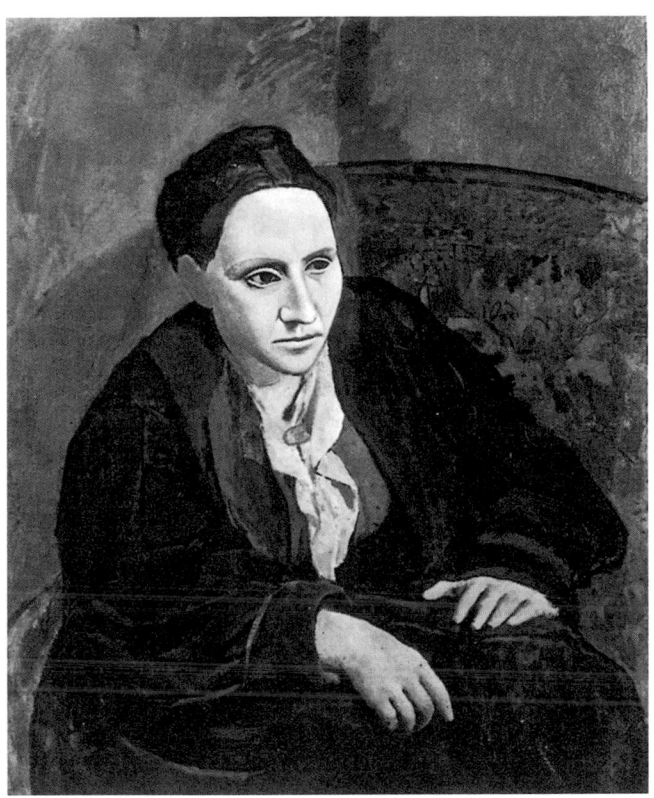

Time and William James

It is obvious that Picasso and Braque would have been familiar with these popularized Bergsonian ideas, so passionately discussed by their peers. We also know concretely that Picasso and Braque were exposed to Bergson's philosophy and that of William James through their relations with Gertrude Stein, a close friend and patron of Picasso who painted her portrait in 1906. Before her arrival in Paris, Stein had taken courses with James at Radcliffe College in Boston, and in his memoirs her brother Leo Stein recalled that James's theories were the subject of repeated discussions at the Steins' Saturday evening *soirées* at 27 rue de Fleurus, frequently attended by the two artists. Bergson was equally influential in these circles: Gertrude's sister-in-law, Sarah Stein, was an avid supporter of Matisse, who had made reference to Bergsonian *durée* in his 1908 text, *Notes of a Painter* ('a rapid rendering of a landscape represents only one moment of its duration'). In 1909 the Bergsonian aesthetician Mathew Stewart Prichard developed a close friendship with both Sarah Stein and Matisse and also frequented the Steins' *soirées*.

88

Literary scholars have traced the formative impact of both Bergson and James on Gertrude Stein's developing prose style, most notably in prewar works such as 'Melanctha', *Three Lives* (1909), *The Making of the Americans* (1902–11), and *Tender Buttons* (1912–14). Study of her notebooks from 1902 to 1908 reveals that she and her brother Leo were engaged in an ongoing debate over James's pragmatism, differing on whether intuition was the best means of grasping an essential 'reality' impenetrable to the intellect. In fact James himself settled the question in favour of intuition in a chapter of his last book, *A Pluralistic Universe* (1909), titled 'Bergson and Intellectualism'. James recognized that Bergson's philosophy lent support to his own critique of the utilitarian function of the intellect and his contention, in *Principles of Psychology* (1890), that temporal change as 'stream of consciousness' and sensate phenomena was the bedrock of all experience. These ideas were a frequent topic of conversation at the Steins' soirées.

We can gain an appreciation of James's impact on Stein by correlating his philosophy with her avant-garde literary innovations, before turning to the art of Picasso and Braque. James's *Principles of Psychology* posited a dualism within human nature premised on a tendency towards 'indiscriminate' absorption of sensory data and the limitation of that sensory intake through 'selective attention'. This 'selective attention' serves utilitarian ends, leading us to value the fixed and unchanging since selectivity facilitates our ability to abstract stable concepts and images from the dynamic and unending flux of phenomena entering the 'stream of consciousness'. Like Bergson, James declared rationalism a mode of philosophizing derived from such utilitarian thinking; at its most extreme, this tendency causes us to overvalue these 'man-made extracts from the temporal flux' as superior to the stream from which they were initially derived. 'The classic extreme', wrote James in *A Pluralistic Universe*, 'is the denial of the possibility of change, and the consequent branding of the world of change as unreal'. Both James in *Principles of Psychology* (1890) and Bergson in *Time and Free Will* (1889) singled out language as an instance of such abstraction. Bergson drew a comparison between words and mathematical symbols. Just as standardized mathematical units of time constitute impersonal representations of our individual experience of time, so words such as 'sad' or 'happy' are impersonal labels applicable to everyone regardless of the individual character of our emotions. As impersonalized representations of the self, words are convenient counters adapted to social discourse; yet from the standpoint of the personality experiencing the emotion, they are impoverished, generalized symbols. James and Bergson thought intuition potentially allowed us to transcend these fixed concepts and symbols to give form to durational processes, including the temporal flux of our individual thoughts and feelings in all their freshness and novelty.

Stein aimed to capture this durational experience by turning language against itself in order to immerse the reader in this durational stream of consciousness. As literary historian Lisa Ruddick has demonstrated, Stein's prewar technique showed signs 'of a progressive disintegration of focus' that figured Stein's rejection of 'selective attention' in favour of the perceptual disinterestedness needed to grasp the stream of consciousness in all its plenitude. This absence of focus refused narrative structure or dramatic highlights; instead her writings treat objects, events and people in a value-neutral, undifferentiated fashion as so much 'casual data'. This mode of disinterestedness differed from the empathetic disposition the Unanimists and the Salon Cubists associated with intuition; as a result Stein's prose lacks the emotional pitch characterizing the poetry of Romains or Arcos. Like her Bergsonian counterparts Stein strips her prose of any literary technique she would associate with 'intellectualism', but this rejection is not accompanied by the empathetic affirmation of a Bergsonian 'life force'. Stein herself claimed that her literary technique was inspired in part by the art of Cézanne, for he 'conceived the idea that in composition one thing was as important as another thing. Each part is as important as the whole, and that impressed me enormously'.

This lack of focal differentiation was augmented in Stein's prose by a deliberate stress on ambiguity rather than clarity. In place of a sequential train of discrete thoughts, Stein presents a complex intermingling of thoughts and ideas that dissolve into each other to form an unbroken, rhythmic 'stream'. Literary historian Steven Meyer has analysed Stein's application of this technique in her 1909 prose portrait of Picasso, published in *Camera Work* (August 1912). In this literary portrait her lines appear to be identical, but on close inspection each overlaps or invades the next, conveying both mental continuity and diversity; their permeability and intricate mutation capture processes of thought. The opening lines of the portrait perfectly convey this process:

One whom some were certainly following was one who was completely charming. One whom some were certainly following was one who was charming. One whom some were following was one who was completely charming. One whom some were following was one who was certainly completely charming.

The second and third sentences are nearly identical to the first, but for the absence of the adverb 'completely' in the second and of 'certainly' in the third. Ironically, Stein uses the adverbial forms of completeness and certainty to suggest partiality and uncertainty. To arrive at a definitive statement, in the Jamesian mode, would be to fix the stream of consciousness by suspending discussion; Stein by contrast wishes to unfold her assessment of Picasso – and to view his art – as a series of unending permutations. 'Something had been coming out of him', wrote Stein, 'and it had meaning, a charming meaning, a solid meaning, a struggling meaning'.

Stein's rejection of 'selective vision' has its counterpart in Braque's and Picasso's radical treatment of form and space. Paintings like Braque's *Violin and Palette* (autumn 1909) and Picasso's *Portrait of Wilhelm Uhde* (spring–autumn 1910) are among the closest visual equivalents to Stein's 'disinterested' prose. In Picasso's work, the figure of the art dealer Wilhelm Uhde appears as a half-length portrait, with sufficient detail for us to recognize his dark hair, parted in the middle; his small mouth, nose, eyebrows and eyes – one in profile, one straight on; his white collar and dark suit jacket. Behind Uhde, canvases lean against a wall, while a table with a drawer and knob appear just to the right. But all the observable forms – body, head, table, canvases, wall – are so broken up into tilted geometric planes, connected through passage, as to nearly dissolve into a play of line and very limited colour: black, white, ochre and their mixture. In Stein's prose, the rhythmic play of repetition and difference acts to undercut the separation of one thought from another. In Picasso's and Braque's paintings the elements of pictorial illusionism serve not to delineate recognizable objects but to confound our expectations, acting to merge objects and personages with their surroundings. The objects we would reduce to 'stock types' by virtue of our linguistic labels – a pitcher and violin in Braque's case, a series of picture frames and an adjacent table in Picasso's – dissolve into the confusing play of solids and voids that permeates each canvas. Picasso, in his portrait of Uhde, subjects his sitter's physiognomy to such ambiguities. Uhde's visage is reduced to a few caricatural elements, such as the pursed lips and angular nose, while others disappear altogether: note for instance the absence of Uhde's right ear or the merger of his faceted forehead with the surrounding environment. Chiaroscuro is used neither to define the borders and edges of objects nor to establish the origin of a single light source. The expectations of such visual logic – the equivalent to 'intellectualism' in the Jamesian vocabulary – are instead overturned by the alternating play of light and shade across

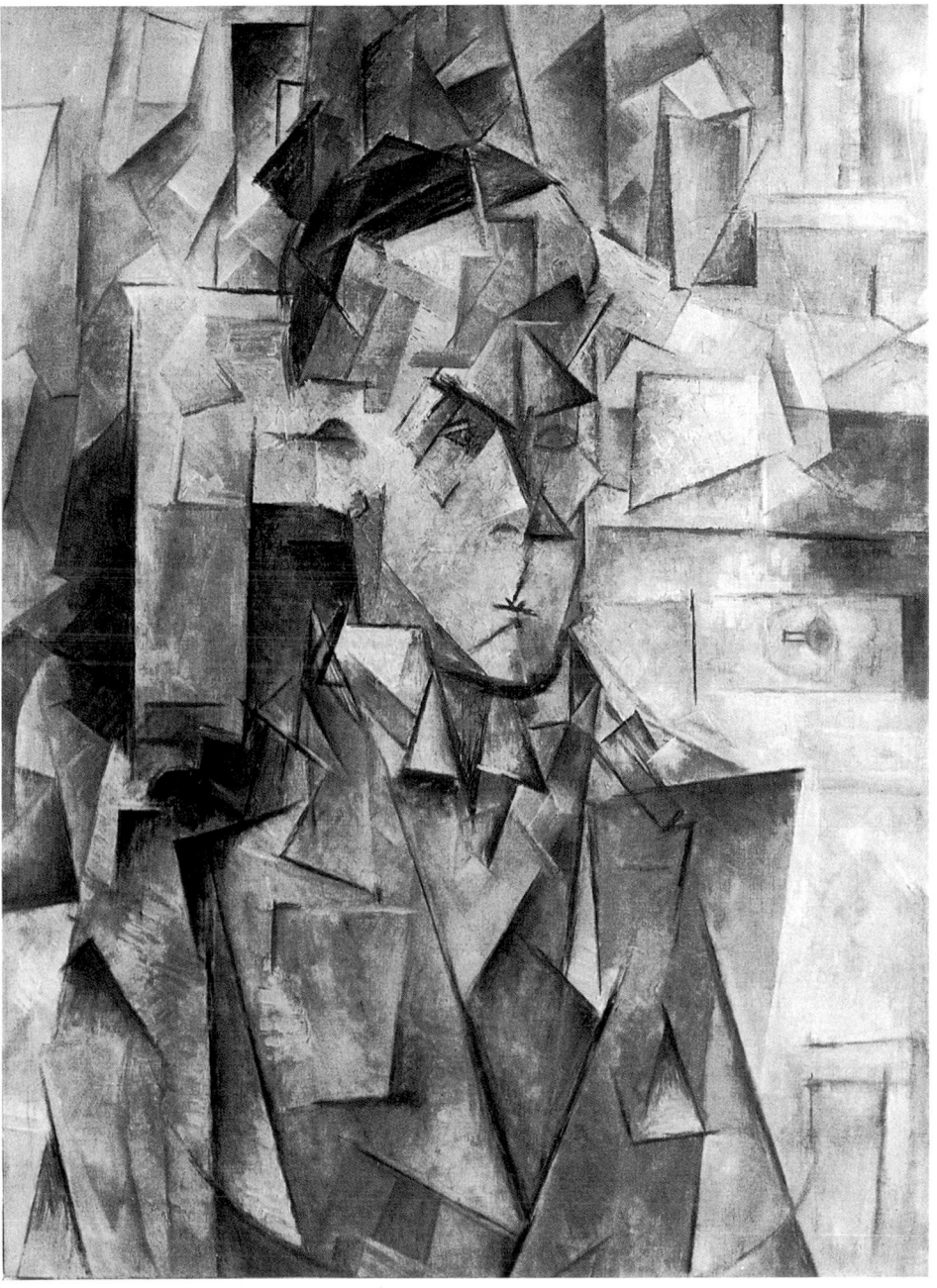

89. **Pablo Picasso**, *Portrait of Wilhelm Uhde*, spring–autumn 1910.

surfaces that may or may not resolve into identifiable objects in our imagination. Braque underscored the contrast by including an illusionistic nail at the top of *Violin and Palette*, while Picasso inserted the cartoonlike drawer knob to Uhde's right.

Just as Stein's literary anti-intellectualism differed from that of the Unanimists, so too Picasso and Braque's painting stood in contrast to that of their Cubist colleagues. The 'disinterestedness' of Stein's prose had its pictorial counterpart in Braque and Picasso's repeated study of mundane still-life objects, as in *Violin and Palette* and Picasso's *The Architect's Table* of early 1912. The latter is a highly complex still life of a table covered with a fringed cloth, whose tassels are visible at lower left. A glass is visible just to the left of centre, with a rectangular outline of its bowl viewed from the side, its contents of dark liquid viewed directly from above as a circle, with a white stem seen straight on, connected at the bottom to a round foot seen from above. To the left a white piece of rectangular sheet music and a white clay pipe appear, and a rope and tassle hold back a curtain in the upper centre. To so describe these elements that Picasso suggests were present, however, is not to deny the tremendous degree of abstraction he has achieved with their help: the very table surface has dissolved into shifting ochre planes that refuse any spatial locations like 'in front of' or 'behind'. Interestingly, the best clues to the objects the viewer beholds are conveyed by words: 'Ma Jolie', written above the lines of the sheet music, is the name of a popular love song; 'Marc', just to the right of the glass's white stem and circular foot, denotes the last, medicinal, pressing of grapes for brandy; and, in the lower right, we find Miss Gertrude Stein's calling card. For both Bergson and James, language acted to 'fix' and 'solidify' perceptual experience, removing us from the 'flux' or 'stream' of consciousness. In Picasso's work, these verbal signs constitute further fragmentary clues to the artist's interests and experience; appearing to float above the objects they escort into the picture, they act as verbal counterparts to the complex and interconnected planes and fragmentary objects that refuse fixity and solidity with equal success.

Such imagery differed dramatically from Le Fauconnier's allegorical celebration of biological fecundity in his *Abundance*, the Unanimist celebration of the city captured in Delaunay's ode to the Eiffel Tower or Léger's rooftop paintings. The 'epic' subjects chosen by these artists both emulated the grand themes of Salon painting and were a suitable counterpart to the life-affirming optimism they associated with Bergsonian intuition and the spirit of empathetic fraternity animating the poetry of the Unanimists. The pictorial

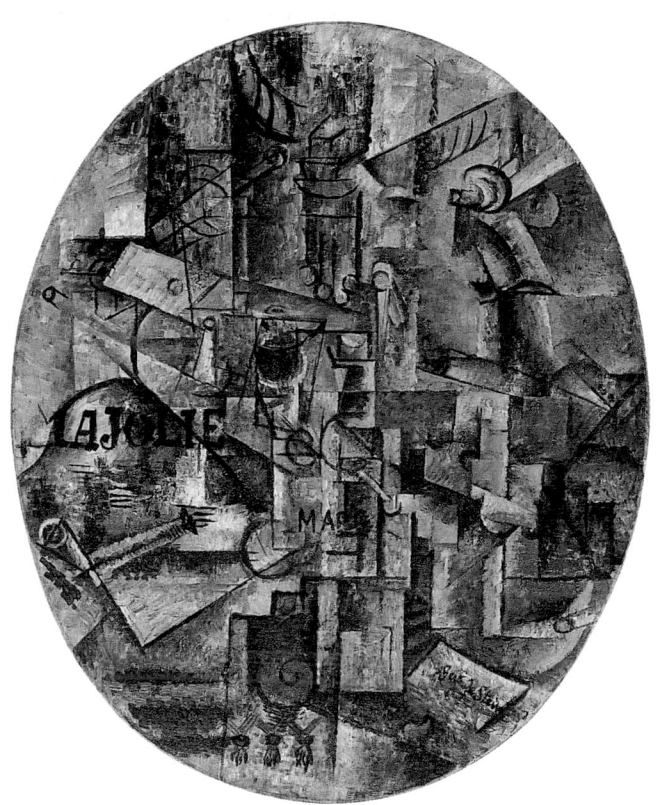

techniques employed by Picasso and Braque were akin to those of the Salon Cubists in their anti-intellectualism, but the vitalist rhythms, associative imagery, monumental subjects, and 'empathetic' consciousness that inspired the art of Gleizes, Delaunay, and Léger did not find a counterpart in the Cubism of Braque and Picasso, nor in the satirical Bergsonism of Marcel Duchamp. Detachment and irony, paroxysm and empathy: these were the two sides of the Cubist revolt against positivism and rationalism.

This contrast even pertained to the early Cubism of Metzinger, whose *Nude* of 1910 closely resembles Picasso's portrait of Uhde. 70, 89 Metzinger's 'Note on Painting' (1910) affirmed this interrelation by outlining the common interests uniting Braque and Picasso with Delaunay and Le Fauconnier. In that text, Metzinger relates Picasso's pictorial innovations to Poincaré's conventionalism and Princet's pronouncements on the new geometry, while Braque's painting 'radiates in time' by virtue of his simultaneous combination of views and the play of warm and cool colours that operate as a 'fluid counterpoint' to this 'dynamic process'. Metzinger then describes Delaunay's *Eiffel Tower* as the artist's Unanimist 'intuition' of the public's reaction to the tower, before concluding that Le Fauconnier situates his 'idea' in 'a vast equilibrium of numbers' in order to achieve 'grandeur'. Metzinger's own allegiance at that point to Picasso and Braque is signalled in the *Nude* by his assimilation of their techniques. His nude possesses pursed lips similar to those in Picasso's *Portrait of Uhde*, and the merger of the figure with the surrounding pictorial space closely approximates Picasso's and Braque's current methods. A key difference, however, is visible in the background where Metzinger has included a clock in the upper right to announce that the simultaneous views in his canvas are the product of Bergsonian duration. *Durée* stands in contrast to the quantified measurement of time and space, and Metzinger's clock, like the timepiece in Gris's *The Watch* (1912) or the illusionistic nail in Braque's *Violin and Palette*, is there to remind us of the intellectualized assumptions governing past pictorial conventions. Metzinger's didactic visual and literary references to Bergson and Poincaré may have more relevance for the art of Metzinger and his Puteaux colleagues than for Picasso and Braque, but they too stand as testimony to the currency of these ideas in Cubist circles. As we shall see, Metzinger's references to 'tradition' in the 'Note on Painting' herald the emergence of another, equally complex dimension of Cubism.

91. **Juan Gris**, *The Watch*, 1912. This is one of Gris's first two collages, in which he plays realism (in the simplified curtain tied back on the left) against abstraction, and mechanical clock time against the subjective flow of time and creativity. In a still life built up through the rhythmic combination of squares and 'Golden Section' rectangles, Gris juxtaposes the watch with the glued-in title of the poem 'Le Pont Mirabeau' by Apollinaire. The poem compares the time it takes to heal the wounds of love to the flowing of the river Seine under the Mirabeau bridge, expressing an organic, human experience of time. The simultaneous views of the still-life objects evoke Gris's own subjective experience of time, emulating the temporal consciousness embedded in Apollinaire's poem.

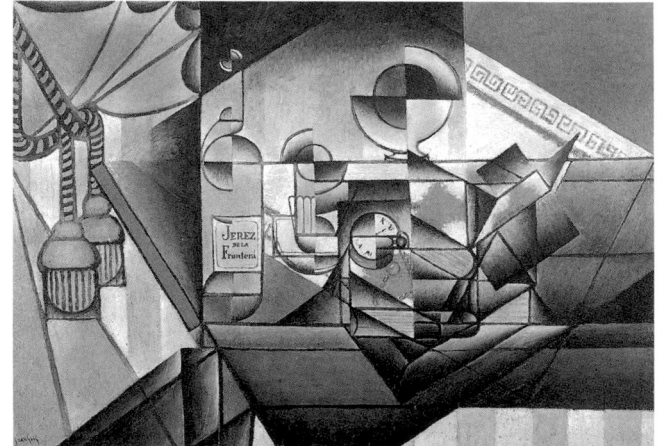

Chapter 3   Political Uses of the Past

The plurality of references to the art of the past appropriated by the Cubists before 1914 bears witness to the role of culture in political discourse. In France figures from a vast political spectrum – including anarchists, republicans, and monarchists – each laid claim to a version of French culture, which meant that art and politics were integral when it came to matters of 'tradition'. The Cubists and their neo-Symbolist allies responded to those claims, which gave rise both to Cubist theories of 'classicism' and to arguments over whether France was in essence 'Latin' or 'Celtic', with a cultural genealogy in the Greco-Roman 'south' or Gothic 'north'. When Roger Allard claimed in 1910 that the Cubists wished to broaden 'tradition in the direction of a future classicism', or when Albert Gleizes in 'Cubisme et la tradition' (1913) claimed that 'Greco-Latin' culture was a foreign incursion that blighted a Gothic tradition supposedly native to 'Celtic' France, both critic and artist were positioning Cubism within this political matrix. Gleizes went so far as to celebrate this Gothic tradition in Cubist terms in his *Chartres Cathedral* of 1912, whose towers with rose windows rise up from the vernacular homes of its builders below, revealing the Gothic to be rooted in French culture, past and present. The disparaging of tradition participated equally in this political discourse. Apollinaire counselled artists to 'innovate violently', thus favouring avant-garde innovation over tradition in all its guises. Various political agendas were encoded in such language; we can begin exploring Cubism's complex politics by examining the competing definitions of 'classicism' found in prewar Paris.

5

Classicism
Long before Cubism made its appearance, Charles Maurras, founder of the royalist and anti-Semitic movement Action Française (founded 1899 in the wake of the Dreyfus Affair), had developed a theory of classicism as the cultural counterpoint to his rejection of republican politics and call for the return of the French monarchy. Claiming that French culture had reached its zenith in

the seventeenth century under Louis XIV, Maurras and his literary allies Pierre Lasserre and Jean-Marc Bernard argued that France should return to the 'rational' order of government and culture during the reign of the Sun King. Cartesian rationalism and the art of Poussin were manifestations of this order, which was part and parcel of France's 'Greco-Latin' heritage, with roots in the south. Maurras's cultural coordinates were reinforced by art historian and Action Française adherent Louis Dimier, who celebrated Francis I's introduction of Italian art into France in a 1900 monograph on the Italian mannerist Primaticcio. After the French Revolution of 1789, argued Maurras, France had fallen victim to the forces of irrationalism: citizenship under the first Republic privileged individual rights over the collective good and the old corporative order that was its counterpart. Under the Republic, base motives such as greed and epicurean indulgence superseded the self-discipline that came with a sense of collective responsibility. In his polemical text Le Romantisme français (1907), Lasserre found a cultural correlate to Maurras's critique in the post-1789 Romantics, who reportedly rejected both classicism in art and monarchism in politics for the celebration of ultra-individualism and emotive self-indulgence.

Besides expounding a Cartesian definition of classicism in the prewar years, Maurras, Lasserre and Bernard condemned the Symbolist movement as antirationalist, exemplified by the Symbolists' allegiance to the intuitionist philosophy of Henri Bergson. In essays published in the monarchist journals Action française (1899–1944) and Les Guêpes (1909–13), Lasserre and Bernard railed against the neo-Symbolist movement. Bernard, who had previously written diatribes against Mallarmé, Mallarmé's neo-Symbolist disciple Jean Royère, Apollinaire, René Ghil and the Unanimists, published his 'Discours sur le symbolisme' in the May 1910 edition of Les Guêpes. Noting that his 'Discours' could have been titled 'Discourse on Romanticism', he claimed that the Symbolists mimicked their ancestors' 'contempt for all established rules', followed 'instinct and taste' when constructing poetry, and therefore fell prey to the 'terrible individualist current' that 'blew in with the Revolution'. Bernard saved his severest criticism for the conservative and Catholic literary critic Tancrède de Visan, whose books Paysages introspectifs (1904) and L'attitude du lyrisme contemporain (1911) claimed that Symbolism as an aesthetic had found its confirmation in Bergson's philosophy.

Such criticism implicated the Cubists, for between 1910 and 1914 the increasingly Bergsonist Gleizes and Metzinger published in neo-Symbolist journals such as Vers et Prose, Les Bandeaux d'or, and

Pan; additionally their literary supporters Allard, Salmon and Apollinaire were all major figures in the neo-Symbolist milieu. In other words, by using Cartesianism to disparage the still vital Symbolist movement, Maurras and his allies were in fact condemning its pictorial bedfellow, Cubism. In response Cubists and their neo-Symbolist allies Allard and Tancrède de Visan self-consciously opposed the royalists' trumpeting of Cartesian classicism with a counter-definition of classicism based on Bergson's anti-Cartesian doctrine of intuition. For example when Allard defined Cubism as leading to a 'future classicism' in the Symbolist journal *L'Art Libre* (November 1910), he did so by claiming that the rhythmic properties of a Cubist canvas reflected the musical structure inherent in *durée* or duration. Allard defined Cubism as classical because he judged the Cubists' innovative style to be representative of their 'intuitive' grasp of the collective *durée* of the French people. Moreover, on the basis of their Bergsonism, Allard and his colleagues claimed that this French spirit could not be rationally discerned and in the process declared Maurras's correlation of classicism with rationality invalid. Thus the Cubists reclaimed 'classicism' from the ultra-right Action Française and self-consciously allied that term with the Bergsonian 'irrationalism' that monarchists identified with the Republican cause.

Such statements account for the 'organicist' integration of tradition – the art of the past – into the Cubist project. Taking their lead from Allard, Gleizes and Metzinger also condemned the imitation of past art and equated classicism with aesthetic innovation, all on the basis of the radical heterogeneity of 'duration', in which no event is absolutely repeatable. Having declared their own creative endeavors the product of duration, the Cubists then rejected any aesthetic principle – including contemporaneous notions of classicism – that would encourage artists to slavishly imitate past masters. The imitation of past art forms, they argued, denied the classical tradition itself, which was nothing but a succession of previous innovations, all attuned to the qualitative *durée* of a given period. As Metzinger put it in his 'Note on Painting' of September 1910, 'Picasso, Braque, Delaunay, Le Fauconnier [are] too enlightened to believe in the stability of any system, even one called classical', and instead 'recognize in the most novel of their creations the triumph of desires that are centuries old'. The following year Metzinger declared the classical tradition to consist of nothing more than a 'series of uninterrupted innovations', adding that the Cubists 'by innovating only want to continue it'. Their chief means of doing so, stated Metzinger, was by infusing their canvases with *durée*. In their

1912 text *Du Cubisme*, Gleizes and Metzinger reiterated this claim, stating that 'imitation is the only error possible in art; it attacks the law of time'.

These statements were part of a shared vocabulary that affected the Cubist-oriented Société Normande de Peinture Moderne (founded 1909), which included Cubists Pierre Dumont (1884–1936), Fernand Léger and the Duchamp-Villon brothers among its membership, all of whom came from Normandy. Over the course of 1911 the Société group had joined Gleizes and his colleagues in the planning of the 'Section d'Or', a joint exhibition held in October 1912 as a counterpart to the contemporaneous 'Maison Cubiste' exhibition at the Salon d'Automne of that year. That summer, concurrent with Salmon's announcement that Bergson was to write the catalogue for the upcoming Section d'Or, the Société Normande held an exhibition in which Gothic subject matter and Cubist distortions were purposely intertwined in paintings like *Chartres Cathedral* of 1912 by Gleizes and *Rouen Cathedral* by 5, 9 Dumont, who was president of the Société. In Dumont's painting, elements of the cathedral, such as the statue of a saint, are spatially divorced from the building's façade, while the cathedral itself merges with its architectural surroundings. In his work, Gleizes subjects Chartres Cathedral to comparable spatial displacements, combining views of the cathedral's transept windows and spires with the building's central nave and the humble buildings flanking the edifice. Vertical planes intersect and unite the architectural and natural forms, which shift their colours and angles with the changing perspectives. In both cases Dumont and Gleizes purposely integrate the cathedral with its urban surroundings to indicate the building's status as an expression of the collective labour of the local community.

While Gleizes and Dumont's shared interest in Gothic architecture indicates their consensus on what constituted the French tradition, the preface for the exhibition stands as further testimony to the impact of Bergsonism on the Cubists. In his preface, the critic Elie Faure stated that the changes in modern thought created 'by the philosophers of constructive and lyrical intuition' were matched by 'young painters' who embraced 'intuitive life with the trembling and joyous desire to submit to its will'. 'It is not up to us', states Faure, 'to impose on the artist the inertia of our vision', rather we should recognize an attempt to transform appearances in response to 'heroic sentiment'. The multiple views found in Gleizes's and Dumont's cathedral paintings presumably captured their intuitive response to these monuments of French culture. In

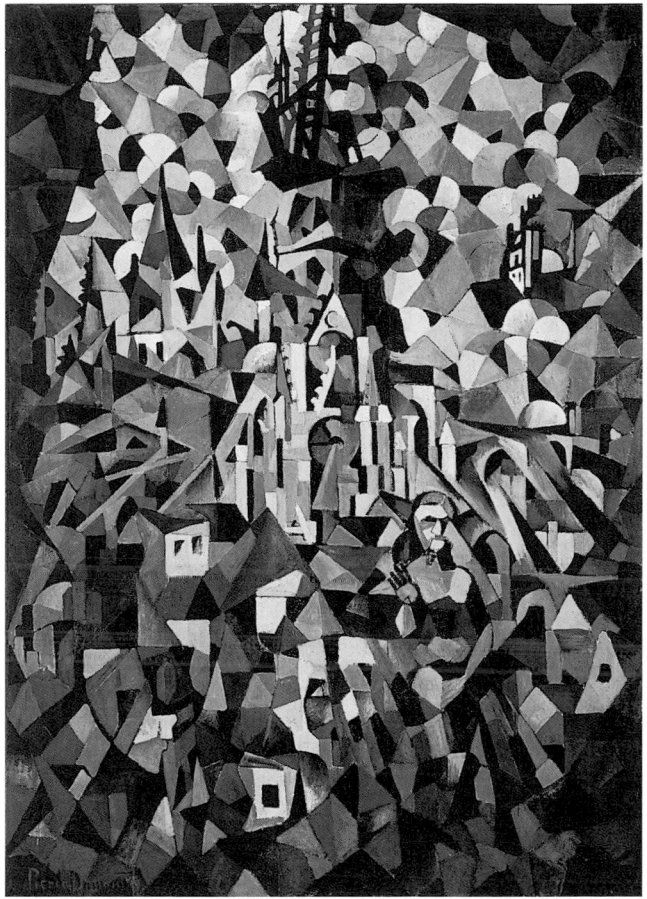

short, the Cubists wished to relate their art to tradition and declare
it classical, since the classical tradition is itself the sum total of past
innovations, the effort of those artists who remained true to their
intuitive abilities. For the Cubists this meant that artists could combine pictorial conventions forged in the past with innovations keyed
to an artist's dynamic *durée*. Metzinger's essay 'Cubism and tradition'
(August 1911) praised Le Fauconnier's *Abundance* (1910–11) for its   93
'indispensible mixture of certain conventional signs with new signs'.
Le Fauconnier depicted a traditional symbol of fecundity in the
female nude carrying a basket of fruit and accompanied by a small
child; both the fruit and the infant symbolize the Bergsonian 'life
force' or *élan vital* celebrated in Bergson's *Creative Evolution* (1907).
By virtue of this subject matter, Metzinger continued, Le Fauconnier
was able to 'magnificently develop what the men of our race are

used to admiring in natural sights, and the power which renders it perceptible to us ... contains enough in the way of unknown elements to impress several generations'. These 'unknown elements' were the novel means by which Cubists unite representational content with durational form.

Abundance depicts an allegorical nude bearing a large basket of fruit, with her son playfully holding some fruit of his own, in a panoramic landscape of the French Alps. All around her are the signs of fecundity in the forest, fields and village – with its herd of sheep – as well as the husbanding of the lush environment, suggested by the three tree stumps that appear as grey circles ringed by brown. All these forms are geometrized and painted with earth

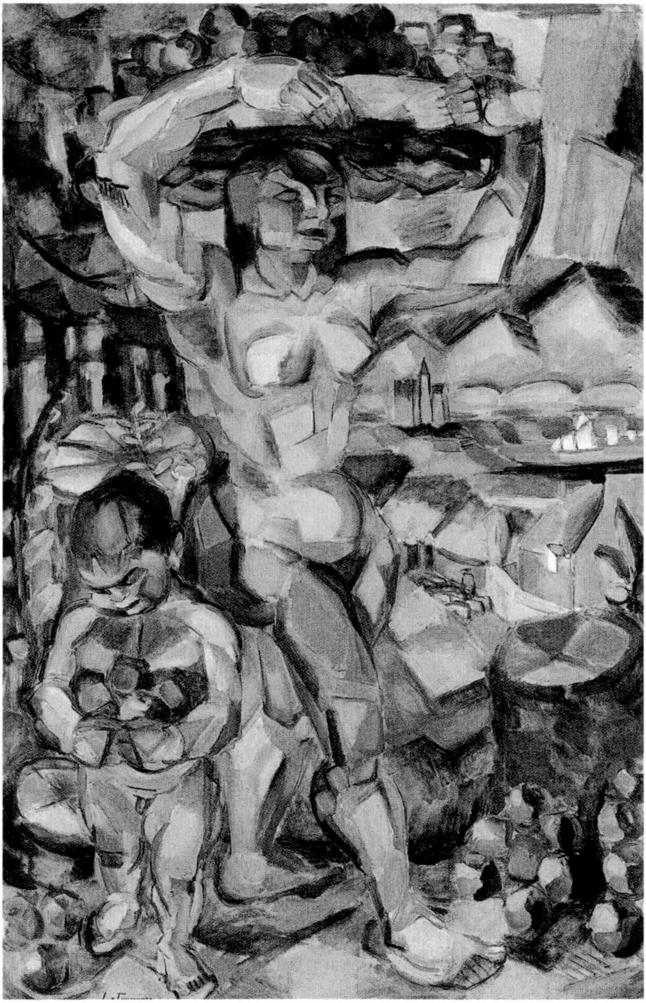

93. **Henri Le Fauconnier**, *L'Abondance (Abundance)*, 1910–11.

94. Henri Le Fauconnier, c. 1911.

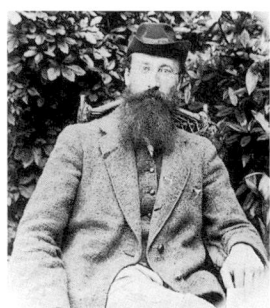

95. **Henri Le Fauconnier,**
The Lake, 1911.
Le Fauconnier underscored the symbolic importance of the château in this panoramic image of Lac d'Annecy. By choosing a viewpoint on the forested slopes above the village of Duingt, Le Fauconnier hides the adjacent town and isolates the château on its peninsula, which juts out dramatically into the lake. Located at the composition's centre, the château's white tower has a commanding presence as the symbolic guardian of the lake, the surrounding landscape and the spiritual essence of France itself.

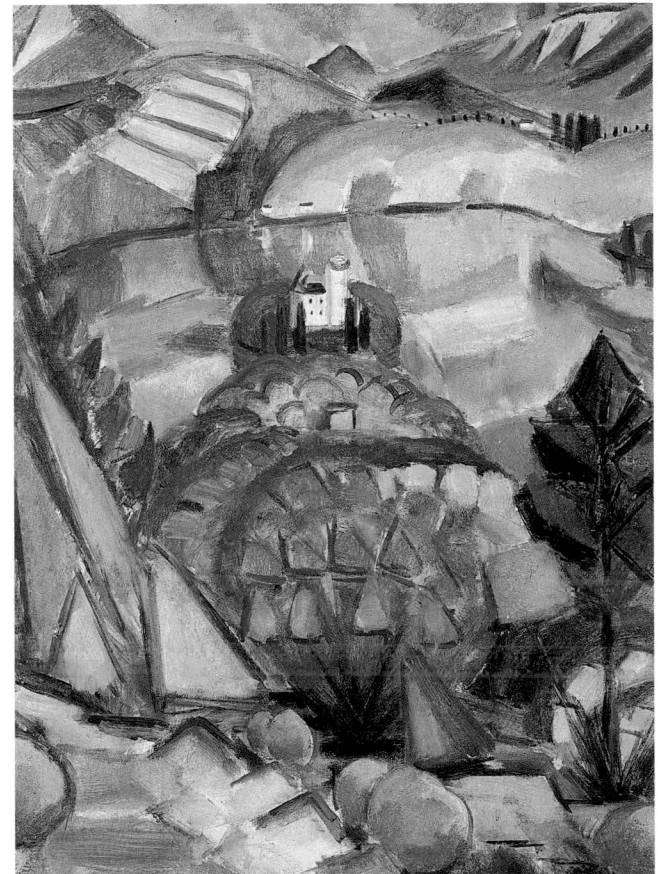

colours, the space compressed though not substantially distorted. In the distance the eleventh-century fortress, Château de Duingt, appears on the shore of Lac d'Annecy. Cézanne had already made the fortress familiar to avant-gardists, and it was a famous historical site associated with the region. With its appearance Le Fauconnier alludes to the well-known role of the castle's owners – the de Sales – in defending the region's Catholic identity during the Protestant Reformation; thus the edifice not only symbolizes antiquity and tradition, but operates as an affirmation of French Catholicism. As a consequence of Le Fauconnier's novel technique, the painting's historical content cannot be grasped instantaneously, but only discerned after a prolonged period of concentrated looking, as if to underscore the interrelation of pictorial form to content: an allegorical image of the Bergsonian *élan vital* nurtured by spiritual values native to France.

This link between Bergsonism, abstract form and historical content had profound implications with regard to the relation of tradition to innovation in Cubist practice. 'We will even willingly confess', state Gleizes and Metzinger in *Du Cubisme*, 'that it is impossible to write without using clichés, and to paint while disregarding familiar signs completely'. For this reason, they add, 'it is up to each one to decide whether he should disseminate them throughout his work'. The relation of this statement to the Cubist conception of tradition becomes clear when considering such works as Metzinger's *Femme à la fenêtre (Maternité)* (1911–12), whose general composition openly derives from Elisabeth Vigée-Lebrun's self-portrait of 1789 in the Louvre, widely known through mass-produced engravings. But this clichéd 'sign' has been recast both in terms of subject matter and style. Although the hair ribbon worn by the mother in Metzinger's rendition of the maternity theme echoes Vigée-Lebrun's neo-Greek attire, her dress is clearly modern. Where Vigée-Lebrun has utilized traditional perspectival techniques, Metzinger has introduced *passage* and multiple views to create a dynamic, durational pictorial space. These multiple views are concentrated in the centre before a flattened schematic space, focusing the artist's (and viewer's) intuition on the tender relation between mother and child, both of whom are viewed in profile as well as frontally. As with Picasso's portraits, Metzinger has purposely based his work on the 'familiar' in order to provide viewers with a point of access. If Metzinger was aware of Vigée-Lebrun's monarchist politics, he may have sought to reclaim her neoclassical style for the French Revolution through his use of the colours of the Republican flag – red, white and blue – repeated throughout the composition.

Raymond Duchamp-Villon also employs this mixture of old and new artistic conventions in his sculpture. For instance, the sidelong glance and gesture of modesty evident in the pose of his 1914 *Seated Woman* relates to the defensive posture found in classical Greek statues of Aphrodite. Like Metzinger, Duchamp-Villon has revised a figural arrangement devised by other artists, and deeply embedded in Western consciousness, through his geometrification of form and the chromatic and reflective treatment of the sculptural surface. Each element of the anatomy is treated as a fully autonomous form, pushed to an extreme of abstract simplification, that is then fitted together, utilizing Cubist innovation to radically update the conception of the Greeks. In keeping with this Bergsonian and Cubist paradigm, the novel form of *Seated Woman* is nothing more than the most recent example in a long line of aesthetic innovations, each of which inspired its successor.

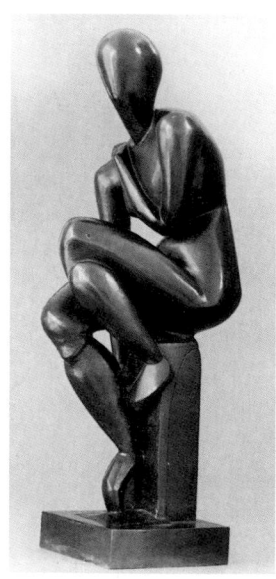

96. Raymond Duchamp-Villon, *Seated Woman*, 1914.

Similarly, in his façade for the Maison Cubiste, Duchamp-Villon 99 combined the structure of an eighteenth-century townhouse with innovative crystalline forms to produce that mixture of new and conventional signs Metzinger found so praiseworthy. The geometric linear and rounded forms completely transform the decorative appearance of the entrance, yet only serve to affirm the imposing overall monumentality of an *hôtel particulier* and its articulation of columns, pilasters and pediments. And like Gleizes in *Chartres Cathedral* (1912), Duchamp-Villon imposed his 'intuitive' Cubist 5 forms on a purposely Gothic substructure in his project for a dormitory of 1914, whose façade incorporated his highly abstract 101 sculptural reliefs into a fenestrated bay and portal modelled after Gothic precedents. The reliefs also transformed Christian motifs into planetary ones, depicting from the bottom stage to the top an abstracted moon, stars and planets. In so doing he remained true to the innovative *élan vital* animating the traditional and the modern. The conflation of the Gothic and the modern was reinforced in other ways as well, for critics commonly associated medieval masons with engineers like Gustave Eiffel, claiming that both adhered to the structural properties of their respective building materials. As a result, artists like Duchamp-Villon and Robert Delaunay drew comparisons between iron structures like the Eiffel Tower and medieval cathedrals, a correlation that inspired Delaunay to paint both the church of Saint-Séverin and the Eiffel Tower. 82

The Gothic

Given that the Puteaux Cubists alluded to the Gothic, classical Greek statuary, neoclassicism and Norman folk art (in the case of the furniture for the Maison Cubiste) at various stages of their development before 1914, we must be cautious about ascribing a particular ideological stripe to their art on the basis of stylistic references alone. Bergsonism, however, is the general paradigm underlying their appropriation of various period styles, and given Action Française's hostility to that philosopher we may assume that the Cubists rejected Maurras's integral nationalism. Furthermore we can draw political distinctions among the Cubists and their supporters; it is unlikely, for instance that Gleizes, who had helped form the anticlerical Association Ernest Renan in 1905, would have shared Le Fauconnier and Visan's enthusiasm for French Catholicism.

Indeed when Gleizes summarized his views on tradition in his 1913 manifesto 'Cubisme et la tradition', published in the journal

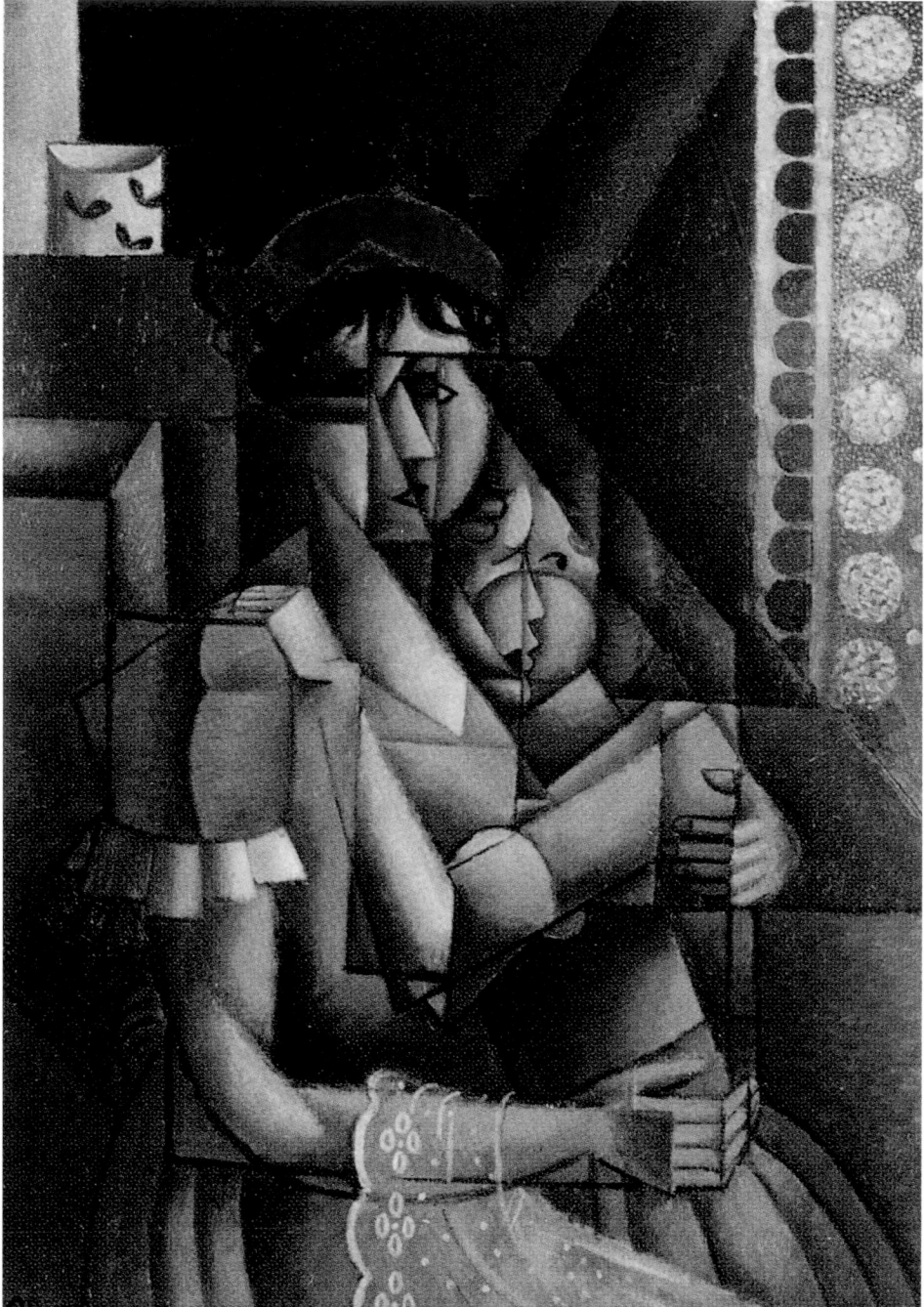

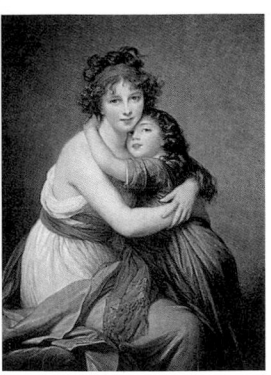

98. Elisabeth Vigée-Lebrun,
Mme Vigée-Lebrun and her Daughter, 1789.

Montjoie! (1913–14), he rejected the 'Latin' south celebrated by artists like the conservative Maurice Denis in favour of the 'Gothic' north. 'Cubisme et la tradition' places Cubism in the context of the antiroyalist, anarcho-syndicalist, racial ideology of an organization known as the Celtic League (founded 1911). In this essay, Gleizes identifies the French proletariat as the incarnation of a 'Celtic' national genius, condemning both 'Latinism' and monarchism as foreign to France's true racial essence. By politicizing the message of *Du Cubisme* (1912), coauthored with Metzinger and resultingly homogenized, Gleizes presents himself as the ideological voice for Cubism in the public sphere, a logical extension of his previous involvement in the Abbaye de Créteil, the anticapitalist commune of artists and writers. His attempt to redefine Cubism politically both signals the central importance of cultural nationalism and reveals the complexity and range of the debate over national identity on the eve of World War I.

Between 1911 and 1913 the notion of Bergsonian classicism charted above became tied to one of Celtic nationalism. The praise of Celtic roots and Gothic culture as 'truly French' in Cubist and neo-Symbolist circles was part of a concerted attempt to counter the trumpeting of Greco-Latin culture by Action Française. This manoeuvre also involved Bergson, whose philosophy of intuition was deemed compatible with the idealist and pantheistic spirit found in Gothic art and Bardic poetry. In the spring of 1911, Robert Pelletier had founded the Ligue Celtique Française and the journal *L'Etendard celtique* to expound the Celtic movement's anti-Greco-Latin agenda. By the time *L'Etendard celtique* had been replaced by *Revue des nations* in February 1913, the league's membership had expanded to include many figures associated with the Puteaux Cubists: Alexandre Mercereau, Gleizes and Metzinger's close friend and founder of *Vers et Prose*; leading Symbolist poet Paul Fort; and the publisher of *Du Cubisme*, Eugène Figuière. Over the course of that year Fernand Divoire (who contributed regularly to Henri-Martin Barzun's journal *Poème et drame* (1912–14) and *Montjoie!*), the art critic Olivier Hourcade, and Bergson's major Symbolist apologist Tancrède de Visan all joined the movement.

Concurrently, Gleizes and Metzinger's criticism became associated with journals promoting the Celtic League's agenda. When an excerpt from *Du Cubisme* was published in the first issue of *Poème et drame*, it was preceded by an article extolling Celtism by linguist and Celtic League member Charles Callet, thus signalling Henri-Martin Barzun's approval of Celtism. Since Barzun had helped found the Abbaye de Créteil, this endorsement was significant among Cubist

97. Jean Metzinger,
Femme à la Fenêtre (Maternité), 1911–12.

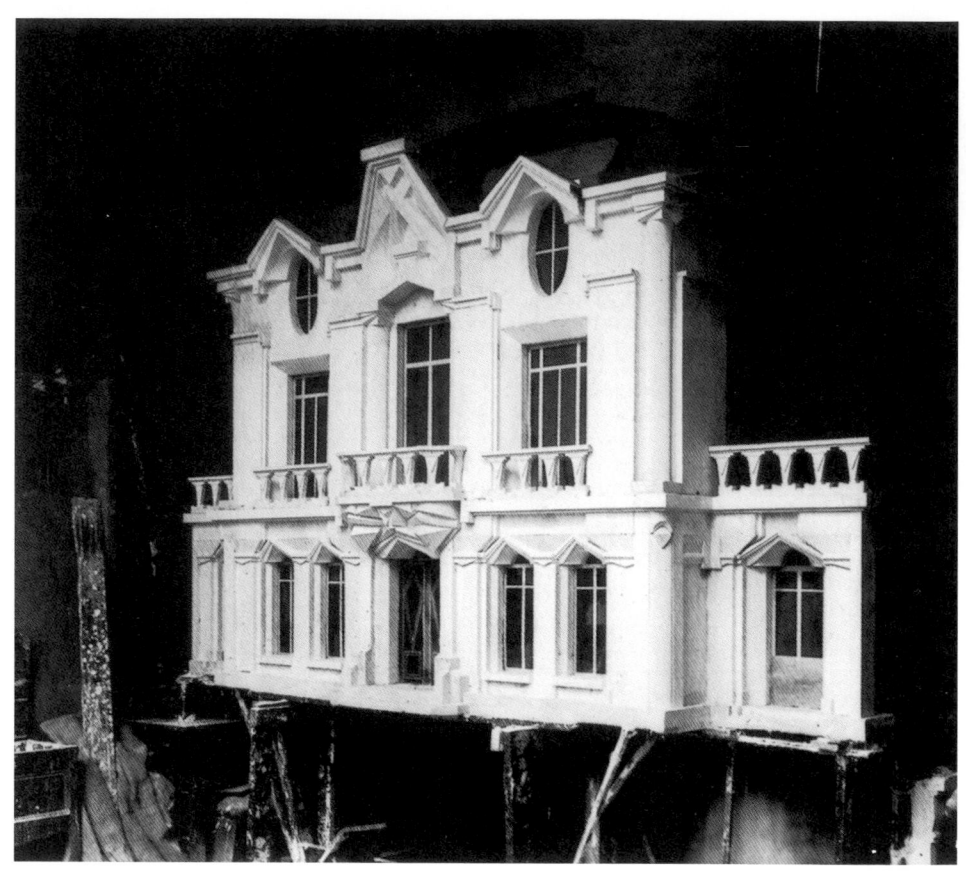

circles. In February 1913, Jacques Reboul, another promoter of Celtic nationalism, helped launch *Montjoie!* as a kind of literary complement to Pelletier's new *Revue des nations*, which began publication that same month. Contributors to the first issue of *Revue des nations* included Fort and Mercereau, and the journal also had a lengthy article on Bergson's philosophical legacy. Pelletier's own inaugural article outlined the League's artistic purpose as the promotion of medieval corporatism, federalism, and the idealist and pantheistic spirit personified by artisans of the Gothic era and the French Primitives of the fifteenth and sixteenth centuries.

Pelletier's synthesis of medieval corporatism and federalism has a resounding echo in Gleizes's 'Cubisme et la tradition'. Between the autumn of 1911 and the publication of 'Cubisme et la tradition' in the February issues of *Montjoie!*, Gleizes's aesthetic views had evolved from an unquestioning trumpeting of Greco-Roman culture to an outright attack on that cultural heritage as 'foreign' to the

99. Raymond Duchamp-Villon, maquette for the Maison Cubiste, 1912.

100. André Mare,
Bed and bedcover for the *petite chambre*, Maison Cubiste, Salon d'Automne, Paris, 1912.
Designer André Mare orchestrated the creation of the Maison Cubiste for the 1912 Salon d'Automne. On passing through an entrance designed by Duchamp-Villon (see plate 99), viewers were confronted with a *salon bourgeois* containing a fireplace by La Fresnaye, paintings by Gleizes, Léger and Metzinger, and decorative mirrors by Laurencin (see plate 114). As David Cottington demonstrates, stylistic references to Norman folk art in the Maison Cubiste – such as this bed for the *petite chambre* – won the approval of critics who allied such features with writer Roger Marx's Republican doctrine of 'social art', which advocated the popularization of rural folk culture among all classes as a symbol of solidarity.

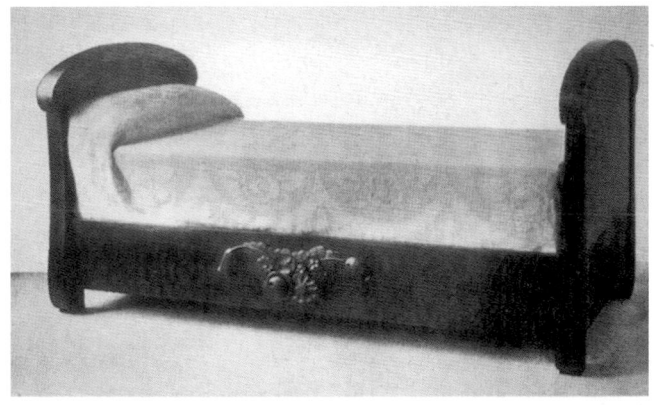

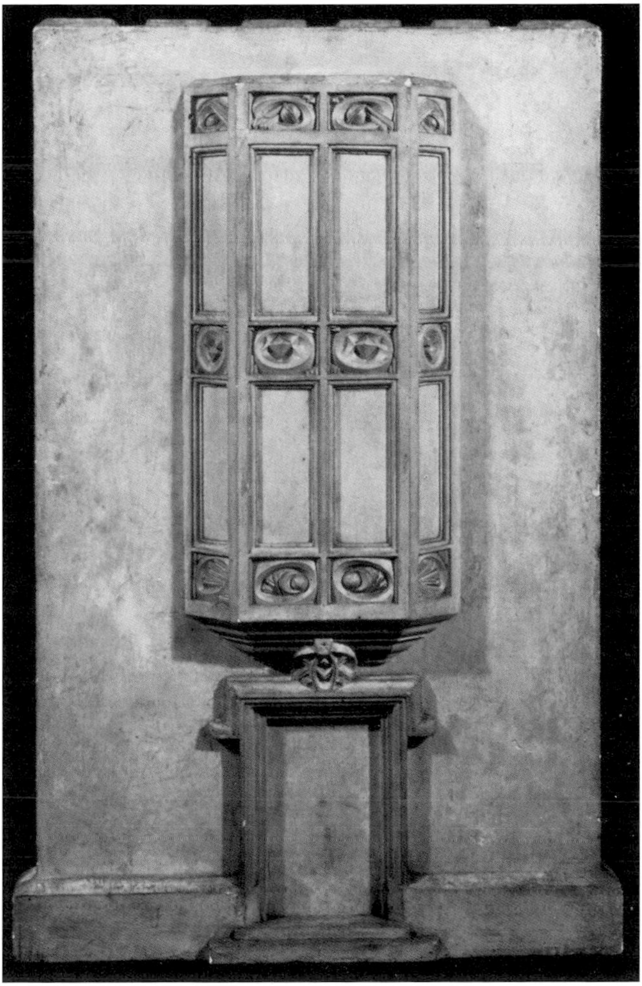

101. Raymond Duchamp-Villon,
Projet d'architecture, 1914.

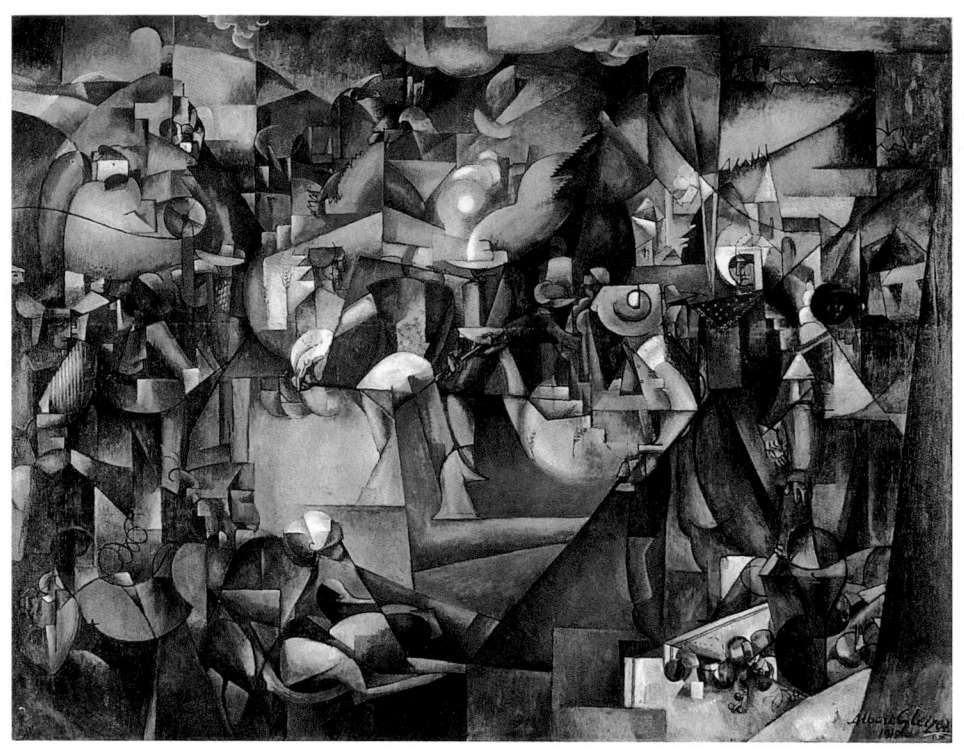

Celtic roots of France. In an early essay of September 1911, Gleizes had identified the contemporary return to 'the French tradition' with qualities of 'grandeur, clarity, equilibrium and intelligence' stemming from the 'Renaissance' and 'Greco-Roman traditions'. Yet by 1912 Gleizes followed Pelletier in vilifying the Renaissance as a period of Italian cultural hegemony over France. Gleizes's 'Cubisme devant les artistes' (1912) even characterizes the Cubists as 'liberators' of a 'French tradition' previously crippled by 'the detestable Italian influence, the sad heritage of the Renaissance of the sixteenth century'. Gleizes traces the lost period of French cultural dominance back to the Gothic era, whose cultural representatives are 'our primitives and our cathedrals'. In 'Cubisme et la tradition' (1913) he describes Gothic art's practitioners as truly embodying the nation's 'Celtic origins'. In turning to the Celtic roots of their own culture, French artists should extract 'the elements which are its essence, and develop them in this spirit; an affair of intuition, of tact, of will'. Gleizes noted in 1912 that spectators can thus 'savour (goûter) the tableau as an organism', as an object 'with its own raison d'être'. Having rediscovered the 'Celtic origins' of

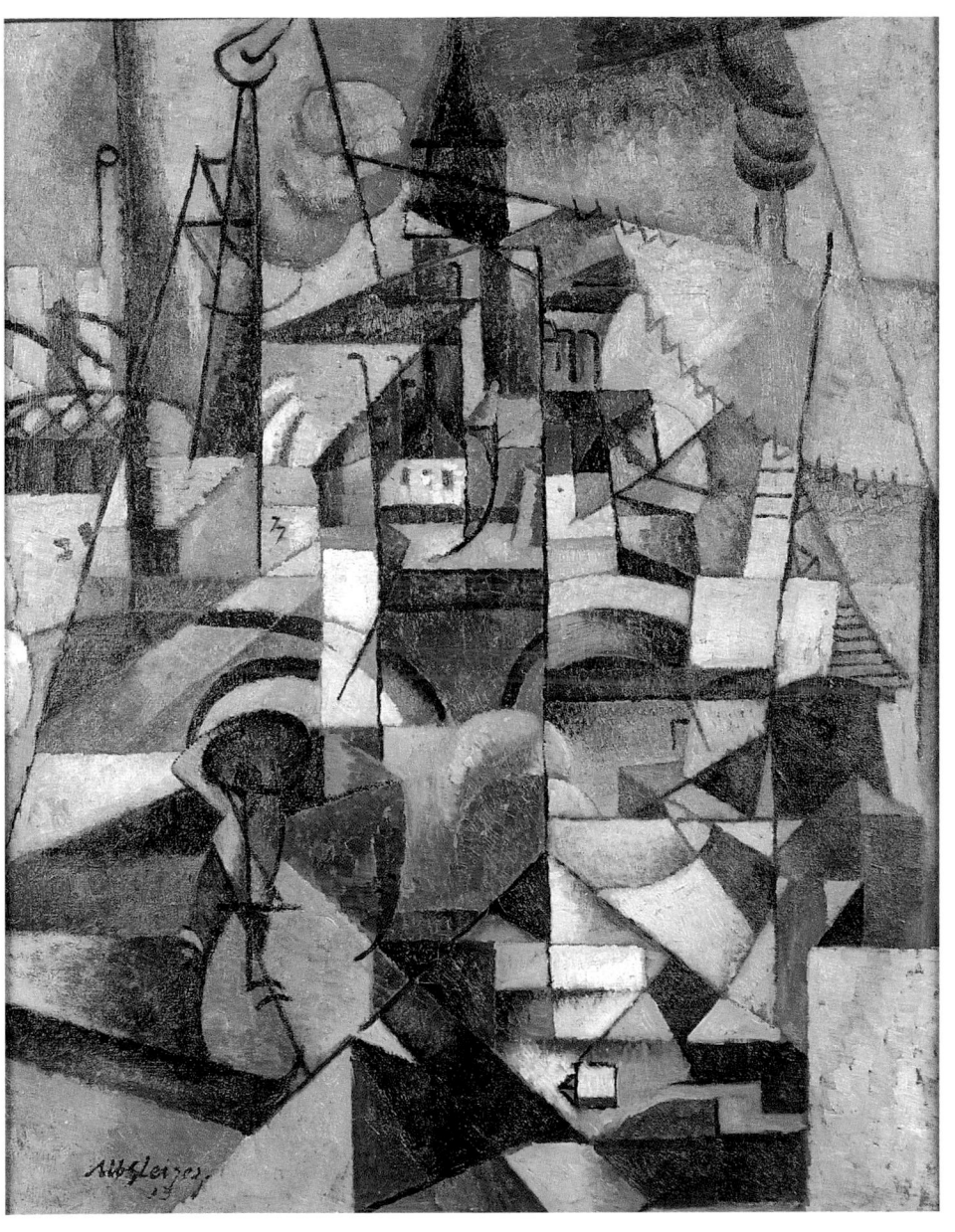

103. **Albert Gleizes**, *The City and the River*, 1913.

French art, Gleizes wanted French artists to 'develop' these origins through intuition, to create an 'organic' art as rooted in the French tradition as the Gothic art of their Celtic forbears.

Besides echoing Pelletier in his condemnation of the harmful effects of the Italian Renaissance on France's Celtic heritage, Gleizes's 'Cubisme et la tradition' replicated Pelletier's analysis of the class divisions stemming from this influence. Gleizes blames royal authority for the imposition in France of an Italian art 'impregnated with Greek antiquity' and hostile to the 'primordial aspirations' of France. Only artists like Jean Clouet, as in his *Francis I, King of France* of 1525, had 'enough belief and courage' to represent the spirit of *le peuple* (the people) by adhering to the 'ancestral truth' of Gothic art. Clouet cultivated the 'plastic values' of design and form championed by Gleizes, resultingly his art captured 'the freshness and naturalness of our origins' rather than the 'affectation and preciousness' of Italian Mannerism.

Gleizes's eulogy to Gothic art and the Celtic roots of plebian culture has its pictorial equivalent in his *Harvest Threshing* (1912), a celebration of peasant life possibly inspired by Barzun's epic poem *La Montagne* (1908), and the centrepiece of the Section d'Or exhibition. Barzun's poetic ode to the collectivity and spiritual harmony inspired by *la vie naturelle* finds a parallel in *Harvest Threshing*. This monumental painting depicts a vast panorama of domesticated

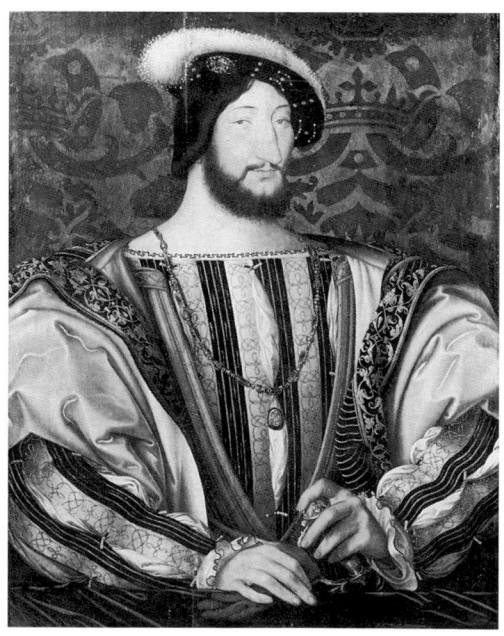

104. **Jean Clouet**,
Francis I, King of France, 1525.

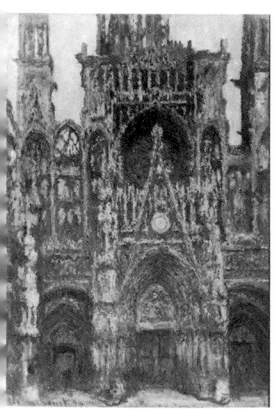

105. Claude Monet,
Rouen Cathedral, Façade (Grey Day),
1892–94.
Monet's numerous depictions of
Rouen Cathedral were precedents
for Gleizes's *City and the River*
(plate 103) and *Chartres Cathedral*
(plate 5) and Dumont's *Rouen
Cathedral* (plate 92). Monet's
anticlerical Republicanism led him
to depict the effects of light on the
exterior façade rather than the
church interior, thus avoiding any
association of light with divine
inspiration. The choice of Rouen
Cathedral underscored this secular
interpretation, for the town itself
was largely working-class by virtue
of its industrialized port. Modern
syndicats or unions were frequently
compared to the medieval guilds
that built the cathedrals, with the
result that artists like Monet,
Pissarro, or Gleizes could interpret
these Gothic edifices as symbols
of working-class solidarity, both
past and present.

nature, with several villages in a mountainous landscape and numerous figures on various scales engaged in harvesting the ripe wheat. Multiple views and geometrizing planes synthesize a complex series of vignettes, in which figures set a harvest table (complete with tablecloth, cherries and pears), reap the wheat or converse in the village. The pictorial rhythms and earthen palette bind the painting into an organic whole and evoke an idealized harmony, wherein the rhythm of human labour is at one with the organic rhythm of the seasons. *Harvest Threshing* pictorially and ideologically confirms Pelletier's praise of the collective spirit and *durée* of the Celtic peasant, which was at the heart of Gleizes's Bergsonian and nationalist cultural agenda by the autumn of 1912.

This association of Celtic *élan vital* with Gothic architecture was celebrated by Gleizes a year later in *The City and the River*, his major painting of 1913. Gleizes's placement of Gothic edifices at the centre of this painting as well as in *Chartres Cathedral* (1912) symbolized the temporal continuity uniting past and present, a continuity additionally signified by the ebb and flow of the Seine in *The City and the River*. Twin spans cross the river in the centre of the canvas in a series of concentric arcs; above this rise the buildings of Paris topped by a Gothic tower. To left and right are smoke stacks, a large green tree and a steel bridge, while below the arcs is the *quai*, still used to this day for industrial activities. On the left is a worker, his right arm raised to balance a heavy load, and between him and the steel bridge on the upper left is a small French tricolour flag, possibly on a barge. To the right, parallel brushstrokes indicate the sparkling water. By placing a Gothic cathedral in the midst of a contemporary urban landscape, complete with iron bridges, French flag and modern worker in the foreground, Gleizes underscored the continuity uniting the modern worker and French society with the medieval artisanal society that had constructed the cathedrals. The collective labour that went into the building of Gothic cathedrals had its modern equivalent in the rural labour depicted in *Harvest Threshing*, or the industrial labour of the urban worker in *The City and the River*. In all these cases the rhythms of human labour, whether rural or technological, were subsumed within the larger organic rhythm of the Celtic race's creative evolution.

Gleizes's association of the Gothic with *le peuple* was also promoted by Léger as a sign of his own socialist allegiances. As Robert Herbert has demonstrated, Léger valued the collaborative spirit of medieval guilds and drew comparisons between Gothic art and his own Cubism, as in *Contrast of Forms* (1913). In 1913 in *Montjoie!*, Léger disparaged the Italianate classicism of southern Europe in

103

5

106

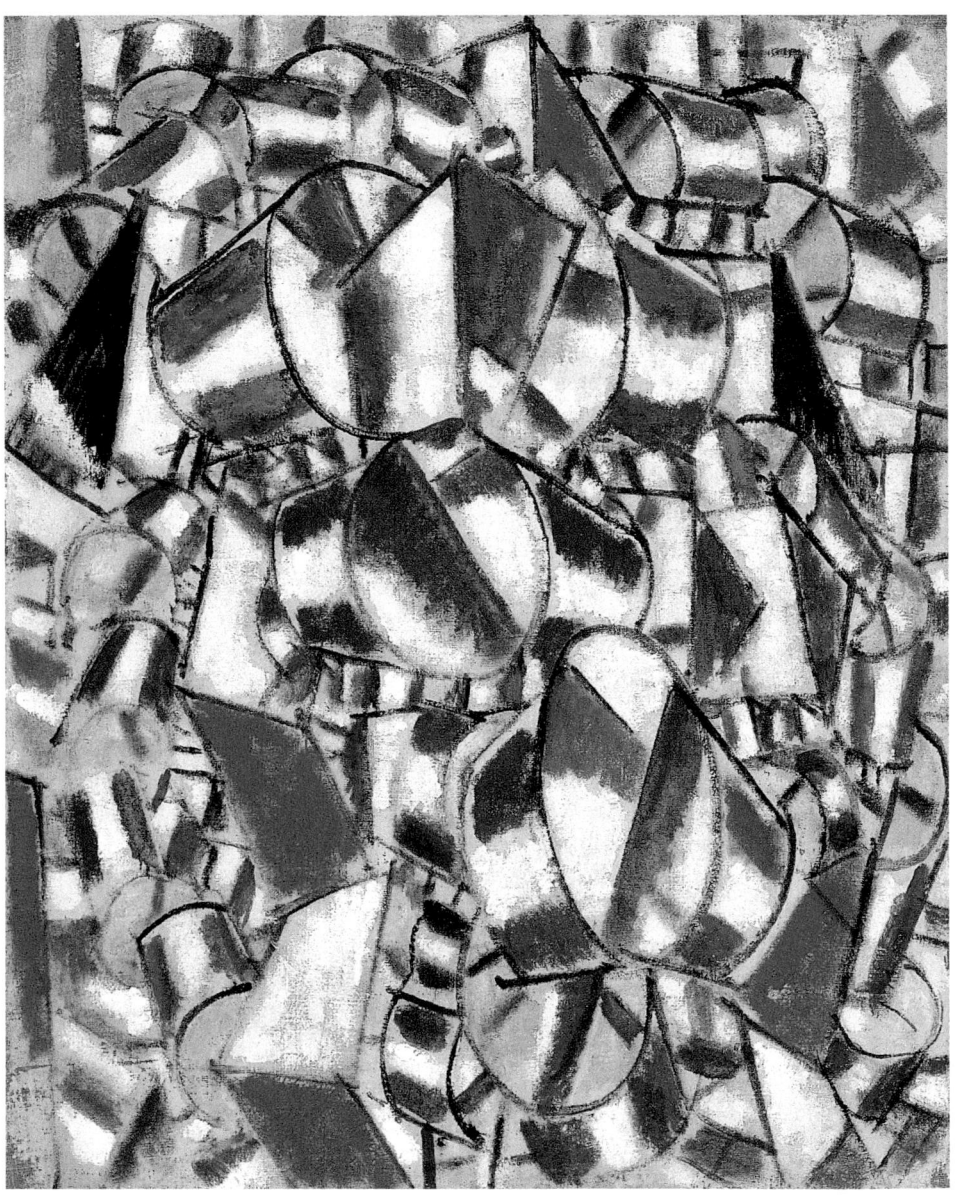

106. **Fernand Léger,**
Contrast of Forms, 1913.

comparison to the art of the 'Gothic' north, concluding that northern artists 'seek their dynamic means through the development of colour'. In his various writings Léger described his turn to abstraction in terms of emulating the art of French Primitives (such as Clouet and Gothic artisans), in contrast to the 'imitative' art of the High Renaissance. Under the influence of Renaissance ideals, Léger asserts, individualism had been championed to the detriment of the collectivism of the anonymous cathedral builders, leading to the triumph of easel painting – designed for individual, bourgeois collectors – over the public art of mural painting that had dominated artistic production before the Renaissance.

Since the latter works were executed in fresco rather than oil on canvas, Léger emulated their matte, 'decorative' surfaces. In contrast to Renaissance artists who used chiaroscuro to create illusions of depth, Léger claimed that the Primitives employed unmodelled surfaces and 'pure colour'; he attempted to modernize such techniques by applying unmixed colours to canvases that he had primed himself in a deliberately rough fashion, which lent a chalky, matte appearance to his colours and a tactile solidity to the forms themselves. Léger regarded his resulting abstractions as the modern equivalent of Gothic ornamentation, deriving his forms from 'popular' culture and making them, in theory, more accessible to the people. Where Gothic artisans had drawn artistic inspiration from *le peuple*, Léger turned to garishly coloured advertisements, the dynamism of the new film medium, and the reflective qualities of metal to develop his own 'popular' mode of abstraction.

In *Contrast of Forms* he has crowded his canvas with a profusion 106 of overlapping drum or barrel-like shapes delineated with heavy black outlines. Seeming to tumble outward, the dynamic forms take on a volumetric quality through his use of white to imitate reflections off 'metallic' or curvilinear surfaces. Like Gleizes, Léger found compatibility between Gothic art and the modern urban landscape, but took industrial machine forms rather than proletarian labour as a point of departure, developing his Cubist innovation to the point of pure abstraction. In the postwar period Léger resuscitated this attack on Renaissance art, writing in 1924 that the sixteenth century was an era of 'nearly total decadence in all the plastic arts'. The Ecole des Beaux-Arts, Léger added, had instituted the 'slavish imitation of art of that period' and was 'opposed to the so-called primitive epoch that is great and immortal precisely because it invented its forms and methods'. Gothic invention, and the collective values associated with that aesthetic, were the models to be emulated.

Anarchist avant-gardism

While the Puteaux Cubists reconciled their abstraction with the art of the past, others in their circle saw Cubist innovation as indicative of a violent rupture with past traditions. This interpretation motivated anarchists who claimed allegiance to the anarcho-individualist doctrine of 'Artistocratie'. First propounded by the anarchist Gérard de Lacaze-Duthiers in 1906, the Artistocratic doctrine was disseminated in a series of journals culminating in the founding of *Action d'art* in February 1913. Over the period before 1914 these anarchists forged links with key figures among the Cubist avant-garde; thus when *Action d'art* published a petition in April 1913 defending artistic freedom from state censorship, the *bande à Picasso* affiliates Apollinaire and Max Jacob signed it, along with Salon Cubists Archipenko, Dumont, Gleizes and Francis Picabia as well as writers Mercereau and Fort. In a July 1913 issue of *Action d'art*, the anarchist and pacifist André Colomer proclaimed Apollinaire's *The Cubist Painters* and Gleizes and Metzinger's *Du Cubisme* amenable to the 'individualistic and anarchically idealist tendencies' expressed in the journal. Appropriately *The Cubist Painters* and *Du Cubisme* – as well as the poetry of Mallarmé – were sold alongside anarchist tracts in the *Action d'art* bookstore. Colomer, the journal's main theorist, associated Cubist innovation with theories of creativity propounded by Mallarmé, Max Stirner, Oscar Wilde and Henri Bergson. For Colomer the Cubists upheld the 'tradition' of avant-gardism, in which the creative transformation of the self initiated a defiance of social conventions. 'The true tradition', wrote Lacaze-Duthiers in October 1912, 'is a tradition of revolt and emancipation. The tradition we represent is the tradition of free ideas. Every idea is revolutionary.... Of past art, all that which was once new, all which was opposed to prejudice and habit, is our tradition'.

This association of aesthetic vanguardism with revolutionary change was shared by those sympathetic to anarchism in the Cubist camp, most notably Apollinaire and Picasso. When Apollinaire called upon artists to 'innovate violently' or Picasso later proclaimed his art to be 'a sum of destructions', both poet and artist related Cubism's departure from academic convention to the Nietzschean creation of new social values. In *The Cubist Painters* (1913) Apollinaire described Picasso as 'newborn', a protean creator who 'orders the universe in accordance with his requirements'. Like Lacaze-Duthiers and André Colomer, both Apollinaire and Picasso identified artistic novelty with a new way of thinking and a concomitant break from a bourgeois order allied to an imitative and thus 'impotent' academicism.

Evidence for Picasso's earlier involvement with anarchists and his embrace of its individualist creed is abundant, not only in his art but in his role as co-editor of a short-lived anarchist journal. *Arte Joven*, founded in Madrid in 1901, published numerous writings by Spain's leading anarchist writers, including Pío Baroja, whose fiction chronicled the plight of the marginalized and unemployed. Advertisements appeared in the journal for translations of Nietzsche's *The Birth of Tragedy* and *The Twilight of the Gods* – works passionately embraced as advocating an absolute freedom for the artist – and for works by the leading European anarchist theorist Peter Kropotkin, including his *Memoirs of a Revolutionist* and *The Conquest of Bread*. Picasso and his co-editor Francisco Asís de Soler reject the past in *Arte Joven*'s outspoken editorial statement:

It is not our intent to destroy anything: our mission is more elevated. We come to construct. The old, the decrepit, the worm-eaten will sooner or later fall down by itself....

We come to the struggle with much enthusiasm, with much energy, with a tenacity that will never be able to spare the old.

This anarchist theme of hostility to tradition and to the past is crucial to understanding Picasso's later work, especially his 'African' period and subsequent Cubism.

Picasso's immersion in the anarchist milieu in Barcelona likewise stamped his life in Paris, where he moved permanently in 1904, seeking out French anarchist circles as well as antigovernment exiles from Spain. In particular he shared anarchist attitudes towards his art with his new friends, the poets and art critics Salmon and Apollinaire, who add an ideological stamp to their avant-gardism. Throughout his prewar work, Picasso's art expresses contempt for bourgeois culture, operating in a relationship of tension and contradiction to the dominant culture that necessarily defined its rebellion. Picasso consistently and purposely inverted and subverted subjects and themes of the academic tradition. As we saw earlier, in 1907, during his africanizing period, he conflated aspects of masks from the French Congo with recognizable Venus motifs, as in *Les Demoiselles d'Avignon*, turning the traditional allegory of beauty in a work like Giorgione's *Sleeping Venus* into something alien and threatening. His *Mother and Child* of 1907 becomes a frightening icon, at once evoking such religious works as Raphael's Madonnas (though more so their myriad later academic imitators) and attacking the forces of Church and State that such works had come to represent for an opponent of the status quo. Transforming the conventional formula for a Madonna and Child – with its infant

22

34

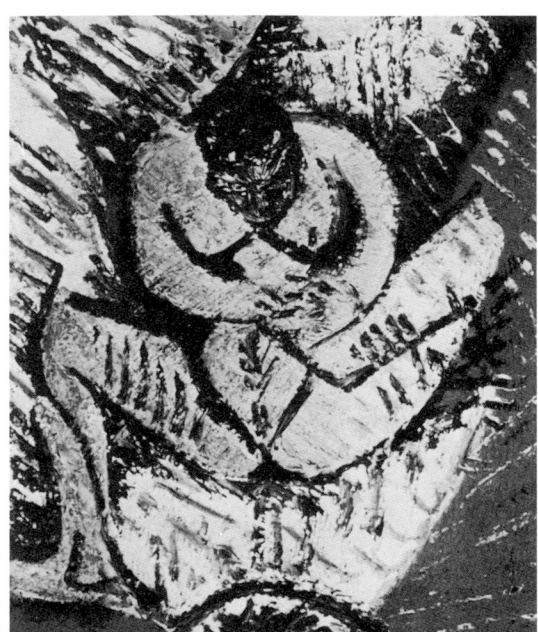

107. **Pablo Picasso**,
Femme accroupie (Seated Woman),
summer 1907.

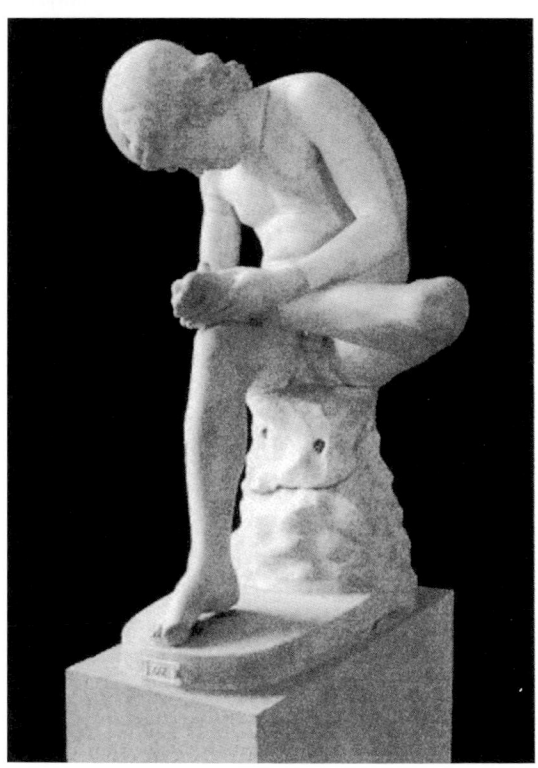

108. *Spinario*, Hellenistic Greece,
4th–3rd century B.C.

contained within the mother's silhouette, her blue robe of heaven and radiating halo — such antitraditional manoeuvres function in subversive relation to the culture of high art, supporting institutions, and religious ideology.

As *Mother and Child* demonstrates, Picasso systematically subjected the most traditional subjects in Western art to stylistic distortions based on precedents from Africa. Even his so-called *Femme* 107 *accroupie (Seated Woman)*, an africanized female figure covered with striation marks and looking at her foot, is a clear reference to the famous Hellenistic statue of a boy with a thorn in his foot, 108 the *Spinario*. Art historian Irving Lavin has noted that Picasso had the theoretical investigations of Albrecht Dürer in mind when he created 'at the birth of Cubism' a new, measured canon based on 109 'primitive' sculpture. Studying Dürer's Dresden sketchbook, first 110 published in 1905, Picasso observed in spring 1907 'the German artist's effort to reconcile the sometimes crass realism of his native tradition to the norms of antiquity'. Picasso's interest in Dürer's surprising conflation of northern naturalism and the art of antiquity may have inspired an appropriation of the art of 'ideal proportion' for his own anti-academic ends.

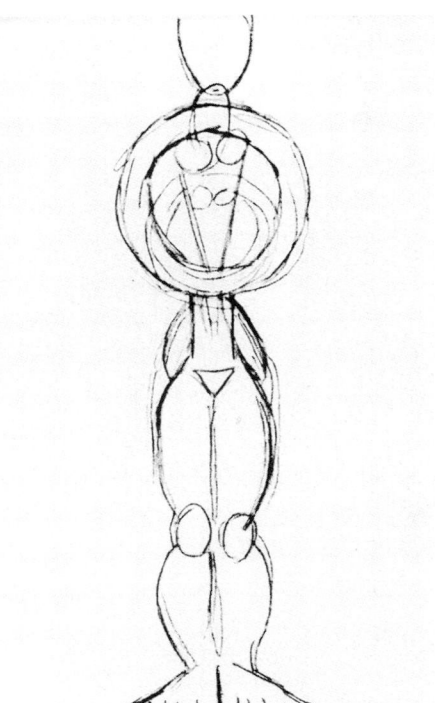
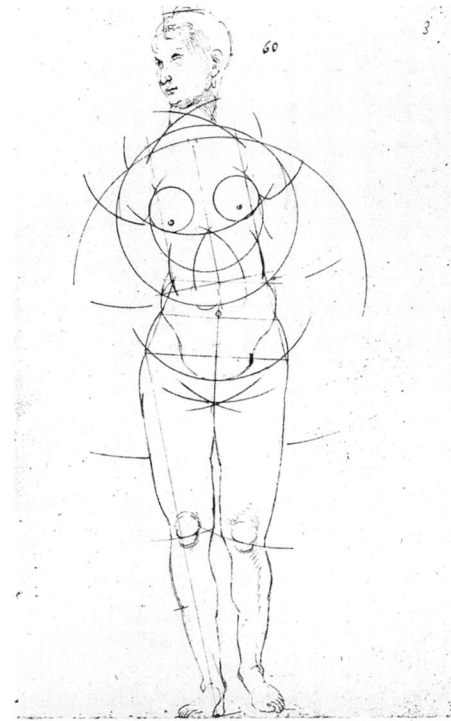

The *Demoiselles*, his manifesto of antitraditionalism, enacted an equally startling conflation of European and African art when he drew on the visionary figural distortions and garish hues found in El Greco's *Apocalyptic Vision* (1608–14), owned at this time by an acquaintance from Spain, the artist Ignacio Zuloaga who lived on the nearby rue Caulaincourt. The blue cloth of the background, crudely edged with white, is strikingly reminiscent of El Greco's treatment of his main figure, possibly echoing the 'Spanishness' or outsiderhood of Picasso's relation to French culture and ironically, even blasphemously, evoking the ecstatic religiosity of the Spanish master. Such meditations on and borrowings from ancient and Renaissance art serve the transformation of past canons into modernist transgressions. Unlike the Salon Cubists, whose references to tradition were safely contained within the geo-political borders of Europe, Picasso's conflation of black Africa and European culture precipitated a profound break from those cultural norms, fully in keeping with the radical approach to innovation promoted within the anarchist movement and a source of continuing influence on Picasso's later collage.

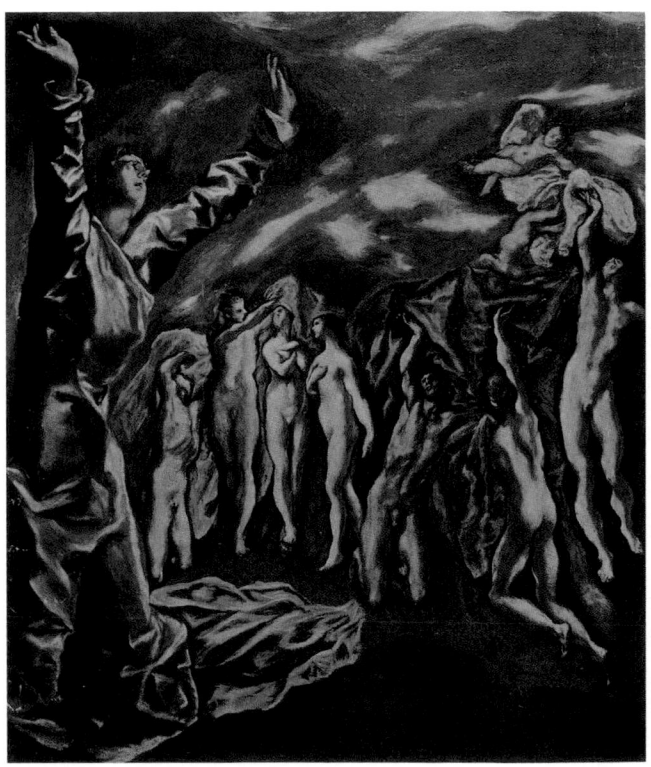

III. **El Greco**,
Apocalyptic Vision, 1608–14.

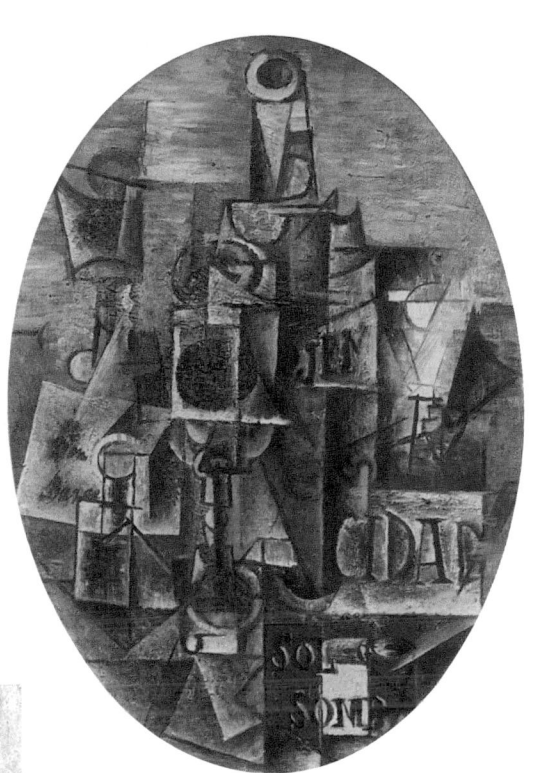

112. **Pablo Picasso**,
Spanish Still Life, spring 1912.

113. **Juan Gris**,
Bottle of Anis del Mono, 1914.
Picasso and Gris frequently wove Spanish
themes into their works, highlighting their
hybrid place in French culture. In *Spanish Still
Life* Picasso includes a ticket to a bullfight
in the unmistakable red and yellow of the
Spanish flag, along with other tokens of a visit
to Barcelona (a letter to Picasso's father, the
masthead of *La Publicidad*). Gris likewise
incorporates a flamboyantly Spanish object
into his *papier collé*: the full label from a bottle
of Anis del Mono with its trademark monkey,
mounted in the centre of a painted field of
diamonds that both evokes the distinctive
pattern of the glass and cleverly establishes
the Cubist rhythms of the work's broken
forms and perspectives. Picasso also included
recognizable images of a bottle of Anis del
Mono in paintings of 1909 (*Still Life with
Liqueur Bottle*) and 1915 (*Bottle of Anis del
Mono, Wineglass, and Playing Card*).

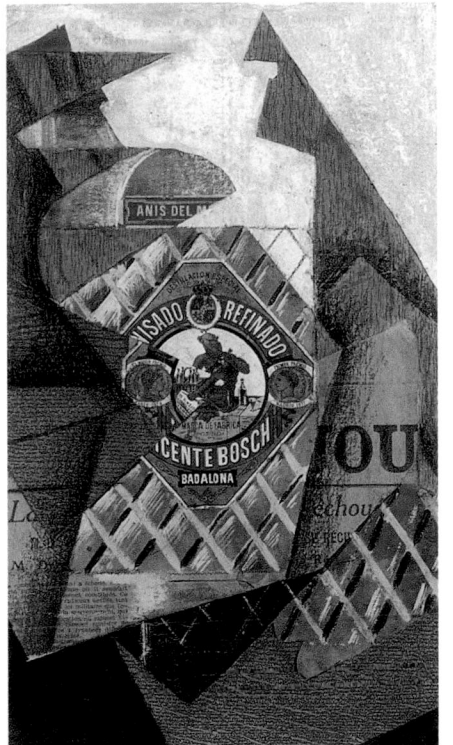

Chapter 4 Gender Codes

The differential relation of the 'masculine' to the 'feminine' within aesthetic discourses of modernism, including that of the Cubist movement, served to support unequal relations between the sexes in the realm of culture. 'Masculine' high art was pitted against 'feminized' mass culture; the male artist's 'sensibility' was deemed superior to the female artist's; and male poets and painters met with more support in the development of their professional careers than their female counterparts. Within Cubism these oppositional dichotomies were frequently endorsed and sometimes challenged. In examining the movement we will pay particular attention to the male Cubists' denigration of the 'decorative arts' in favour of the 'fine arts'; the gendered assumptions informing Cubist representations of men and women; and the role gender played in the careers of related male and female artists associated with the Cubist movement.

The decorative
We can begin by examining the Cubists' gendered valorization of 'fine art' as opposed to 'decoration', and its impact on exhibition practices. Art historian Nancy Troy has considered the conflation

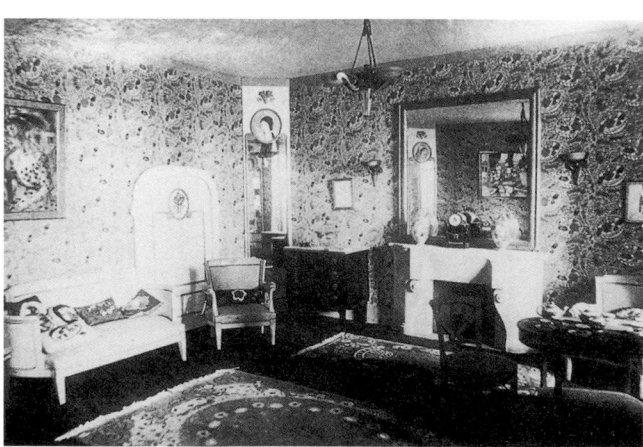

114. **André Mare et al.,**
Salon bourgeois, Maison Cubiste,
Salon d'Automne, 1912.

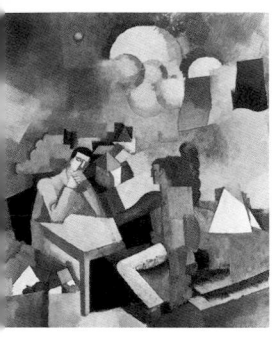

115. **Roger de La Fresnaye**, *Conquest of the Air*, 1913. La Fresnaye coupled his interest in the decorative arts with paintings in a Cubist idiom celebrating French nationalism and exhibited with the Puteaux group at the Salons. The prominent French tricolour flag on the upper right signals the patriotic theme of this work, which eulogizes French aviation. By painting this work in a Cubist style – geometrizing the forms and using Cézannesque *passage* to unite them – La Fresnaye suggests a link between modernist style and industrial progress. As Kenneth Silver has written, 'Where Picasso's iconoclasm visually undermined such obviously bourgeois ideologies as nationalism, from the very start La Fresnaye had managed to separate Cubism's pictorial subversions from its thematic and ideological ones'.

of the decorative with the domestic in Cubist discourse and the concomitant condemnation of the decorative as part and parcel of a wider consumer culture divorced from the 'spiritual' values the Cubists associated with their own painting. Gleizes and Metzinger explicitly reject, in *Du Cubisme* (1912), the decorative integration of an easel painting with its surrounding environment; instead they claimed each painting was an independent 'organism' with 'its own raison d'être'. An artist's decorative integration of a painting with an interior could therefore be seen as a sign of artistic 'impotence', suggestive of a passive and feminized domestic space antithetical to the Cubists' own 'virile' aesthetic and active masculine sphere. This serves to confirm literary historian Andreas Huyssen's argument that the modernist celebration of the aesthetic 'autonomy' of painting was part of a gendered discourse pitting masculine 'high art' against the feminized realm of 'mass', consumer culture.

Consumerism and high art, however, collided head-on when the Salon Cubists collaborated with decorative designer André Mare in creating the Maison Cubiste at the Salon d'Automne in 1912. Behind a plaster building façade designed by Duchamp-Villon were three rooms, including a principal parlour known as the *salon bourgeois*. While Mare was responsible for designing the furniture, a host of female and male modernists collaborated on other objects in the *salon*. The Cubist painter Roger de La Fresnaye designed the woodwork, fireplace and chandelier with highly simplified forms, while Jean-Louis Gampert designed the wallpaper, Sabine Desvallières the firescreen, Jacques Villon the tea service, and Maurice Marinot the enamelled glassware, all with less radical features of modernism. Marie-Thérèse Lanoa was responsible for the rugs, and Marie Laurencin executed the oval paintings of primitivized women's heads inserted above mirrors in the four corners of the room. Although both men and women created the decorative elements integral to the interior, it was men alone who contributed the paintings that hung on the walls. Among them were Cubist works by Duchamp, Gleizes, Léger, Metzinger and La Fresnaye as well as sculptures by Duchamp-Villon. In effect the inclusion of these paintings and sculptures in Mare's decorative, domestic interior confused the very gendered divisions Gleizes and Metzinger claimed to enforce. As Troy notes, 'the independent organism was embedded in a simulated bourgeois environment designed, like the department store display, to arouse desire on the part of the consuming audience so the masculine force of the *tableau de chevalet* [easel painting] was overwhelmed by the feminizing associations of decoration and the decorative arts'.

114
100

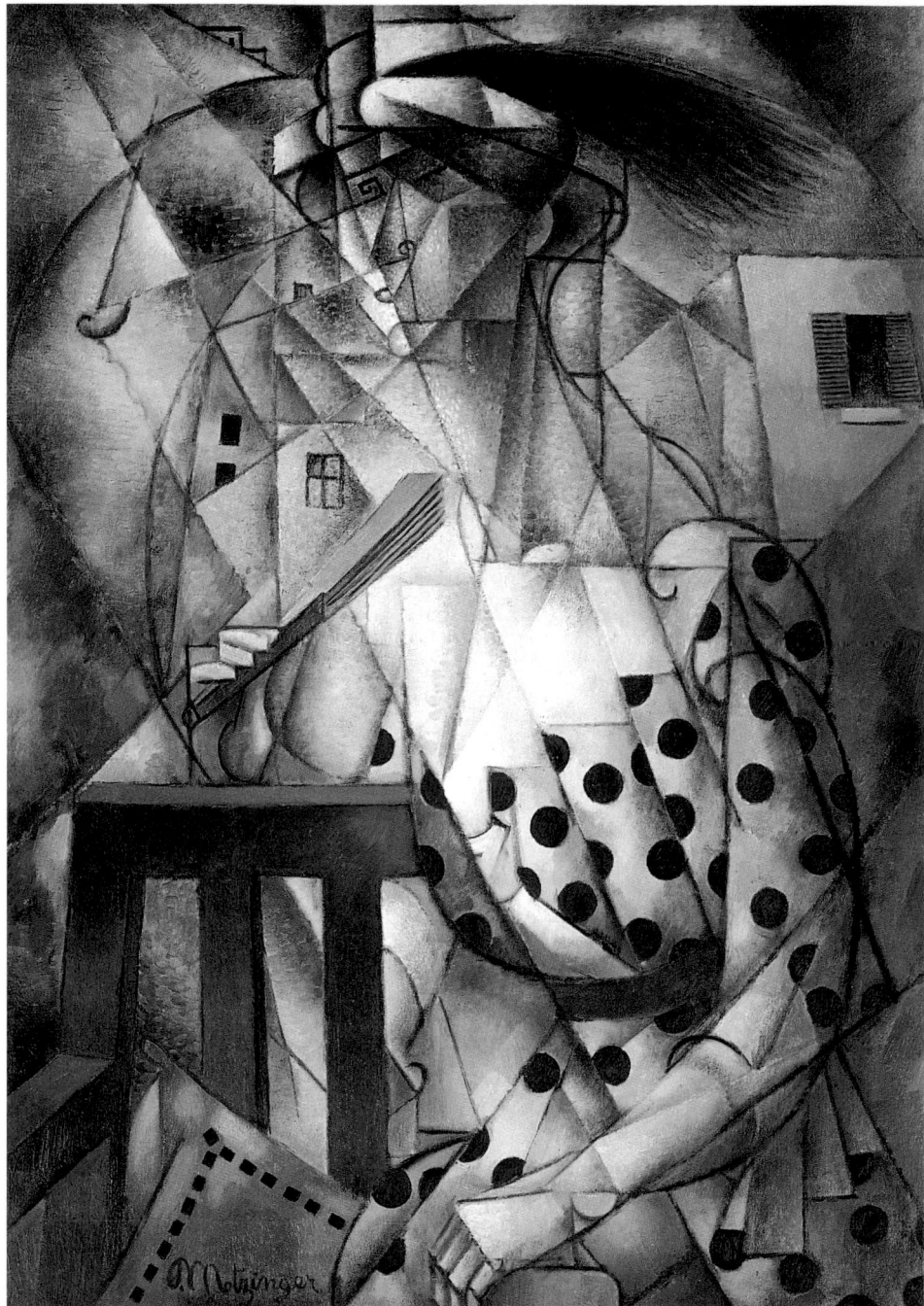

On the other hand, examination of Metzinger's contribution to the Maison Cubiste – his *Woman with Fan* (1912) – indicates that the 116 gendered condemnation of the decorative in *Du Cubisme* may reflect Gleizes's biases more than Metzinger's. The decorative in Metzinger's painting takes the form of an elegantly dressed woman seated on a park bench, with a highly fashionable hat and fan. Metzinger's work recalls Edouard Manet's equally fashion-conscious portrait of Madame and Monsieur Guillemet, known as *In the Conservatory* (1879). Art historian Robert Herbert has analysed 117 Manet's use of decorative properties associated with painting – for instance, an emphasis on the flat planarity of the canvas – which allude to the sitters' own status in the world of fashion as proprietors of an upscale clothing store in the *haute bourgeois* district of Paris. Having positioned the Guillemets amidst the highly artificial arrangement of exotic plants in a conservatory, Manet creates a decorative effect by setting his figures in a shallow illusionistic space defined by a background 'screen' of foliage. Madame Guillemet's pleated dress fans out as if to augment the regulated planarity created by the slats and rods of the bench, thematically linking fashion, decoration, and femininity. Metzinger achieves similar results by superimposing a rhythmic pattern of diagonal lines on the dress and physiognomy of the woman, combining slightly shifting viewpoints that extend to conjoin the sitter with the houses of her urban environment. The dots on the dress shift subtly from purple to black and create an alternative decorative pattern that affirms the painting's surface. These Cubist treatments of form and space contrast strikingly with the straightforwardly rendered green bench

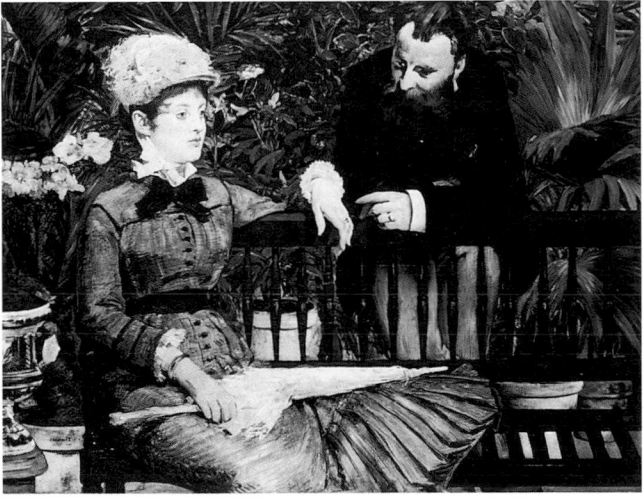

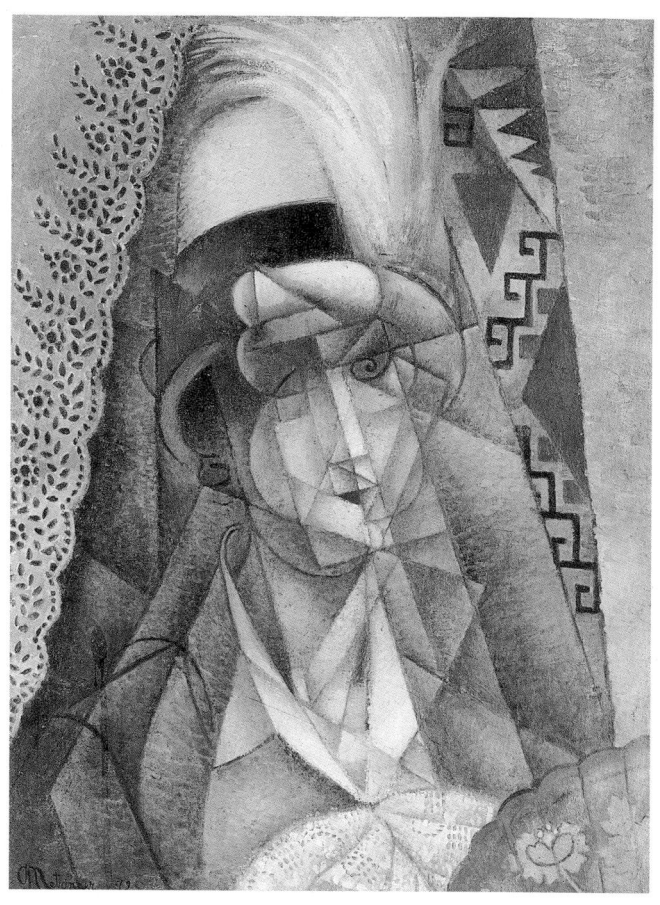

and fan, which operate somewhat like Braque's nail in *Violin and Palette*. Metzinger's preoccupation with the decorative led him to paint several Cubist images of fashionably dressed women such as *Woman with Hat* (1912–13) and *The Yellow Feather* (1912), complete with such feminine decorative accoutrements as lipstick, lace, dyed feathers, decorative fans and primitivist fabrics. Metzinger continued to develop the style of decorative Cubism that became his hallmark over the decade that followed, thus his inclusion of *Woman with Fan* in the *salon bourgeois* may well indicate his dissent from the theoretical strictures laid out in *Du Cubisme* that same year and his valorization of his sitter's own exercise of decorative taste.

The contradiction between gendered theory and praxis signalled by the Maison Cubiste was only exacerbated in 1913 when Gleizes, Metzinger, Léger and other Salon Cubists agreed to show their work in a travelling exhibition organized by department stores in the United States. Sponsored by the Gimbel Brothers chain headquartered in Milwaukee, Wisconsin, the exhibition travelled to stores in Cleveland, Pittsburgh, New York and Philadelphia during the summer of 1913. Here works including Metzinger's *Portrait of an American Smoking* (c. 1912) and Gleizes's *Women Sewing* (1913) were displayed in the very emporia condemned by writer Emile Zola and other modernists for creating a culture of mass consumption, attuned to the 'female' desire for fashionable goods. Metzinger's American, with his short haircut, tattersall jacket, pipe, and fashionable beer appears as the consummate consumer himself; a comfortably North American version of bourgeois, he is combined through the use of multiple views and passage with his possessions: a conventional painting of a sailboat, the miniature portrait of an ancestor, and a large 'art' vase of the sort included in the Maison Cubiste. Gleizes's work, alternatively, depicts three women sewing in a garden or courtyard under a tree, a village or city visible through an archway. The very means by which Gleizes denies spatial recession combines the figures of the working women – in their simple country hats and dresses – with the town beyond, suggesting both their communal labour and the relation of their work to its commercial destination.

119. **Jean Metzinger,** *Portrait of an American Smoking,* 1912.

120. **Albert Gleizes,** *Women Sewing,* 1913.

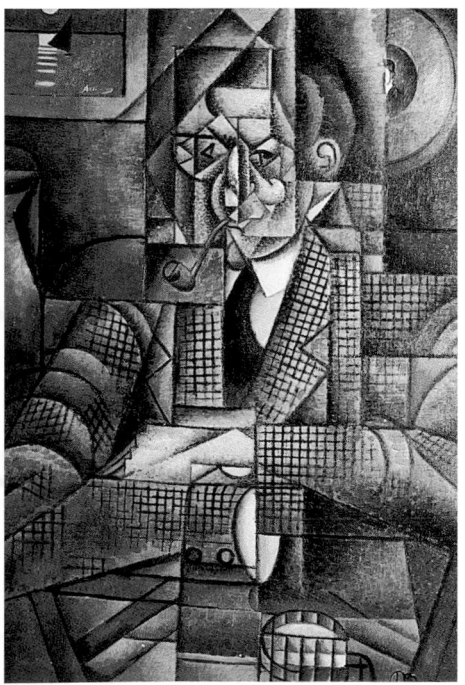
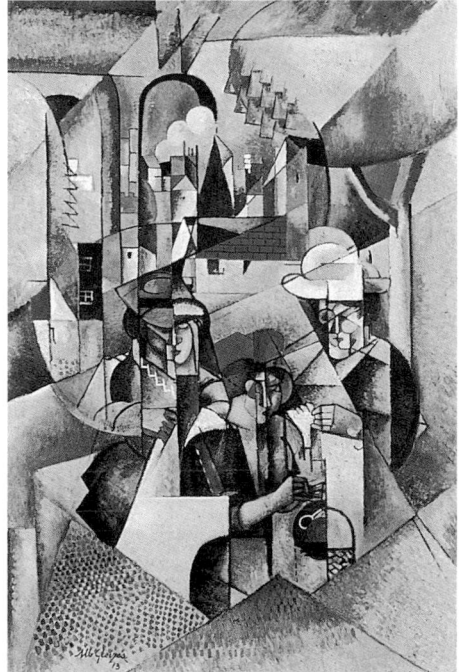

Exhibition practices such as these were pointedly rejected by the art dealer Kahnweiler, whose contractual arrangements with Braque, Picasso and Gris prevented them from exhibiting alongside the Salon Cubists in Paris after 1912. Instead Kahnweiler exhibited their work in the 'masculine space' of his gallery. An austere environment, Kahnweiler's exhibition space was devoid of the ornate furnishing found in most galleries, and the plain sackcloth that served as a backdrop to the art was meant to signal the dealer's disdain for decorative accoutrement, preferring the 'cerebral' to the material value of the art on display. Visitors complained that there were not even places to sit. Kahnweiler may not have been able to banish 'decoration' entirely, however, as Braque introduced into his art (to be quickly copied by Picasso and Gris) techniques he had learned as a house-decorator's son. Artificial woodgrain, or faux-bois, can be made with special 'combs' drawn through the paint, as in Braque's *Fruit Dish, Ace of Clubs* (early 1913), or skilfully painted freehand (as with artificial marble), a technique Braque first included in a still life with a violin on a table, entitled *Homage to J.S. Bach* (winter 1911–12). Picasso responded with his *Still Life (Memory of Le Havre)* of May 1912. These artisanal tricks began the introduction of myriad techniques that all tend to affirm the flatness of the picture plane: letters, numbers, planes of flat colour and, eventually, commercial papers, including decorative wallpaper, simply glued on. These techniques and materials operate simultaneously to introduce the decorative as a theme both into the Cubism of Braque, Picasso and Gris and into Kahnweiler's 'masculine space'. But unlike Metzinger, invoking specifically femininized notions of decoration-as-taste, Braque appropriates the masculinized arena of the modern-day artisan, a male profession not indicative of female decorative sensibility.

121. **Pablo Picasso**, *Still Life: Au Bon Marché*, spring 1913. Picasso adapted the decorative aesthetic of collage to gendered ends in this parody of the female's dual role as a consumer and as 'goods for sale'. A pasted box lid from the lingerie department of the store Au Bon Marché combines with decorative wallpaper, a glass on the right, a decanter on the left, and a newspaper clipping above to evoke a fashionable woman's boudoir. Using an ad with a conventional illustration of just such a consumer, Picasso cuts the newsprint so as to isolate the woman, with her modern haircut and gesture of vanity. A number of elements cut off from their context in the newspaper then combine to suggest her availability: the price '2.85', and the words above announcing 'METHODS OF PAYMENT' and 'MASSAGE'.

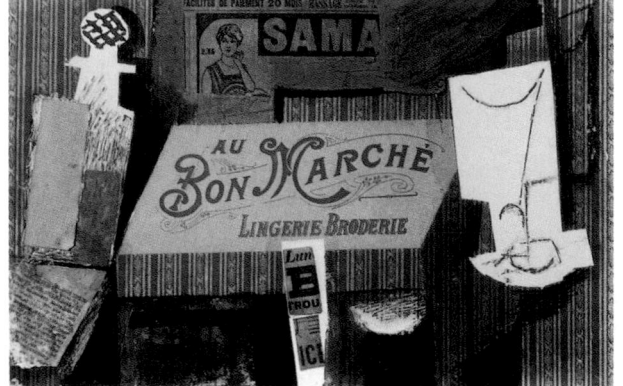

Creativity

The movement's developing views on gender also implicate Cubist theories of creativity. The gendered assumptions culturally inherited by these artists, and reinforced by their readings of Nietzsche and Bergson, disposed them to associate female reproductive processes with Bergson's concept of the *élan vital*, thus defining feminine creative capacities as synonymous with those found in nature. This narrow correlation denied women the power to realize their creative potential in spheres of cultural production such as art. As anthropologist Sherry Ortner has shown, the identification in patriarchal societies of biological reproduction as a woman's primary creative capacity has stood in stark contrast to the type of creativity attributed to the male, who 'lacking natural creative functions, must assert his creativity externally', that is, through cultural means. In this schema, social functions like child-rearing are declared 'natural' to women by virtue of an identification of such care 'as an extension of her natural nursing bond with children'. This tendency to restrict a woman's activities to those deemed 'natural' to her in effect subsumes women within the realm of the 'instinctual', the 'animal' or 'primitive' and privileges the male gender as uniquely capable of transcending such natural functions to create cultural artifacts. Bergsonian Cubists like Gleizes, Metzinger or Le Fauconnier, however, wanted to interrelate cultural production and productive forces in nature. In keeping with Ortner's paradigm they identified women as the product of natural forces, by declaring female fecundity an example of the *élan vital*'s productivity. But whereas women were the product of this *élan*, men, by virtue of their intuitive powers, were both its product *and* its producer. The male Cubists not only associated their own artistic capacities with the conversion of *élan vital* into forms of cultural production, but extended this attribution to other male activities like boxing or rugby, subjects frequently portrayed in their paintings. That such activities were associated with the national 'regeneration' of French male *volonté*, or 'will', in writings of the period is further evidence of the gendered import of such imagery.

In this thinking these Cubists expanded upon the female-as-nature/male-as-culture dichotomy prevalent among Symbolists of the previous generation. The Symbolists, including Gauguin and the critic Albert Aurier, related male creativity to a desired state of mental instability, even while they declared women biologically bereft of this creative capacity. The supposed inability of women to focus such a mental state into channels of creativity was said to result in 'hysteria', a term whose etymological root in the Greek word for womb, *hysteron*, makes plain its gendered origin. In the subsequent period leading to World War I, however, nationalist writers like Henri Massis and Ernest Psichari attributed a declining French birthrate to the neurasthenic dandyism of the previous generation and raised worries about a lack of military preparedness. These writers and many Cubist artists turned to Bergson's vitalist doctrine of *élan vital* and looked for evidence of its resurgence in a youthful generation who had rejected the 'lethargy' of the older Symbolists.

In the art of Cubism's male practitioners, the *élan vital* is identified with iconic images of the female nude, symbolic of the biological fecundity permeating the natural world. The most famous Cubist example of such imagery is Le Fauconnier's *Abundance*, exhibited in the 1911 Salon des Indépendants. The preceding year Arcos, Gleizes, Mercereau and others had followed the painting's development during weekly meetings in Le Fauconnier's studio, and the theme of fecundity symbolized by the monumental nude had a counterpart in the poetry written by Mercereau and Arcos. In Le Fauconnier's image, the nude female not only gathers nature's fruit, she is accompanied by a child, the organic product of her own fecundity (the abdomen of Le Fauconnier's allegorical female is placed at the centre of the picture to highlight this theme). Rooted in the land, both child and mother are painted in earth colours and the angular treatment of their anatomy echoes that of the panoramic landscape. The themes of regeneration and fruitfulness in the painting echo Mercereau's Bergsonian ode to female fecundity in his *Paroles devant la vie* (1911), as both men embraced Bergson's association of organic regeneration and evolution with duration.

When the Cubists developed a male counterpart to images like *Abundance* they invariably represented a cultural activity, usually competitive sports. Indeed, in 1912 Bergson himself described the revived interest in sport among the French as evidence of the *volonté créatrice* (creative will) animating the younger generation. Bergson's correlation between male *volonté*, sport, and the creative capacities of French youth was taken up in Agathon's *Les jeunes gens d'aujourd'hui* (*The Young People of Today*) (1913), a highly popular book that employed Bergson's terminology in a promotion of French nationalism. Citing Bergson, Agathon associated the youth's 'life energy' with their 'anti-intellectual' attitude and love of sport. 'Sport', we are told, has created a 'patriotic optimism among young men'; moreover 'collective sports like football' produce a 'spirit of solidarity' reflective of 'military virtues'. As historian John Bowditch has shown, Agathon's description of this Bergsonian *esprit de corps*

122. **Jean Metzinger**,
The Cyclist, 1913.
Metzinger celebrated the salutory effects of exercise on the male population in his *Cyclist*, which focused on a sport that historian Eugen Weber has described as a French creation, and one affordable to the French working class by 1900. Metzinger underscored its patriotic origins by flanking the cyclist with a poster advertising the Paris-Rouen Race, a reference to the first long-distance race inaugurated by the French in 1869. The transparent planes of the cyclist's face suggest the simultaneity of his action with that of the crowd, while the flag of the Republic flies on the upper right.

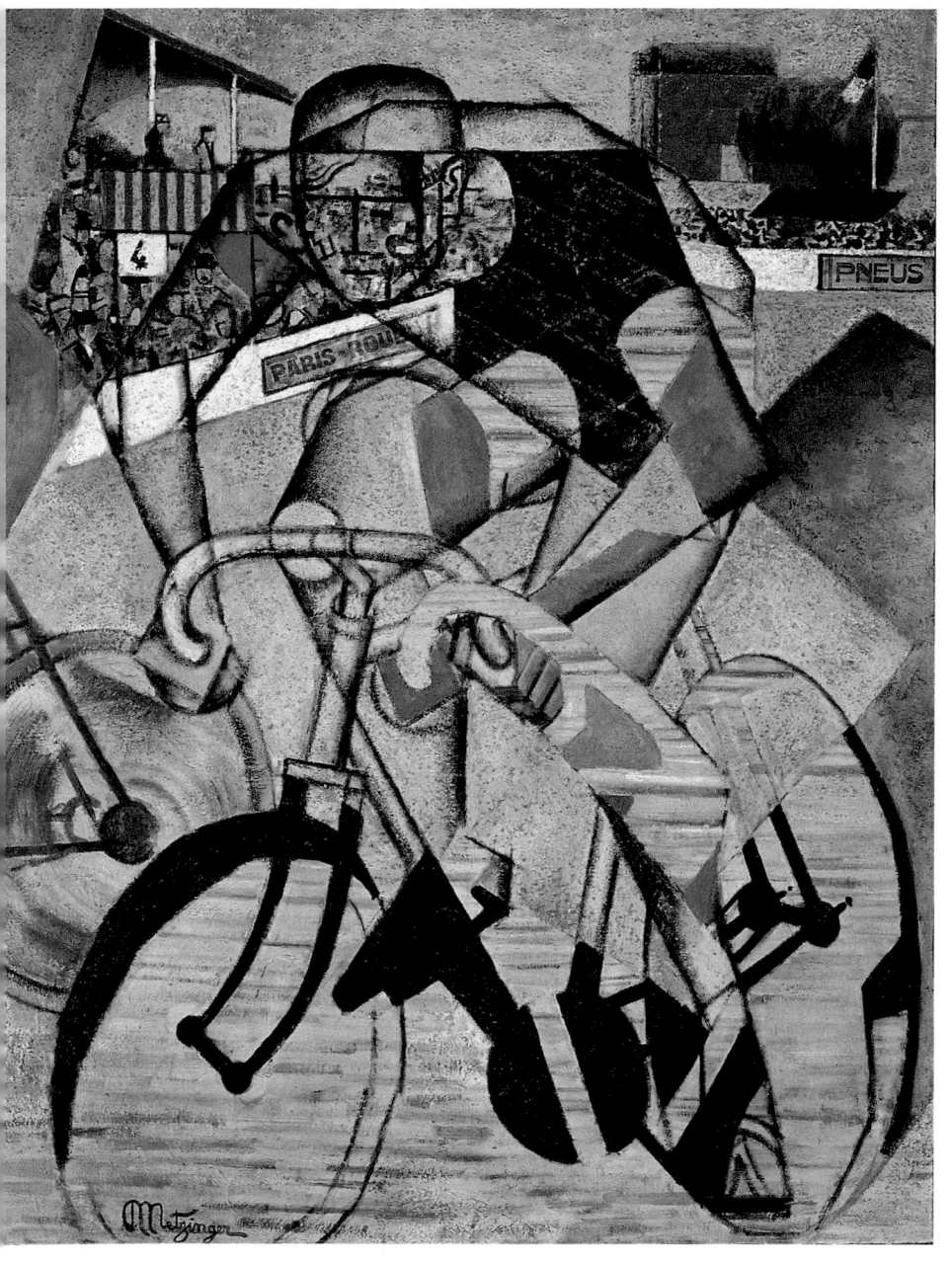

echoed contemporary military rhetoric, which eulogized the 'qualitative' *élan vital* of the French soldier as a psychological weapon able to compensate for any shortage in numbers when compared to the Germans, a delusion that tragically failed to be borne out in the war itself.

Art historian David Cottington has considered Agathon's nationalistic promotion of sport as the inspiration behind Gleizes's *Football Players* (1912–13), a painting Apollinaire described as 'vigorous', with *élan* as its subject matter. (The precedent of Henri Rousseau may also participate in this discourse; his *Football Players* of 1908 likewise depicts the game of rugby – just beginning to be popular in France – and was painted the first year that the France–England match was held in Paris.) In Gleizes's painting, volumetric forms and large diagonal planes jut forward, augmenting the dynamic rush of the rugby players towards the viewer, in stylistic unity with the urban setting of iron bridges and industrial smoke. In 1913 Delaunay painted his own ode to rugby in his *Cardiff Team*, a composite image juxtaposing the players with such modern icons as a Ferris wheel, billboard advertisements, an airplane, and the Eiffel Tower. Such homages to contemporary male virility had a sculptural counterpart in works like Archipenko's *Boxing (Boxers,*

123. **Albert Gleizes**,
The Football Players, 1912–13.

124. **Robert Delaunay**,
Cardiff Team, 1913.

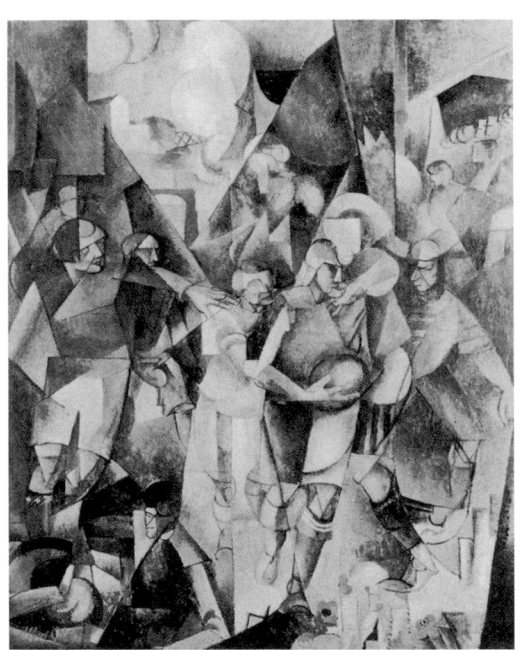

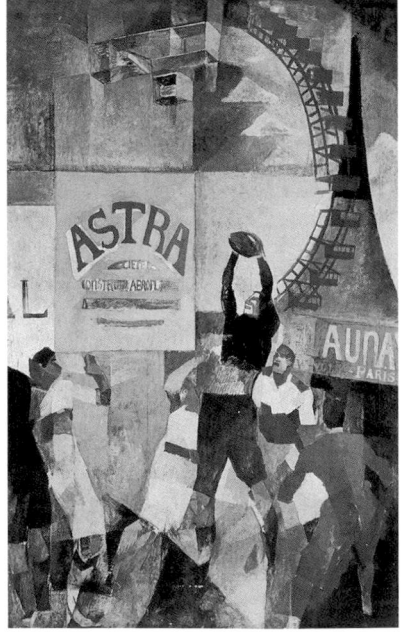

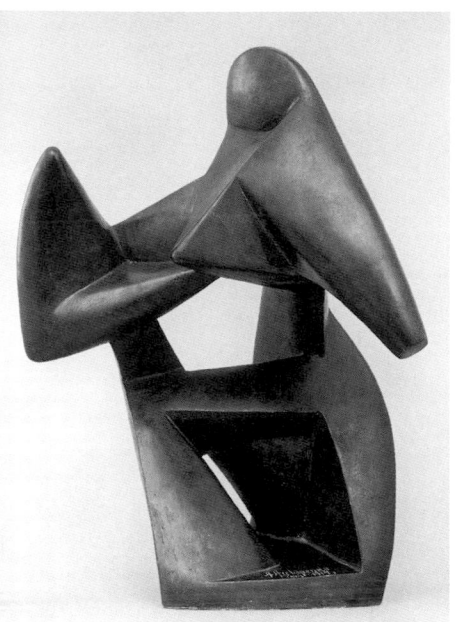

125. **Alexander Archipenko**,
Boxing (Boxers, Struggle), 1914.

126. **Alexander Archipenko**, *Repose*, 1912.

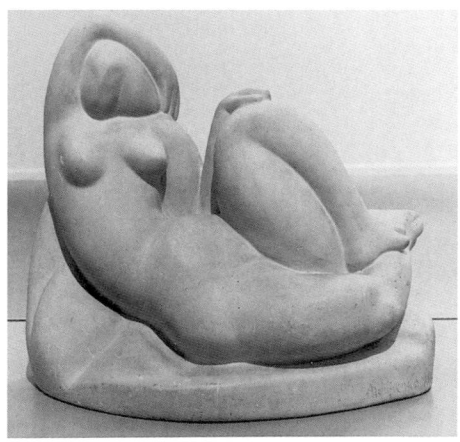

Struggle) (1914). Using plaster painted black, jutting forms abstractly [125] convey the thrusts and energy of powerful boxers. Archipenko's image of 'cultural warfare' differed dramatically from his contemporaneous representations of female nudes, such as *Repose* (1912) or [126] *Woman Combing Her Hair* (1915). In contrast to the male dynamism [83] signified by the hard-edged angularity and black coloration of *Boxing* (possibly signifying the ethnicity of the boxers themselves), Archipenko's pink-tinted *Repose* casts the woman in the passive role of a languid bather, her abstract rounded forms suggesting both her fecundity and her connection with the similar forms of the earth on which she rests. The blue patina and curvaceous hips of *Woman Combing Her Hair* evoke her status as a modern Venus, newly emerged from the aquamarine of the Mediterranean.

The full import of Gleizes's or Archipenko's images of sport, however, only emerges when these odes to male power are considered in relation to their female Bergsonian counterparts, such as Le Fauconnier's *Abundance*. That male *élan* signified a cultural activity [93] like sport, with its metaphorical relation to armed combat, is the counterpart to a discourse that would restrict the feminine *élan* to biological reproduction. And as Ortner states, this formulation speaks:

> to the great puzzle of why male activities involving the destruction
> of life (hunting and warfare) are often given more prestige than the
> female's ability to give birth, to create life ... we realize it is not the
> killing that is the relevant and valued aspect of hunting and warfare;
> rather it is the transcendental (social, cultural) nature of these
> activities, as opposed to the naturalness of the process of birth.

The precepts linking Le Fauconnier's *Abundance* to Gleizes's *Football Players* thus served to define unequal relations between genders. Bergsonism, in its Cubist manifestations, constitutes yet another example of the subordination of women in the realm of cultural production.

Careers

Gender shaped not only Cubist imagery, but the development of artistic careers, including creative partnerships between male and female artists. Relationships between male and female Cubists were fraught with tension and frequently resulted in the subordination of the female partner's career in the service of the other. To better understand the conditions under which these women laboured as artists, we need to recognize how gendered stereotypes informed the partnerships of female Cubists like Sonia Terk Delaunay and Alice Halicka with their male counterparts, Robert Delaunay and Louis Marcoussis.

Sonia Terk arrived in Paris from her native Russia in 1905; shortly after her arrival she studied art at the Académie de la Palette, alongside Dunoyer de Segonzac and Amédée Ozenfant. By 1907 she had developed a unique synthesis of Fauvism, Expressionism and Russian folk art, and an exhibition of these paintings at Wilhelm Uhde's gallery in 1908 consolidated her reputation among the avant-garde. That same year she met Robert Delaunay, and following their marriage in 1910 they embarked on an artistic collaboration that extended over thirty years. Upon entering this relationship Terk temporarily abandoned painting in favour of embroidery as a creative outlet, and her subsequent application of her Cubist aesthetic to the decorative arts and clothing design as well as easel painting led critics to judge her oeuvre of secondary importance when compared to the purely 'high art' production of Robert Delaunay. The very commercial success Terk achieved in adapting her Cubist designs to the world of fashion was deemed a sign of her failure as an artist. In fact her decision to take up embroidery was encouraged by her husband who unwittingly reaffirmed the gendered tradition in which men produce art, while women

127. **Robert Delaunay**,
Simultaneous Windows, 1912.

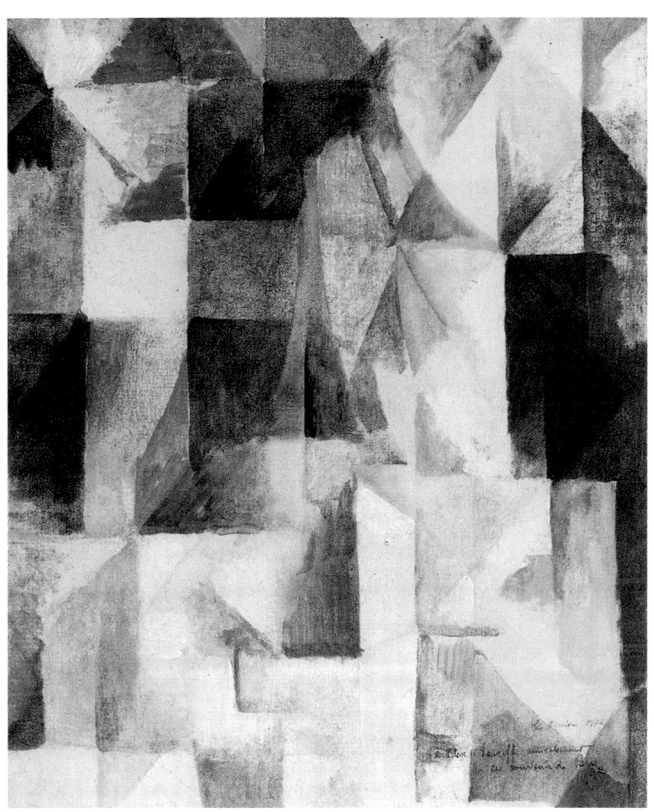

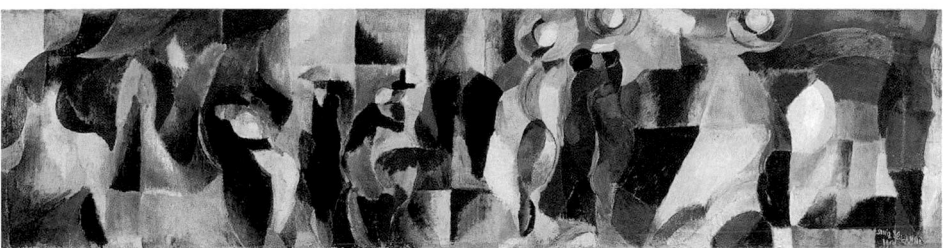

128. **Sonia Terk Delaunay**,
Le Bal Bullier, 1913.

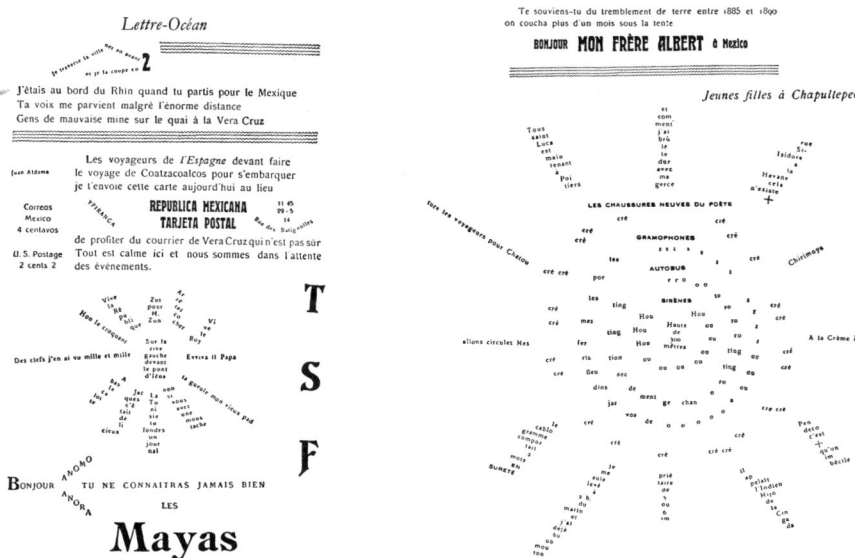

129. Guillaume Apollinaire, 'Lettre-Océan', *Les Soirées de Paris*, June 1914.

---

129. Guillaume Apollinaire, 'Lettre-Océan', *Les Soirées de Paris*, June 1914. This ideogram, or 'calligram', evokes on the left the Eiffel Tower – both in form (the placement of the words suggests a view of the tower from above) and in function as a telegraph tower – and on the right the Grande Roue, a huge Ferris wheel built for the Universal Exposition of 1900. Apollinaire uses free verse and the visual imagery of word placement to parallel what he celebrated in Delaunay's work as 'Orphism' or 'Simultanism'. Comparing the extreme combination of abstract form and brilliant colour in Delaunay and the Czech painter František Kupka with the abstraction of Wassily Kandinsky in Germany and Piet Mondrian in the Netherlands, Apollinaire introduced a crucial new concept in *The Cubist Painters* that goes well beyond the aims of Cubism itself: 'The works of the Orphic artists must simultaneously present pure aesthetic pleasure, a self-evident construction, and a sublime significance.... This is pure art.'

decorate the domestic environment. Although the reasons for Terk's decision to take up satin-stitch embroidery remain obscure, it may well be that burgeoning competition with Delaunay, exacerbated by the critical success of Terk's exhibition at Uhde's gallery, may have led her to take a different but parallel path towards abstraction.

Comparing the artist's embroidered quilt of 1911 to Delaunay's *Window* series of the same period, art historian Whitney Chadwick has noted that both artists utilized the term *métier* or craft to describe their interest in their aesthetic medium, but that Terk's work suffered from critical neglect due to her association of such terminology with the 'feminized' field of the decorative arts. In Delaunay's painting the frame operates as a window onto an outside world dominated by the central image of the green-coloured Eiffel Tower, interpenetrated with a spectral range of colour contrasts suggestive of the dynamism of the modern city. Delaunay utilized the window motif as a symbolic bridge between the private interior and public exterior space, and the Eiffel Tower proclaimed the relation of his abstraction to that public icon of modernity.

Terk's quilt by contrast broke down hierarchical relations that would separate the aesthetic concerns associated with oil painting from those of the 'domestic sphere' and reaffirmed her earlier

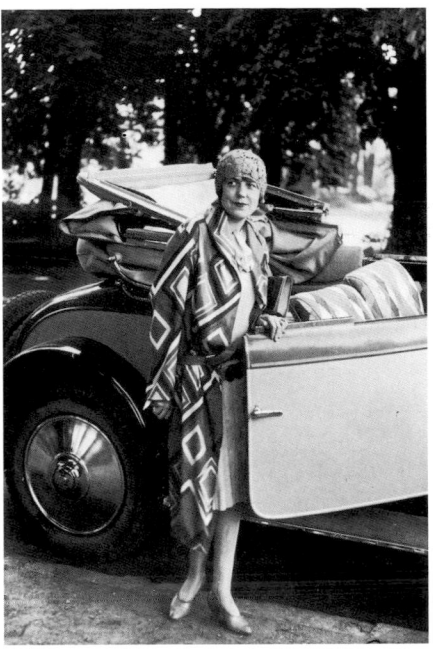

130. Dress by Sonia Terk Delaunay, modelled against an automobile, 1926.

primitivizing interest in Russian 'folk' culture. By crossing that symbolic divide, Terk's work challenged received assumptions and transgressed the gendered categories endorsed by contemporaneous art criticism. For instance the quilt's geometric combination of high-keyed reds, yellows, greens, pinks and purples encoded both her memory of Russian peasant quilts and her exploration, along with Delaunay, of the developing vocabulary of Cubist painting. By 1913 her production encompassed both the 'high art' medium of oil on canvas – signalled by *Le Bal Bullier* of 1913 – as well as the *haute couture* of contemporary fashion, exemplified by her design of 1913 for a 'simultaneous dress'. The arabesque forms coursing through *Le Bal Bullier* were inspired by Terk's experience of the undulating rhythm of the tango danced at a Parisian night club, a primitivizing motif indicative of her continued interest in vernacular culture. Similarly her application of the colour contrasts found in her painting to women's fashion affirmed the contemporaneous celebration of the role female clothing played in adding an aesthetic dimension to the public 'spectacle' of the Parisian boulevard. In his *Aesthetic of the Street* of 1901 the Symbolist writer Gustave Kahn had already lauded the appearance of polychromy in women's clothing, and Terk's own designs serve to ally Cubist aesthetics to this feminized realm of popular culture.

128

Sonia Terk's strategic turn to the decorative arts as a creative outlet closely resembles the artistic trajectory chosen by Alice Halicka, though the latter did not achieve Terk's commercial success. Halicka arrived in Paris from Poland in 1912 and began her studies at the Académie Ranson, under the tutelage of the Symbolists Maurice Denis and Paul Sérusier. By the end of 1912 she had entered into a relationship with fellow Pole Louis Marcoussis, who introduced her to members of the Cubist movement, including Apollinaire, Braque, Gris, Jacob, Salmon, the critic Maurice Raynal and others. Like Marcoussis, Halicka began to experiment with Cubist still life, and works such as her *Cubist Still Life with Guitar* of 1916 – with its dark hues and technique of breaking objects with long horizontal and vertical lines – closely resemble still lifes by her partner. The majority of Halicka's Cubist output occurred during World War I, when Marcoussis had given up painting while serving in the army. Halicka's success may have precipitated rivalry with Marcoussis, who following his return home in 1919 discouraged his partner from signing a contract with the dealer Zborowski. Halicka

131. **Alice Halicka,**
Cubist Still Life with Guitar, 1916.

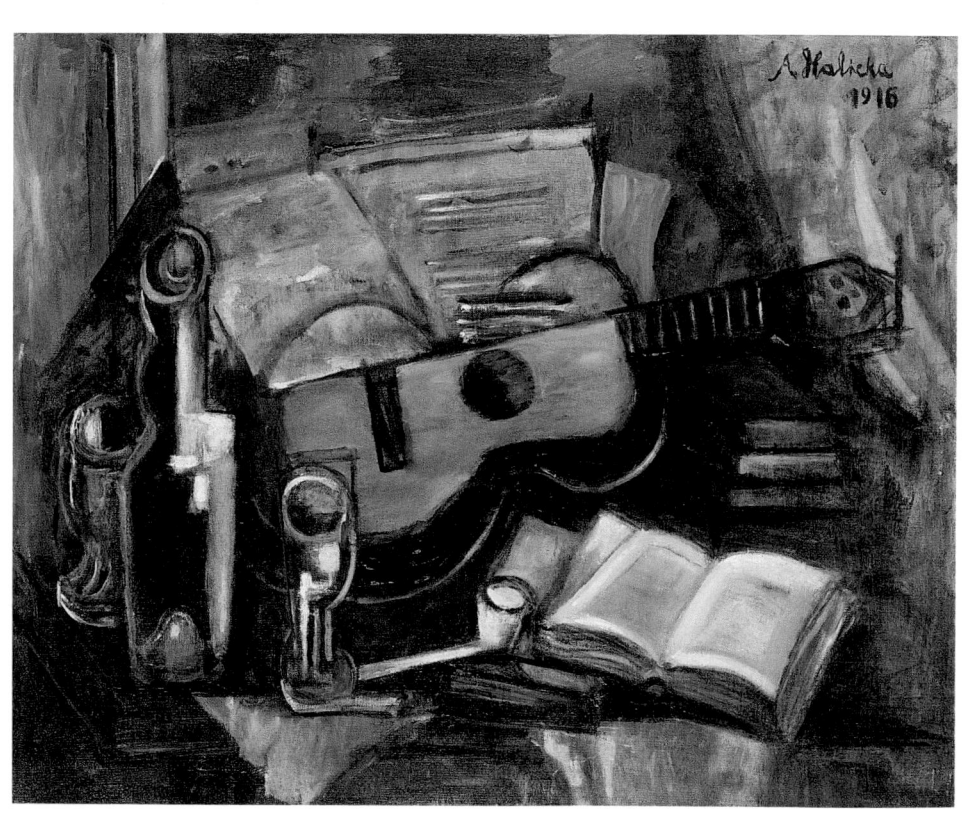

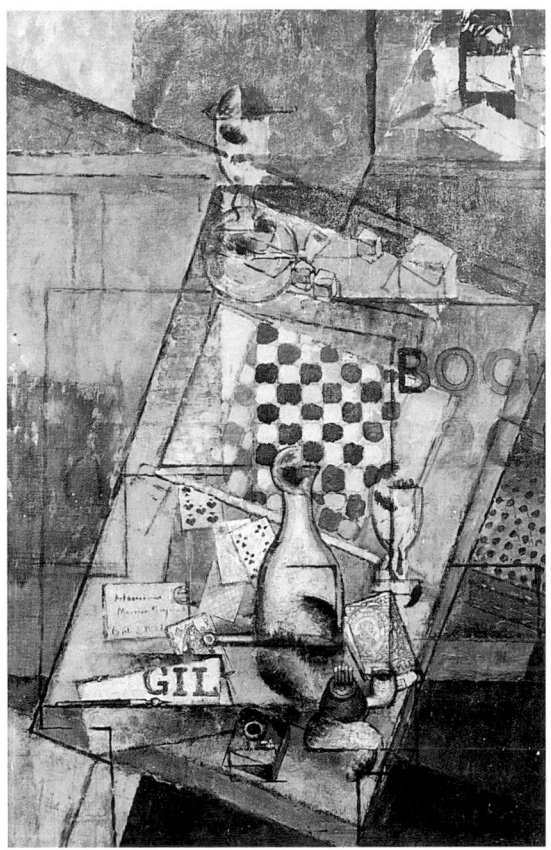

then abandoned her wartime Cubist style, first returning to more figurative styles, then developing a combination of needlework and collage she called *Romances capitonnées* ('Quilted Romances').

Reflecting on Halicka's Cubist phase in a 1927 book on modernist art, Raynal wrote the following: 'From Cubism she took not the aesthetics, but the discipline and practical methods. In effect her feminine sensibility prevented her from taking on the conception of pure creation, an art detached in its basic principles from all conscious intention'. As art historian Gill Perry observed, Raynal's concept of 'pure painting' bestowed a spiritual dimension on the Cubist pursuit of abstraction and aesthetic autonomy that no female artist was deemed capable of emulating. In effect female artists were caught in a double bind: if they successfully took up the Cubist idiom, they were condemned for betraying their 'female' sensibility, but if they applied Cubist techniques to the 'feminine' realm of the decorative arts, their art was considered of minor

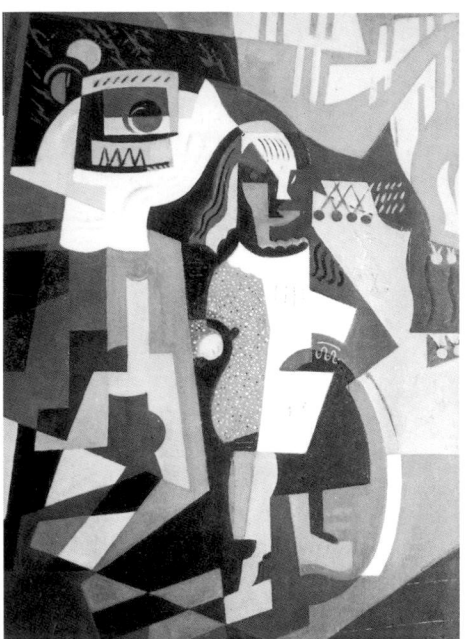
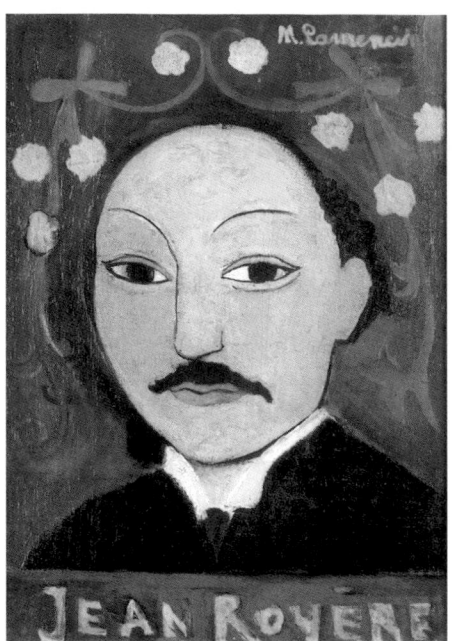

importance when compared to the oil-on-canvas production of their male colleagues. A turn to the decorative arts may have curtailed professional competition with a well-established partner, but it effectively undermined the status of women like Terk and Halicka within the male-dominated avant-garde.

Even female artists who worked exclusively in oil-on-canvas made compromises as to subject matter if not medium. One such figure is Maria Blanchard whose Cubist paintings were often devoted to domestic subjects, particularly the theme of childhood as in her *Child with a Hoop* (1915). While they were part of the repertoire long associated with successful female artists, including Berthe Morisot and Mary Cassatt, Perry is right to conclude that such subjects may have contributed to her marginalization in histories of Cubism. Critics like Raynal saw such 'sentimental' subjects as antithetical to the conceptual rigour of 'pure painting' despite Blanchard's obvious debt to the hard-edged abstraction of Raynal's favourite artist, Juan Gris, and despite the frequency of the subject of children through-out Picasso's pre- and post-Cubist work.

Raynal's reference to Halicka's 'feminine sensibility' serves to remind us of Apollinaire's claim that the art of Marie Laurencin was quintessentially feminine and thus qualitatively distinct from that of her male Cubist peers. Laurencin began her artistic career as a porcelain painter at the Ecole de Sèvres in 1902 before taking up painting as a student at the Académie Humbert, where she met Braque. In 1907 Braque introduced her at the Bateau Lavoir in Montmartre, but even before this date Laurencin had attended meetings of the Abbaye de Créteil. Laurencin began exhibiting at the Salon des Indépendants in 1907, and by the spring of 1910 Apollinaire designated her work Cubist, thus numbering her among the movement's progenitors.

Before this date, however, Laurencin was inspired by the self-taught 'naive' artist Henri Rousseau, as well as the primitivizing aesthetic of Henri Matisse. Laurencin signalled her allegiance to Matisse in her 1908 portrait of Jean Royère, a neo-Symbolist supporter of Fauvism who edited the journal *La Phalange* (1906–14). Laurencin's painting closely resembles Matisse's portrait of his daughter Marguerite of the previous year; indeed, both Matisse and Laurencin paint their subjects in matte colours, with the name of the sitter inscribed in naïve lettering on the canvas. Between 1908 and 1912 she became romantically involved with Apollinaire and proclaimed her allegiance both to him and to Picasso in her *Group of Artists* of 1908, which portrays Laurencin, Picasso's lover Fernande Olivier, Picasso, and his dog Fricka gathered around the seated Apollinaire. Although Laurencin was undoubtedly familiar with the africanized primitivism of Picasso's *Demoiselles d'Avignon,* the simplification in *Group of Artists* or her contemporaneous portrait of Royère owes more to Rousseau and the Fauvism of Matisse.

134

135

22

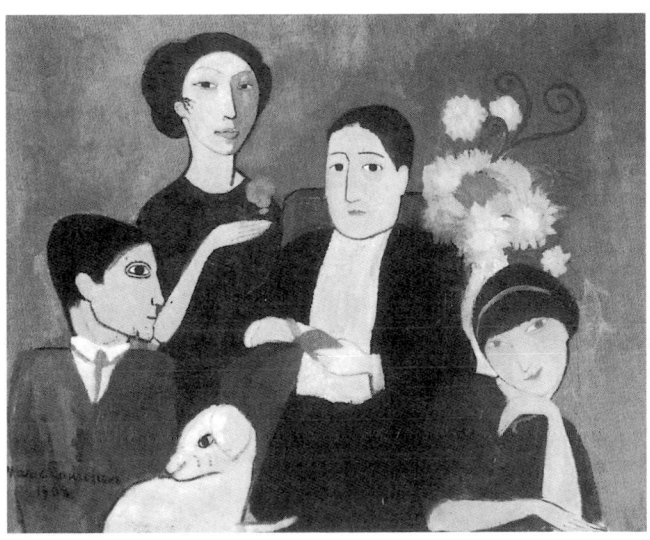

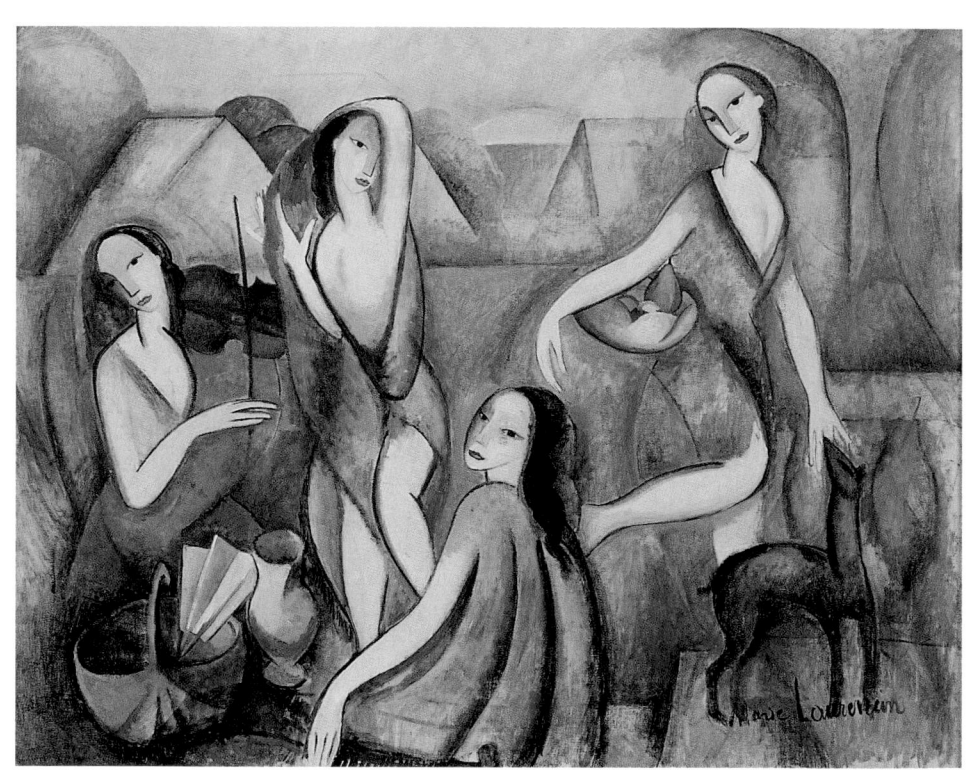

136. **Marie Laurencin**, *Les Jeunes Filles (Young Girls)*, 1910–11.

In subsequent years Laurencin developed a hybrid aesthetic that conflated Cubist techniques, africanized motifs and decorative elements to create a style that defied categorization. Like Sonia Terk she worked in the decorative arts: before contributing her painted *trumeaux* (oval panels) to the Maison Cubiste in 1912, she had executed a series of tapestries for chair covers and created a decorative panel for a fireplace designed by fellow Cubist La Fresnaye. Although Apollinaire repeatedly declared Laurencin's art to be an expression of her 'feminine' sensibility, and celebrated her predilection for a pastel palette as evidence of her allegiance to the 'charm' and 'grace' of the French Rococo, there were other aspects of Laurencin's persona and art that transcended these narrow aesthetic parameters. The physiognomic distortions found in Laurencin's *Les Jeunes Filles* (*Young Girls*) (1910–11) and her *Head of a Woman* (1909) clearly derive from the same Fang masks from Gabon that inspired the primitivism of Derain and Picasso, while the background buildings in *The Young Girls* closely resemble the geometrized houses and Cézannesque colours in Braque's *Houses at L'Estaque* of 1908. Though such stylistic references speak to Laurencin's ambitions as a modernist, Perry has noted that the treatment of the female body in this and subsequent works had very specific gender connotations. [114] [136] [47]

The idea of a 'feminine' style of painting was frequently conflated with the representation of a 'feminine' image, which led critics like Louis Vauxcelles to associate the young girls repeatedly found in Laurencin's art with the coquettish social type known as the *femme-enfant* (woman-child). Childlike in her physical slenderness and adolescent in her playful flirtatiousness, the *femme-enfant* constituted an unthreatening form of the 'new woman' for her modern male counterpart; moreover, critics came to attribute such naive qualities to Laurencin herself. By combining Cézannesque *passage*, Cubist abstraction, and the earth palette of Braque's *Houses at L'Estaque* with the arabesque, elongated forms of these *femmes-enfants*, Laurencin in *Young Girls* effectively allied her 'feminine sensibility' to the aesthetic prerogatives of the Bateau Lavoir circle.

This calculated hybridity was asserted in other ways as well, for Laurencin claimed a Creole ancestry that accounted for her native 'affinity' to the art of Africa, while she incorporated the arabesque into her work to signal her interest in the decorative 'Oriental exoticism' of Arab cultures. Despite Apollinaire's claim in 1912 that her artistic genealogy could be traced to the French Primitives and the art of Watteau, Fragonard and Morisot, Laurencin's own primitivist self-fashioning encompassed Europe, the 'Orient', and Africa, thereby confounding any strict associations of her painting and persona with definitions of European femininity or *l'art féminine*. Laurencin's close friend Jean-Emile Laboureur underscored that difference in a 1914 print of Laurencin in the process of painting *Le Bal élégant* (1913). Laurencin's long checked skirt and the angularity of her clothing contrast dramatically with the fictional dancers in her painting, whose transparent pastel-coloured gowns and elongated forms exemplified the 'feminine' attributes critics associated with Laurencin herself.

Laurencin's art instigated what art historian Bridget Elliott has termed a 'tactical indeterminacy', allowing her to problematize a gendered discourse that has retrospectively distorted our understanding of Laurencin's contribution to Cubist aesthetics. No less a central player than Picasso included her name on a list of Cubists to include along with himself in the Armory Show in New York (1913), though this fact is frequently overlooked. When we re-examine the art of the Cubists from a feminist perspective we better understand the social forces that shaped the careers of the female Cubists and their efforts to overcome the prejudicial barriers of their era.

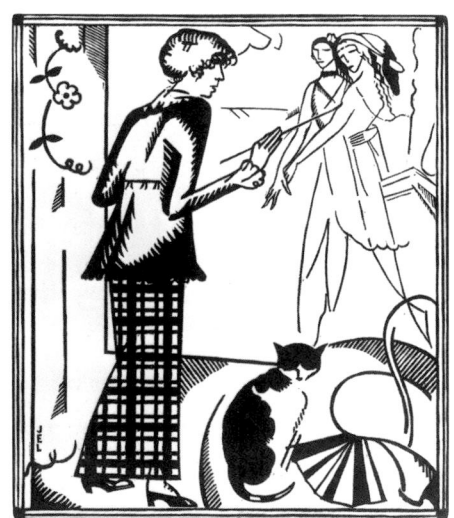

137. **Jean-Emile Laboureur**, *Portrait of Marie Laurencin*, 1914

Chapter 5 Pasted Papers and Revolution

Any art can be profitably considered in relation to its social context, but this is more than a truism in Paris before the Great War, where discussion of the arts was quite self-consciously political. To read the art criticism of the prewar period in dailies and journals representing the entire range of political opinion from right to left is to realize the extent to which French life in this period was saturated in a politicized rhetoric that insisted on the ideological implications of everything, especially art, and above all a self-consciously rebellious avant-garde art. From 1908 until after the war, Cubism was consistently attacked – or celebrated – in terms that took it for granted that traditional artistic canons were continuous with stable social conventions and that, as the Symbolist poet Gustave Kahn (1859–1936) wrote, 'in shattering a fragment of the artistic façade [the artist] touches the social façade'. One important conclusion we must draw is that artists who 'shattered the artistic façade' knew in advance what their reception would be. It is in this environment that we can understand not only Cubism but the even more radical invention of collage.

The French verb *coller* means 'to glue' and was traditionally used to refer to making paper valentines, hanging wallpaper, or posting advertisements on billboards (new at the end of the nineteenth century), all of which are germane to Cubist uses of the medium. The term *collage* thus refers to works in which various kinds of mass-produced or handcoloured papers, printed oilcloth, or objects – such as commercial labels or calling cards – are pasted or otherwise incorporated into the work of art (the term *papiers collés* refers to collages made of various kinds of papers only). Although the artists who primarily exploited this new medium were Braque, Picasso and Gris, all of the Cubists embraced aspects of its resulting influence. Indeed, the invention of this medium within Cubism is now considered to be the most important historical legacy of the movement for later twentieth-century art, and, not surprisingly, controversy has raged over its meaning. If we can agree that debates are good for getting us all to think more deeply, then collage represents an ideal opportunity to consider questions of interpretation.

The practice of collage invented by the Cubists was unique in several important ways. First, collage represented a deliberate rejection of the traditional and stable materials of which painting had been made since the Renaissance – oil paint on canvas – in favour of the literal incorporation of ordinary, lowly, impermanent and often industrially mass-produced materials accessible to anyone. Secondly, the use of glue, influenced by Braque's training as a house decorator, equally defied traditional notions of the *métier* (craft) of high art. Thirdly, collage problematized the presence of the 'hand' of the artist by shifting the 'master's touch' from the profoundly mystified act of painting to cutting, placing, and gluing, with drawing often used not to inspire admiration of its facility or

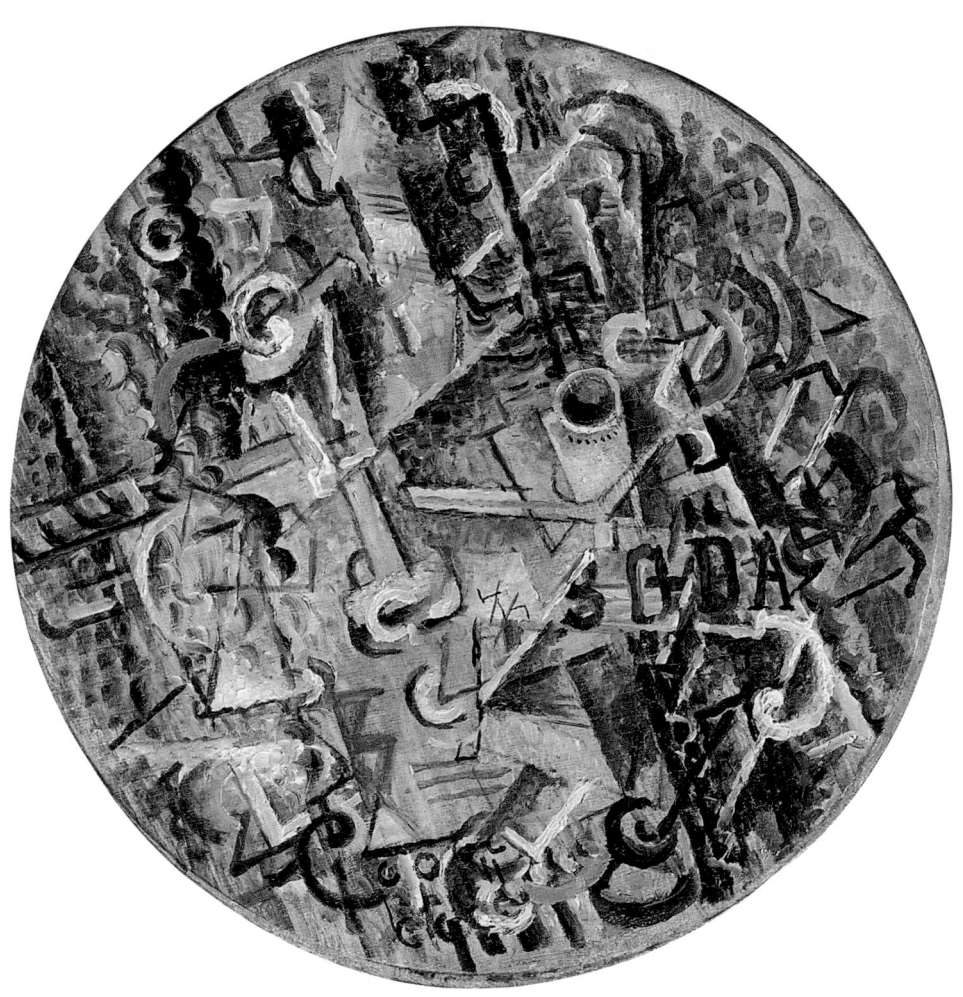

elegance, but to falsify appearances of the cut edges of the various papers. Lastly, and most significantly, collage allowed a more perfect abandonment of illusionism, however radical had become Cubism's depiction of three-dimensional forms in space, in favour of the literal incorporation of objects (wallpaper, calling cards, coffee packets) that might once have been fictionally depicted. The resulting combination of residual illusionism – used to bring these glued objects into relation to each other – and the striking appearance of 'reality' broke down the traditional distinction between 'art' and 'life', and therefore fulfilled one of the loudest cries of modernists in all media. Resultingly, collage allowed for a more profound meditation on the very means and language of art.

Numbers, letters and signs

For Braque and Picasso, the shockingly abstract style of their Cubist paintings was never entirely divorced from subjects and themes already familiar from their earlier work. Images from figures to musical still lifes, from cityscapes to the café, represent more than mere pretexts for the solution of formal problems. Nevertheless, the most difficult and 'hermetic' Cubist canvases came to hover on the brink of complete abstraction, as in Braque's *Soda* of spring 1912. 138 In this work a small conical glass on the left, a white clay pipe in the centre right, and the word 'SODA' are all that is 'readable' in a bewildering field of repetitious black and white forms on an ochre ground. Stippled areas fill the space between these forms in a way that refuses a reading into depth, despite the temptation to see some darker areas as 'shadows' and some white areas as 'objects'. The ideas, discussed in earlier chapters, that encouraged such individualized expression and helped overthrow an inherited and shared vocabulary of illusionism have here led to a work that seems almost to resist the notion of its own audience. How do we 'enter' such a work, much less understand it? Collage offered a route away from the obscure and hermetic character of works like *Soda* to a style that was at once more abstract and therefore more outrageously avant-garde, yet conjured with seeming more concrete and connected, literally, to life.

138. **Georges Braque**, *Soda*, spring 1912.

139. **Georges Braque,**
The Portuguese, 1911–12.

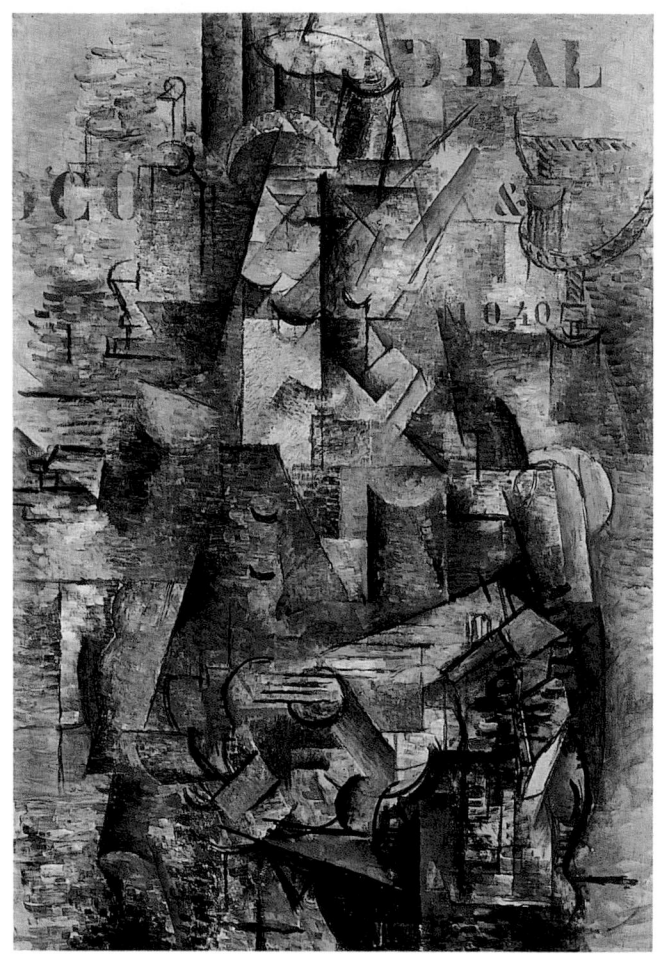

Picasso and Braque introduced numbers and letters into their canvases as early as August 1911. Braque's *The Portuguese* (autumn 1911–early 1912) represents a singing guitarist, with letters and numbers – 'D BAL' from *GRAND BAL*, 'OCO' from *CHOCOLAT*, and the price '10,40' – appearing as elements in a café, a location affirmed by the curtain loop and tassels on the upper right. Such signs import ready-made cultural symbols into otherwise illusionistic environments (however abstract that illusionism has become), analogous in some ways to the nail in Braque's *Violin and Palette*, which juxtaposed a traditional form of illusion with an alternative Cubist one. Simultaneously these letters and numbers, perhaps through the idea of their presence as advertisements stencilled on a glass entrance wall, seem to sit on the 'picture plane' (fictional planar surface immediately in front of the depicted recessional space of a painting), breaking any unity of recessive depth.

To the calculated contrast between whimsy and abstraction of the sometimes caricatural figural elements in the works between 1909 and 1911, such as *The Portuguese* or Picasso's *Portrait of Kahnweiler*, is now added a host of new elements. Braque had grown up in a family of highly skilled house painters and at 17 had been apprenticed to a 'painter-decorator' in Paris, where he learned how to imitate textured surfaces such as woodgrain (*faux-bois*) and marble. In early 1912 Braque and Picasso introduced such elements as simulated woodgrain (done with a decorator's comb, another technique Braque taught to Picasso), sand mixed into paint to give physicality to selected areas, puns and settings introduced through stenciling recognizable words or fragments of words, and bright colour, especially in ways that likewise affirm the picture plane, as in *Still Life (Memory of Le Havre)* (May 1912). Such disruptions to the unity within Cubist painting, in both space and symbolic form, constitute early steps towards a 'collage aesthetic'.

Well before the flurry of activity in autumn 1912 resulting in a full exploration of collage, Picasso had already produced the first Cubist oil paintings with foreign elements pasted onto the canvas: *The Letter* of spring 1912 (location unknown), onto which he glued an Italian stamp, and *Still Life with Chair Caning* of May 1912. In the latter work, he added a piece of commercial oilcloth imitative of chair caning, thus introducing into an otherwise consistently Cubist oil

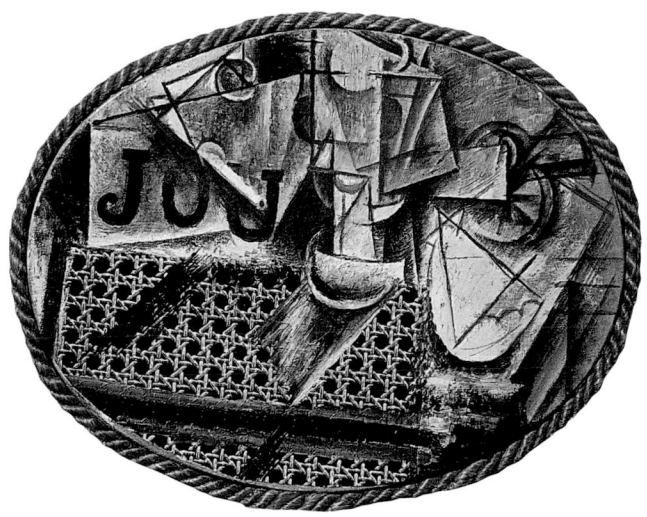

140. **Pablo Picasso**,
Still Life with Chair-Caning, May 1912.

painting a cheap and common material itself fully reflective of the conventions of illusionism or *trompe l'oeil* ('fool the eye'). The cultural association of mass consumer products with decoration and the feminine suggests Picasso's further breaking of academic codes, as oil painting was treated in the critical literature of the day as a 'masculine' arena. A rope frame likewise ironizes traditional artistic materials, replacing the usual gilt frame it wittily echoes. The still-life objects – glass, newspaper and white clay pipe – sit on a café table and are depicted in a visual system pointedly at odds with the fictive literalness of the chair caning. Several possibilities suggest themselves for a 'reading' of this work: a round café table with these objects placed upon the printed tablecloth, with the oval format operating as the perspective view of a customer seated at the table; alternatively, the still-life objects may be placed upon a glass table, through which we view the seat of a caned chair, or on a mirrored surface reflecting the back of a caned chair. In any reading, we understand the tension between the illusion and the canvas as a literal presence on which the oilcloth is glued and the paint brushed. As art historian Christine Poggi observes, 'the grey smears of paint on the surface heighten the confusion of alternative paradigms, since they may be read as shadows on an opaque surface or as reflections of light on a glass or mirror surface. By multiplying the alternatives, Picasso denies a direct, transparent relation between his pictorial signifiers and their referents in the external world. He thereby points to the arbitrariness of those signifiers in the absence of a single governing interpretive context or paradigm', leaving us free to experience our own subjective response.

Sculpture
Further important experiments of this period include first Braque's (1911) and later Picasso's (1912) paper sculptures, which played an important role in encouraging the artists' introduction of bright colour and texture into their works. For Braque's sculptures, none of which survives unfortunately, he evidently cut, shaped and painted paper. In *Fruit Dish and Glass* of September 1912, Braque incorpor- 14
ated pieces of artificial woodgrain paper he found in a decorator's shop near his summer retreat, waiting to buy it for several days until Picasso had left town so that he could experiment in private. When his friend returned a week later, Braque surprised him with the first *papier collé*, beginning a two-year period of intensive investigation of the new medium by both artists (Gris did not make his collages until just before the war, in the wake of Picasso and Braque). *Fruit Dish and Glass* employs the woodgrain paper in the upper half to signify

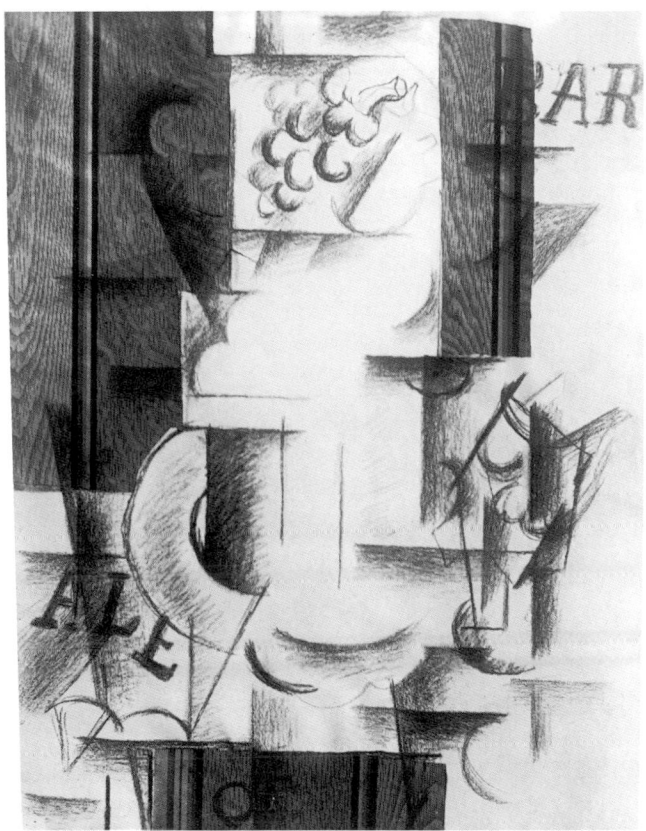

either the paper itself as wallpaper, such as could be found in cheap working-class cafés, or as wood panelling in a somewhat higher-class establishment. The same paper below signifies the table upon which the fruit dish with grapes and the wineglass sit, while the words 'BAR' and 'ALE' locate the still life definitively in a public as opposed to private space. The compositional elements are tied together with charcoal lines and planes of *passage*, but the overall effect is one of increased, indeed elegant, simplicity, with wonderfully complicated tensions and contradictions between realism and abstraction, the 'real' and the artificial.

On 9 October 1912, Picasso wrote to Braque: 'My dear friend Braque, I am using your latest paperistic and powdery procedures. I am in the process of conceiving a guitar and I am using a little dust against our horrible canvas'. The work in question was almost certainly Picasso's paper sculpture, *Guitar* of October 1912 (later 142 constructed with metal and wire), and it is important to recognize

142. **Pablo Picasso**,
Maquette for *Guitar*, October 1912.

143. Grebo mask,
Ivory Coast or Liberia.

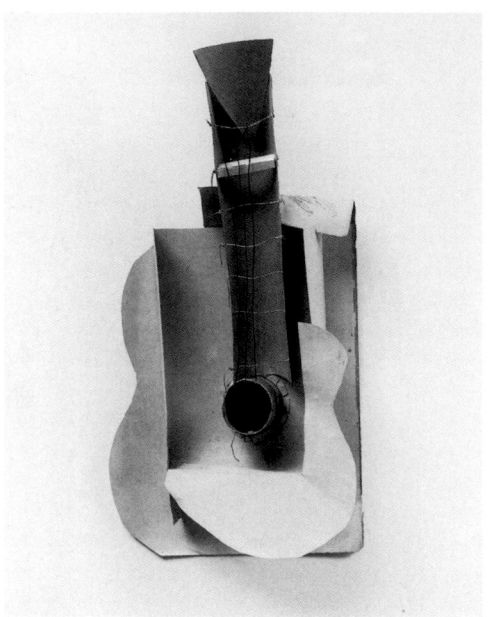

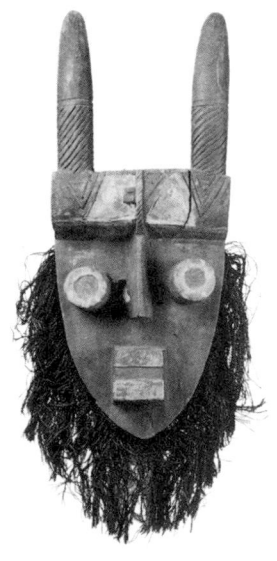

both his acknowledgment of the role of Braque's lost paper sculptures in this development and the mention of their attack on the 'horrible canvas' as both the precondition of *métier* and the ground of illusionism. This work also reveals Picasso's study of African sculpture, specifically a Grebo mask he purchased in August of that year, with its projecting cylinders, rectangles and triangular wedge of the most uncompromising geometricity. Such radically abstract forms nonetheless readily read as 'eyes', 'lips' and 'nose', sharply revealing their arbitrariness as signs for a face. But rather than bringing this lesson to the construction of a comparable head, Picasso made a reconceived *Guitar*, with its recessive sound hole projecting forwards and the planes of its body – on two different scales to suggest differences in depth – cut away to reveal transparent openings onto its interior spaces. A ground plane – a wall on which the guitar hangs – curls over the upper body, defying our desire to view it logically. Picasso likewise hangs this work on the wall as he did his collection of African masks, which was certainly not the way masks operated in their original culture, where they were 'danced' and used in ritual performances rather than being displayed as visual objects. The same, of course, is true of guitars. Nonetheless, the radicalism and ingenious simplicity of this work borrows something from the language of the 'primitive' in its extreme simplicity and directness of expression.

A new form of Cubist sculpture emerged from this fresh encounter with African sculpture, one that broke with the unity of form and material of earlier sculpture such as Picasso's *Doll* of 1907 or Derain's *Cat* of 1908 and led to the three-dimensional equivalent of collage: assemblage. In *Guitarist with Sheet Music* of spring 1913, a paper high-relief sculpture, Picasso whimsically creates the figure of a female guitarist, playing on the witty comparison between the shape of her head and her guitar, as well as placing the hole of the guitar in the most suggestive spot. This sort of sexual punning is repeated in several collages by both Picasso and Braque.

33
17
144

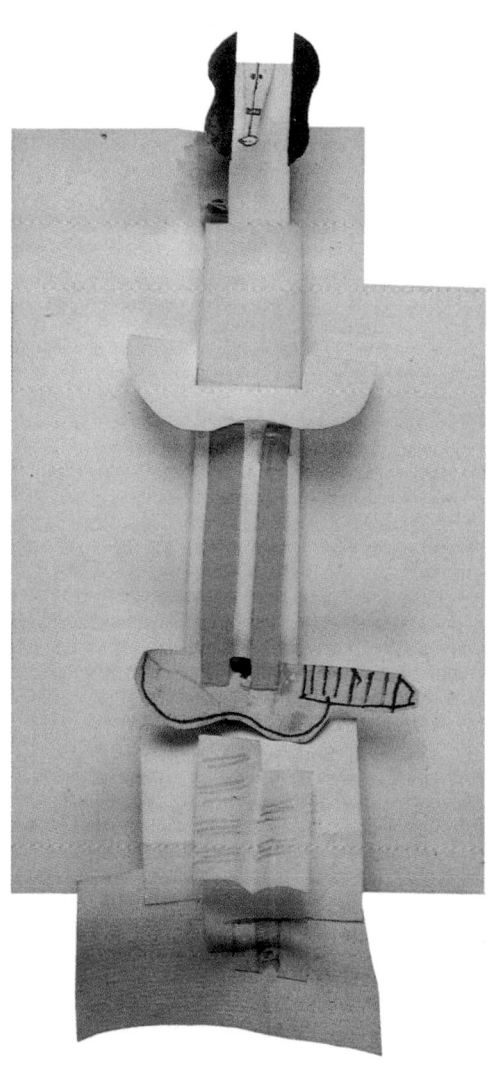

144. **Pablo Picasso**,
Guitarist with Sheet Music,
spring 1913.

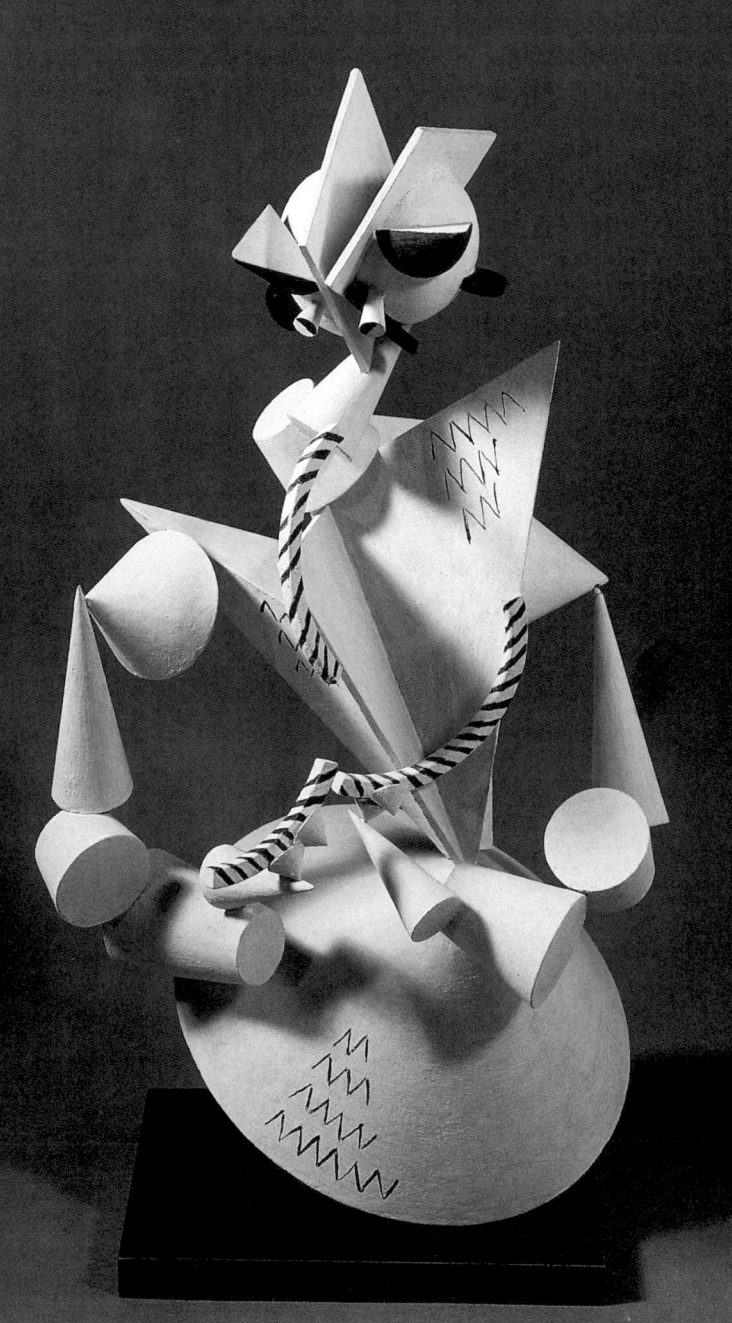

145. **Henri Laurens,**
The Clown, 1915.

146. **Pablo Picasso,**
Still Life, early 1914.
Here Picasso brings together
traditional and non-traditional
materials in a witty balancing act
between 'realism' and 'illusion'.
A Cubist construction of painted
wooden sections, this relief
presents the plane of a table
against a wall with a knife and
bread on its surface, while its
edge has a real tapestry fringe
attached, such as appears in
photographs of Picasso's studio
and throughout domestic spaces
at this time.

Archipenko's *Médrano II (Dancer)* of 1913, assembled from painted tin, wood and glass, is equally primitivist in conjuring into motion a circus dancer, that urban and proletarian version of the 'primitive'. With its transparent planes of glass and metal arcs of tin, the high-relief sculpture traces the dancer's movements through time in characteristically fragmented fashion; the paint brings her body and costume to life, while the word 'Médrano' painted on the base of the relief locates her in the daily Médrano circus attended so enthusiastically by Archipenko, Apollinaire, Braque, Picasso and many others. Although all of Braque's paper sculptures are lost, he continued to work with the medium as is evident in a surviving photograph of 1914. Here he cleverly uses a corner as two relief planes into which his cardboard and newsprint fit, and as Poggi observes 'the word "ART" is legible, ironically appearing just where one might expect the label on the cardboard bottle to identify its contents'.

Other sculptors to follow this Cubist path included Henri Laurens and Jacques Lipchitz. Laurens, born into poverty, was only able to study art in evening classes. His early sculpture showed the influence of Rodin, but a developing friendship with Braque brought

147

8

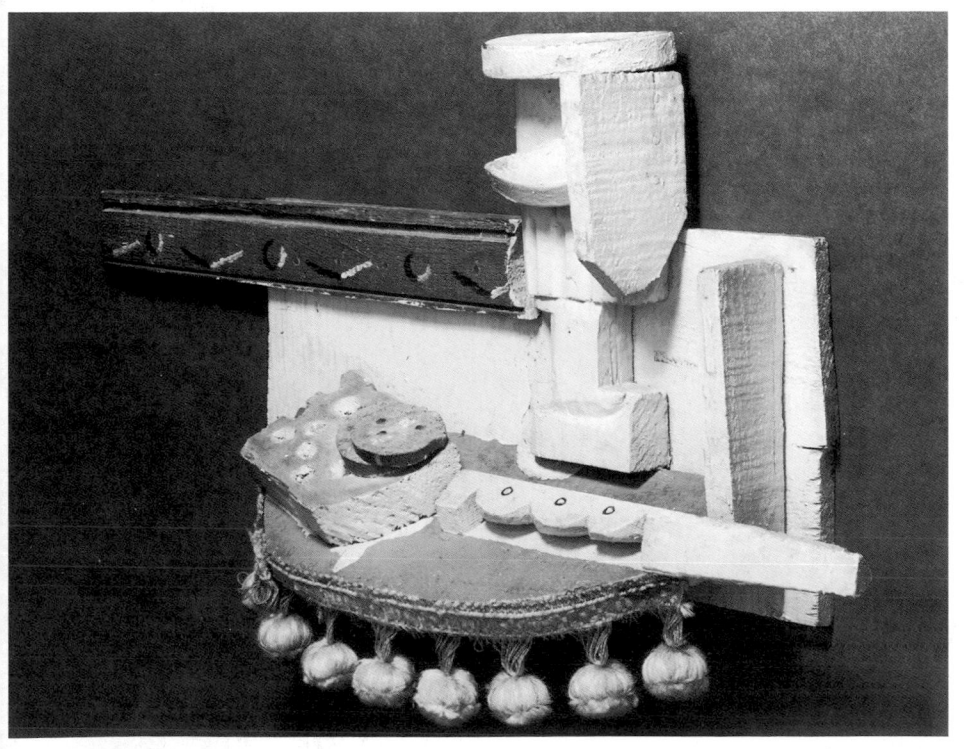

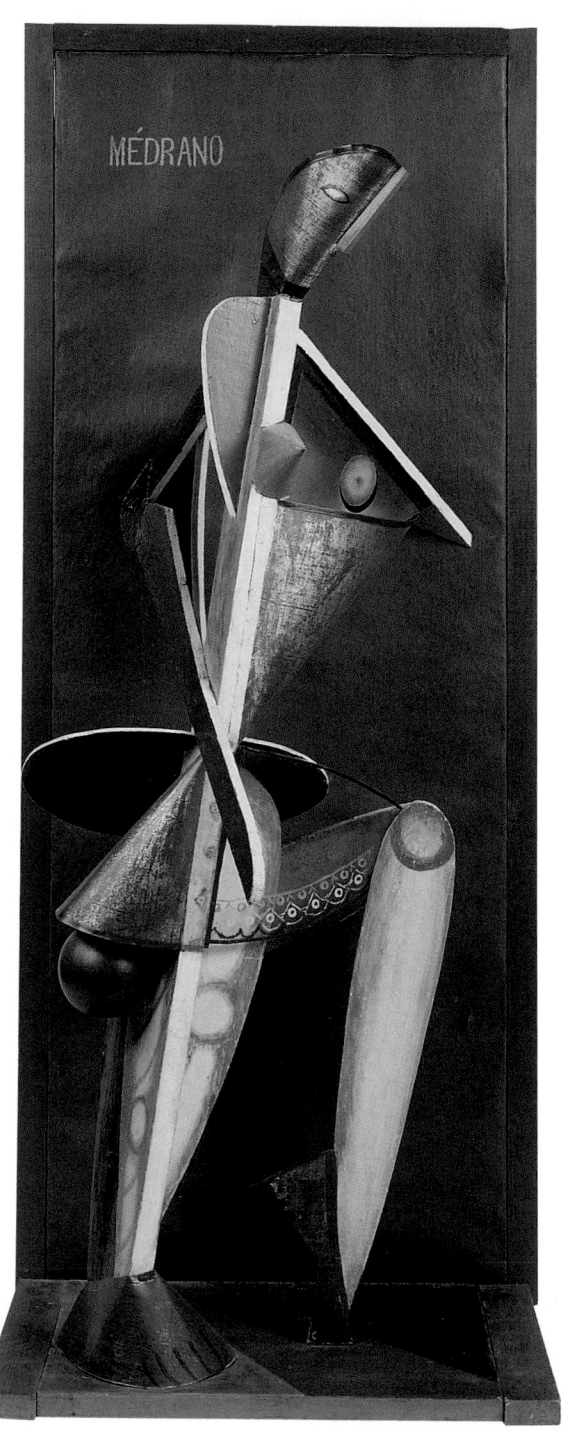

147. Alexander Archipenko,
Médrano II (Dancer), 1913.

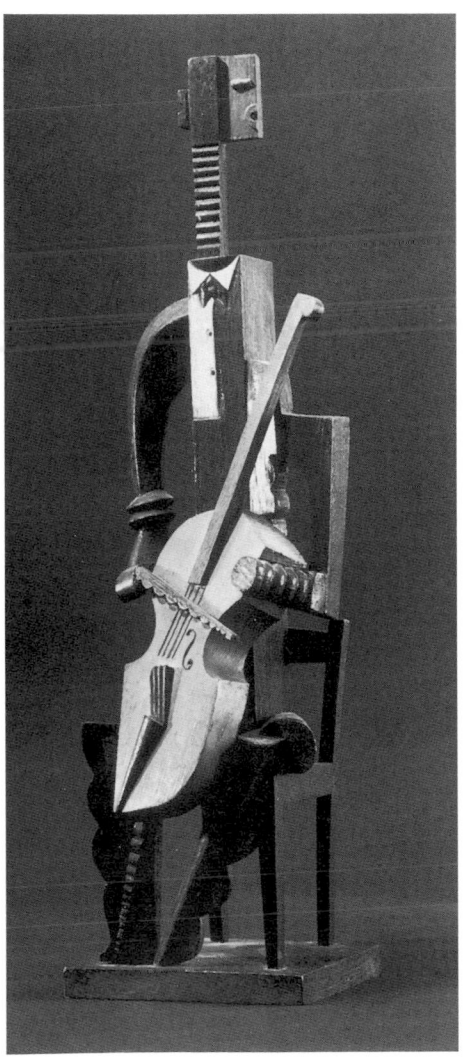

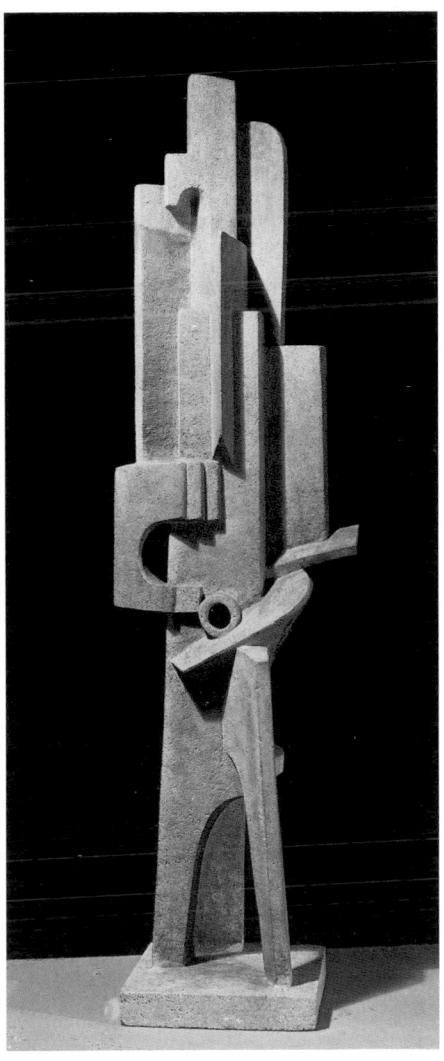

him into Cubist circles. Laurens's first Cubist works are now lost, but some polychromed Cubist constructions survive from 1914 and 1915, including *The Clown* (1915). This freestanding assemblage of painted wood studiedly responds to Archipenko's controversial *Médrano II* in its joined three-dimensional geometric forms – such as the triangle of the lapel and the cone of the hips – and its playful application of paint as well as the circus theme.

Lipchitz was born in Lithuania and came to Paris in 1909 to study sculpture. Diego Rivera introduced him to Picasso in 1913, and from 1916 he was close to Juan Gris. At first unsympathetic to Cubism, by 1915 he had abandoned a simplified form of primitivism for a Cubist vocabulary, experimenting with open geometric forms and layered planes as in *Detachable Figure (Seated Musician)* of 1915 and *Man with a Guitar* of 1916. In the first work Lipchitz combines the painted-wood image of a tuxedoed cello player – the ultimate high-art musician – with a masklike unpainted wooden head alluding to African sculpture, complete with 'ritual' feathers and plants. This overt combination of Western and non-Western is more subtly encoded in his *Man with a Guitar* of a year later. Here the musician plays a folk instrument in a staccato rhythm echoed by the forms of the figure; the movement of the spectator around the free-standing sculpture as well as changes in light would only enhance this effect.

Mass culture

The boldness of the paper *Guitar* experiment, and the model of Braque's *Fruit Dish and Glass* of September, led Picasso directly to collages such as *Guitar, Sheet Music and Glass* of November 1912, which plays with the paper *Guitar*'s inventions, but in two dimensions. On a ground of cheap commercial wallpaper, the artist has combined aspects of a guitar: a piece of painted or manufactured woodgrain paper (either an imitation or an imitation of an imitation) cut into the double curve of a guitar's silhouette; a piece of paper painted black, representing the bottom curve of the guitar but on a larger scale than the double curve, as if closer to the viewer; a piece of blue paper standing in for the neck of the guitar; and the sound hole of the guitar as a circle of white paper. By virtue of its whiteness this last necessarily reads as the ground upon which all the other papers are glued, and as the sound hole of the guitar it also implies a recessive space. But both these illusions are at odds with its material placement on top of the other pieces of paper. Such conundrums shared with the paper *Guitar* continue, for between the bottom, side and neck of this guitar is a transparent plane revealing the wallpaper upon which the object may fictively hang.

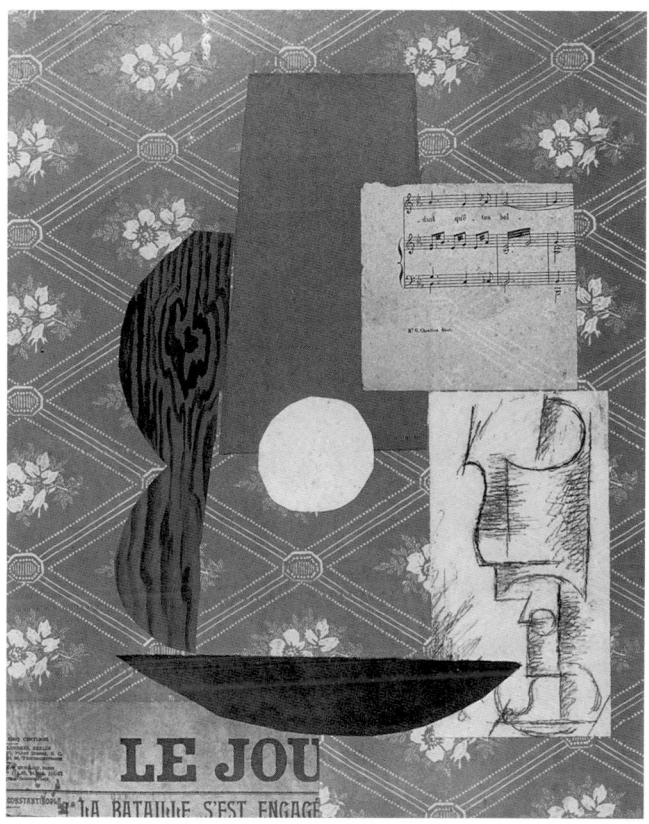

An actual fragment of a popular song, such as might be played upon the guitar, is glued overlapping the neck, while a glass and newspaper complete the café setting.

The popular sheet music (1912's version of a new CD), the humble guitar and the cheap wallpaper – printed in only one colour – suggest a working-class café, where newspapers are provided free for the customers. In every way this collage evokes the vernacular life of the people (including artists), who came to cafés for whole evenings to meet their friends, listen to music and discuss the issues of the day. The newsprint itself, in fact, is the largest hint that this work wishes to engage, in the most immediate sense, the historical present of Parisian culture. The newspaper is the most flamboyantly 'unworthy' artistic material in the collage and constituted for the artists a fresh and startling way of introducing subjects that summoned current ideas and themes – and for Picasso radical ideologies and controversies consonant with his anarchism – to play a renewed role in their art. As a product of modern industrialized

HUIT PAGES. — CINQ CENTIMES

FILS SPÉCIAUX : LONDRES, BERLIN

LE JOURNAL, 100, RUE DE RICHELIEU, PARIS

Téléphone

LE JOURNAL

F. XAU, Directeur.

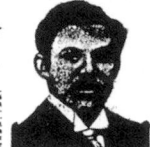

Un Cortège de Cholériques

UN AFFREUX CHARNIER

Hadernkeui, 12 novembre. (Par dépêche de notre envoyé spécial.)...

PAUL ERIO.

LA BATAILLE S'EST ENGAGÉE FURIEUSE
sur les Lignes de Tchataldja

UNE SOUDAINE OFFENSIVE DES BULGARES EST VIGOUREUSEMENT REPOULSÉ

Monastir est serrée de près par les Serbes et les Grecs

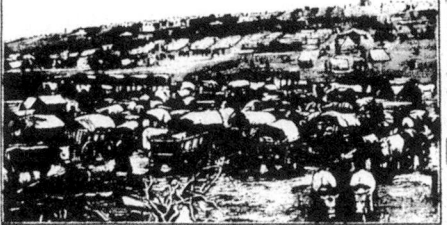

UN CAMP SERBE SUR UNE HAUTEUR DEVANT MONASTIR (Photo de notre envoyé spécial Henry ERNEST.)

L'ENVOYÉ SPÉCIAL DU "JOURNAL" aux Avant-Postes Turcs

Hadernkeui, 17 novembre, 9 heures du matin. (Par dépêche de notre envoyé spécial.)...

PAUL ERIO.

Les journaux turcs annoncent une grande victoire

Constantinople, 17 novembre...

Les Serbes s'avancent vers Monastir

Skoplje (Uskub), 16 novembre. (Par dépêche de notre envoyé spécial.)...

HENRY BARBY.

LA SITUATION

Un télégramme officiel parvenu hier...

SAINT-BRICE.

Pourquoi l'Horloger a-t-il coupé le cou à sa Femme ?

GILBERT HARDY

Le Meurtrier

Deux cris dans la nuit

ÉCHOS

— LE BOUCHON DE CRISTAL —

Le Meeting du Pré-Saint-Gervais contre la Guerre

Au retour, une Bagarre s'est produite, place du Combat, entre Anarchistes et Agents

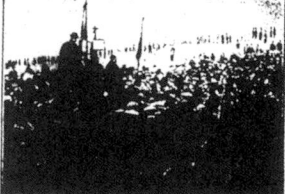

Un coin du meeting du Pré-Saint-Gervais

France, newsprint automatically imports mass culture into the collage and arrives already structured by the larger discourses of French culture. Given that these artists drew almost exclusively upon the most widely circulated and politically centrist daily papers, they could be said to be ironically conjuring with and playing against the dominant discourse such journals embodied.

Viewing newsprint as a dominant discourse in turn-of-the-century France suggests a way of recognizing the life of newsprint as a cultural force both in the collages and in the culture at large. Newspapers purport simply to convey the truth, never acknowledging that that 'truth' represents the world as viewed through the values of the newspaper's owners and editors. Newspaper language represents itself as value-neutral, its prose in the style of 'objectivity'. Between 1830 and 1880, newspaper circulation had increased by some 4000 percent, from about 50,000 to some 6 million copies per day. What this marked after 1880 was an ubiquitous merging of the political with the commercial, and the newspaper was perhaps the first purposely perishable consumer commodity.

Literary historian Richard Terdiman discusses a secret system that developed – known only to the trade – governing the sale of four kinds of space within the commercial newspaper, which perverted the public's credulous distinctions between the different modes of discourse based on their location within the paper. The cheapest was the *annonce*, something like a classified ad and always found on the last of the newspaper's four pages. The next was the *réclame*, a larger ad on page 3 equally frank in proclaiming its commercial status. The paid *fait divers* or news item appeared on page 2, where 'the disguised colonization of "objective" informational discourse by the commercial began'. But the greatest deception occurred on the front page:

'Editorial publicity' on page 1 completely disguised its status as advertisement. It could consist of a recommendation, within a nominally factual chronique *[report], of a stock share, or of a particular recent book within a literary* compte-rendu *[review]. From within the world of journalism, this system induced a generalized cynicism concerning the interchangeability of facts, opinions, and money. Villemessant, the notorious editor of* Le Figaro *during the Second Empire [1852–70], declared that he was satisfied with an issue of his paper only when every single line* within it had been bought and paid for in some way.

The layout of the paper additionally controlled its discourse, contributing to the fragmentation and neutralization of information and emphasizing its distance from the readers' experience. With

151. Front page of *Le Journal*, 18 November 1912.

politics, the arts, and the commercial overlapping on every page, the 'message' of the mass-circulation newspaper is overtly mixed. Their juxtaposition neutralizes what would otherwise be their cumulative and interconnected logic; as Terdiman writes, newspapers systematically 'rationalize disjunction; they are organized *as disorganization*'. Thus for nineteenth-century writers newsprint came to stand for the commercialized and dishonest discourse of the bourgeoisie, against which the Romantic poet Charles Baudelaire (1821–67) and the Symbolist poet Stéphane Mallarmé (1842–98) staked their identities. Terdiman quotes Baudelaire in 'Mon coeur mis à nu' ('My Heart Laid Bare'): 'I don't understand how an uncorrupted hand could touch a newspaper without a convulsion of disgust'.

Interestingly, the question of Picasso's relation to Mallarmé and his hatred of newsprint has become an interpretive flashpoint for scholars and critics of collage. Rosalind Krauss has argued for an exclusively semiotic reading of Picasso's collages, cogently observing that differences in scale for different parts of an object operate as a linguistic sign for 'depth' while the busy black and white of the newsprint surface operates as a sign for 'light'. Such elements of the language of art do not attempt to 'represent' depth or light in a traditional sense, hence collage becomes a unique form of modernism and the artist a uniquely self-conscious manipulator of signs. Indeed, Picasso's success in 'transmut[ing] the grey drone of the marks on the page into the very sign or constellation for light' rises to a Mallarméan purity that redeems the hated newsprint, 'showing that the newspaper can … be made to yield – for the new art – the very qualities Mallarmé condemned it for lacking'. Poggi grounded this question more historically by discussing the commodification of culture represented by the daily paper that led Mallarmé to reject everything to do with it, and she argues how and why Picasso in turn rejected Mallarmé's aestheticist strategy, though both sought to counter bourgeois commodification of art and life. David Cottington alternatively notes that the radical appearance of the collages increasingly narrowed their audience to a subcultural group of self-styled bohemians and bourgeois collectors. In this view the abstraction of the collages reflects a general retreat into an apolitical aestheticism in the face of the growing dominance of nationalist discourse in post-1906 France.

The question remains whether these artists nonetheless imagined their art as resisting nationalism in the name of the avant-garde and of anarchism. For example, the Puteaux Cubists embraced

Mallarméan Symbolism as part of a larger critique of the right-wing politics of the royalist Action Française. And Picasso's anarchist aesthetics could justify such individual acts of stylistic radicalism *as* political; the anarchist writer Pierre Quillard urged in 1892, 'Whoever communicates to his brothers in suffering the secret splendour of his dreams acts upon the surrounding society in the manner of a solvent and makes of all those who understand him, often without their realization, outlaws and rebels'. Quillard was not alone in espousing such views, as was demonstrated in 1913 in *Action d'art* (Art Action) by the anarchist theorist André Colomer, who incorporated Cubist avant-gardism into a blueprint for revolution based on a transformation of individual consciousness and, subsequently, of society. Such 'revolutionary' gestures as may be encoded in Picasso's collages ultimately lacked the power to change European society or to effect a social revolution, and it may be tempting to read back into its history modernism's failure in this regard. But we should also keep in mind the modernists' sometimes grandiose ambitions and recognize the fundamental difference of a historical period when art could be imagined to have such powers within its reach.

Picasso and Politics
The newsprint Picasso incorporated into his collages had a great deal of cultural complexity, even before he appropriated it for a work like *Guitar, Sheet Music and Glass*. Here things get even more complicated, because the actual piece of newsprint in this work – as is evident on the front page of *Le Journal* from which it was cut – refers to the current Balkan War, which plunged Europe, and Picasso's bohemian milieu not least, into anxious preoccupation with the possibility of war engulfing the Continent. In 1912 and 1913 Picasso made approximately eighty collages, of which fifty-two contain newsprint texts; of these, at least half deal with the Balkan Wars and the economic and political state of Europe. During November and December of 1912, when the political crisis was at its peak, collages – most incorporating newsprint – nearly supplanted the activity of painting in his work. Of all two-dimensional works executed in the autumn and winter of 1912, thirty-nine were collages while only twelve were paintings, including oil, watercolour and gouache. The political reports glued into these early collages had special resonance for an artist deeply tied to the anarchist, antimilitarist traditions of Barcelona and daily exposed to, if not immersed in, the raging arguments over the coming pan-European war.

150

151

In order to understand the allusions in the collages and to grasp Picasso's concern with such issues, it is important briefly to review contemporary political events. In France in the years leading up to the war, frequent clashes between strikers and the government – which increasingly used the army to break strikes – forced attention on the plight of the workers. One result of the repression of the labour movement and the persecution of its leaders was the growth and increasing militancy of the anarchist movement and the Confédération Générale du Travail, the labour movement or syndicalist arm of the anarchist movement, which recorded 300,000 members in 1906, 400,000 in 1908, and 600,000 in 1912. At the same time, the more moderate socialists were gaining voters and seats in Parliament.

The other major crisis of these years was the First Balkan War. When Raymond Poincaré became French prime minister in 1912, partly on a platform of revenge for France's defeat in the Franco-Prussian War of 1870, he rapidly began to gear up for war with Germany, which would be 'short but glorious'. One of his first moves was to support Russian designs on the Balkans, which involved supporting the Serbians and Bulgarians against the Ottoman and Austro-Hungarian Empires, bound by treaty to Germany. On 15 October 1912, Montenegro, Serbia, Bulgaria and Greece declared war on the Ottoman Turks, who had occupied their lands since the sixteenth century. After expelling the Turks, in November Serbia laid claim to a large part of Albania in the Austro-Hungarian Empire, which then mobilized. But because Russia's military preparations were incomplete, treaty discussions began in London and dragged on until May 1913. The Second Balkan War amounted to a few weeks' skirmish and ended in a 'final' treaty in August 1913. When World War I did break out a year later, the immediate event that sparked it was the assassination of Austria-Hungary's Archduke Francis Ferdinand by a Serbian nationalist.

A burning issue for both anarchists and socialists was whether the workers would fight in the war that now seemed inevitable. Jean Maitron cites the following 'notice to conscripts' distributed by the International Antimilitarist Association (AIA), founded in 1904:

When they command you to fire your guns on your brothers in misery ... workers, soldiers of tomorrow, you will not hesitate, you will not obey.... When they send you to the border to defend the coffers of the capitalists against other workers, abused as you are yourselves, you will not march. All war is criminal. At the mobilization order, you will answer with an immediate strike and with insurrection.

Although the AIA was soon crushed by the government, its recommendations were embraced with increasing frequency. Desertion and absenteeism in the French Army grew at an extraordinary rate in response to this powerful and widely disseminated critique of the military establishment: 5991 in 1902; 14,067 in 1907; 12,000 to 13,000 in 1912. The anarchists and socialists organized demonstrations so huge and enthusiastically critical of the government that Premier Barthou threatened to crack down further on the labour movement. In the end, though, the government ignored the message from the left with impunity, and the French nation in a patriotic fever marched off to a war ultimately more destructive than could possibly have been imagined.

It would have been nearly impossible in Paris in those years to have remained oblivious to the scope of this left-wing antiwar movement, which drew attention to the plight of workers as well as to the machinations of armaments manufacturers and government ministers. While the fever of patriotism in France grew around him and the press became more and more hysterical, Picasso explored these issues through 'quoting' with the newsprint he selected and through juxtaposition of such quotations with the still-life images in his collages of 1912 and 1913. Such associations range from black humour to black horror; as the newsprint in *Guitar, Sheet Music and Glass* says, 'The Battle Has Begun'. 150

A reading of the newspaper clippings in Picasso's collages from November and December of 1912 reveals many of them to be reports and accounts of events with special political meaning, as is evident in *Glass and Bottle of Suze*, filled with clippings – nearly bulletin board style – from the same page of 18 November. Most were carefully cut out to preserve legibility, and sometimes whole columns of print remained intact. Where Picasso cut into the text of an article, he usually clearly retained its sense. Furthermore, the clippings did not innocently register front page news but were selected from all parts of the newspaper, including the financial pages. In fact, it seems likely that the very development of the use of newsprint in Picasso's collages – a full year before Braque added newsprint to his *papiers collés* – was directly motivated by a desire to work these political issues into his art. 153 151

Glass and Bottle of Suze contains a report of the Serbian advance towards Monastir in Macedonia, including accounts of the wounded, descriptions of battle movements, and speculations on how long the besieged city of Adrianople can hold out against famine. Picasso includes gruesome descriptions of the victims of war:

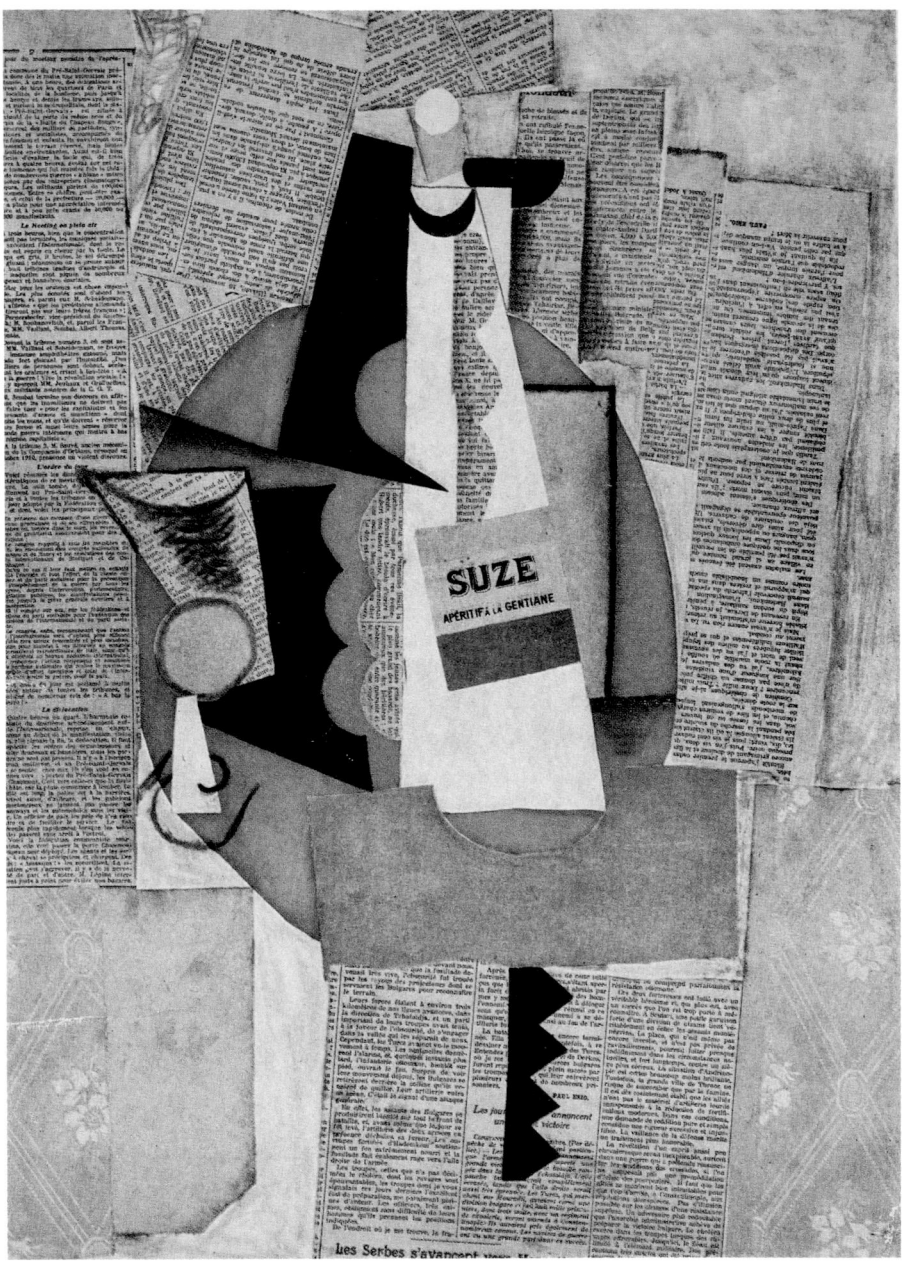

152. **Pablo Picasso**,
1947 reproduction of *Glass and Bottle of Suze*,
November 1912, showing the original colours
that echo the French *tricolore*.

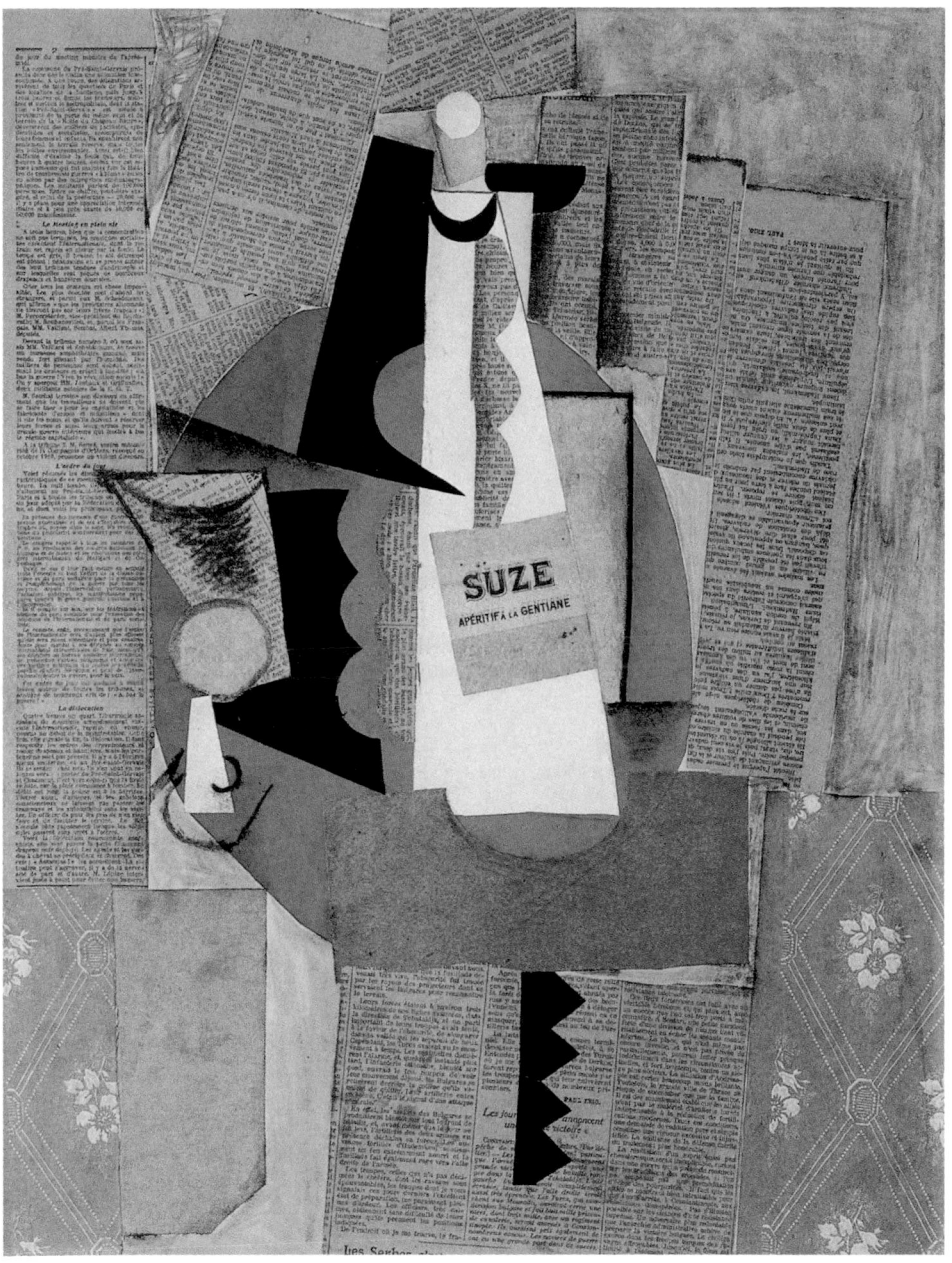

153. Pablo Picasso,
Glass and Bottle of Suze, November 1912.
This recent reproduction shows how the
coloured label in the centre has faded with time.

Before long I saw the first corpse still grimacing with suffering and whose face was nearly black. Then I saw two, four, ten, twenty; then I saw a hundred corpses. They were stretched out there where they had fallen during the march of the sinister convoy, in the ditches or across the road, and the files of cars loaded with the almost dead were stretched out everywhere on the devastated route....
But I had seen nothing yet.

These vivid descriptions placed upside down in the still life – an image of the world turned on its head – are forced into a dialogue with a report on the right-hand side of the collage of a mass socialist/anarchist/pacifist meeting, with lengthy quotations from the speakers that, in effect, voice the leftist position. This article – right-side up in the composition – reports that 'the most listened-to speakers were at first the foreigners, and among them M. Scheidemann [a leading German Socialist], who affirmed "that the German proletarians will not fire on their French brothers".... M. Sembat ended his speech affirming that the workers ought not to seek death "for the capitalists and the manufacturers of arms and munitions".'

Thus reading the newsprint in *Glass and Bottle of Suze* renders an enormous amount of volatile information, including part of a serial novel satirizing upper-class libertines. Picasso incorporates these articles from *Le Journal* into an image of a white triangular bottle with a scalloped neck in the centre, complete with its original label; a glass to the left with a newsprint bowl (the only piece obscured by shading), white stem and charcoal foot; newspaper on a blue oval café table; and the same cheap wallpaper used in *Guitar, Sheet Music and Glass*, within a 'systematic disorganization' of the elements of conventional illusionism. The newsprint surrounds the signified glass and bottle, while its information saturates the conceptual field, evoking a series of associations from the ghastly preview of war, to its powerful resistance at home, to the escapist frivolities of the class that will benefit from military conquest. Picasso subverts the layout of the mass-distribution dailies, wherein the political implications of a column reporting a pacifist rally are defused by its submersion in a patchwork of commodified information, from the sensationalist, to the trivial, to the commercial.

By retrieving columns from different parts of the newspaper, Picasso reunites reports that now echo meaningfully, critiquing – from an anarchist perspective – the discourse that would disjoin them in a pretence of political neutrality. This reorganization constitutes a counter-discourse, subverting the original ideological formation of the newsprint, and does so furthermore in the setting of a proletarian café, that locus of friendship, argument, sedition, and police surveillance that according to historian Scott Haine 'sustained the political, cultural and social ferment of *fin-de-siècle* and *belle époque* Paris'. At the same time, Picasso breaks down visual conventions of pictorial representation that for the vast French public embodied 'order' and 'unity', celebrating instead the seemingly random and disorderly, what critics called the 'ugly', the 'primitive', the 'anti-aesthetic' and the 'anti-French'. What is for the bourgeoisie a disorderly work is for the leftist avant-garde a work whose unity resides in the very subversion of the conventions of academic illusionism and the illusions paraded in bourgeois newsprint. Thus both form and content play important roles in the overall practice of the collages. Indeed, it was through the language of avant-garde abstraction that Cubist theorists (and their anarchist allies) proposed to transform consciousness, and with it, society.

Current reproductions of the *Bottle of Suze* show the label as close in colour to the newsprint, so that it seems to play a relatively unimportant visual role in the overall work. A close inspection of the collage in the original, however, reveals that the Suze label was initially a bright red. This is confirmed by a surviving fifty-year-old colour reproduction of this collage, made before the volatile ink of the label 152 faded. Comparing this image to the one made recently, the bottle of Suze suggests both its role in the daily life of the artist and – with its blazing red juxtaposed with the white bottle and blue table – the tricolour flag of the French Republic. Picasso frequently used colour symbolism, including during his Cubist period, and he more than once used the colours of the French flag in various ways. A number of possible readings might be suggested. The one-colour wallpaper has already alerted us to the still life's location in a working-class café; if debates relating to issues in the newspaper take place around the table, rather like different voices, the flag summons the ways a variety of positions can all mantle themselves in forms of allegiance. Indeed, the tricolour evokes a range of symbolic political associations, as both the flag of the current government, the Third Republic – which was variously supported or critiqued for the war preparations protested at the demonstration – and the flag of the French Revolution of 1789, which produced the first French Republic and as such stood for 'Liberté, Egalité, Fraternité' – Liberty, Equality, Fraternity – those revolutionary principles that leftists thought the Third Republic had betrayed. The subject evoked in the collage – debating political issues with friends in a public place – problematizes notions of what constitutes 'public' vs. 'private' and foregrounds antimilitarist politics through the medium of collage.

Picasso was later asked by Pierre Daix whether he had incorporated the column reporting the mass demonstration on purpose; Picasso replied: 'Of course I did it on purpose, because it was an important event involving a hundred thousand people.... Oh yes, I found that in the newspaper, and it was my way of showing I was against the war'.

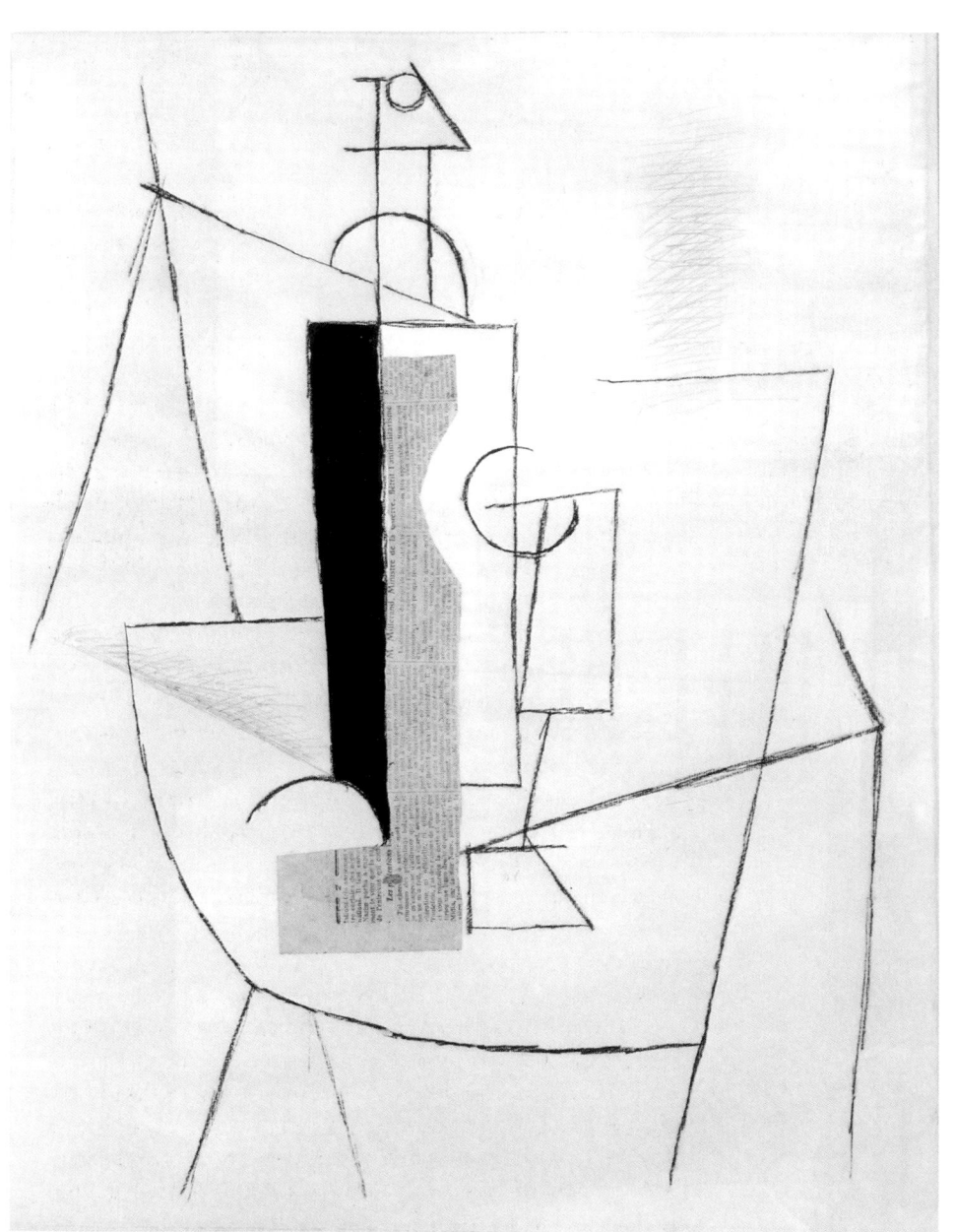

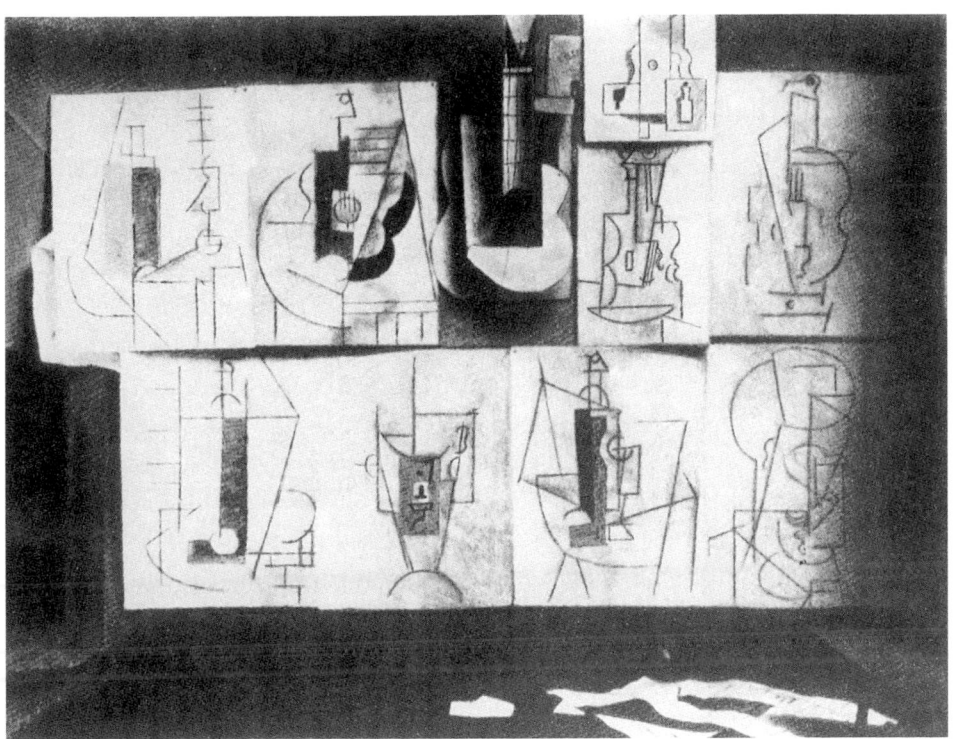

In *Still Life: Bottle and Glass on Table*, we read that M. Millerand, once a leading socialist but now Minister of War (a contradiction in terms for the Party faithful), has 'blasted' the antimilitarists in the Chamber of Deputies for resisting the passage of a law expediting the French military build-up. This work appears in the lower centre of a photograph of Picasso's studio at this time, revealing – both in the multiple works surrounding the paper sculpture of the *Guitar* and in the cut-up piece of newspaper on the floor – a working method clearly conceiving of these newsprint collages as inter-related groups. Some have newsprint already glued in; others are complete or nearly complete drawings awaiting the incorporation of pasted papers. Clearly Picasso could plan, exchange and manipulate the varieties of news he chose to glue in with such a working method. This is affirmed in the overwhelming readability of the news items he incorporated in the works of this period, including not just political news but items suggestive of private as well as public madness – murders, suicides, accidents – and items of interest to the Cubists' artistic and bohemian circles, such as theatre listings or cures for syphilis.

154

155

185

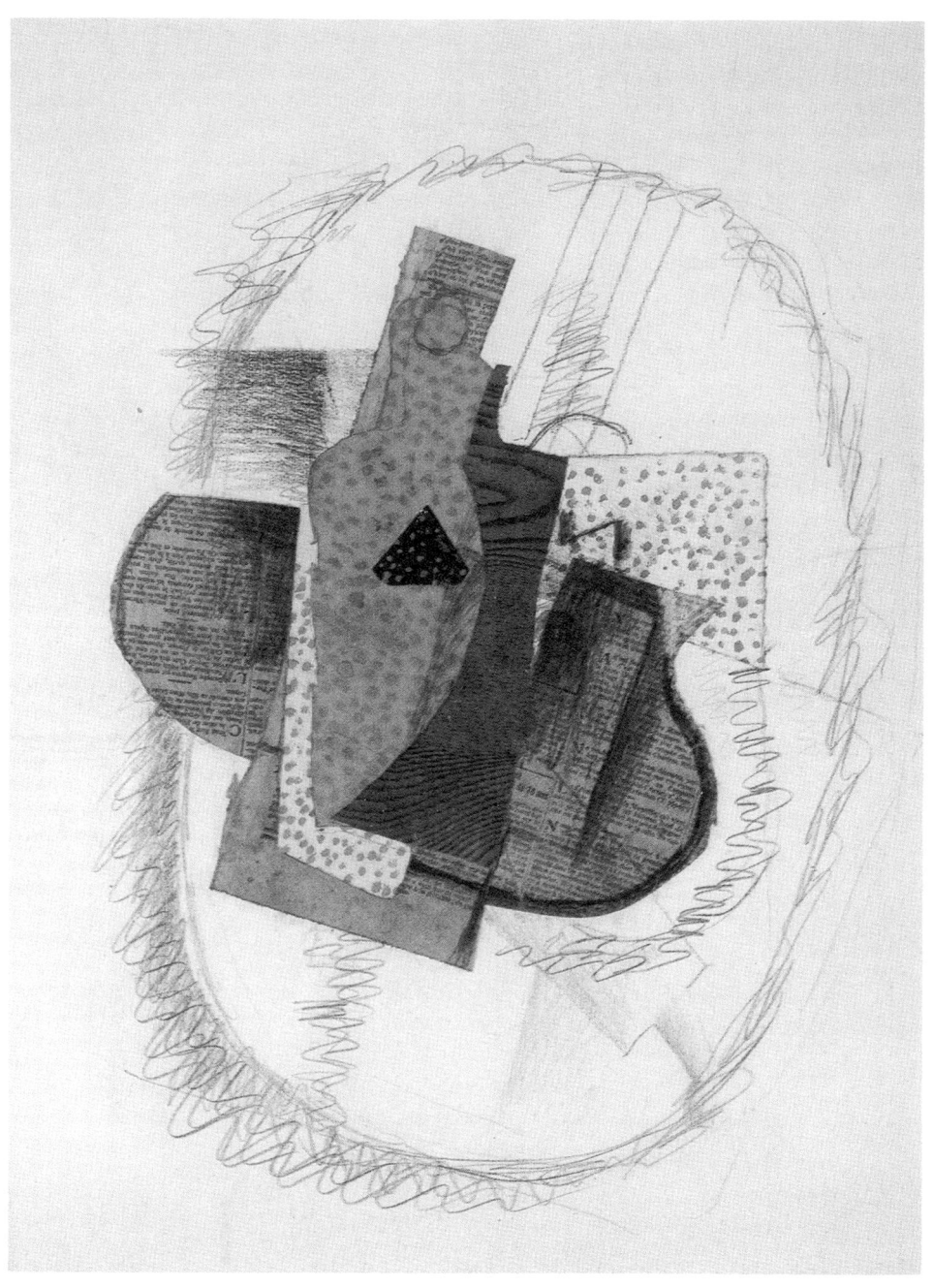

156. Georges Braque,
Still Life with Bottle, January 1914.

Braque and Gris

Braque's use of newsprint in his collages differed from Picasso's frequent use of texts, though he sometimes included short articles or *petites annonces*, such as an article on the election of Henri Bergson to the French Academy in January 1914 in *Still Life with Bottle*. In this work, in fact, the literally 'Bergsonian' newspaper constitutes the body of a guitar, while the woodgrain paper separately signifies both the guitar's and the table's woodenness, viewed as distorted through a glass bottle. Braque freely draws the oval of the table in charcoal, and decorates white and beige papers with dots of paint in a mock neo-Impressionist pointillism perhaps signifying 'the decorative' much the way the wallpaper does in *Bottle of Suze*. 156 153

Both artists repeatedly employed large-scale headlines for puns and allusions. For example Picasso's pun on the fragment 'JOU' from the masthead of *Le Journal* in *Guitar, Sheet Music and Glass* suggests 150 the verb *jouer*, 'to play', as in *jouer du guitare*: the proximity of the guitar and the letters 'JOU' bring the music to life. Braque's *Still Life* 158 *with Tenora* of summer 1913, arranged as a still life of a wineglass and a tenora – a clarinet-like Catalan instrument – on a table, plays cleverly with the pasted papers, each one bringing a separate attribute of the subject. The papers overlap each other, with black paper serving as the wallpaper etched with white chalk moulding overlapped

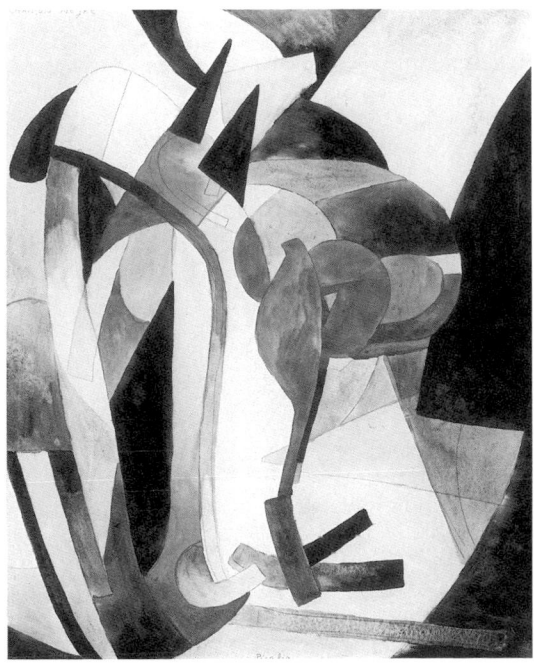

157. **Francis Picabia**,
Chanson nègre (Negro Song), 1913.
Picabia travelled to New York City around the time of the Armory Show (1913), which introduced European modernism to America, and visited a nightclub with a band and tap dancers. In his Cubist evocation of this experience, geometric shapes and abrupt colour changes suggest the intense vitality and rhythm of music and dance in abstract visual terms.

159. Georges Braque in his studio, 5 impasse de Guelma, c. 1911.

by the artificial woodgrain paper, which in turn lies under a corner of the newspaper; the tenora elusively lies above and below, in front of and behind the woodgrain paper. The woodgrain signifies the texture of the table, but also wittily evokes the wood of which the tenora, a woodwind instrument, is made. The headline, 'L'Echo d'A[rt]', is from an art, literature, music and theatre review, whose presence suggests a critical audience while also introducing the word 'echo', evocative of music. Being an 'echo of art', however, analogizes the music with visual art – including the very work we are contemplating, neatly framed with paint – overriding a merely musical 'theme' to suggest not just music but creativity as the subject, appropriately aided by wine. The very rhythms of the simplified geometric forms, with their abrupt and contradictory relations in space, suggest their relations to the tenora as a folk instrument, playing the unpretentious and 'authentic' folk music Braque would have remembered from the summer and autumn of 1911 he spent in Céret, near the Pyrenees in the French part of Catalonia. Thus the cheap materials of which the collage is made are perfectly of a piece with the popular music evoked by its forms.

158. **Georges Braque**, *Still Life with Tenora*, summer 1913.

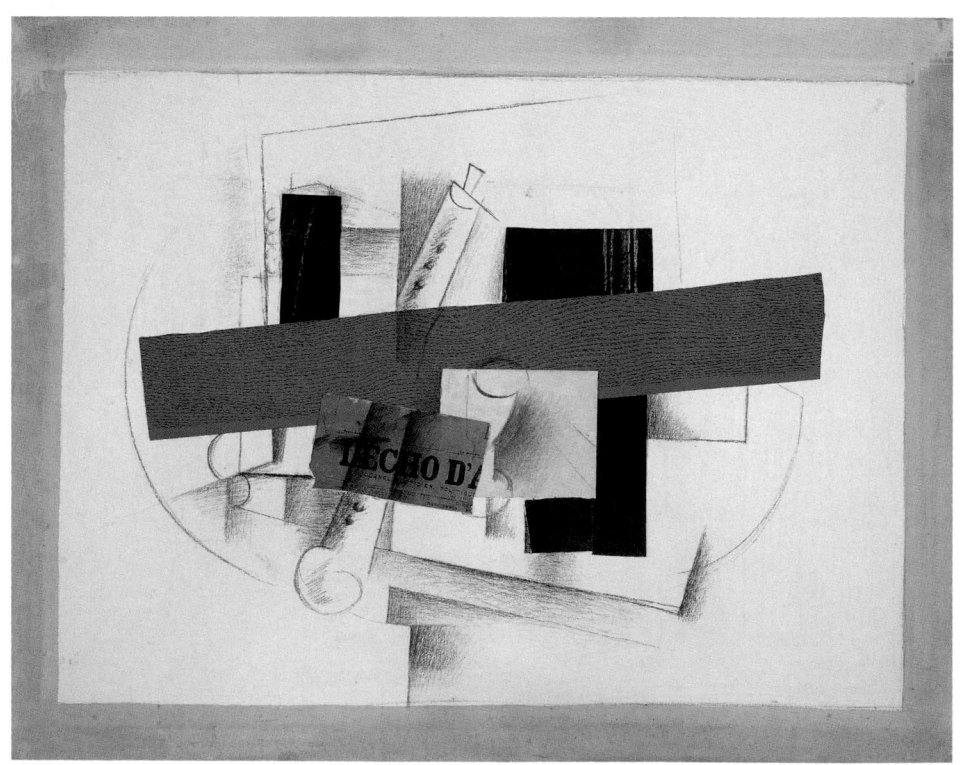

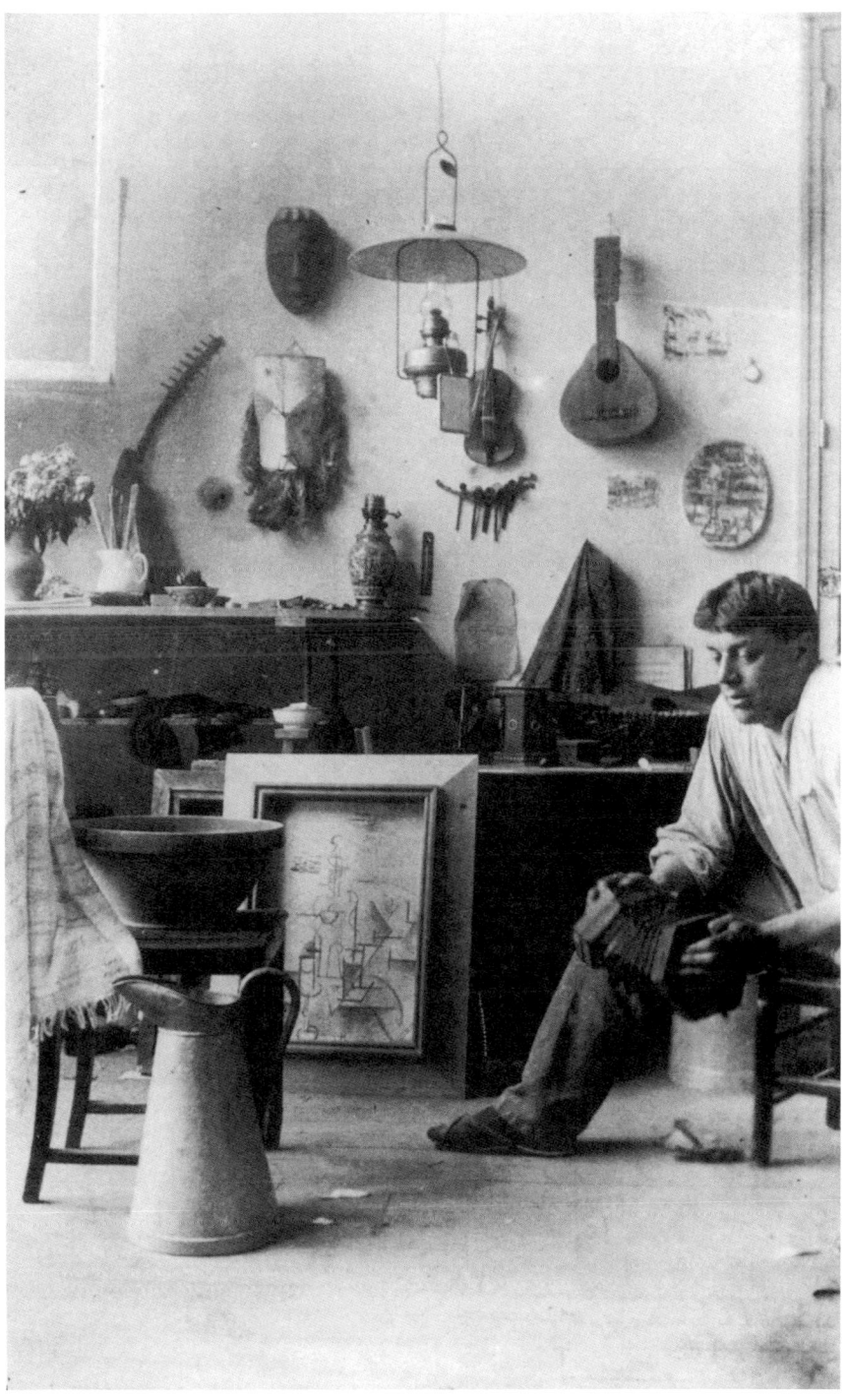

Music and popular culture were by no means new themes for Picasso and Braque. Unlike the Puteaux Cubists, from 1909 on they concentrated on still lifes and figures, who often play musical instruments, as for example Braque's *Violin and Palette* (1909), *The Portuguese* (1911–12) or *Still Life with Bottle* (1914) and Picasso's numerous 'guitars'. If music informed the rhythms of Cubist painting, that music was primarily jazz, which was all the rage in Paris in those years. Art historian Jody Blake has detailed the influence of the African-American musicians and dancers – from the cakewalk and ragtime to a whole range of hybrid 'African'/European 'animal dances' – which introduced to Paris syncopated rhythms saturated in primitivist aesthetics.

Folk music was another aspect of popular culture embraced by modernists, whether the urban version rife in the cabarets and dancehalls of Montmartre or the rural version of small French towns; witness Braque's own claim to folk culture in his mastery of the humble concertina – with which he entertained his friends according to numerous reports – visible in a photograph of Braque in his studio (c. 1911). As with the *Portrait of Kahnweiler*, the rhythmic repetition of the stepped shape of an accordion's bellows structures Picasso's *Accordionist* of summer 1911, while the separate touches of paint gaily beat a supporting counter rhythm. This evocation of jazz, which was taken to be 'African' by critics and viewers alike, and folk music is not just for fun, though that is one aspect. Its deep presence in the work analogizes Cubist painting with 'authentic' and spontaneous folk culture, an attitude informing Cubism from the start. Despite the obvious difficulty of 'seeing' this kind of painting, and its resultingly small and elite group of viewers, such analogies aim to ally the new art with 'the people' as against the bourgeois art of the salons.

160. **Pablo Picasso**,
Accordionist, summer 1911.
This is an especially difficult painting to 'read', yet Picasso allows us to orient ourselves within the composition of a traditional half-length seated figure in an armchair. The large dark isosceles triangle in the middle of the painting contains the figure; its apex, pointing to the right, outlines the figure's left arm, bent at the elbow and held just above the scroll of the chair's arm. The lower point of this triangle marks the figure's right arm, whose elbow rests above the other armchair scroll. At the top of the painting the curves of forehead and closed eyes suggest the location of the head – in a transport of musical inspiration – while the white areas below indicate the location of the shirt and the hands playing the accordion. Such details allow viewers to bring their own senses and memories into play in responding to the work.

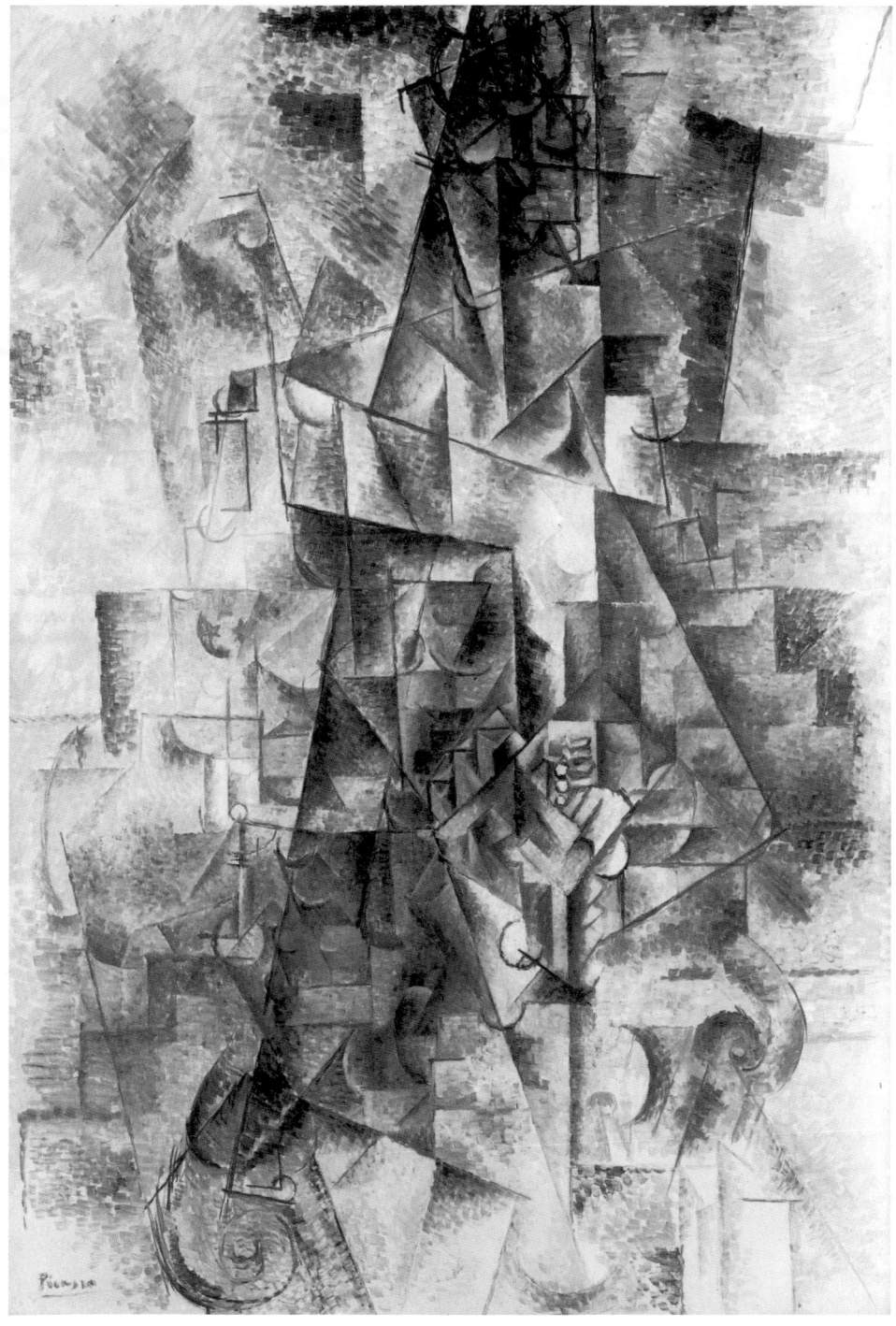

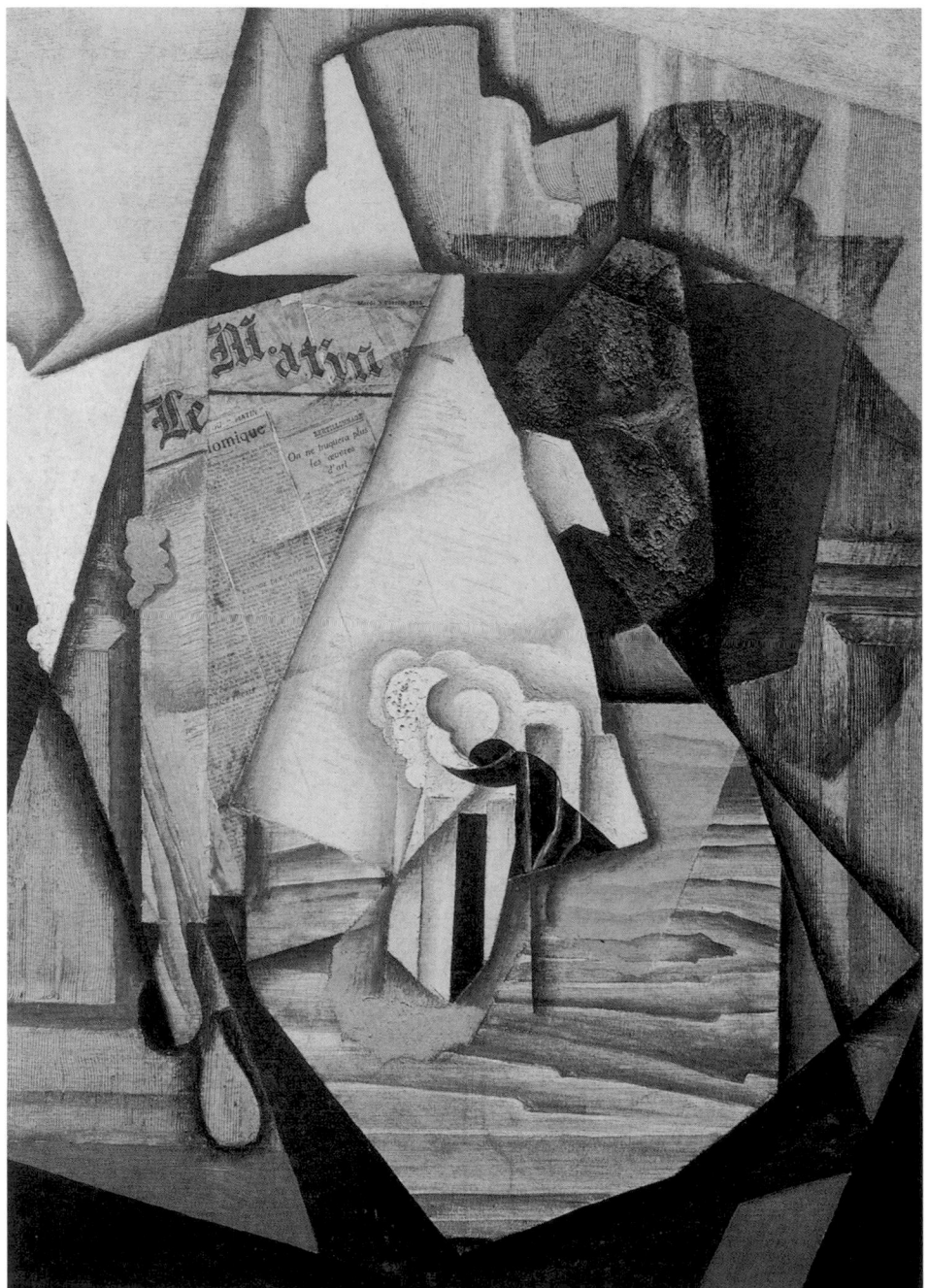

Gris inherited a complex and, in Picasso's hands, politicized version of collage when he began to concentrate on *papiers collés* in the summer and autumn of 1914, on the eve of war. A comparison of Picasso's use of newsprint with Gris's is quite telling. In Gris's *Man at the Café* (1914), a figure sits at a table drinking a beer and reading the news. However, here the 'news' is not an intrusion from the political world, but a carefully selected fragment from some other paper brought together with the masthead of *Le Matin*, which plays on the concept of illusion versus reality so wittily juggled in the work itself, with its industrial artificial woodgrain paper – both 'real' and carefully faked with paint – and its literal newsprint: the headline reads, 'There will be no more faking of works of art'.

161

161. Juan Gris,
Man at the Café, 1914.
In this work Gris combines the colours and textures of a table and wood panelling to depict a figure sandwiched between these two spatial regions. Devices from his days as a cartoonist are used to signify the figure's hand (in the blue strip to the left of the newspaper *Le Matin*), the wonderfully sinister shadow of the hatted figure on the upper right and the beer stein foaming over at the top. The contrast between these highly readable images and the profoundly abstract and disorienting space constitutes Gris's signature style in this period.

162. Juan Gris,
The Table, spring 1914.
The headline pasted into *The Table* announces 'The True and the False', a witty act of artistic self-reference. In this paradoxical image, texture as a property has become completely independent of the objects depicted. The woodgrain representing the texture and material of the table floats away from the table's charcoal outline and its cut shape is used instead to describe the transparent glass and bottle above. Below, a cartoon key opens the drawer of the wooden table, which the absence of woodgrain has left starkly and absurdly white, revealing the 'truth' of the primed canvas beneath. Gris conjures here with 'truth' and 'falsehood' on several levels: all art is illusion, even when it abandons traditional three-dimensional illusionism as a way of trying to arrive at a deeper truth.

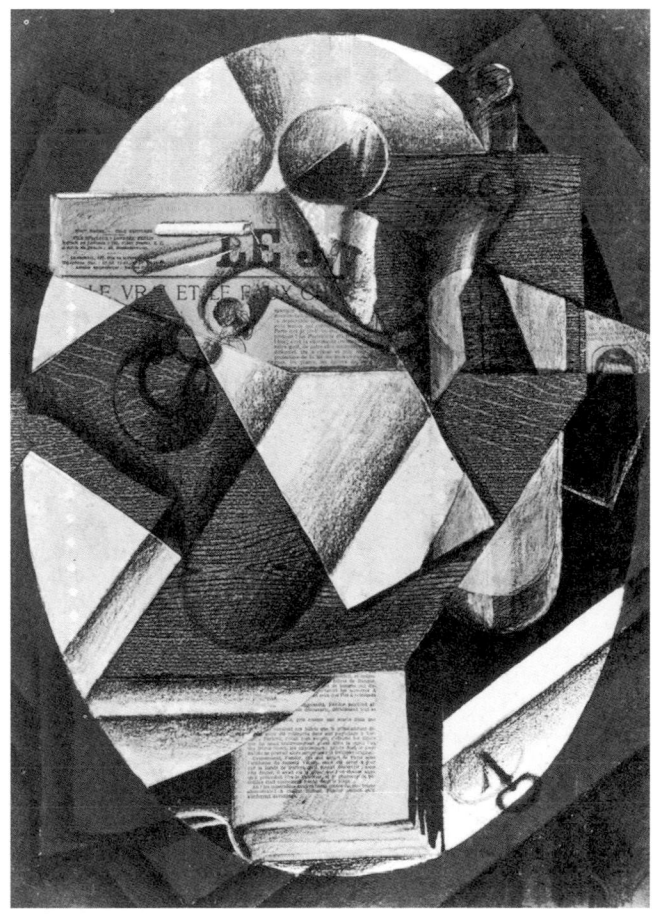

In the *Musician's Table* (1914), Gris brilliantly counterbalances illusionism and abstraction, utilizing to the full his cartoonlike illustrational style to contrast with his Cubist exploration of space. In fact, it is Gris's very use of illustration, for instance the clarity of the mildly distorted graphite violin, that allows such an extreme reduction of spatial structure to planes of colour and pattern, revealed through the violin's transparency. The black plane of the table top, the separate plane of its woodgrain texture, the faked sheet of music, all occupy distinct and incompatible positions in space. According to Christopher Green, such innovations had their origins in Poincaré's separation of qualities in *Science and Hypothesis*. Thus the detachment of signifiers from referents – woodgrain from tabletop – may stand as another instance of Poincaré's impact on the pictorial innovations of the Cubists. The resulting combination of visual confusion and revelation serves a meditation on the nature of creativity suggested by the partly emptied bottle of liquor, the demotic presence of the daily paper, and the violin and sheet music, empty and waiting for the composer's inspiration, which will be jazz if the music has anything in common with the style of the collage. The comparison between music and Gris's own investigations into Cubist transformations of reality is both a conscious echo of similar works by Picasso and Braque and a significant claim to originality in its departure from their treatments of the theme. This time Gris's headline informs us that 'Explorers in disaccord accuse each other of having explored nothing'. The metaphorical comment on his friendly rivalry with Picasso and others again refers to the creative process and to the dialogue between a small group of artists and himself, carefully defusing the political potential Picasso manipulates so cleverly. Indeed, in *Breakfast* (1914), Gris playfully wins this artistic contest by pasting his own name under the headline in *Le Journal*'s morning news, read over the breakfast table in the privacy of his own home, as we can tell from the small packet of coffee.

Thus the deliberation of their approaches to collage speaks as much to Gris's careful avoidance of the political as to Picasso's purposeful deployment of anarchist themes – war, pacifism, armaments profiteering, strike-breaking – at a moment of international crisis. Gris represents an interesting example of an artist whose leftist politics, inspiring the expressive power of his cartoons, nourished his subsequent painting, but who wanted to strip his avant-garde art of those politics at a time when they were most intensely unacceptable, as we discuss in the next chapter.

Whether meditating on themes of aesthetic language or social conflict, the collages reject the commodification of art in important

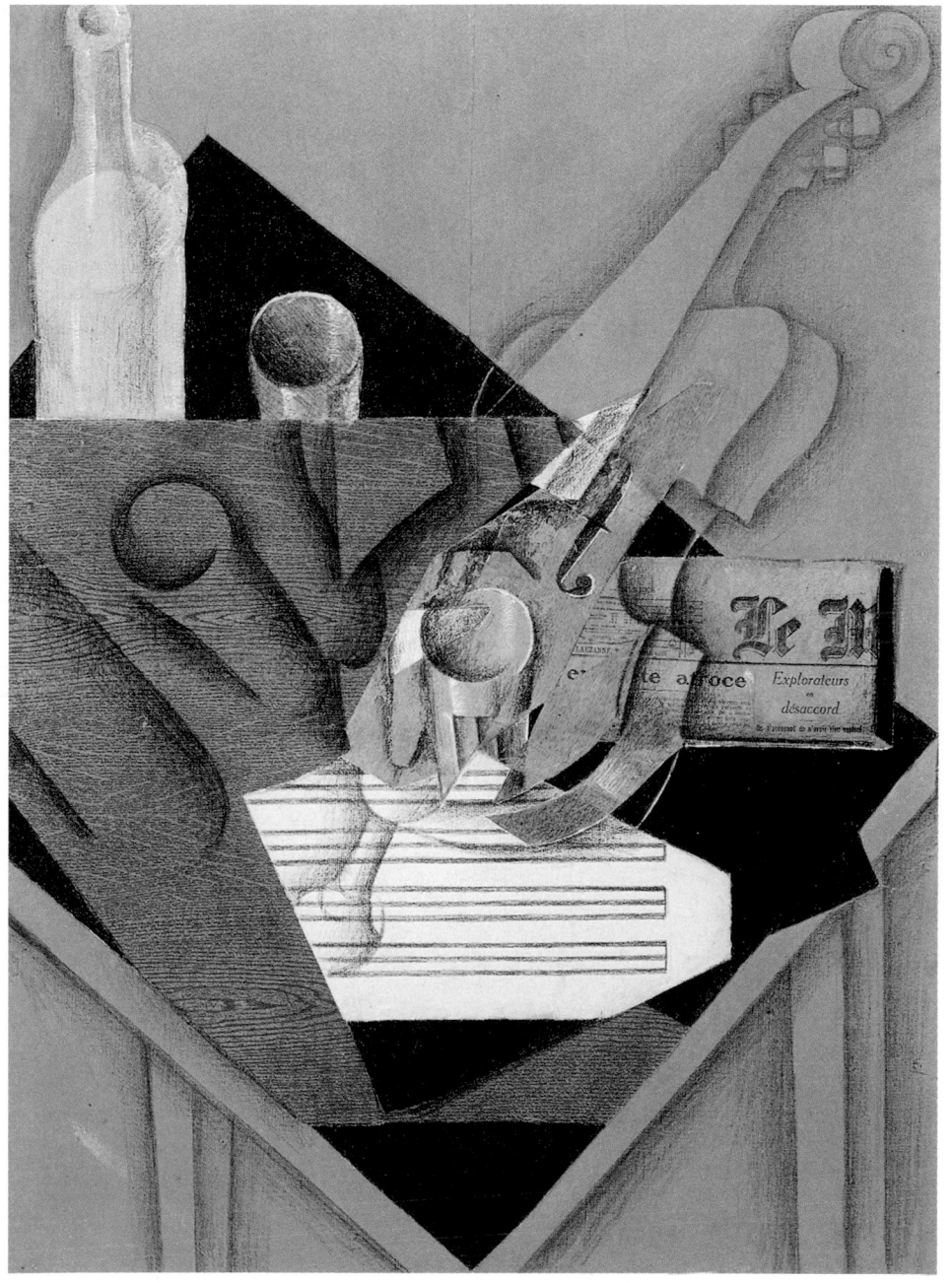

163. **Juan Gris**, *Musician's Table*, 1914.

ways. The ephemeral materials of which they are made not only disdain the condition of saleability, they flamboyantly mock the concept of 'fine' art and craftsmanship. To literally incorporate newsprint itself – the very figure of commodification and impermanence – into a work of 'high' art is to subvert the notion of bourgeois collectability, to fly in the face of the conservatives' noisy lament over the absence of *métier* in contemporary art. Given that newsprint in strong light turns brown in an afternoon, these artists necessarily envisaged its decay, its temporality, as part of the meaning of such works, in addition to the subversive choices they made in incorporating ephemeral newsprint, advertisements, the cheapest wallpaper, sticky bottle labels, tattered bits of popular song-sheets, all the detritus of an industrial and commercial culture increasingly dominant in Paris and more than usually visible to outsiders in the city. Art historian Thomas Crow, in 'Modernism and Mass Culture in the Visual Arts', has pointed to the political relevance of such antibourgeois subversions as the introduction of mass-produced materials and artisanal techniques into 'high' art: 'As such surfaces soon degrade, peel, flake, and fade, as newsprint and handbills turn brown and brittle, so collage disrupts the false harmonies of oil painting by reproducing the disposability of the late-capitalist commodity. The principle of collage construction itself collapses the distinction between high and low by transforming the totalizing creative practice of traditional painting into a fragmented consumption of already existing manufactured images'. The newsprint, more than any other of the collage elements, suggests Apollinaire's meaning in his explanation of the appearance of 'actual objects' in the collages: 'new in art', he wrote in *The Cubist Painters*, 'they are already soaked with humanity'.

Chapter 6   Cubism at War

The period from the outbreak of World War I in early August 1914 to its conclusion in November 1918 radically transformed every aspect of French society. The French, indeed all of Europe, entered the war enthusiastically, assuming it would be 'over by Christmas', but after only three months it was already clear that any chance of a decisive military victory for either side had been lost and that the war was a stalemate. Unbroken parallel strings of well-fortified defensive trenches on either side of a 'no-man's-land' – its width determined by the range of the machine gun – stretched hundreds of miles from Switzerland to Belgium; this siege warfare guaranteed a war of attrition, regularly punctuated by massive and fruitless assaults by one side or the other, resulting in human slaughter on a historically unprecedented scale.

The British assault on the Somme in July 1916 was typical: a weeklong barrage of over a million and a half shells succeeded in turning the front into a muddy quagmire. But of the 12,000 tons of shell delivered onto the German side, only about 900 tons represented high explosive, hence the Germans in their deep dugouts harboured safely until the end of the bombardment, then quickly set up their machine guns. As military historian John Keegan writes:

The battle was about to begin. And its first, and indeed decisive,
act was to be the 'race for the parapet' – a race which for the British
ran from their own front trench to the other side of no-man's-land,
for the Germans from the bottom to the top of their dug-out steps.
Whoever first arrived at the German parapet would live. The side
which lost the race would die.

Soldiers involved in such suicidal frontal attacks were expected to run towards enemy lines carrying 66-pound packs and make their way through the fresh mud and barbed-wire entanglements amid ceaseless machine-gun fire. 60,000 were killed or wounded on the first day of the Somme, and as British writer and participating soldier Edmund Blunden later remembered, 'By the end of the day both sides had seen, in a sad scrawl of broken earth and murdered men, the answer to the question. No road. No thoroughfare. Neither race had won, nor could win, the War. The War had won, and would go on winning'. By the time the Somme campaign

164

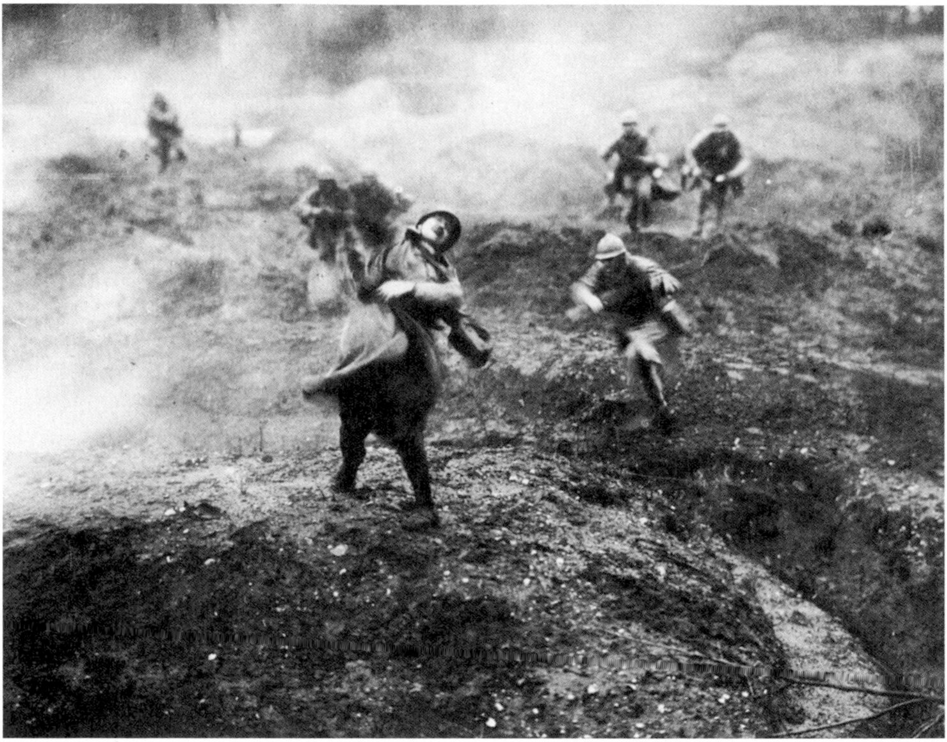

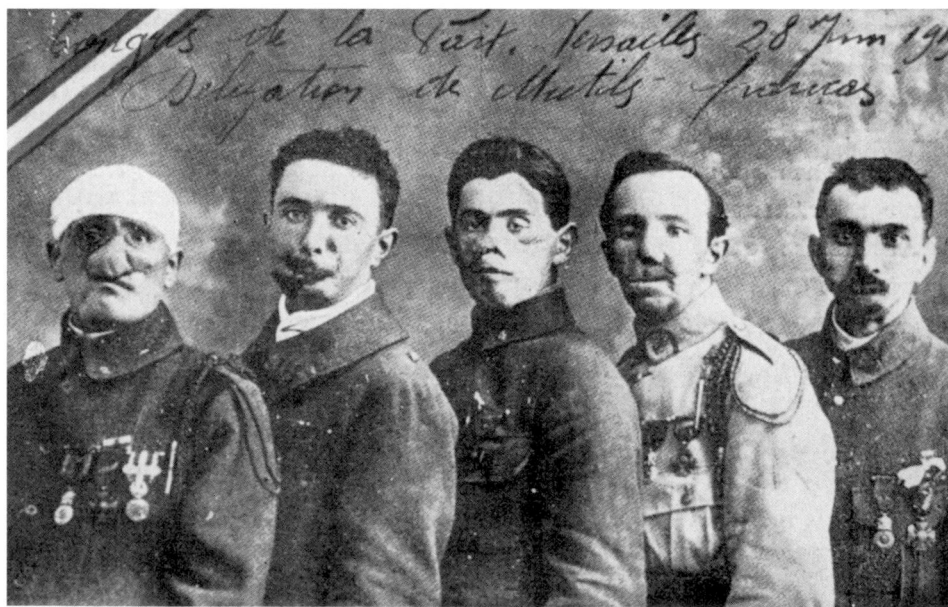

officially ended on 18 November, 419,654 British and nearly 200,000 French soldiers were casualties.

These horrific numbers were possible partly because of the technological innovation of the machine gun and partly because of a shift from volunteer armies to much vaster armies of draftees. Such wholesale conscription forced the participation of each country's entire able-bodied male population, introducing the phenomenon of 'total war'. From 1917 onwards French morale was sorely tested by army mutinies on the front in May of that year, and a series of strikes in Paris and the provinces in March and April 1918 revealed mounting protest against the war. After the war's conclusion, citizens were constantly reminded of the cost of victory by the return of wounded mutilated veterans to civilian life. By the war's end on 165 11 November 1918, more than 1,350,000 French soldiers had been killed and another 4,250,000 wounded, a toll that would have been unimaginable at the start of hostilities. Physical devastation only added to the suffering: the entire north-east of France lay in ruins, 166 with over a thousand cities and villages completely destroyed, another twelve hundred towns rendered uninhabitable, and three million acres left unfit for cultivation.

France's cultural and political elite responded to these events in a manner that was understandable, but frequently deplorable. Henri Bergson quickly turned the conflict into a spiritual battle

164. The leading wave of a French infantry assault on the German trenches, Western Front, 1916.

165. Delegation of French Mutilés de Guerre, Congress of Versailles Treaty, 28 June 1919, postcard.

166. Verdun, rue Mazel, after the bombardment of 1916, postcard.

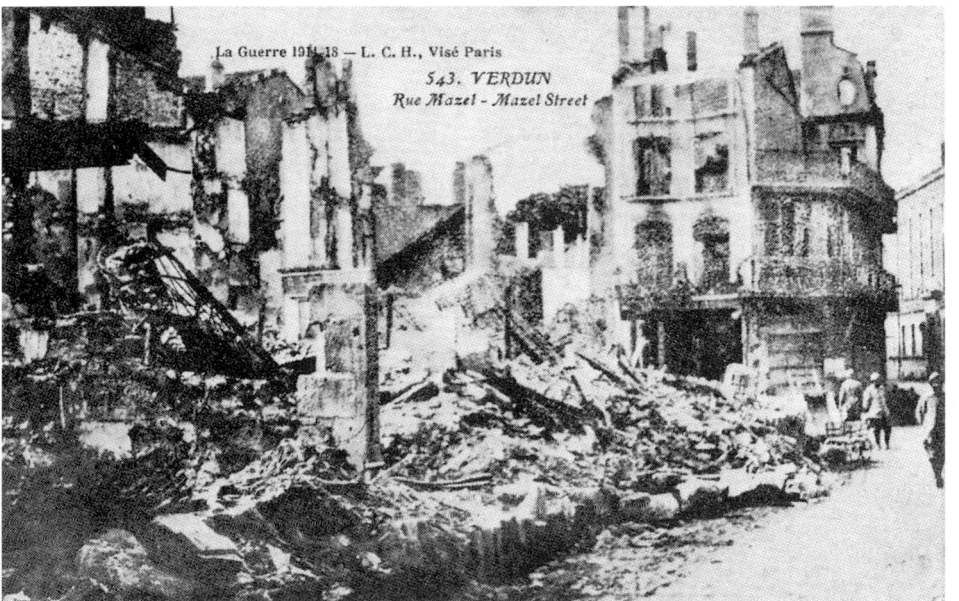

199

between the forces of despotism (Germany) and those of freedom (France), disseminating his views in the 4 September 1914 issue of the *Bulletin des armées de la République*; even worse, the French historian Félix Sartiaux wrote in *Morale kantienne et morale humaine (Kantian Ethics and Human Ethics)* that one of the 'most subtle traits of the German character is its hypocrisy' for the Germans were 'a race of born liars'. Sartiaux's anti-Kantianism was shared by others: Action Française railed against his influence, and the French cleric Monseigneur Pons even declared Kant anti-Catholic and anti-French in his book of 1915, *La Guerre et l'âme française (The War and the French Soul)*. Bergson's ethical interpretation of the conflict was seconded by figures like the anarchist Peter Kropotkin, who supported the French war effort as a defence of the revolutionary tradition against the forces of political reaction. Kropotkin was not alone in rejecting international class solidarity in the name of 'higher values': in early August 1914 the anarcho-syndicalist union Confédération Génerale du Travail (C.G.T.) appealed to all workers to rally to the war effort. In December 1912 the C.G.T. had fomented a general strike against the jingoistic buildup of armaments in France, but on 4 August 1914 the C.G.T. leader Léon Jouhaux declared the war a battle for justice and republican liberty against German militarism. It was only with the Zimmerwald Conference – held in neutral Switzerland in September 1915 – that leftists throughout Europe again united in their opposition to the war.

The Cubists and their literary supporters were not exempt from the cataclysmic sweep of events, which transformed the Parisian cultural landscape in which Cubism had flourished. Art historian Kenneth Silver in his book on the Parisian avant-garde and the war years has charted the impact: while Gris and Picasso – in default of their Spanish military service – remained non-combatants throughout the conflict, the vast majority of Cubists either volunteered or were conscripted. Braque, Derain, Duchamp-Villon, La Fresnaye, Gleizes, Léger, Metzinger and Villon were all at the front by the first winter of the war. While some foreigners, such as the Poles Apollinaire and Marcoussis, rejected their countries' neutrality and joined the French troops, those of German citizenship were either arrested or forced to flee: Kahnweiler was in Italy when the war broke out and sought refuge in Switzerland; his property – including his stock of Cubist artworks – was confiscated, to be auctioned off by the French state after the war. Laurencin, who had married a German in June 1914, fled to neutral Spain for the war's duration. Still others signalled their opposition by leaving France: the Delaunays for instance were in Portugal and Spain throughout the

167. Lodewijk Schelfhout and Piet Mondrian in Schelfhout's studio, 26 rue du Départ, Paris, 1912. Le Fauconnier's choice of the Netherlands as a place of refuge was in large part motivated by his circle of friends, as well as his artistic prominence there. Before the war the Dutch artist Schelfhout and artist-critic Conrad Kickert had promoted Le Fauconnier in Dutch circles, which culminated in a retrospective at the 1912 Moderne Kunstkring exhibition in Amsterdam. The leading Dutch modernist Piet Mondrian's first exposure to Cubism was mediated by Kickert and Schelfhout, who introduced him to Le Fauconnier and Léger. At the war's outbreak Le Fauconnier was in Dutch Zeeland on a painting trip with Kickert and Mondrian; remaining in Holland until 1919, Le Fauconnier participated in the left-wing pacifist movement Het Signal.

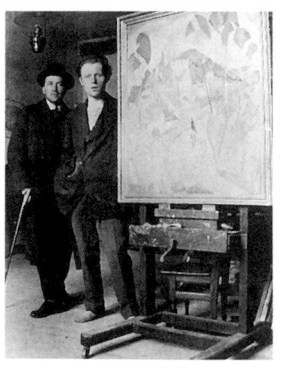

war, Le Fauconnier settled in the neutral Netherlands, Marcel ¹⁶⁷ Duchamp left France for the still-neutral United States in 1915, and Gleizes did the same when he was demobilized the same year. Given that Duchamp-Villon and Apollinaire both died by the end of the conflict as a long-term consequence of war injuries, Braque was lucky only to have been wounded, though it took him many years ¹⁶⁸ to recover.

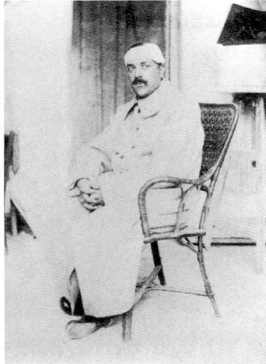

168. Photograph of Georges Braque in Henri Laurens's studio, taken by Laurens, 1915.

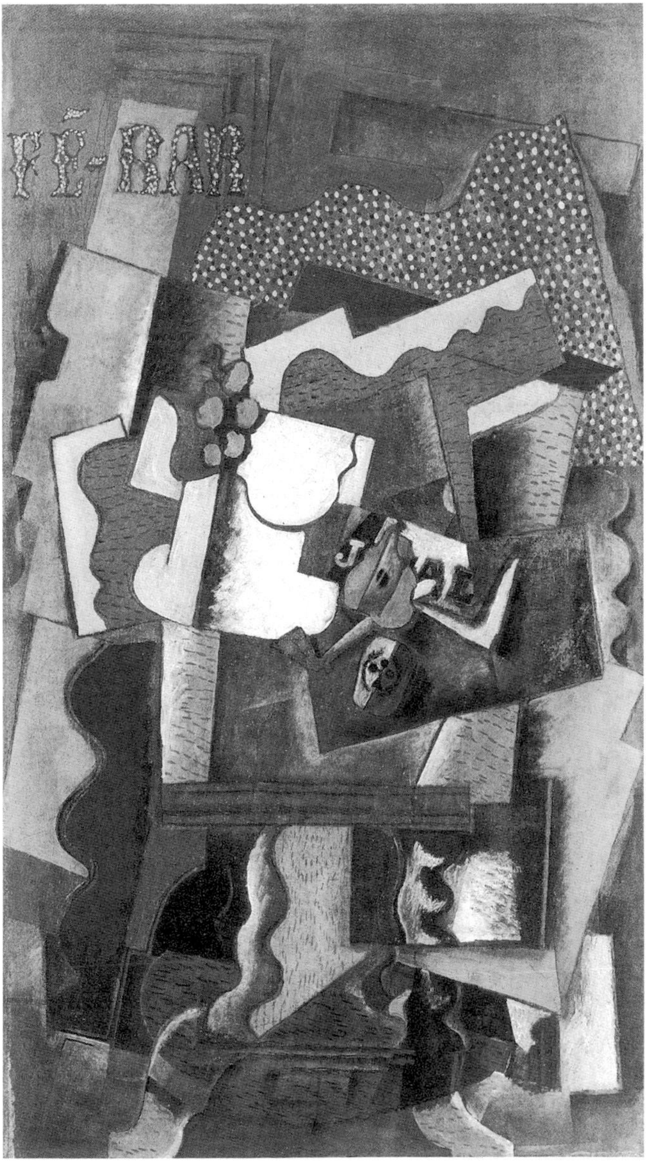

169. **Georges Braque**,
The Pedestal Table, 1918.
Though wounded in the war, Braque eventually recovered and began to paint again, establishing by 1918 a style that points the way to his later work. Drawing on the 'lessons of collage', with its layering of space and decorative play with pattern and colour, he developed a curvilinear form of late Cubism. Embracing Gris's wartime work, such as *The Table* (plate 162), Braque suggests two different colours and textures of wood, overlapping with, yet distinct from, the structure of the table. The pear, playing card, white clay pipe, folded newspaper and fruit dish with grapes on a square pedestal table remain objects with their own integrity, but negotiate a fully Cubist space. Initiating the use of a dark ground, Braque manages to juxtapose the gaiety of a café-bar and its exuberant confetti patterns with deeper notes of brooding mystery.

Although historians rightly align protest against the war with the emergence of Dada at the Cabaret Voltaire in Zurich in 1916, Cubism also played a role in the cultural politics of wartime resistance. Protest against the conflict was prevalent among former members of the Abbaye de Créteil. Before the war the Unanimists argued that the multinational makeup of modern cities and the cross-cultural communication facilitated by modern technology meant that the collective fraternity resulting from *la vie unanime*, or 'unanimous life', would break down national prejudices and establish harmony in Europe. With the outbreak of hostilities many Unanimists protested the war in the name of such transnational ideals. For instance Alexandre Mercereau published an antiwar manifesto in 1914, while René Arcos railed against the conflict in 1915 as a journalist for the *Chicago Daily News* before moving to Switzerland in 1916. In Geneva, Arcos founded a press and collaborated with the artist Frans Masereel (1889–1972) in producing antiwar publications. In books such as Arcos's *Le Sang des autres* (1920), Pierre Jean Jouve's *Heures, livre de la nuit* (1919), Jules Romains's *Europe 1914–16* (1916), and Charles Vildrac's *Chants du désespéré* (1920), these poets lamented the human carnage and called upon combatants to resuscitate and prolong the internationalist camaraderie integral to Unanimism. Masereel's Cubist-inspired frontispiece for Arcos's volume captures the epic proportions of the war by depicting a swarm of dying and fighting combatants, a city subject to aerial bombardment, and sinking ships on a distant sea. In effect Masereel's Unanimist vision has encompassed the global scale of the conflict, and the looming cannon on the right – inscribed with the initials 'F.M.' – is there to underscore the mechanized efficiency of the war's violence.

Gleizes celebrated the survival of these Unanimist values in a painting of 1917 titled *In Port. In Port* was completed in New York, 171 shortly before the United States joined the war, but was first conceived in 1916 when Gleizes frequented a circle of war resisters in Barcelona that included the deserter Max Goth (Maximilien Gauthier, art critic for *Les Hommes du jour*), the Delaunays and Laurencin. As art historian Christopher Green notes, *In Port* combined imagery from New York harbour with that of Barcelona, symbolizing the role of neutral America and Spain in promoting international trade and cultural communication. The surrounding grey-blue sea, signified by scallop-shaped waves, frames the colourful port. On the left a series of harbour buildings are paired with the jutting bows of docked boats seen from a variety of perspectives, and the star on a ship's funnel is placed above the fragmented stern

170. **Frans Masereel**, Frontispiece for René Arcos, *Le Sang des autres*, 1920. The Belgian artist Masereel (1889–1972) was a committed pacifist, most famous for his woodblock prints. Having studied art in Paris, he signalled his antiwar stance by moving to Switzerland in 1914; following the war he settled in Germany where he was prominent in anarchist and communist circles.

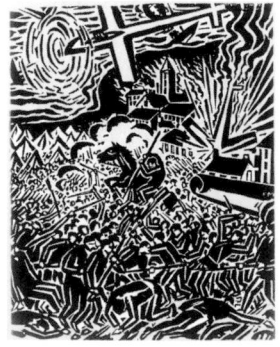

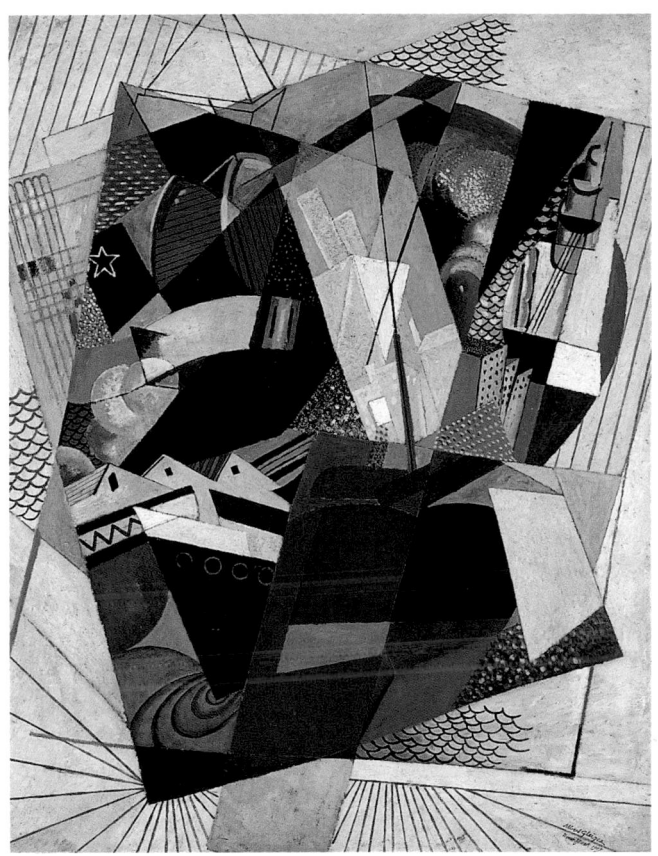

171. **Albert Gleizes,**
In Port (Overlooking a Port), 1917.

of a ship. Gleizes conflates Barcelona and New York by basing his composition in part on earlier images of Barcelona's port, including numerous towers and sharp prows, but adds the tension cables that appeared in his earlier images of the Brooklyn Bridge. The combined features of these two world harbours remind us that international cooperation and economic prosperity could still persist in the midst of the deprivations caused by war. By providing a safe haven for an international intelligentsia opposed to the war, these countries nurtured the Unanimist spirit during a moment of profound crisis.

In neutral Switzerland the art dealer Daniel-Henry Kahnweiler launched his own rebuttal of wartime xenophobia in his text of 1915, *Der Weg zum Kubismus (The Rise of Cubism)* (published in 1920). Kahnweiler's book championed the philosophy of Immanuel Kant as the key to an understanding of the art of Picasso and

Braque. He deployed the Kantian term 'analytic' to describe their Cubist treatment of form in works from 1910 to 1912 – such as Braque's *The Portuguese* – and the Kantian term 'synthetic' to signify the 'additive' methods following from the invention of collage in 1912, such as Braque's *Fruit Dish, Ace of Clubs* of early 1913. Kahnweiler's application of Kantian precepts to the art of Braque and Picasso may well be part and parcel of his ongoing attempt to separate his artistic 'stable' from their potential rivals among the Salon Cubists. Kahnweiler's Kantian terminology gained wide currency after the war, yet we should recognize the boldness – both philosophical and political – of his theoretical stance at this historical juncture.

By promoting Kant, Kahnweiler explicitly rejected the philosophical premises of prewar Cubism, whose practitioners had embraced the anti-Kantian precepts of Bergson, James and Poincaré. Indeed, the celebration of radical subjectivity and the temporal qualities of consciousness accounts for the Cubists' dismissal before the war of critics who would associate Cubist innovation with Kantian terminology. For instance, Olivier Hourcade, in an essay of February 1912, claimed that Kant's distinction between 'the phenomenon and the thing in itself' accounted for Gleizes's departure from 'optics' and 'perspective', while Jacques Rivière in an August 1912 essay recast this Kantian distinction in terms of 'conception and vision', asserting that the Cubists grasped the 'absolute' by rejecting erroneous sensory data. In *Du Cubisme* Gleizes and Metzinger censured such 'well-meaning critics' by deriding concepts of 'absolute form' and calling 'naive' the related portrayal of 'things not as they appear, but as they are'. Such Kantian notions were antithetical to Poincaré's conventionalism, Bergsonian temporality, and Nietzschean 'will to power' to which these Cubists turned in developing their art. From a political standpoint Kahnweiler's Kantian apologia for Cubism would have been an open declaration that the roots of Cubism resided in a broader European culture. As we have seen, in the minds of French nationalists Kantian thought epitomized the pernicious influence of Germanic culture on France; moreover socialists in Switzerland utilized Kant's philosophy to justify wartime pacifism, for Kant was among the first to advocate a 'United States of Europe' as a solution to European conflict. While in Switzerland, Kahnweiler moved among exiled German socialists, and his friendship with artist Hans Arp and poet Tristan Tzara exposed him to the anarchist politics of the Zurich Dada movement. Pacifists in Switzerland allied Kant to their cause, and Kahnweiler's own politics assured his familiarity with such thinking. Thus Kahnweiler's *The Rise of Cubism* could well be a philosophical response to the wartime politics that had forced him into exile and destroyed his livelihood.

In France proper, the wartime policy of *union sacrée*, or sacred union, not only caused the left and right to close ranks, it facilitated the cultural subordination of leftist cultural politics to a right-wing nationalist agenda. The impact of the royalist Action Française on wartime cultural discourse had important consequences for the Cubist movement. During the war years royalists like Maurras claimed that French culture derived from a spirit of reason and order, with roots going back to classical Greece and Rome; by contrast Germany had embraced the irrational and its cultural corollary, the Gothic. According to Maurras, German society, having rejected the Latinate classicism that had spawned European civilization, could only descend into the barbarism exemplified by war. When Italy entered the conflict on the side of France in May 1915 this crude dichotomy between Latinate classicism and Gothic barbarism took on the mantle of political legitimacy, for the cultural alliance between Latin nations was now matched by a military one. Wartime nationalists utilized such terminology against Cubism, citing the movement's internationalism and inclusion of Eastern Europeans and Germans among its membership as evidence of its corrosive effect on the Latinate roots of French culture. Cubism was now viewed as part of a prewar cultural invasion of Paris that had undermined the French spirit and prepared the way for the military invasion that followed.

The Cubists responded in a variety of ways to such attacks. Gleizes temporarily abandoned his own antiroyalist allegiance to the Gothic tradition and 'Celtic nationalism' in favour of Unanimist imagery, while Léger waited to promote his own leftist condemnation of Italian art in favour of Gothic 'primitivism' until the postwar era. Duchamp-Villon avoided Italianate classicism altogether and instead turned to the victorious Gallic Cock – a venerable symbol of both the French Republic and the revolutionary tradition – to signal his wartime patriotism. In this painted plaster medallion, 173 designed to ornament a theatre set up to entertain troops, Duchamp-Villon has portrayed a triumphant rooster whose right claw rests on a rising sun. Rays of light sculpted in relief radiate through the background, suggesting a future victory over Germany. The forms of the cock itself, while simplified and geometrized, retreat from the abstraction of his immediately preceding works, such as *Seated Woman*, perhaps to appear modern without also 96 appearing to be Cubist.

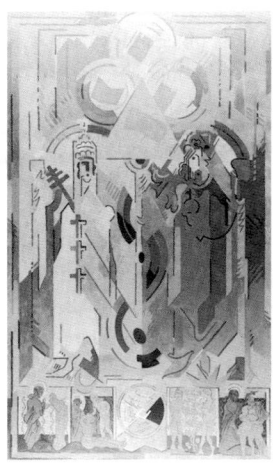

172. **Albert Gleizes**, *Spiritual Authority and Temporal Power*, 1939–40.
In the interwar years Gleizes resuscitated his Celtic nationalism and called for a return to medieval aesthetics and artisanal production as a protest against industrial capitalism. Having embraced Catholicism anew in 1918, Gleizes and a number of followers founded the artists' community of Moly-Sabata (1927–51), outside a village south of Lyons, where they applied his aesthetic precepts to handcrafted pottery as well as large-scale mural painting.

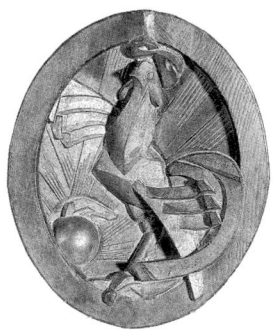

173. **Raymond Duchamp-Villon**, *Rooster (Gallic Cock)*, 1916.

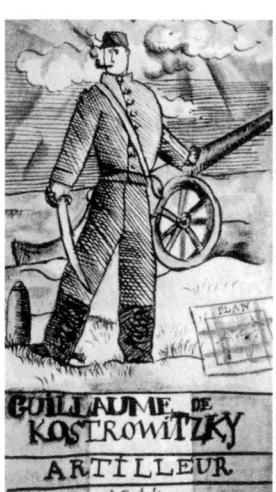

174. Pablo Picasso,
Guillaume Apollinaire, Artilleryman,
1914.

In his 1914 portrait of Apollinaire as an artilleryman, Picasso utilized the aesthetic language of French folk culture to ally the foreign-born poet to the patriotism of the common footsoldier or *poilu*. Drawn in a crude format imitative of *Images d'Epinal*, folkish woodblock prints produced in the region of Epinal from the sixteenth century onward, Picasso overlays Apollinaire's foreign surname 'Kostrowitzky' with the tricolour of the French flag to announce the poet's new-found national allegiance (Apollinaire would be granted French citizenship in March 1916). This playful dialogue with French culture – complete with phallic cannon – gave way, however, to a more serious politics of appeasement by 1915, indicative of Picasso's suppression of his prewar anarchist sympathies. In works such as his *Portrait of Ambroise Vollard*, Picasso abandoned the language of Cubism in favour of a style reminiscent of the ultra-conservative Ingres, the nineteenth-century artist most celebrated by the reactionary right. Yet concurrently Picasso painted a series of figures, such as *Guitar Player* of 1916, taking the 'lessons' of collage to the point of greatest abstraction, with the figural forms and surrounding space literally flattened into darkly coloured intersecting and overlapping rectangles and rhomboids, interrupted by a few sparing curves and circles. This severely Cubist style seems to signal that his alternative retreat from abstraction was a strategic manoeuvre at a time when non-combatants were subject to public ridicule and Cubism was under attack as *bôche*, a derogatory word for 'German'. Apollinaire, in a March 1915 article written from the front, underscored the point by announcing that Picasso, 'whose health is too weak to allow him' to fight had 'outdone Ingres' in his recent drawings. By lamenting Picasso's 'illness' Apollinaire created a fiction that accounted for his status as non-combatant during a period when pacifists were labelled *défaitiste* (defeatist). It is telling, therefore, that Apollinaire praises Picasso's emulation of Ingres, rather than his continued exploration of Cubism, as a sign of his wartime contribution. In the absence of Picasso's military service, his 'defence' of French culture in the guise of Ingresque portraits could stand in as evidence of his cultural loyalty.

For artists at the front the situation was radically different. Largely unaffected by the 'culture wars' that preoccupied non-combatants in Paris, artists like Fernand Léger proclaimed Cubism the style best able to convey the impact of modern warfare. Léger, who served as a sapper in the Argonne and as a stretcher-bearer at Verdun, claimed that his creation of aesthetic dissonance through multiple contrasts in his prewar painting anticipated the mechanized violence of the war itself. In a letter of October 1916, written

175. **Pablo Picasso**,
Guitar Player, 1916.

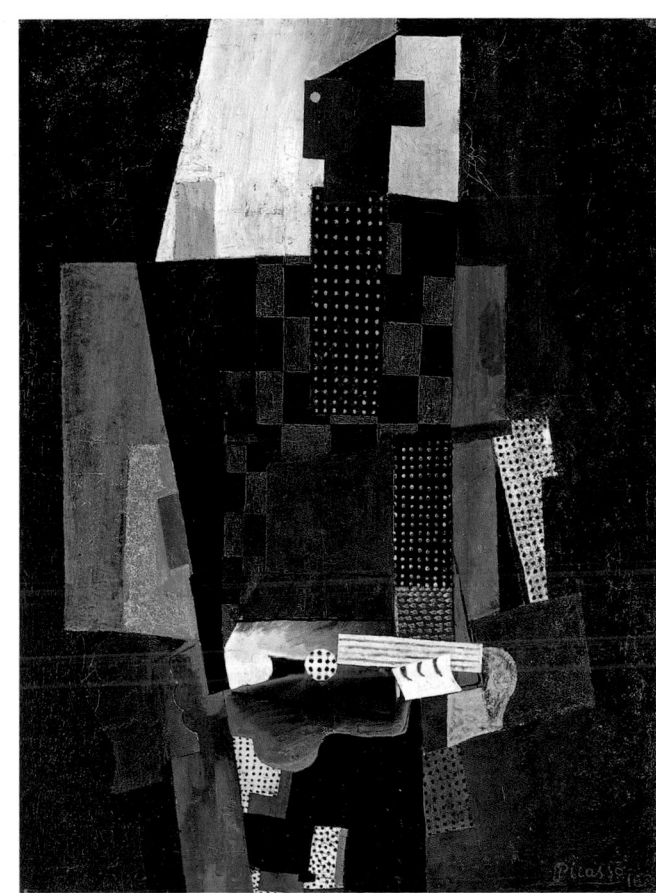

176. **Pablo Picasso**,
'Manager from New York',
costume for *Parade*, 1917.
During the war Picasso
collaborated with a new circle of
artists. Jean Cocteau introduced
him to Sergei Diaghilev, director
of the provocative yet fashionable
Ballets Russes, and Picasso became
a stage and costume designer for
Cocteau's ballet *Parade*, with music
by Erik Satie and choreography by
Léonide Massine. This Cubist
'Manager' with his attached New
York skyscrapers parallels Satie's
inclusion of dance-hall music in a
'high-art' context, but the attempt
to produce a modernist ballet
during the war resulted in disaster.
With the audience crying
'treason' and threatening to riot,
Apollinaire's appearance on
stage – bandaged and in uniform –
saved the day, according to several
witnesses.

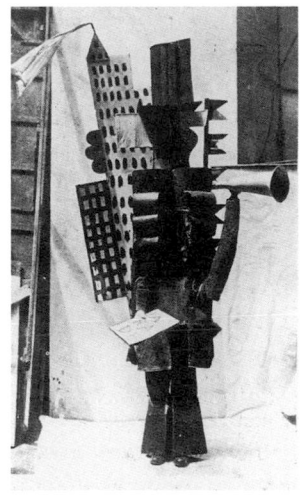

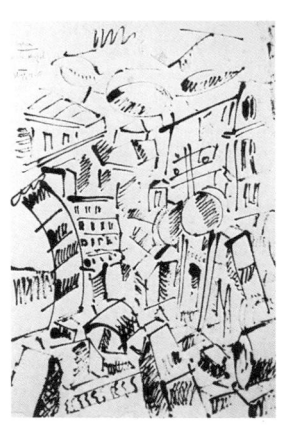

177. **Fernand Léger,**
Verdun, la rue Mazel, 1916.

from the front near Verdun, Léger exalted the synchronization of soldiers' movements with the rhythm of their artillery: 'the gunners were like madmen', Léger exclaimed, before noting that the frenetic pace of the bombardment caused officers and *poilus* to join in a concerted effort 'to hurry things along'. In portraying the ruined city of Verdun in 1916 Léger utilized his prewar aesthetic to convey the shattered quality of the urban landscape, while his painting of a card party in the trenches fused the soldiers' anatomy with the metallic sheen of instruments of war. As Eric Michaud has argued we should see the transformation of these soldiers into machine forms as a celebration of the precision, synchronized movement and military discipline that, to Léger's mind, served to efface differences of class and rank among soldiers in the trenches.

Although Cubism had came under attack during the war, its greatest challenge emerged four days after the November 1918 Armistice, when the artists Amédée Ozenfant (1886–1966) and Charles-Edouard Jeanneret (who became the architect Le Corbusier) (1887–1965) published a manifesto of postwar and 'post-Cubist' aesthetics titled *After Cubism*. Drawing an absolute divide between Cubism and art of the postwar era, Ozenfant and Le Corbusier summarized the difference between their new aesthetic precepts and those governing prewar Cubism:

Art before the great test was not living enough to invigorate the idle, nor to interest the vigorous; society then was restless, because the directive of life was too uncertain, because there was no great collective current to force to work those who had to work, nor to tempt to work those who did not have to…. Gone are those times, at once too heavy and too light.

Uncertainty, restlessness, lack of vigour: these were the metaphorical corollaries to 'defeatism' that had been displaced by the collective discipline and heroic labour that went into the war effort. During the war itself Ozenfant had already signalled his own aesthetic 'vigour' by founding a journal, *L'Elan* (1915–16), whose masthead alluded to the celebrated *élan vital* of the French soldier. Then in 1920, Ozenfant and Le Corbusier founded *L'Esprit Nouveau* (1920–25), 'the new spirit', adopting another wartime slogan – coined by none other than Apollinaire – to signal their contribution to postwar reconstruction.

The March 1920 issue of *L'Esprit Nouveau* contained a manifesto announcing the creation of a new movement known as 'Purism'. Ozenfant and Le Corbusier's tract contrasts tellingly with the antipositivist precepts governing prewar Cubism:

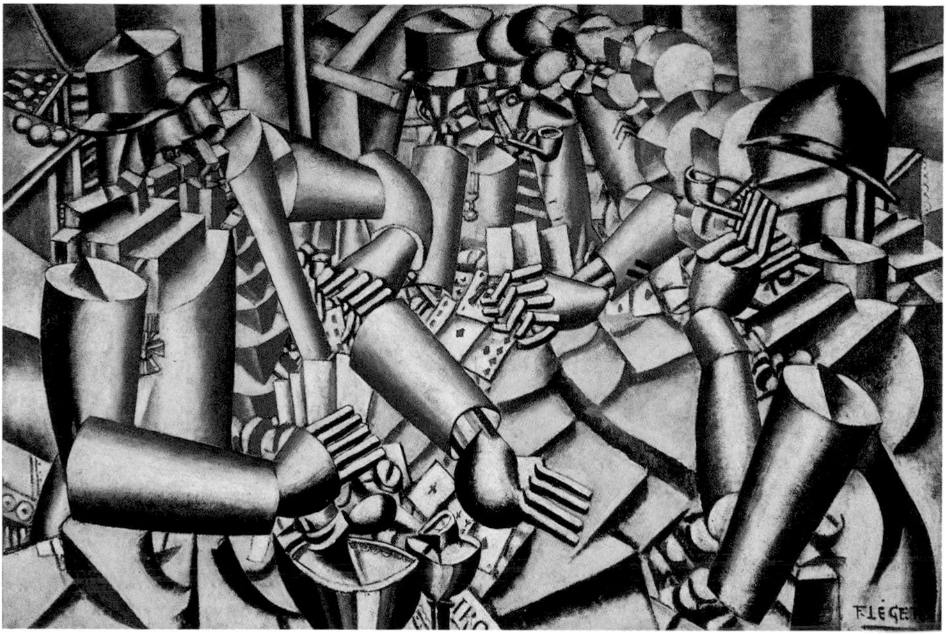

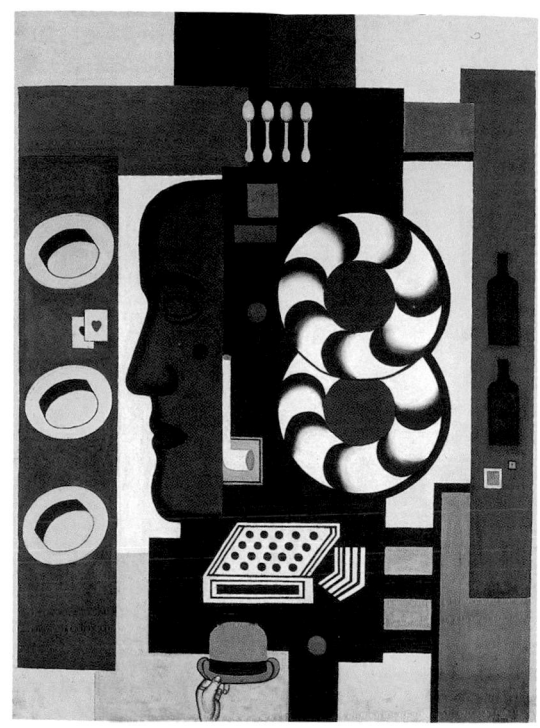

178. **Fernand Léger**,
The Card Party, 1917.

179. **Fernand Léger**,
Composition with Hand and Hats, 1927.
In the 1920s Léger signalled his populism
by turning to department-store window
displays as a source of inspiration.
Created by a new kind of artisan, such
displays were meant to appeal to the
aesthetic sense of the general public;
for this reason Léger saw them as a new
artistic form geared to the modern
city. By giving a central role to mass-
produced commodities, drawn with
cartoonlike precision, Léger attempted
to make Cubism an 'art of the people'.

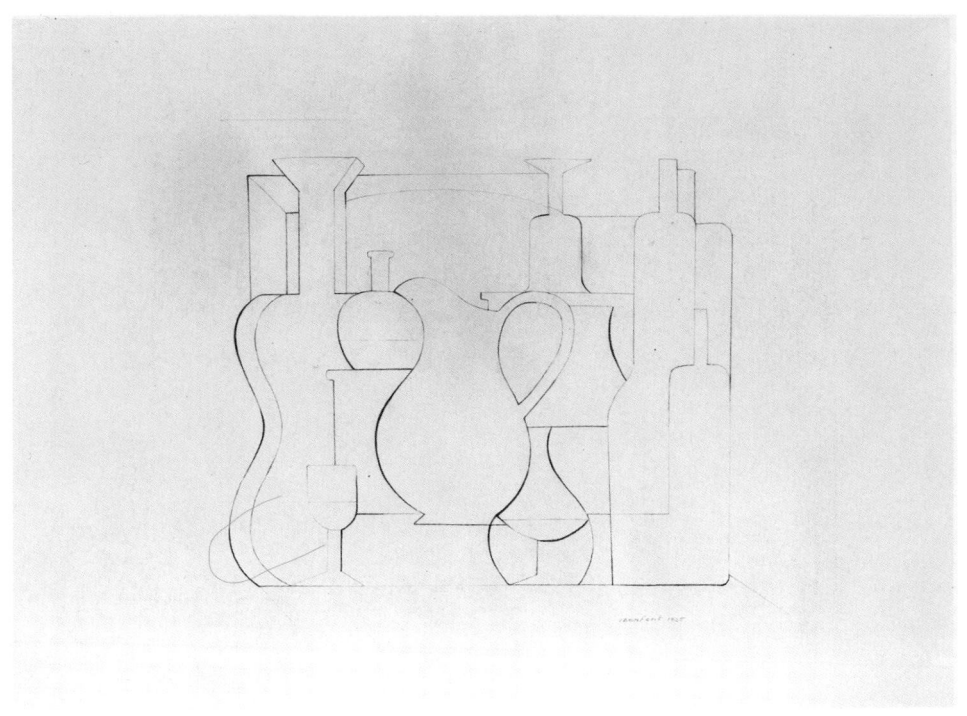

Logic, born of human constants, and without which nothing is human, is an instrument of control, and for him who is inventive, a guide towards discovery: it controls and corrects the sometimes capricious march of intuition and permits one to go ahead with certainty. There are obviously those arts whose sole ambition is to please the senses, we call them arts of pleasure. Purism offers an art that is perhaps severe, but one that addresses itself to the elevated faculties of the mind.

This desire to subject 'intuition' and unbridled sensuality to the intellectual 'control' of Purist 'logic' signalled the death knell of Cubism. The irrationalism associated with Bergsonian intuition and sensual individualism were now signs of moral decay, no longer tenable in the wake of World War I.

We can measure the distance between Purism and Cubism by comparing Picasso's *Still Life (Memory of Le Havre)* of 1912 with Ozenfant's *Composition (Fugue)* of 1925 and Le Corbusier's *Still Life with Pile of Plates* of 1920. The subject of Picasso's work – *Memory of Le Havre* – marks it as a meditation on his subjective experience of a certain time and place, recovered from the *durée* of his own consciousness. Through a bewildering network of interpenetrating diagonal planes, we are presented with a cacophony of fragmented

180. **Amedée Ozenfant,** *Composition (Fugue)*, 1925.

181. Reproduction of paintings by Charles-Edouard Jeanneret (Le Corbusier) and Amedée Ozenfant in *L'Esprit Nouveau*, no. 17 (1922).

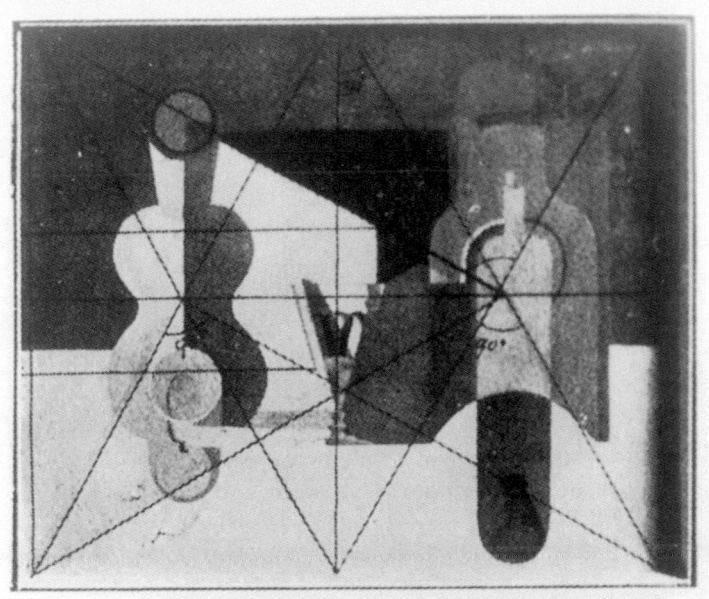

JEANNERET

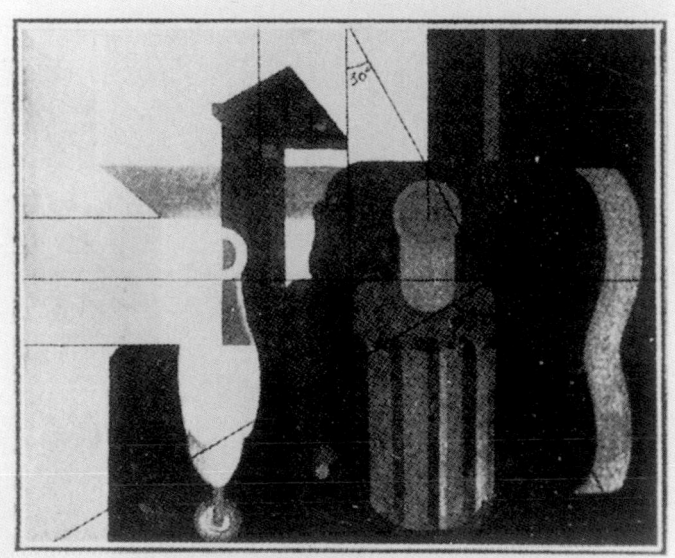

OZENFANT

still-life objects inhabiting a nebulous space, including a glass, scallop shells and a bottle of 'OLD JAM[AICA]' rum on a table, signified by his first attempt at faux-bois. Picasso's signature brushstroke is present throughout the canvas, which appears to have been repeatedly gone over as he worked towards combining his memories of a trip to Braque's hometown. The Purists' studied rejection of such idiosyncratic imagery and obfuscatory techniques is evident in the form and content of their still lifes. Ozenfant has drawn his still-life objects with rule and compass, thus subjecting his drawing to a degree of regularity, anonymity and standardization reminiscent of an architect's or engineer's blueprint. Le Corbusier, in *Still Life with Pile of Plates*, is just as exacting in his delineation of form, effacing all evidence of the artist's touch in order to create an unmodulated, matte surface. Picasso's obfuscating diagonal planes, his use of *passage*, and his fragmented forms have been replaced by a regimented frieze of still-life objects subjected to uniform illumination and composed of repeated shapes: cylinders and circles, horizontals and verticals. The very 'appearance' of disorder created by Picasso's

182. **Charles-Edouard Jeanneret (Le Corbusier)**, *Still Life with Pile of Plates*, 1920.

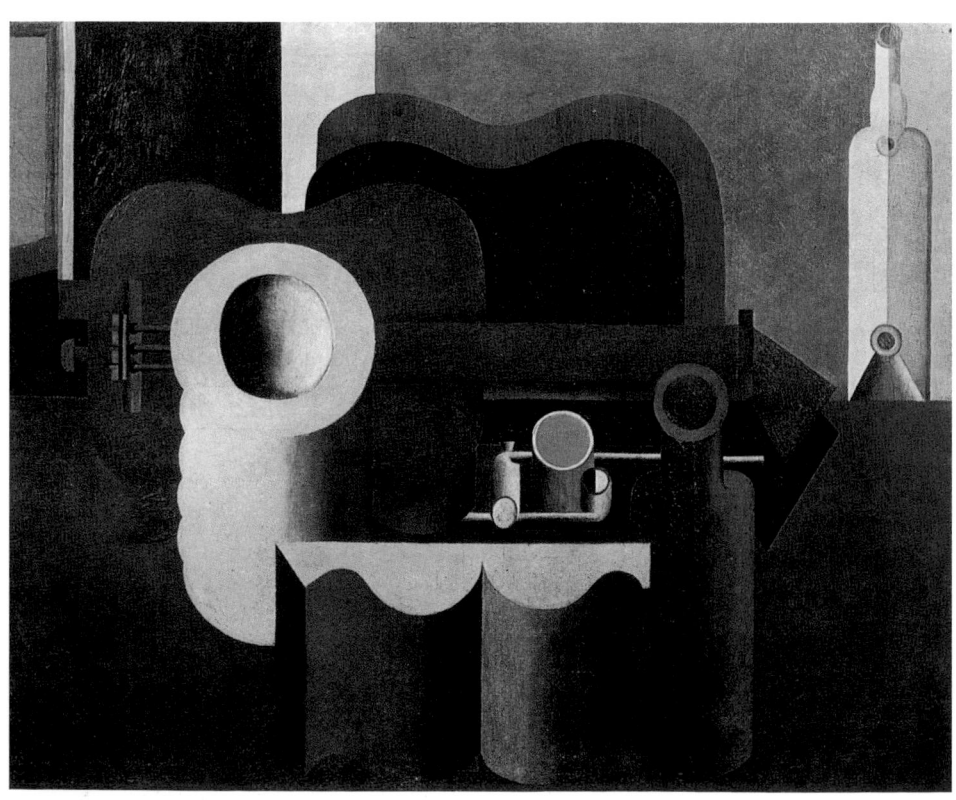

still-life memorabilia was banished, for the placement of plates and bottles in Le Corbusier's still life was predetermined by 'general' laws of geometry, as evidenced by the proportional grids overlaying Purist paintings in *L'Esprit Nouveau*. 181

Ozenfant and Le Corbusier would have likewise despised the affront to collective order and logic signified by Marcel Duchamp's *Three Standard Stoppages*, as well as Duchamp's embrace of the anarchist Max Stirner. Indeed the Purist manifesto registered their political sympathies by reiterating tropes utilized by ultra-nationalists who condemned the cultural ambience before the war. In his book *The Undying Spirit of France* (1917) the reactionary Maurice Barrès had anticipated the Purists, claiming that the French before 1914 'had come to be regarded as jaded triflers' who 'were supposed to allow impulses and passion to determine the course of their lives, pleasure being the supreme good sought'. Happily the war had intervened to transform society, just as Purism would now utilize the 'lessons' of the war to transform art. The war substituted military discipline, logic and order for the vagaries of intuition and sensual self-indulgence; similarly individual rights were subordinated to the collective good through the introduction of passports to control movement and conscription. 64

Having embraced the discipline of logic, the Purists purged their art of sensual individualism and subjected it to 'universal' laws indicative of 'collective' values. Whereas Gleizes's and Metzinger's *Du Cubisme* (1912) had described the Cubist picture as 'a sensitive passage between two subjective spaces', the Purists rejected such intimate encounters: 'The clear perception of the great general law is superior to the brute pleasure of the senses. The highest delectation of the mind is the perception of order, and the greatest human satisfaction is the feeling of collaboration or participation in this order.' This 1920 homage to order contrasts dramatically with the Nietzschean celebration of individual freedom codified in *Du Cubisme* (1912):

> *[Cubism rejects] that negative truth, the mother of morals and everything insipid which, true for the many, is false for the individual.... Let the forms which the Cubist discerns and the symbols in which he incorporates their qualities be sufficiently remote from the imagination of the crowd to prevent the truth which they convey from assuming a general character.*

Since the Purists lauded the replacement of handcrafted objects by standardized forms, the plates and bottles found in their still lifes are the interchangeable products of the industrial process. Shaped by the machine rather than the individual hand, their appearance is the result of what the Purists refer to as 'mechanical selection', an impersonal cultural parallel to Darwin's theory of natural selection. By couching these industrial objects within the rationalized aesthetic of Purism, Ozenfant and Le Corbusier emulated the wartime introduction of methods of 'scientific management' into the factories for the purpose of augmenting armaments production on the home front. In 1915 alone 500,000 soldiers were subjected to such management techniques when put to work in French munitions factories, thereby fulfilling Minister of War Alexandre Millerand's January 1915 declaration: 'There are no more workers' rights, no more social laws. There is nothing now but war'. Pictorial organization, like industrial organization, argued the Purists, should utilize the lessons of war to further discipline French culture.

In another article published in *L'Esprit Nouveau* the Purists subsumed French society as a whole into this process, claiming that 'the social contract that has evolved through the ages fixed standardized classes, function, needs, producing standardized products'. An authoritarian message resides in such statements, for the Purists numbered themselves among an emerging technocratic elite destined to suppress all forms of dissent and marshal wartime propaganda and its organizational methods to transform French culture and society irrevocably. Such a grotesque vision was the complete antithesis of Cubism, a cosmopolitan movement whose cultural values and aspirations were effaced by the enormous social and cultural upheaval of the war, leaving only the residue of a stylistic 'influence'. 'Cubism, Vorticism, Imagism and all the rest', wrote Ford Madox Ford in 1915, 'never had their fair chance amid the voices of the cannon'.

Select Bibliography

Introduction

Among the most historically significant memoirs, period overviews and eyewitness criticisms of the Cubist movement are G. Apollinaire, *Méditations ésthetiques: les peintres cubistes* (Paris 1913), trans. L. Abel (New York 1970); E. Florian-Parmentier, *La littérature et l'époque: histoire de la littérature française de 1885 à nos jours* (Paris 1914), 311–58; A. Gleizes, 'The Abbey of Créteil, a Communistic Experiment', *The Modern School* (October 1918), 300–15; Gleizes, *Souvenirs: Le Cubisme, 1908–1914* (Lyons 1957); Gleizes and J. Metzinger, 'Du Cubisme', trans. R. Herbert, *Modern Artists on Art* (Englewood Cliffs 1964), 1–18; H. Le Fauconnier, 'La sensibilité moderne et le tableau', in *Moderne Kunstkring: Catalogue des ouvrages de peinture, sculpture, dessin, gravure, exposés au Musée Munissipal Suasso à Amsterdam du 6 octobre au 7 novembre 1912* (Amsterdam 1912); D.-H. Kahnweiler, *The Rise of Cubism* (Munich c. 1920), trans. H. Aronson (New York 1949); Metzinger, *Le Cubisme était né· Souvenirs* (Chambéry 1972); M. Raynal, *Anthologie de la peinture en France de 1906 à nos jours* (Paris 1927); A. Salmon, *La Jeune peinture française* (Paris 1912); Salmon, *Souvenirs sans fin, première époque (1903–1908)* (Paris 1955); G. Severini, *The Life of a Painter*, trans. J. Franchina (Princeton 1995); G. Stein, *The Autobiography of Alice B. Toklas* (New York 1933). For translations of primary documents, see M. Antliff and P. Leighten, *A Cubism Reader* (Chicago 2002) and E. Fry, *Cubism* (London 1966).

The most accessible historical introduction to the period is B. Tuchman, *The Proud Tower: A Portrait of the World Before the War, 1890–1914* (New York 1966). Secondary studies that readably bring important aspects of the period to life include C. Green, *Art in France 1900–1940* (New Haven and London 2000); S. Kern, *The Culture of Time and Space* (Cambridge, Mass. 1983); R. Shattuck, *The Banquet Years: The Origins of the Avant-Garde in France, 1885 to World War I* (rev. ed. New York 1968); and J. Warnod, *Washboat Days*, trans. C. Green (New York 1972).

Recent art historical studies include M. Antliff, *Inventing Bergson: Cultural Politics and the Parisian Avant-Garde* (Princeton 1993); D. Cottington, *Cubism in the Shadow of War: Avant-Garde and Politics*

in *Paris, 1905–1914* (New Haven 1998); F. Frascina, 'Realism and Ideology: An Introduction to Semiotics and Cubism', in *Primitivism, Cubism, Abstraction*, eds. C. Harrison et al. (New Haven 1993), 87–183; M. Gee, *Dealers, Critics and Collectors of Modern Paintings: Aspects of the Parisian Art Market Between 1910 and 1930* (New York 1981); Green, *Cubism and Its Enemies: Modern Movements and Reaction in French Art, 1916–1928* (New Haven 1987); L. Henderson, *The Fourth Dimension and Non-Euclidean Geometry in Modern Art* (Princeton 1983); Leighten, *Re-Ordering the Universe: Picasso and Anarchism, 1897–1914* (Princeton 1989); *Picasso and Braque: A Symposium*, ed. L. Zelevansky (New York 1992); C. Poggi, *In Defiance of Painting: Cubism, Futurism, and the Invention of Collage* (New Haven 1992); D. Robbins, 'The Formation and Maturity of Albert Gleizes', Ph.D. diss. (New York University 1975); K. Silver, *Esprit de Corps: The Art of the Parisian Avant-Garde and the First World War, 1914–1925* (Princeton 1989); W. Rubin, *Picasso and Braque: Pioneering Cubism* (New York 1989); V. Spate, *Orphism: The Evolution of Non-Figurative Painting in Paris 1910–1914* (Oxford 1979); N. Troy, *Modernism and the Decorative Arts in France. Art Nouveau to Le Corbusier* (New Haven 1991); J. Weiss, *The Popular Culture of Modern Art: Picasso, Duchamp, and Avant-Gardism* (New Haven 1994). The best formalist treatments of Cubism remain J. Golding, *Cubism: A History and An Analysis, 1907–1914* (rev. ed. London 1988) and R. Rosenblum, *Cubism and Twentieth-Century Art* (London and New York 1961).

Primary source cited: 'Lan-Pu-Hé', 'Cubist Bar', *Fantasio* (15 October 1912), 195.

Chapter 1: European Primitives

Theoretical and historical considerations of primitivism include M. Antliff and Leighten, 'Primitive', in *Critical Terms in Art History*, eds. R. Nelson and R. Shiff (Chicago 1996), 170–84; J. Clifford, *The Predicament of Culture* (Cambridge, Mass. 1988); F. Connelly, *The Sleep of Reason: Primitivism in Modern European Art and Aesthetics, 1725–1907* (University Park 1995); J. Fabian, *Time and the Other: How Anthropology Makes its Object* (New York 1983); S. Gilman, *Difference and Pathology: Stereotypes of Sexuality, Race and Madness* (Ithaca 1985); C. Miller, *Blank Darkness: Africanist Discourse in French* (Chicago 1986); and E. Said, *Orientalism* (New York 1979).

Secondary sources useful for this subject include *André Derain: Le peintre du 'trouble*

moderne', ed. S. Pagé (Paris 1994); R. Benjamin, 'Fauvism in the Landscape of Criticism: metaphor and scandal at the salon', in *Fauve Landscape*, ed. J. Freeman (Los Angeles and New York 1990); *Les Demoiselles d'Avignon*, ed. H. Seckel (Paris 1988); J. Elderfield, *The 'Wild Beasts': Fauvism and Its Affinities* (New York 1976); J. Fineberg, *The Innocent Eye: Children's Art and the Modern Artist* (Princeton 1997); *Henri Rousseau*, eds. M. Hoog, C. Lanchner and W. Rubin (New York 1985); J. Herbert, *Fauve Painting: The Making of Cultural Politics* (New Haven 1992); M. Hoogendonk, A. Lighart and W. Schipper, *Henri Le Fauconnier: Kubisme en Expressionisme in Europa* (Bussum 1993); Leighten, *Re-Ordering the Universe: Picasso and Anarchism*; Leighten, 'The White Peril and l'art nègre: Picasso, Primitivism and Anticolonialism', *The Art Bulletin* 72 (December 1990); M. Leja, '"Le Vieux marcheur" and "les deux risques": Picasso, Prostitution, Venereal Disease and Maternity, 1899–1907', *Art History* 8 (March 1985), 66–81; G. Perry, 'Primitivism and the "Modern"', in *Primitivism, Cubism, Abstraction*, eds. Harrison et al. (New Haven 1991); *'Primitivism' in 20th-Century Art: Affinity of the Tribal and the Modern*, ed. Rubin, 2 vols. (New York 1984); Robbins, 'Henri Le Fauconnier's Mountaineers Attacked by Bears', *Rhode Island School of Design: Museum Notes* (1996), 24–53; C. Rhodes, *Primitivism and Modern Art* (London 1994); Rubin, 'Cézannisme and the Beginnings of Cubism', in *Cézanne – The Late Work* (New York 1977); Shiff, *Cézanne and the End of Impressionism* (Chicago 1984); P. Smith, 'Joachim Gasquet, Virgil and Cézanne's landscape: "My beloved Golden Age"', *Apollo*, 148/439 (October 1998); L. Steinberg, 'The Philosophical Brothel', *Art News*, Part I (September 1972), 20–9 and Part 2 (October 1972), 38–47; R. Thompson, *Flash of the Spirit: African and Afro-American Art and Philosophy* (New York 1984).

Primary sources cited: Apollinaire, 'The Beginnings of Cubism', *Le Temps* (14 October 1912), trans. L. Breunig, *Apollinaire on Art* (New York 1972); Apollinaire, 'Le Douanier', *Les Soirées de Paris* (15 January 1914); Apollinaire, 'Actualités', *Les Arts à Paris* (15 July 1918); G. Burgess, 'The Wild Men of Paris', *Architectural Record* 27 (January–June, 1910), 401–14; C. Estienne, 'Des Tendances de la peinture moderne: Entretien avec M. L. Vauxcelles', *Les Nouvelles* (20 July 1909), 4.; P. Picasso and F. Asís de Soler, 'Arte joven', *Arte Joven* (15 March 1901), 1.

Chapter 2:
Philosophies of Space and Time

Relevant studies in the history of ideas include H. Hughes, *Consciousness and Society* (New York 1961) and Kern, *The Culture of Time and Space.*

Useful secondary sources for this subject include D. Ades, N. Cox and D. Hopkins, *Marcel Duchamp* (London 1999); W. Agee and G. Hamilton, *Raymond Duchamp-Villon, 1876–1918* (New York 1967); A. Antliff, 'Anarchy, Politics, Dada' in *Making Mischief: Dada Invades New York*, eds. F. Naumann and B. Venn (New York 1996); M. Antliff, *Inventing Bergson; A. Archipenko, Fifty Creative Years, 1908–1958* (New York 1960); Gleizes, *Souvenirs: Le Cubisme, 1908–1914*; Green, *Juan Gris* (New Haven 1992); Green, *Léger and the Avant-Garde* (New Haven 1976); Henderson, *Duchamp in Context: Science and Technology in The Large Glass and Related Works* (Princeton 1998); Henderson, *The Fourth Dimension and Non-Euclidean Geometry in Modern Art*; Henderson, 'Modern Art and the Invisible: The Unseen Waves and Dimensions of Occultism and Science', in *Okkultismus und Avantgarde 1900–1915*, ed. I. Ehrhardt (Frankfurt 1995); K. Jánsky Michaelsen and N. Guralnik, *Alexander Archipenko: A Centennial Tribute* (New York 1987); S. Meyer, 'Writing Psychology Over: Gertrude Stein and William James', *The Yale Journal of Criticism*, 8 (1995), 133–63; I. Raaschou-Nielsen, 'The Ambiguous Painting: Jean Metzinger's *Woman with a Horse* (1911–12) and Henri Bergson', *Statens Museum for Kunst Journal*, 1 (1997), 127–35; Robbins, 'The Formation and Maturity of Albert Gleizes'; Robbins, 'Jean Metzinger at the Center of Cubism', in *Jean Metzinger in Retrospect* (Iowa City 1985), 9–23; *Robert Delaunay 1906–1914: De l'Impressionisme à L'Abstraction*, J. Ameline and P. Rousseau et al. (Paris 1999); L. Ruddick, '"Melanctha" and the Psychology of William James', *Modern Fiction Studies* 28/4 (winter 1982–83), 545–56; Ruddick, 'William James and the Modernism of Gertrude Stein', in *Modernism Reconsidered*, eds. R. Kiely and J. Hildebidle (Cambridge, Mass. 1983); Spate, *Orphism: The Evolution of Non-Figurative Painting in Paris 1910–1914*; J. Sund, 'Fernand Léger and Unanimism: Where There's Smoke...', *Oxford Art Journal* 7/1 (1984), 49–56; M. Teuber, 'Formvorstellung und Kubismus oder Pablo Picasso und William James', in *Kubismus*, ed. S. Gohr (Cologne 1982), 9–57.

Primary sources cited: R. Allard, 'Au Salon d'Automne de Paris', *L'Art libre* (Lyons) (November 1910), 441–3; R. Arcos, *Ce qui nait* (Paris 1911); H. Bergson, *Creative Evolution*, 1907, trans. A. Mitchell (New York 1911); Bergson, 'The Introduction to Metaphysics', 1903, in *The Creative Mind*, trans. M. Andison (New York 1946); Bergson, 'Laughter', 1900, trans. in *Comedy*, ed. W. Sypher (Baltimore 1956, rpt. 1980); Bergson, *Matter and Memory*, 1896, authorized trans. N. M. Paul and W. S. Palmer (London 1911; rpt. New York 1970); Bergson, *Time and Free Will*, 1889, authorized trans. F. L. Pogson (New York 1910; rpt. New York 1960); W. James, *A Pluralistic Universe* (New York 1909); James, *The Principles of Psychology* (New York 1890); E. Jouffret, *Traité élémentaire de géométrie à quatre dimensions* (Paris 1903); Kahnweiler, *The Rise of Cubism*; A. Mercereau, 'Pour Bergson', *Paris-Journal* (3 September 1912); Metzinger, *Le Cubisme était né: Souvenirs*; Metzinger, 'Notes sur la peinture', *Pan* (October–November 1910), 649–52; H. Poincaré, *La science et l'hypothèse* (Paris 1902); J. Romains, *La vie unanime: Poèmes 1904–1907* (Paris 1983); Salmon, 'Bergson et les cubistes', *Paris-Journal* (29 November 1911); Salmon, 'Courrier des ateliers', *Paris-Journal* (10 May 1910), 4; Salmon, 'La Section d'Or', *Gil Blas* (22 June 1912); G. Stein, 'Pablo Picasso', *Camera Work* (August 1912), 29–30; L. Stein, *Appreciation: Painting, Poetry, and Prose* (New York 1947); T. de Visan, 'Sur l'oeuvre de Maurice Maeterlinck', *Vers et Prose* (December 1906–February 1907), 82–93; Visan, 'La philosophie de M. Bergson et le lyrisme contemporain', *Vers et Prose* (April–June 1910), 125–40.

Chapter 3:
Political Uses of the Past

Important historical studies relevant to French cultural politics include R. Sonn, *Anarchism and Cultural Politics in Fin-de-Siècle France* (Lincoln 1989); E. Weber, *Action Française: Royalism and Reaction in Twentieth-Century France* (Stanford 1962); and Weber, *My France: Politics, Culture, Myth* (Cambridge, Mass. 1991).

Relevant secondary sources include M. Antliff, *Inventing Bergson*; M. Antliff, 'Cubism, Futurism, Anarchism: The Aestheticism of the Action d'Art Group', *Oxford Art Journal* 21/2 (1998), 99–120; M. Antliff, 'Organicism against itself: Cubism, Duchamp-Villon, and the contradictions of Modernism', *Word & Image* 12/4 (1996), 366–88; D. Cottington, *Cubism in the Shadow of War*; Green, *Art in France 1900–1940*; R. Herbert, 'Léger, the Renaissance, and the "Primitive"', in *Hommage à Michel Laclotte: Etudes sur la peinture du Moyen Age et de la Renaissance* (Paris 1994), 642–7; I. Lavin, *Past-Present: Essays on Historicism in Art from Donatello to Picasso* (Berkeley and Los Angeles 1993); Leighten, *Re-Ordering the Universe: Picasso and Anarchism*; K. Murphy, 'Cubism and the Gothic Tradition' in *Architecture and Cubism*, eds. E. Blau and N. Troy (Cambridge, Mass. 1997), 59–76; *Picasso and the Spanish Tradition*, ed. J. Brown (New Haven 1996); J. Richardson, *A Life of Picasso, vol. 2, 1907–1917* (New York 1996); Robbins, 'The Formation and Maturity of Albert Gleizes'; Robbins, 'Henri Le Fauconnier's Mountaineers Attacked by Bears', *Rhode Island School of Design: Museum Notes* (1996), 24–53.

Primary sources cited: J.-M. Bernard, 'Discours sur le Symbolisme', *Les Guêpes* (May 1910), 200–13; A. Colomer, 'A Notre librairie', *L'Action d'art*, no. 9 (25 July 1913), 4; E. Faure, 'Préface', *Catalogue de la Troisième Exposition de la Société Normande de Peinture Moderne*, 15 June–15 July 1912 (Rouen); Gleizes, 'L'Art et ses représentants: Jean Metzinger', *Revue Indépendante*, 4 (September 1911), 161–72; Gleizes, 'Les Beaux-Arts: à propos du Salon d'Automne', *Les Bandeaux d'or*, 4/13 (1911–1912), 42–51; Gleizes, *Souvenirs: Le Cubisme, 1908–1914*; G. Lacaze-Duthiers, 'L'Artistocratie', *L'Idée Libre* (October 1912), 153–5; P. Lasserre, 'La Philosophie de M. Bergson', *L'Action Française* (March 1911), 165–83; F. Léger, 'The Machine Aesthetic: The Manufactured Object, the Artisan, and the Artist', *Bulletin de l'Effort Moderne*, 1/2 (1924), in *Functions of Painting by Fernand Léger*, ed. E. Fry, trans. A. Anderson (New York 1973), 52–61; Léger, 'The Origins of Painting and its Representative Value', *Montjoie!* nos. 8–10 (1913), in *Functions of Painting by Fernand Léger*, 3–10; C. Maurras, 'A Propos de Bergson', *Action Française* (11 February 1914), 1; Metzinger, 'Cubisme et tradition', *Paris-Journal* (16 August 1911); Metzinger, 'Notes sur la peinture', *Pan* (October–November 1910), 649–52; Salmon, 'La Section d'Or', *Gil Blas* (22 June 1912).

Chapter 4: Gender Codes

On the importance of 'gender' in the study of history, see J. Scott, 'Gender: A Useful Category of Historical Analysis', in *Gender and the Politics of History* (New York 1988) and S. Ortner, 'Is Female to Male as Nature is to Culture?', in *Woman, Culture, and Society*, eds. M. Lamphere and M. Rosaldo (Stanford 1974), 67–87. The most useful study of gender and French cultural politics, though it primarily addresses a later period, is M. Roberts, *Civilization Without Sexes: Reconstructing Gender in Postwar France, 1917–1927* (Chicago 1994).

Secondary sources relevant to the study of gender and Cubism include M. Antliff, *Inventing Bergson*; J. Blake, *Le Tumulte noir: Modernist Art and Popular Entertainment in Jazz-Age Paris, 1900–1930* (University Park 1999); J. Bowditch, 'The Concept of Elan-Vital: A Rationalization of Weakness', in *Modern France: Problems of the Third and Fourth Republics*, ed. E. Earle (Princeton 1951), 32–43; Paula J. Birnbaum, 'Alice Halicka's Self-Effacement', in *Diaspora and Visual Culture: Representing Africans and Jews*, ed. N. Mirzoeff (London 2000), 207–23; S. Buckberrough, *Robert Delaunay: The Discovery of Simultaneity* (Ann Arbor 1982); Cottington, *Cubism in the Shadow of War*; W. Chadwick, 'Living Simultaneously: Sonia & Robert Delaunay', in *Significant Others: Creativity & Intimate Partnership*, eds. Chadwick and I. de Courtivron (London 1993), 31–48; B. Elliott, 'The "Strength of the Weak" as Portrayed by Marie Laurencin', *Genders*, 24 (1996), 69–109; Elliott and J. Wallace, *Women Artists and Writers: Modernist (im)positionings* (London 1994); R. Herbert, *Impressionism: Art, Leisure and Parisian Society* (New Haven 1988); P. Mathews, *Passionate Discontent: Creativity, Gender, and French Symbolist Art* (Chicago 1999); E. Otto, 'Marie Laurencin and the Gendering of Cubism, 1904–1914' (M.A. thesis, Queen's University 1997); Perry, *Women Artists and the Parisian Avant-Garde* (Manchester 1995); *Robert Delaunay 1906–1914: de l'Impressionisme à L'Abstraction*; A. Sheon, '1913: Forgotten Cubist Exhibitions in America', *Arts Magazine* (March 1983), 93–107; Spate, *Orphism*; Troy, 'Domesticity, Decoration and Consumer Culture: Selling Art and Design in Pre-World War I France', in *Not at Home: The Suppression of Domesticity in Modern Art and Architecture*, ed. C. Reed (London 1996), 113–29.

Primary sources cited: Apollinaire, 'Art News: The Decorative Arts and Female Painting' (March 1912) and 'Through the Salon des Indépendants' (March 1913), in *Apollinaire on Art*, ed. L. Breunig (New York 1972), 208–10 and 286–93; Raynal, *Anthologie de la peinture en France de 1906 à nos jours*.

Chapter 5: Pasted Papers and Revolution
Important general works on collage include *Collage: Critical Views*, ed. K. Hoffman (Ann Arbor 1989); P. Daix and J. Rosselet, *Picasso, the Cubist Years 1907–1916: a Catalogue Raisonné of the Paintings and Related Works* (London 1979); I. Monod-Fontaine, *Braque: the Papiers Collés* (Washington 1982), 53–8; and Poggi, *In Defiance of Painting: Cubism, Futurism, and the Invention of Collage*.

Of theoretical relevance are M. Bakhtin, 'Discourse in the Novel', *The Dialogic Imagination: Four Essays* (Austin 1981) and Frascina, 'Collage: Conceptual and Historical Overview', *Encyclopedia of Aesthetics* (New York 1999), 382–4; R. Terdiman, *Discourse/Counter-Discourse: The Theory and Practice of Symbolic Resistance in Nineteenth-Century France* (Ithaca 1985).

Relevant historical studies include S. Haine, '"Café Friend": Friendship and Fraternity in Parisian Working-Class Cafés, 1850–1914', *Journal of Contemporary History*, 27 (1992), 607–26; J. Maitron, *Histoire du mouvement anarchiste en France (1880–1914)* (Paris 1951); and T. Zeldin, *France, 1848–1945*, vol. 2 (Oxford 1973–77).

For debates on interpretation of collage, see Cottington, *Cubism in the Shadow of War*; T. Crow, *Modern Art in the Common Culture* (New Haven and London 1996); Frascina, 'Realism and Ideology: An Introduction to Semiotics and Cubism'; R. Krauss, 'Re-Presenting Picasso', *Art in America* 68 (December 1980), 91–6; Krauss, *The Picasso Papers* (New York 1998); Leighten, 'Cubist Anachronisms: Ahistoricity, Cryptoformalism, and Business-As-Usual in New York', *Oxford Art Journal*, 17/2 (1994), 91–102; Rosenblum, 'Picasso and the Typography of Cubism', in *Picasso in Retrospect*, eds. R. Penrose and J. Golding (London 1973); Poggi, 'Mallarmé, Picasso, and the Newspaper as Commodity', *The Yale Journal of Criticism*, 1 (fall 1987); Shiff, 'Picasso's Touch: Collage, *Papier collé*, Ace of Clubs', *Yale University Art Gallery Bulletin* (1990), 38–47.

Useful secondary sources include Blake, *Le Tumulte noir: Modernist Art and Popular Entertainment in Jazz-Age Paris*; J. Boggs, *Picasso & Things* (Cleveland 1992); Y.-A. Bois, 'Kahnweiler's Lesson', *Representations* 18 (spring 1987), 33–68; W. Camfield, *Francis Picabia: His Art, Life, and Times* (Princeton 1979); Green, *Juan Gris*; Leighten, *Re-Ordering the Universe: Picasso and Anarchism*; L. Nochlin, 'Picasso's Color: Schemes and Gambits',

Art in America, 68 (December 1980), 105–23 and 177–83; A. Parigoris, 'Les Constructions cubistes dans "Les Soirées de Paris": Apollinaire, Picasso et les clichés Kahnweiler', *Revue de l'art*, no. 82 (1988), 61–74; J. Weiss, *The Popular Culture of Modern Art*.

Primary sources cited: G. Kahn, *Premiers poèmes* (Poitiers 1897); P. Quillard, 'L'Anarchie par la littérature', *Entretiens politiques et littéraires* (April 1892), 150–1; Salmon, *La Terreur noire, chronique du mouvement libertaire* (Paris 1959).

Chapter 6: Cubism at War
Useful historical and cultural studies include P. Bernard and H. Dubief, *The Decline of the Third Republic, 1914–1938* (Cambridge and New York 1988); C. Brosman, *Visions of War In France: Fiction, Art, Ideology* (Baton Rouge 1999); *European Culture in the Great War: the Arts, Entertainment and Propaganda, 1914–1918*, eds. A. Roshwald and R. Stites (New York 1999); P. Fussell, *The Great War and Modern Memory* (New York 1975); N. Goldberg, 'French Pacifist Poetry of World War One', *Journal of European Studies* 21 (December 1991), 239–58; Green, *Art in France 1900–1940*.

For the most comprehensive studies of Cubism and wartime cultural politics, see Green, *Cubism and Its Enemies: Modern Movements and Reaction in French Art* and K. Silver, *Esprit de Corps: The Art of the Parisian Avant-Garde and the First World War*. Other recent art-historical studies include M. Affron, 'Léger's Modernism: Subjects and Objects', in *Fernand Léger*, ed. C. Lanchner (New York 1998), 121–48; A. Antliff, *Anarchist Modernism: Art, Politics and the First American Avant-Garde* (Chicago 2001); Green, 'Albert Gleizes', in *The European Avant-Gardes: Art in France and Western Europe 1904–1945* (London 1995), 206–11; Green, 'Out of War: Léger's Painting of the War and the Peace, 1914–1920', in *Fernand Léger 1911–1924: The Rhythm of Modern Life*, ed. D. Kosinski (Munich and New York 1994), 45–55; Leighten, *Re-Ordering the Universe: Picasso and Anarchism*; E. Michaud, 'Art, War, and Competition: The Three Battles of Fernand Léger', in *Fernand Léger*, ed. Kosinski, 57–63.

Primary source cited: A. Ozenfant and C. Jeanneret, 'Le Purisme', *L'Esprit Nouveau* (March 1920), 369–86, trans. in *Modern Artists on Art*, 59–73.

List of Illustrations

Measurements are in centimetres, followed by inches, height before width before depth

1 Georges Braque, *Fruit Dish, Ace of Clubs*, 1913. Oil, gouache and charcoal on canvas, 81 x 60 (31⅞ x 23⅝). Musée national d'art moderne, Centre Georges Pompidou, Paris. © ADAGP, Paris and DACS, London 2001; **Dedication** Kenneth Allen, *Night-Window No. 3*, 1985–90. Oil on board, 59.6 x 46.9 (23½ x 18½). Private collection; **2** Photograph, 'Le Meeting du Pré-Saint-Gervais contre la Guerre', *Le Journal*, 18 November 1912. Bibliothèque nationale, Paris; **3** Pablo Picasso, *Head with Scarification*, 1907. Oil on wood panel, 17.5 x 14 (6⅞ x 5½). Collection Claude Picasso, Paris. © Succession Picasso/DACS 2001; **4** Jean Metzinger, Study for *Portrait of Albert Gleizes*, 1911. Pencil on cream paper, 21.0 x 15.5 (8⅜ x 6⅛). Musée national d'art moderne, Centre Georges Pompidou, Paris. © ADAGP, Paris and DACS, London 2001; **5** Albert Gleizes, *Chartres Cathedral*, 1912. Oil on canvas, 73.6 x 60.3 (29⅜ x 24⅛). Sprengel Museum, Hanover. © ADAGP, Paris and DACS, London 2001; **6** Sonia Terk Delaunay, *Couverture (Quilt)*, 1911. Appliquéd fabric, 109 x 81 (42⅞ x 31⅞). Musée national d'art moderne, Centre Georges Pompidou, Paris. L & M SERVICES B.V. Amsterdam 20010409; **7** Juan Gris, *Breakfast*, 1914. Papier collé, crayon and oil on canvas, 80.9 x 59.6 (31⅞ x 23½). Museum of Modern Art, New York, acquired through the Lillie P. Bliss Bequest. Photograph © 2001 The Museum of Modern Art, New York; **8** Georges Braque, *Construction*, 1914. Cardboard and newsprint. No longer extant. © ADAGP, Paris and DACS, London 2001; **9** Juan Gris, *Hommage à Picasso*, 1912. Oil on canvas, 74.3 x 93.3 (29¼ x 36¾). Gift of Mr Leigh B. Block, Art Institute of Chicago; **10** Pablo Picasso, *Portrait of Ambrose Vollard*, 1915. Pencil on paper, 46.7 x 31.9 (18⅜ x 12⅝). The Metropolitan Museum of Art, New York. © Succession Picasso/DACS 2001; **11** Installation photograph of the Salon d'Automne, October 1912. Keystone; **12** Paul Gauguin, *Vision After the Sermon*, 1888. Oil on canvas, 73 x 92 (28¾ x 36¼). National Gallery of Scotland, Edinburgh; **13** Jean Metzinger, *Portrait of Apollinaire*, 1910. Oil on canvas, 130 x 97 (51⅛ x 38⅛). Private collection, Germany. © ADAGP, Paris and DACS, London 2001; **14** Pablo Picasso, Photograph of Guillaume Apollinaire in Picasso's studio, *c.* 1910. © Succession Picasso/DACS 2001; **15** Photograph of Gino Severini at the Marlborough Gallery, London, 1913; **16** Photograph of the Bateau Lavoir, 13 rue Ravignan, Paris. Courtesy Mr Stanley Jernow; **17** Photograph of André Derain in his studio, 1908. Originally reproduced in 'The Wild Men of Paris', Gelett Burgess, *Architectural Record*, 1910; **18** Photograph of Pablo Picasso in his rue Ravignan studio, 1908. Courtesy Mr Stanley Jernow; **19** Georges Braque, *Grand Nu (Large Nude)*, 1907–8. Oil on canvas, 140 x 100 (55¼ x 39½). Collection Alex Maguy, Paris. © ADAGP, Paris and DACS, London 2001; **20** Georges Braque, Drawing for *Large Nude*, 1907–8. Ink on paper. Location unknown, originally reproduced in 'The Wild Men of Paris', Gelett Burgess, *Architectural Record*, 1910. © ADAGP, Paris and DACS, London 2001; **21** André Derain, *Bathers*, 1907. Oil on canvas, 132.1 x 195 (51¼ x 75⅞). The Museum of Modern Art, New York, William S. Paley & Abby Alrich Rockefeller Funds. © ADAGP, Paris and DACS, London 2001; **22** Pablo Picasso, *Les Demoiselles d'Avignon*, 1907. Oil on canvas, 243.9 x 233.7 (96 x 84). Museum of Modern Art, New York, acquired through the Lillie P. Bliss Bequest. Photograph © 2001 The Museum of Modern Art, New York. © Succession Picasso/DACS 2001; **23** Pablo Picasso, *Three Women*, 1907–8. Oil on canvas, 200 x 179 (78¾ x 70½). The State Hermitage Museum, St Petersburg. © Succession Picasso/DACS 2001; **24** Henri Matisse, *Le Bonheur de vivre (Joy of Life)*, 1905–6. Oil on canvas, 174 x 238 (68½ x 93¾). © The Barnes Foundation, Merion, Pennsylvania. © Succession H. Matisse/DACS 2001; **25** André Derain, *Three Trees, L'Estaque*, 1906. Oil on canvas, 100.3 x 80 (39½ x 31½). Private collection. © ADAGP, Paris and DACS, London 2001; **26** Fang mask, Gabon (former French Congo). Painted wood, height 42 (16½). Musée national d'art moderne, Centre Georges Pompidou, Paris; **27** Photograph of André Derain's studio with Fang mask on wall, *c.* 1912–13. Courtesy Michel Kellerman; **28** Henri Matisse, *The Blue Nude (Souvenir of Biskra)*, 1907. Oil on canvas, 92 x 140 (36¼ x 55⅛). The Baltimore Museum of Art, Cone Collection. © Succession H. Matisse/DACS 2001; **29** *Head of a Man*, Iberian, Cerro de los Santos, 5th–3rd century B.C. Stone, height 21 (8¼). Musée des antiquités nationales, Saint-Germain-en-Laye; **30** Pablo Picasso, *Self-Portrait with a Palette*, 1906. Oil on canvas, 92 x 73 (36¼ x 28¾). Philadelphia Museum of Art, A.E. Gallatin Collection. © Succession Picasso/DACS 2001; **31** Kota reliquary, People's Republic of the Congo (former French Congo). Wooden mask with sheet brass and copper, height 50 (19⅝). Herbert Ward Collection, Smithsonian Institute, Washington, D.C.; **32** Teke figure, People's Republic of the Congo (former French Congo). Wood, height 29.9 (11¾). Musée de l'homme, Paris; **33** Pablo Picasso, *Doll*, 1907. Painted wood with metal eyes, height 23.5 (9¼). Art Gallery of Ontario, Toronto. © Succession Picasso/DACS 2001; **34** Pablo Picasso, *Mother and Child*, 1907. Oil on canvas, 81 x 60 (31⅞ x 23⅝). Musée Picasso, Paris. © Succession Picasso/DACS 2001; **35** Jean-Auguste-Dominique Ingres, *Venus Anadyomene*, 1808–48. Oil on canvas, 192 x 92 (76 x 36¼). Musée Condé, Chantilly, France; **36** Photograph of 'Congolese village', International Exposition, Paris, 1900. V. Champier, *Chefs d'oeuvre de l'Exposition Universelle*, 1900. Bibliothèque nationale, Paris; **37** 'Human Sacrifices in Dahomey', etching published in Dr Repin, 'Voyage au Dahomey', *Tour du Monde*, VII, 1863. Bibliothèque nationale, Paris; **38** Juan Gris, 'Guided by a need', from *L'Assiette au beurre*, 29 August 1908. Lithograph. Bibliothèque nationale, Paris; **39** Pablo Picasso, Study for *Les Demoiselles d'Avignon*, spring 1907. Pencil and pastel on paper, 48 x 63 (18⅞ x 24¾). Öffentliche Kunstsammlung Basel, Kupferstichkabinett. © Succession Picasso/DACS 2001; **40** Henri Le Fauconnier, *Breton Girl*, 1908. Oil on canvas, 55.0 x 46.5 (21⅝ x 18¼). Musée des Beaux-Arts, Lyons; **41** Henri Le Fauconnier, *Village in the Rocks*, 1908. Oil on canvas, 73 x 93 (29⅛ x 36⅝). Gemeentemuseum, The Hague; **42** Henri Rousseau, *The Poet and His Muse (Portrait of Guillaume Apollinaire and Marie Laurencin)*, 1909. Oil on canvas, 146 x 97 (57½ x 38⅛). Öffentliche Kunstsammlung Basel, Kunstmuseum Basel; **43** Paul Cézanne, *Mont Sainte-Victoire*, 1885–87. Oil on canvas, 66 x 90 (26 x 35⅜). Courtauld Institute Galleries, London; **44** Paul Cézanne, *Five Bathers*, 1885–87. Oil on canvas, 65.5 x 65.5 (25⅞ x 25⅞). Öffentliche Kunstsammlung Basel, Kunstmuseum Basel; **45** Georges Braque, *Olive Trees*, 1907. Oil on canvas, 38.1 x 46.2 (15 x 18⅜). Worcester Art Museum, Massachusetts, Gift of the estate of Mrs Aldus Chapin Higgins. © ADAGP, Paris and DACS, London 2001; **46** Georges Braque, *Terrace of Hôtel Mistral*, 1907.

Oil on canvas, 80 x 61 (31½ x 24). Private collection, New York. © ADAGP, Paris and DACS, London 2001; **47** Georges Braque, *Houses at L'Estaque*, 1908. Oil on canvas, 73 x 60 (28¾ x 23½). Kunstmuseum, Bern, Hermann and Margrit Rupf Foundation. © ADAGP, Paris and DACS, London 2001; **48** Pablo Picasso, *Reservoir at Horta*, summer 1909. Oil on canvas, 60 x 50 (23¾ x 19¾). Private collection, New York. © Succession Picasso/DACS 2001; **49** Georges Braque, *Harbour in Normandy*, 1909. The Art Institute of Chicago. © ADAGP, Paris and DACS, London 2001; **50** Fernand Léger, *Woman Sewing*, 1909–10. Oil on canvas, 72 x 54 (28⅜ x 21¼). Musée national d'art moderne, Centre Georges Pompidou, Paris. © ADAGP, Paris and DACS, London 2001; **51** Paul Cézanne, *La Femme à la cafetière (Woman with a Coffeepot)*, c. 1890–94. Oil on canvas, 130.5 x 95.5 (51⅜ x 38). Musée d'Orsay, Paris; **52** Pablo Picasso, Photograph of Daniel-Henry Kahnweiler in Picasso's studio, boulevard de Clichy, c. 1910. © Succession Picasso/DACS 2001; **53** Pablo Picasso, *Nude*, 1910. Oil on canvas, 97.8 x 76.2 (38½ x 30). Albright-Knox Art Gallery, Buffalo, New York. © Succession Picasso/DACS 2001; **54** Pablo Picasso, *Portrait of Daniel-Henry Kahnweiler*, 1910. Oil on canvas, 100.5 x 72.6 (39⅝ x 28⅝). Art Institute of Chicago, Gift of Mrs Gilbert W. Chapman in memory of Charles B. Goodspeed. © Succession Picasso/DACS 2001; **55** Georges Braque, *Violin and Palette*, 1909. Oil on canvas, 91.7 x 42.8 (36⅛ x 16⅞). The Solomon R. Guggenheim Museum, New York. Photograph Lee B. Ewing © The Solomon R. Guggenheim Foundation, New York. © ADAGP, Paris and DACS, London 2001; **56** Jean-Baptiste-Siméon Chardin, *Musical Instruments and Parrot*, c. 1732. Oil on canvas, 117.5 x 143.5 (46¼ x 56½). Private collection, Paris; **57** Albert Gleizes, *Portrait of the Publisher Figuière*, 1913. Oil on canvas, 143 x 102 (56¼ x 40⅛). Musée des Beaux-Arts, Lyons. © ADAGP, Paris and DACS, London 2001; **58** Jean-Léon Gérôme, *The Snake Charmer*, 1880. Oil on canvas, 83.8 x 122.1 (33 x 48). © Sterling and Francine Clark Art Institute, Williamstown, Massachusetts, USA; **59** Albert Gleizes, *Passy (ponts de Paris)*, 1912. Oil on canvas, 58.3 x 72.7 (23 x 28⅝). Museum Moderner Kunst, Stiftung Ludwig, Vienna. © ADAGP, Paris and DACS, London 2001; **60** Photograph of Albert Gleizes, c. 1912; **61** Photograph of Jean Metzinger, c. 1912; **62** Riemannian geometry represented on a sphere; **63** Jean Metzinger, *Cubist Landscape (The Village)*, c. 1911–12. Oil on canvas, 81.3 x 99 (32 x 39). Sidney Janis Gallery, New York. © ADAGP, Paris and DACS, London 2001; **64** Marcel Duchamp, *Three Standard Stoppages*, 1913. Three threads glued onto three glass panels, each 125.4 x 18.4 (49⅜ x 7¼); three flat wooden strips repeating the curves of the threads, average length 114 (45); wooden box, 28.2 x 129.2 x 23 (11⅛ x 50⅞ x 9). The Museum of Modern Art, New York. © Succession Marcel Duchamp/ADAGP, Paris and DACS, London 2001; **65** Marcel Duchamp, *Portrait of Chess Players*, 1911. Oil on canvas, 101 x 101 (39¾ x 39¾). Philadelphia Museum of Art, Louise and Walter Arensberg Collection. © Succession Marcel Duchamp/ADAGP, Paris and DACS, London 2001; **66** Photograph of the Duchamp-Villon brothers in Puteaux, 1913. Philadelphia Museum of Art, Louise and Walter Arensberg Collection; **67** Jean Metzinger, *Le Goûter (Tea-time)*, 1911. Oil on wood, 75.5 x 69.5 (29¾ x 27⅜). Philadelphia Museum of Art, Louise and Walter Arensberg Collection. © ADAGP, Paris and DACS, London 2001; **68** Jean Metzinger, *The Port*, c. 1911–12. Location unknown. © ADAGP, Paris and DACS, London 2001; **69** Juan Gris, *Landscape at Céret*, 1913. Oil on canvas, 92 x 60 (36¼ x 23⅝). Moderna Museet, Stockholm; **70** Jean Metzinger, *Nude*, 1910. Dimensions and whereabouts unknown. © ADAGP, Paris and DACS, London 2001; **71** Henri Le Fauconnier, *Village in the Mountains*, 1911–12. Oil on canvas, 100 x 80.5 (39⅜ x 31⅝). Museum of Art, Rhode Island School of Design, Providence. Photography Cathy Carver; **72** Albert Gleizes, *Portrait of Jacques Nayral*, 1911. Oil on canvas, 161.9 x 114 (63¾ x 44⅞). Tate Collection, London. © ADAGP, Paris and DACS, London 2001; **73** Jean Metzinger, *Woman with a Horse*, 1911–12. Oil on canvas, 162 x 130.5 (63¾ x 51⅜). Statens Museum for Kunst, Copenhagen. Photograph Hans Peterson. © ADAGP, Paris and DACS, London 2001; **74** Gino Severini, *Travel Memories*, 1910–11. Oil on canvas, 81.2 x 99.8 (32 x 39¼). Private collection. © ADAGP, Paris and DACS, London 2001; **75** Pablo Picasso, *Still Life (Memory of Le Havre)*, 1912. Oil on canvas, 92 x 65 (36¼ x 25⅝). Private collection, Basel. © Succession Picasso/DACS 2001; **76** Photograph of members of the Abbaye de Créteil. Fondation Albert Gleizes, Paris; **77** Albert Gleizes, *Portrait of René Arcos*, 1910. Fondation Albert Gleizes, Paris. © ADAGP, Paris and DACS, London 2001; **78** Albert Gleizes, *At the Market*, 1908. Indian ink and pencil, 50 x 60 (19⅝ x 23⅝). Current location unknown. © ADAGP, Paris and DACS, London 2001; **79** Fernand Léger, *Les Fumées sur les toits (Smoke over the Roofs)*, 1911. Oil on canvas, 60.3 x 96.0 (23¾ x 37¾). Richard Weil Collection, St Louis/Minneapolis Institute of Arts. © ADAGP, Paris and DACS, London 2001; **80** Fernand Léger, *The Wedding*, 1910–11. Oil on canvas, 257 x 206 (160½ x 128¾). Musée national d'art moderne, Centre Georges Pompidou, Paris. © ADAGP, Paris and DACS, London 2001; **81** Francis Picabia, *Procession, Seville*, 1912. Oil on canvas, 122 x 122 (48 x 48). Herbert and Nanette Rothschild Collection, New York. © ADAGP, Paris and DACS, London 2001; **82** Robert Delaunay, *Eiffel Tower*, 1911. Oil on canvas, 202.0 x 138.4 (79½ x 54½). The Solomon R. Guggenheim Museum, New York. Gift, Solomon R. Guggenheim 1937. Photograph Sally Ritts. © The Solomon R. Guggenheim Foundation, New York; **83** Alexander Archipenko, *Woman Combing Her Hair*, 1915. Bronze with blue patina, height 62.2 (24½). North Carolina Museum of Art. © ARS, New York and DACS, London 2001; **84** Alexander Archipenko, *Woman with a Fan*, 1914. Painted wood, painted sheet metal, glass bottle and metal funnel; support: oil on burlap, and oil on oilcloth, mounted on wood panels, 108 x 61.5 x 13.5 (42½ x 24¼ x 5). Collection of the Tel Aviv Museum, Jerusalem, gift of the Goeritz family, London, 1956; **85** Marcel Duchamp, *The Bride Stripped Bare by Her Bachelors, Even (The Large Glass)*, 1915–23. Oil, varnish, lead foil, lead wire, 272 x 176 (107⅛ x 69¼). Philadelphia Museum of Art, Bequest of Katherine C. Dreier. © Succession Marcel Duchamp/ADAGP, Paris and DACS, London 2001; **86** Marcel Duchamp, *Bottlerack*, 1913–14. 1961 replica of 1914 original. Galvanized iron, 59 x 36.8 (23¼ x 14½). Private collection. © Succession Marcel Duchamp/ADAGP, Paris and DACS, London 2001; **87** Juan Gris, *Man in a Café*, 1912. Oil on canvas, 127.6 x 88.3 (50¼ x 34¾). Philadelphia Museum of Art, Louise and Walter Arensburg Collection; **88** Pablo Picasso, *Portrait of Gertrude Stein*, 1906. Oil on canvas, 99.6 x 81.3 (39¼ x 32). The Metropolitan Museum of Art, New York, bequest of Gertrude Stein. © Succession Picasso/DACS 2001; **89** Pablo Picasso, *Portrait of Wilhelm Uhde*, 1910. Oil on canvas, 81 x 60 (31⅞ x 23⅝). Collection of Mr and Mrs Joseph Pulitzer, Jr. © Succession Picasso/DACS 2001;

90 Pablo Picasso, *The Architect's Table*, 1912. Oil on canvas, mounted on oval panel, 72.6 x 59.7 (28⅝ x 23½). Museum of Modern Art, New York, The William S. Paley Collection. Photograph © 2001 The Museum of Modern Art, New York. © Succession Picasso/DACS 2001;
91 Juan Gris, *The Watch*, 1912. Oil and papier collé on canvas, 65 x 92 (25⅝ x 36¼). Private collection; **92** Pierre Dumont, *Rouen Cathedral*, 1912. Oil on canvas, 192.4 x 139 (75¾ x 54⅝). Milwaukee Art Museum, anonymous gift. Photograph Larry Sanders. © ADAGP, Paris and DACS, London 2001; **93** Henri Le Fauconnier, *L'Abondance (Abundance)*, 1910–11. Oil on canvas, 191 x 123 (75 x 48). Gemeentemuseum, The Hague;
94 Photograph of Henri Le Fauconnier, *c.*1911. Photograph courtesy of M. Didier Sevin, Carpentras; **95** Henri Le Fauconnier, *The Lake*, 1911. Oil on canvas, 84 x 61 (33 x 24). The State Hermitage Museum, St Petersburg;
96 Raymond Duchamp-Villon, *Seated Woman*, 1914. Bronze, 71 x 22 x 28 (28 x 8⅝ x 11). Musée national d'art moderne, Centre Georges Pompidou, Paris;
97 Jean Metzinger, *Femme à la Fenetre (Maternité)*, 1911–12. Oil on canvas, 91.4 x 64.8 (36 x 25½). Collection of Roger L. Yaseen. © ADAGP, Paris and DACS, London 2001; **98** Elisabeth Vigée-Lebrun, *Mme Vigée-Lebrun and her Daughter*, 1789. Oil on canvas, 130 x 94 (51⅛ x 37). Musée du Louvre, Paris. Photo Giraudon/Bridgeman Art Library, London; **99** Raymond Duchamp-Villon, *La Maison Cubiste*, 1912. Plaster maquette. Musée national d'art moderne, Centre Georges Pompidou, Paris; **100** Andre Mare, Bed and bedcover for the *petite chambre*, Maison Cubiste, Salon d'Automne, Paris, 1912. Musée national d'art moderne, Centre Georges Pompidou, Paris. © ADAGP, Paris and DACS, London 2001;
101 Raymond Duchamp-Villon, *Projet d'architecture*, 1914. Plaster maquette, 56 x 34 (22 x 13⅜). Philadelphia Museum of Art; **102** Albert Gleizes, *Harvest Threshing*, 1912. Oil on canvas, 269 x 353 (105⅞ x 139). Private collection, Paris. © ADAGP, Paris and DACS, London 2001; **103** Albert Gleizes, *The City and the River*, 1913. Oil on canvas, 80 x 63.5 (31½ x 25). Ursula and R. Stanley Johnson Collection, Chicago. © ADAGP, Paris and DACS, London 2001; **104** Jean Clouet, *Francis I, King of France*, 1525. Oil on wood, 96 x 74 (37¾ x 29⅛). Musée du Louvre, Paris; **105** Claude Monet, *Rouen Cathedral, Façade (Grey Day)*, 1892–94. Oil on canvas, 107 x 73 (42⅛ x 28¾). Musée d'Orsay, Paris; **106** Fernand Léger, *Contrast of Forms*, 1913. Oil on canvas, 100.3 x 81.1 (39½ x 32). The Museum of Modern Art, New York, Philip L. Goodwin Collection. Photograph © 2001 The Museum of Modern Art, New York. © ADAGP, Paris and DACS, London 2001;
107 Pablo Picasso, *Femme accroupie (Seated Woman)*, summer 1907. Oil on wood, 17.6 x 15 (7 x 5⅞). Musée Picasso, Paris. © Succession Picasso/DACS 2001;
108 *Spinario*, Hellenistic sculpture. Marble, 4th–3rd century B.C. Pergamon Museum, Berlin, Germany. Photo The Bridgeman Art Library, London;
109 Pablo Picasso, *Study of Nude with Annular Torso and Arms*, 1907. Carnet no. 7, folio 59. Private collection. © Succession Picasso/DACS 2001;
110 Albrecht Dürer, *Nude Figure Constructed with Annular Torso.* Drawing MS R-147, fol. 163. Sächsische Landesbibliothek, Dresden; **111** El Greco, *Apocalyptic Vision*, 1608–14. Oil on canvas, 222.2 x 193.0 (87½ x 76). The Metropolitan Museum of Art, New York; **112** Pablo Picasso, *Spanish Still Life*, spring 1912. Oil on canvas, 46 x 33 (18⅛ x 13). Musée d'art moderne, Villeneuve-d'Ascq, gift of Genevieve and Jean Masurel. © Succession Picasso/DACS 2001; **113** Juan Gris, *Bottle of Anis del Mono*, 1914. Papier collé, oil and charcoal on canvas, 41.8 x 24.0 (16⅜ x 9½). Judith Rothschild Collection; **114** Andre Mare et al., Photograph of the *salon bourgeois*, Maison Cubiste, Salon d'Automne, Paris 1912. Photo Archive Andre Mare, Paris. © ADAGP, Paris and DACS, London 2001; **115** Roger de La Fresnaye, *Conquest of the Air*, 1913. Oil on canvas, 235.9 x 195.0 (92⅞ x 76¾). Museum of Modern Art, New York, Mrs Simon Guggenheim Fund. Photograph © 2001 The Museum of Modern Art; **116** Jean Metzinger, *Woman with Fan*, 1912. Oil on canvas, 90.7 x 64.2 (35¾ x 25¼). Solomon R. Guggenheim Museum, New York. Gift, Solomon R. Guggenheim, 1938. Photograph David Heald © Solomon R. Guggenheim Foundation. © ADAGP, Paris and DACS, London 2001; **117** Edouard Manet, *In the Conservatory*, 1879. Oil on canvas, 115 x 150 (45¼ x 59). Nationalgalerie Staatliche Museen, Preussischer Kulturbesitz, Berlin; **118** Jean Metzinger, *The Yellow Feather*, 1912. Oil on canvas, 73 x 54 (28¾ x 21¼). Ursula and R. Stanley Johnson Collection, Chicago. © ADAGP, Paris and DACS, London 2001; **119** Jean Metzinger, *Portrait of an American Smoking*, 1912. Oil on canvas, 93 x 65 (40 x 26). Photograph 1997. Previously Lawrence University, present whereabouts unknown. All Rights Reserved. © ADAGP, Paris and DACS, London 2001; **120** Albert Gleizes, *Women Sewing*, 1913. Oil on canvas, 185.5 x 126 (73 x 49⅝). Rijksmuseum Kröller-Müller, Otterlo, Netherlands. © ADAGP, Paris and DACS, London 2001;
121 Pablo Picasso, *Still Life: Au Bon Marché*, 1913. Oil and pasted paper on cardboard, 23.5 x 31.0 (9¼ x 12¼). Ludwig Collection, Aachen. © Succession Picasso/DACS 2001;
122 Jean Metzinger, *The Cyclist*, 1913. Oil and collage on canvas, 130.4 x 97.1 (51¼ x 38¼). Peggy Guggenheim Collection, Venice; The Solomon R. Guggenheim Foundation, New York. Photograph David Heald © 2001 The Solomon R. Guggenheim Foundation. © ADAGP, Paris and DACS, London 2001;
123 Albert Gleizes, *The Football Players*, 1912–13. Oil on canvas, 226 x 183 (89 x 72). National Gallery, Washington D.C. © ADAGP, Paris and DACS, London 2001; **124** Robert Delaunay, *Cardiff Team*, 1913. Oil on canvas, 195.5 x 132 (77 x 52). Stedelijk Van Abbe Museum, Eindhoven; **125** Alexander Archipenko, *Boxing (Boxers, Struggle)*, 1914. Plaster painted black, 61 x 46 x 46 (24 x 18⅛ x 18⅛). The Solomon R. Guggenheim Museum, New York. © ARS, NY and DACS, London 2001; **126** Alexander Archipenko, *Repose*, 1912. Plaster tinted pink, 39 x 36 (15⅜ x 14⅛). Collection of the Tel Aviv Museum of Art, Jerusalem, gift of the Goeritz family, London, 1956. © ARS, New York and DACS, London 2001; **127** Robert Delaunay, *Simultaneous Windows*, 1912. Oil on canvas, 45.7 x 37.5 (18 x 14¾). Tate Gallery, London; **128** Sonia Terk Delaunay, *Le Bal Bullier*, 1913. Oil on mattress ticking, 109 x 81 (42⅞ x 31⅞). Musée National d'art Moderne, Paris. L & M SERVICES B.V. Amsterdam 20010409; **129** Guillaume Apollinaire, 'Lettre-Océan', 1914, from *Calligrammes*, © Editions Gallimard 1925;
130 Photograph of a Sonia Terk Delaunay dress modelled against an automobile, 1926. Coll. JD/PR, Paris;
131 Alice Halicka, *Cubist Still Life with Guitar*, 1916. Oil on canvas, 59.5 x 72.5 (23⅜ x 28½). Petit Palais, Musée d'art moderne, Geneva. © ADAGP, Paris and DACS, London 2001; **132** Louis Marcoussis, *Nature Morte au Damier*, 1912. Oil on canvas, 139 x 93 (59¾ x 36½). Musée national d'art moderne, Centre Georges Pompidou, Paris. © ADAGP, Paris and DACS, London 2001; **133** Maria Blanchard, *Child with a Hoop*, 1915. Oil on canvas, 128 x 95 (50⅜ x 37⅜). Petit Palais, Musée d'art moderne, Geneva. © DACS 2001;
134 Marie Laurencin, *Portrait of Jean*

Royère, 1908. Oil on board, 33 x 23.5 (13 x 9¼). Musée Marie Laurencin, Nagano-ken, Japan. © ADAGP, Paris and DACS, London 2001; **135** Marie Laurencin, *Group of Artists (Les Invités)*, 1908. Oil on canvas, 64.8 x 81 (25½ x 31⅞). The Baltimore Museum of Art, Cone Collection. © ADAGP, Paris and DACS, London 2001; **136** Marie Laurencin, *Les Jeunes Filles (Young Girls)*, 1910–11. Oil on canvas, 115 x 146 (45¼ x 57½). Moderna Museet, Stockholm. Photograph Tord Lund. © ADAGP, Paris and DACS, London 2001; **137** Jean-Emile Laboureur, *Portrait of Marie Laurencin*, 1914. Woodcut. Cabinet des Estampes, Bibliothèque nationale, Paris. © ADAGP, Paris and DACS, London 2001; **138** Georges Braque, *Soda*, spring 1912. Oil on canvas, diameter 36.2 (14¼). Museum of Modern Art, New York. Acquired through the Lillie P. Bliss Bequest. Photograph © 2001 The Museum of Modern Art, New York. © ADAGP, Paris and DACS, London 2001; **139** Georges Braque, *The Portuguese*, 1911–12. Oil on canvas, 117 x 81 (46 x 32). Kunstmuseum Basel, gift of Raoul La Roche, 1952. © ADAGP, Paris and DACS, London 2001; **140** Pablo Picasso, *Still Life with Chair-Caning*, 1912. Collage of oil, oilcloth and pastel paper, edged with rope, 27 x 35 (10⅝ x 13¾). Musée Picasso, Paris. © Succession Picasso/DACS 2001; **141** Georges Braque, *Fruit Dish and Glass*, 1912. Papier collé and charcoal on paper, 62 x 45 (24 x 17½). Private collection, formally Douglas Cooper Collection. © ADAGP, Paris and DACS, London 2001; **142** Pablo Picasso, Maquette for *Guitar*, 1912. Cardboard, string, wire (restored), 65.1 x 33.0 x 19.0 (25¾ x 13 x 7½). The Museum of Modern Art, New York, gift of the artist. Photograph © 2001 The Museum of Modern Art, New York. © Succession Picasso/DACS 2001; **143** Grebo mask, Ivory Coast or Liberia. Wood, white paint, plant fibres, length 64 (25¼). Musée Picasso, Paris, gift of Marina Ruíz Picasso; **144** Pablo Picasso, *Guitarist with Sheet Music*, spring 1913. Paper construction, 22.0 x 10.5 (8⅝ x 4⅛). Private collection, Paris. © Succession Picasso/DACS 2001; **145** Henri Laurens, *The Clown*, 1915. Painted wood, 53 x 29.5 x 23 (20⅞ x 11⅝ x 9). Moderna Museet, Stockholm. © ADAGP, Paris and DACS, London 2001; **146** Pablo Picasso, *Still Life*, 1914. Painted wood with upholstery fringe, 25.4 x 45.7 x 9.2 (10 x 18 x 3⅝). Tate Gallery, London. © Succession Picasso/DACS 2001; **147** Alexander Archipenko, *Medrano II (Dancer)*, 1913. Painted tin, wood, glass, and painted oilcloth, 126.6 x 51.5 x 31.7 (49⅞ x 20¼ x 12½). The Solomon R. Guggenheim Museum, New York. Photograph David Heald © The Solomon R. Guggenheim Foundation. © ARS, New York and DACS, London 2001; **148** Jacques Lipchitz, *Detachable Figure (Seated Musician)*, 1915. Painted wood, height 50.2 (19¾). Yulla Lipchitz Collection; **149** Jacques Lipchitz, *Man with a Guitar*, 1916. Limestone, 97.2 x 26.7 x 19.5 (38¼ x 10½ x 7¾). Museum of Modern Art, New York, Mrs Simon Guggenheim Fund (by exchange). Photograph © 2001 The Museum of Modern Art; **150** Pablo Picasso, *Guitar, Sheet Music and Glass*, November 1912. Collage with charcoal, 47.9 x 36.5 (18⅞ x 14⅜). Marian Koogler McNay Art Museum, San Antonio. © Succession Picasso/DACS 2001; **151** Front page of *Le Journal*, 18 November 1912. Bibliothèque nationale, Paris; **152** Pablo Picasso, 1947 reproduction of *Glass and Bottle of Suze*, 1912. Pasted papers, gouache and charcoal on paper, 65.4 x 50.2 (25¾ x 19¾). © Succession Picasso/DACS 2001; **153** Pablo Picasso, *Glass and Bottle of Suze*, 1912. Pasted paper, gouache and charcoal, 65.4 x 50.2 (25¾ x 19¾). Washington University Gallery of Art, St Louis, University purchase, Kende Sale Fund 1946. © Succession Picasso/DACS 2001; **154** Pablo Picasso, *Still Life: Bottle and Glass on a Table*, December 1912. Charcoal, ink and pasted newspaper, 65.0 x 47.3 (25⅝ x 18⅝). The Metropolitan Museum of Art, New York, Alfred Stieglitz Collection 1949. © Succession Picasso/DACS 2001; **155** Photograph of Pablo Picasso's studio with collages on the wall, boulevard Raspail, Paris, 1912. Editions Cahiers d'Art, Paris. © Succession Picasso/DACS 2001; **156** Georges Braque, *Still Life with Bottle*, January 1914. Pencil, pasted paper and gouache, 63 x 47 (24¾ x 18½). Private collection. © ADAGP, Paris and DACS, London 2001; **157** Francis Picabia, *Chanson nègre (Negro Song)*, 1913. Watercolour on paper, 66 x 55.9 (26 x 22). The Metropolitan Museum of Art, New York. © ADAGP, Paris and DACS, London 2001; **158** Georges Braque, *Still Life with Tenora*, 1913. Pasted paper, oil, charcoal, chalk and pencil on canvas, 95.2 x 120.3 (37½ x 47⅜). The Museum of Modern Art, New York, Nelson A. Rockefeller Bequest. Photograph © 2001 The Museum of Modern Art, New York. © ADAGP, Paris and DACS, London 2001; **159** Photograph of Georges Braque in his studio, 5 impasse de Guelma, c. 1911. Archives Laurens; **160** Pablo Picasso, *Accordionist*, 1911. Oil on canvas, 130.0 x 89.5 (51¼ x 35¼). The Solomon R. Guggenheim Museum, New York. © Succession Picasso/DACS 2001; **161** Juan Gris, *Man at the Café*, 1914. Oil and papier collé on canvas, 99.1 x 71.8 (39 x 28¼). Private collection, New York; **162** Juan Gris, *The Table*, spring 1914. Collage, charcoal and gouache on canvas, 59.5 x 44.5 (23.5 x 17.5). Philadelphia Museum of Art; **163** Juan Gris, *Musician's Table*, 1914. Graphite and coloured pencil on papier collé on canvas, 81 x 59.5 (31⅞ x 23½). Private collection, New York; **164** Photograph, *The Leading Wave of a French Infantry Assault on German Trenches*, Western Front, 1916. Hulton Getty; **165** Postcard, *Delegation of French Mutilés de Guerre, Congress of Versailles Treaty*, 28 June 1919; **166** Postcard, *Verdun, la rue Mazel, after Bombardment of 1916*; **167** Photograph of Lodewijk Schelfhout and Piet Mondrian in Schelfhout's studio, 26 rue du Départ, Paris, 1912. Rijksbureau voor Kunsthistorische Documentatie, The Hague; **168** Henri Laurens, Photograph of Georges Braque in Laurens' studio, 1915. Henri Laurens. © ADAGP, Paris and DACS, London 2001; **169** Georges Braque, *The Pedestal Table*, 1918. Oil on canvas, 129.5 x 74.3 (51 x 29¼). Philadelphia Museum of Art, Louise and Walter Arensburg Collection. © ADAGP, Paris and DACS, London 2001; **170** Frans Masereel, frontispiece for René Arcos, *Le Sang des autres*, 1920. Woodcut. Bibliothèque nationale, Paris © DACS 2001; **171** Albert Gleizes, *In Port (Overlooking a Port)*, 1917. Oil and sand on wood, 153 x 120 (60¼ x 47¼). © Museo Thyssen-Bornemisza, Madrid. © ADAGP, Paris and DACS, London 2001; **172** Albert Gleizes, *Spiritual Authority and Temporal Power*, 1939–40. Oil on canvas, 336 x 203 (132¼ x 79⅞). Musée des Beaux-Arts, Lyons. © ADAGP, Paris and DACS, London 2001; **173** Raymond Duchamp-Villon, *Rooster (Gallic Cock)*, 1916. Painted plaster, 44.5 x 37.0 x 7.0 (17½ x 14⅝ x 2¾). Musée des Beaux-Arts, Rouen; **174** Pablo Picasso, *Guillaume Apollinaire, Artilleryman*, 1914. Ink and watercolour, 23 x 12.5 (9⅛ x 5). Private collection, Paris. © Succession Picasso/DACS 2001; **175** Pablo Picasso, *Guitar Player*, 1916. Oil and sand, 130 x 97 (51⅛ x 38⅛). Moderna Museet, Stockholm. Photograph Pers Anders Allsten. © Succession Picasso/DACS 2001; **176** Pablo Picasso, 'Manager from New York', costume for *Parade*, 1917. Bibliothèque nationale, Paris. © Succession Picasso/DACS 2001; **177** Fernand Léger, *Verdun, la rue Mazel*, 1916. Ink drawing, 30.0 x 19.0

(11¾ x 7½). Galerie Jean Bucher, Paris. © ADAGP, Paris and DACS, London 2001; **178** Fernand Léger, *The Card Party*, 1917. Oil on canvas, 129 x 193 (50¾ x 79). Rijksmuseum Kröller-Müller, Otterlo, Netherlands. © ADAGP, Paris and DACS, London 2001; **179** Fernand Léger, *Composition with Hand and Hats*, 1927. Oil on canvas, 162.0 x 130.1 (63¾ x 51¼). Musée national d'art moderne, Centre Georges Pompidou, Paris. © ADAGP, Paris and DACS, London 2001; **180** Amedée Ozenfant, *Composition (Fugue)*, 1925. Pencil on paper, 45.7 x 61 (18 x 24). Museum of Modern Art, New York, Gift of the artist. Photograph © 2001 The Museum of Modern Art, New York. © ADAGP, Paris and DACS, London 2001; **181** Reproduction of paintings by Charles-Edouard Jeanneret (Le Corbusier) and Amedée Ozenfant. *L'Esprit Nouveau*, no.17 (1922), p.1993. © FLC/ADAGP, Paris and DACS, London 2001 and © ADAGP, Paris and DACS, London 2001; **182** Charles-Edouard Jeanneret (Le Corbusier), *Still Life with Pile of Plates*, 1920. Oil on canvas, 81 x 100 (31⅞ x 39⅜). Öffentliche Kunstsammlung Basel, Kunstmuseum Basel. © FLC/ADAGP, Paris and DACS, London 2001

Index